FOR DUMMIES™
BESTSELLING BOOK SERIES

CIW™ Foundat...
For Dummies...

MW00354492

Abbreviations You Should Know

Term	Description
TCP (Transmission Control Protocol)	Manages session between computers; helps break down and reassemble packets; ensures packets are reassembled in correct order; makes sure no data is duplicated. Stateful.
IP (Internet Protocol)	Provides Internet addressing for each computer involved in transmission. (For more on IP addressing, see Chapter 3.) Stateless.
UDP (User Datagram Protocol)	Provides Datagram form of communication; it's stateless, so it uses a best effort method of data transfer: doesn't guarantee reliability.
ARP (Address Resolution Protocol)	Matches IP addresses to physical addresses or determines which computer goes with which IP address.
IPX/SPX (Internetwork Packet Exchange/Sequenced Packet Exchange)	Novell's version of the TCP/IP suite. Early versions of Novell Netware supported IPX/SPX instead of TCP/IP; Netware 5 uses TCP/IP as its default protocol though it still supports IPX/SPX. **Note:** IPX/SPX is backwards compared to TCP/IP: IPX=IP and SPX=TCP. Though TCP/IP is the Internet standard, IPX/SPX is actually more efficient.
NetBEUI (NetBIOS Extended User Interface)	Enables different computers using different programs to communicate using NetBIOS (Network Basic Input/Output System). Used primarily on small Microsoft networks such as a peer-to-peer. Limited use because it's nonroutable. (See Routable protocols in Chapter 19.)
FTP (File Transfer Protocol)	Commonly used to publish Web pages. Also used to provide access to larger files on the Internet or within a company.
TFTP (Trivial File Transfer Protocol)	Less-capable relative of FTP, TFTP uses UDP where FTP uses TCP. Often used for initializing diskless systems, it works with BOOTstrap (BOOTP) protocol.

Common HTML Tags

Tag	What It Does
`<HTML>`	Specifies the document is an HTML document.
`<HEAD>`	Creates the header section of an HTML document.
`<TITLE>`	Holds the title of the document, which displays in the title bar.
`<BODY>`	Defines the body of the document where most content goes.
`<P>`	Breaks the current line and inserts a blank line.
` `	Breaks the current line.
`BGCOLOR=`	Attribute that holds color value `<BODY BGCOLOR=#AAFF33>`. Can appear in the `<BODY>`, `<TABLE>`, `<TR>`, `<TD>`, and `<TH>` tags.
`A HREF=`	Creates a hyperlink. `<A HREF="www.boguscompanyname.com">Click Me</A>`
`IMG SRC=`	Inserts an image. `<IMG SRC="myimage.gif">`
`ALT=`	Attribute in `<IMG>` tag that creates an alternate representation for the image. `<IMG SRC="myimage".gif ALT="My text">`
`<TABLE>`	Defines a table area.
`<TR>`	Defines a row in a table.
`<TD>`	Defines a cell in a row.
`<TH>`	Creates a header cell at the top of a table. Any text in this cell will appear in bold.
`<DIV>`	Creates a divided area in a page to apply formatting to. `<DIV ALIGN=Center>...</DIV>`

CIW™ Foundations For Dummies®

Common Networking Hardware

Hardware	What It Does
Network Interface Card (NIC)	A NIC, also called a network adapter card, is the device that allows a computer to connect to a network; usually contains a transceiver, a device that sends and receives signals. Works at the Data Link Layer of the OSI/RM.
Hub	A hub connects computers in a star topology; several can be hooked together or daisy-chained; often acts as a repeater.
Repeater	Device that amplifies a signal traveling along a network; prevents signal from degrading so computers can be placed farther apart.
Bridge	Connects two LANs with the same protocol; can divide one network into two segments to reduce traffic; can connect different network segments such as a token-ring to an Ethernet network. Bridges use MAC addresses to determine where to send packets; works at the Data Link Layer of the OSI/RM.
Router	Connects two or more networks; uses network addresses such as an IP to determine where to send packets; different protocol structures need different routers, for example one router reads IP addresses, a different type reads SPX addresses; works at the Network Layer of the OSI/RM.
Brouter	Combines functionality of a bridge and a router; can connect two different types of networks; protocol-independent; works at the Network and Data Link Layers of the OSI/RM.
Switch	Can do everything a hub, bridge, or router can do, but faster; utilizes entire bandwidth between sending and receiving machines so it eliminates bottlenecks; switches can work at any one of the first four OSI/RM layers.
Modem	Converts digital signals from a computer into analog signals that can travel over a phone line, and then converts analog signals from the phone line into digital signals so that your computer can understand them.
Channel Service Unit/Data Service Unit (CSU/DSU)	Terminates digital signals that are sent over digital carrier lines and converts them into a format that computers and networks can understand. All dedicated carrier lines, such as T1 and T3, must use a CSU/DSU. Also called a digital modem.

Internet Address Classes

Address Class	IP Address Range	Default Subnet Mask
Class A	0.0.0.0 to 127.255.255.255	255.0.0.0
Class B	128.0.0.0 to 191.255.255.255	255.255.0.0
Class C	192.0.0.0 to 233.255.255.255	255.255.255.0
Class D	224.0.0.0 to 239.255.255.255	Not applicable
Class E	240.0.0.0 to 247.255.255.255	Not applicable

Copyright © 2002 Hungry Minds, Inc. All rights reserved.

Cheat Sheet $2.95 value. Item 1635-3.

For more information about Hungry Minds, call 1-800-762-2974.

For Dummies: Bestselling Book Series for Beginners

 TM

References for the Rest of Us!®

BESTSELLING BOOK SERIES

Are you intimidated and confused by computers? Do you find that traditional manuals are overloaded with technical details you'll never use? Do your friends and family always call you to fix simple problems on their PCs? Then the For Dummies® computer book series from Hungry Minds, Inc. is for you.

For Dummies books are written for those frustrated computer users who know they aren't really dumb but find that PC hardware, software, and indeed the unique vocabulary of computing make them feel helpless. For Dummies books use a lighthearted approach, a down-to-earth style, and even cartoons and humorous icons to dispel computer novices' fears and build their confidence. Lighthearted but not lightweight, these books are a perfect survival guide for anyone forced to use a computer.

> *"I like my copy so much I told friends; now they bought copies."*
> — *Irene C., Orwell, Ohio*

> *"Quick, concise, nontechnical, and humorous."*
> — *Jay A., Elburn, Illinois*

> *"Thanks, I needed this book. Now I can sleep at night."*
> — *Robin F., British Columbia, Canada*

Already, millions of satisfied readers agree. They have made For Dummies books the #1 introductory level computer book series and have written asking for more. So, if you're looking for the most fun and easy way to learn about computers, look to For Dummies books to give you a helping hand.

Hungry Minds™

CIW™ Foundations
FOR
DUMMIES®

by Sharon Roark
with Tom Devine

Hungry Minds™

Best-Selling Books • Digital Downloads • e-Books • Answer Networks • e-Newsletters • Branded Web Sites • e-Learning

New York, NY ◆ Cleveland, OH ◆ Indianapolis, IN

CIW™ Foundations For Dummies®

Published by
Hungry Minds, Inc.
909 Third Avenue
New York, NY 10022
www.hungryminds.com
www.dummies.com

Library of Congress Control Number: 2002101814

ISBN: 0-7645-1635-3

Printed in the United States of America

10 9 8 7 6 5 4 3 2 1

1B/QZ/QU/QS/IN

Distributed in the United States by Hungry Minds, Inc.

Distributed by CDG Books Canada Inc. for Canada; by Transworld Publishers Limited in the United Kingdom; by IDG Norge Books for Norway; by IDG Sweden Books for Sweden; by IDG Books Australia Publishing Corporation Pty. Ltd. for Australia and New Zealand; by TransQuest Publishers Pte Ltd. for Singapore, Malaysia, Thailand, Indonesia, and Hong Kong; by Gotop Information Inc. for Taiwan; by ICG Muse, Inc. for Japan; by Intersoft for South Africa; by Eyrolles for France; by International Thomson Publishing for Germany, Austria and Switzerland; by Distribuidora Cuspide for Argentina; by LR International for Brazil; by Galileo Libros for Chile; by Ediciones ZETA S.C.R. Ltda. for Peru; by WS Computer Publishing Corporation, Inc., for the Philippines; by Contemporanea de Ediciones for Venezuela; by Express Computer Distributors for the Caribbean and West Indies; by Micronesia Media Distributor, Inc. for Micronesia; by Chips Computadoras S.A. de C.V. for Mexico; by Editorial Norma de Panama S.A. for Panama; by American Bookshops for Finland.

For general information on Hungry Minds' products and services please contact our Customer Care Department within the U.S. at 800-762-2974, outside the U.S. at 317-572-3993 or fax 317-572-4002.

For sales inquiries and reseller information, including discounts, premium and bulk quantity sales, and foreign-language translations, please contact our Customer Care Department at 800-434-3422, fax 317-572-4002, or write to Hungry Minds, Inc., Attn: Customer Care Department, 10475 Crosspoint Boulevard, Indianapolis, IN 46256.

For information on licensing foreign or domestic rights, please contact our Sub-Rights Customer Care Department at 212-884-5000.

For information on using Hungry Minds' products and services in the classroom or for ordering examination copies, please contact our Educational Sales Department at 800-434-2086 or fax 317-572-4005.

For press review copies, author interviews, or other publicity information, please contact our Public Relations Department at 317-572-3168 or fax 317-572-4168.

For authorization to photocopy items for corporate, personal, or educational use, please contact Copyright Clearance Center, 222 Rosewood Drive, Danvers, MA 01923, or fax 978-750-4470.

About the Authors

Sharon Roark (Master CIW Designer) has been working with computers for more than 15 years. She has been involved with the Internet and World Wide Web full time for more than five years as a trainer, teacher, developer, merchant, and end user. Sharon has conducted Web and Internet seminars throughout the United States, Australia, Scotland, and England. She is the owner of her own Web design company, CIW Design, and leads seminars for CompuMaster, a worldwide leader in the computer seminars industry.

Before she entered the computer industry full-time, Sharon worked in broadcast news and public relations. She lives close to all her immediate family, in the Kentucky area. In her spare time, she enjoys white-water rafting, scuba diving, and performing in local and regional theater productions.

Tom Devine (CIW Professional, CCNA) has been a Webmaster since 1995. As co-founder of AffordableFurniture.com in 1996, Tom pioneered secure online retailing in the home furnishings sector. He has been involved in nearly every aspect of the Web, including Web site design, information architecture, e-commerce platform construction and deployment, enterprise resource planning, customer relationship management, network administration and security, and Internet marketing. Tom also conducts technology-related conferences and training seminars across the United States on behalf of the Affordable Interactive Corporation of Forney, Texas.

Prior to his adventures on the Web, Tom served his community for several years as a firefighter/paramedic. An on-duty injury forced an early retirement from that great profession, opening the doorway to the brave new world of the Internet. He currently lives in the beautiful ranchland of East Texas, spending free time outdoors with his wife and two daughters.

Dedication

Sharon Roark: To all my family members, especially my sister Jennifer, who put up with me during the last few months I worked on this book (and could barely think of anything else). To Becca and Ryan, who provide joy to all those whose lives they touch, and my Mom and Dad, for always providing a safe haven to return to when the world gets too hectic.

I would like to dedicate this book to all of the small-town boys and girls who dare to dream bigger dreams than those around them. I want to encourage all those who are tempted to settle for less than they deserve to keep reaching for the stars. I also have to mention my wonderful fellow trainers, who continually amaze me with the depth of their knowledge and their patience in dealing with my daily ice cream-seeking adventures!

Tom Devine: My efforts on this book are dedicated to my loving and patient wife, Valerie, and my two darling daughters, Annie and Molly. Without their support and understanding over the past several years, none of this would have been possible.

I dedicate this book, as with everything else that I do, to all of the brave men and women of the fire service who put their lives on the line every day to protect and serve us all.

Authors' Acknowledgments

Sharon Roark: I would like to thank all the wonderful people at Hungry Minds who have given me the opportunity to write this book. I'd especially like to thank Steve Hayes, for keeping me sane when I was tempted to go off the deep end. I also want to thank Nicole Haims for her patience, Dan Barker for his eagle eye for technical details, Rebecca Senninger for her thorough editing, and Kim Darosett for making sure my Kentucky-isms don't confuse readers.

I also want to the thank Tom Devine, who stepped in with technical assistance during the last-minute time crunch, and Laura Moss and Travis Silvers, for helping me put together a fantastic companion CD.

Tom Devine: I would like to thank Sharon Roark, first and foremost, for providing me the opportunity to work on this exciting project. Sharon is one of the most intelligent, resourceful, and charming colleagues that I have ever had the pleasure working with.

Many thanks also to the great folks at Hungry Minds. Steve Hayes, Nicole Haims, and all of the Hungry Minds team made this challenge an enjoyable experience.

Publisher's Acknowledgments

We're proud of this book; please send us your comments through our Hungry Minds Online Registration Form located at www.dummies.com.

Some of the people who helped bring this book to market include the following:

Acquisitions, Editorial, and Media Development

Senior Project Editor: Nicole Haims

Senior Acquisitions Editor: Steven Hayes

Copy Editor: Rebecca Senninger

Technical Editor: Dan L. Barker

Editorial Manager: Leah Cameron

Permissions Editor: Laura Moss

Media Development Specialist: Travis Silvers

Media Development Manager: Laura VanWinkle

Media Development Supervisor: Richard Graves

Editorial Assistant: Amanda Foxworth

Production

Project Coordinator: Ryan Steffen

Layout and Graphics: Joyce Haughey, Jackie Nicholas, Barry Offringa, Betty Schulte, Jeremey Unger, Mary J. Virgin

Proofreaders: Laura Albert, Andy Hollandbeck, Charles Spencer, TECHBOOKS Production Services

Indexer: TECHBOOKS Production Services

Special Help: Nicole Laux, Rebecca Huehls, Kim Darosett

General and Administrative

Hungry Minds Technology Publishing Group: Richard Swadley, Vice President and Executive Group Publisher; Bob Ipsen, Vice President and Executive Publisher; Joseph Wikert, Vice President and Publisher; Barry Pruett, Vice President and Publisher; Mary Bednarek, Editorial Director; Mary C. Corder, Editorial Director; Andy Cummings, Editorial Director

Hungry Minds Manufacturing: Ivor Parker, Vice President, Manufacturing

Hungry Minds Marketing: John Helmus, Assistant Vice President, Director of Marketing

Hungry Minds Production for Branded Press: Debbie Stailey, Production Director

Hungry Minds Sales: Michael Violano, Vice President, International Sales and Sub Rights

Cartoons at a Glance

By Rich Tennant

"What I'm looking for are dynamic Web applications and content, not Web innuendoes and intent."

page 401

"It's okay. One of the routers must have gone down and we had a brief broadcast storm."

page 253

"We sort of have our own way of mentally preparing our people to take the CIW Foundations exam."

page 7

"I'll be right there. Let me just take care of this user. He's about halfway through a 3 hour download."

page 29

"Give him air! Give him air! He'll be okay. He's just been exposed to some raw HTML code. It must have accidently flashed across his screen from the server."

page 141

Cartoon Information:
Fax: 978-546-7747
E-Mail: richtennant@the5thwave.com
World Wide Web: www.the5thwave.com

Contents at a Glance

Table of Contents

Introduction

*I*f you've bought or are thinking of buying this book, you must be interested in becoming CIW certified. (Either that or you were browsing around the bookstore and this book fell off the shelf and hit you in the head.) The purpose of this book is to help you study for and pass the CIW Foundations exam. This introductory section will give you an overview of what's covered on the exam and how the book is put together.

Even if you paid big bucks to attend a week or so of classes that cover the information you need to know for the Foundations exam, you'll find this book a great help. It summarizes topics for easy comparison and weeds out the extra stuff instructors seem compelled to include but isn't necessarily relevant to the exam. It's like having a well-organized compilation of the notes you took in class.

If you have no idea what the CIW Foundations exam is all about, the next few sections will help you get a handle on it. If you already know what the Foundations exam is and why you might want to take it, you can skip the next few sections where I tell you all the reasons why this is the reference tool you can't live without.

About This Book

This book, like all *For Dummies* books, is a simple, no-nonsense approach to passing the CIW Foundations exam. I'm especially proud of it because I think it's better than any other book currently out on this topic. (Yes, my modesty is showing.) I don't waste time explaining arcane topics that you don't need to know for the exam, and I explain some very complicated concepts in the most basic way I know how. And, lucky you, you've got this book to help you study! (I wish I'd had it to help me study, but that wouldn't have been possible, would it?)

If you use this book as a study aid, and not as a means of learning material for the first time, you're going to be fine. At the beginning of each chapter, I lay out the primary objectives of that chapter. Also, throughout each chapter, I point out specific questions that you might face on a topic. I do this because I care. Well, I'm being paid to care. But at least I care! Hey, you're the one shelling out $125 for the exam. I'd rather you study too much and pass the exam on the first try than take it too lightly and have to sit for the exam — and pay for it — twice. Here are some other hints on how to use this book to help you study for the exam:

✔ If it's in the book, it's on the test. Because not everyone who takes the test gets the same questions, you may not get any questions on certain technologies. I wrote this book, however, to cover all the topics you may be faced with. So if you end up not getting any questions on one of the topics you're not sure of, don't get mad at me for asking you to study it — just count yourself lucky!

✔ I suggest you spend most of your time with this book studying the areas you're least familiar with. The most challenging area for most test candidates is the Networking Fundamentals section. I caution you, though, to review *all* the sections of the book, no matter how much background and experience you have.

I know people who have failed the test because they didn't review the (seemingly easy) Internet Fundamentals section. I also know several people who missed enough HTML questions to fail because they figured they didn't need to review this topic because they'd been coding HTML for a while.

✔ This book contains Quick Assessment questions at the beginning of each chapter and Prep Test questions at the end of each chapter. Use them to help you determine how much time you need to spend on each chapter. You can also find quite a few Web sites with good sample questions. I list ten sites in Part V and several others on the CD.

✔ Highlight the tables, definitions, and diagrams in this book. Some of these are major topics that I spend a lot of time on; some are definitions you just need to memorize for the exam and probably won't ever use in real life. That's just how certification exams are — they always include some information that doesn't seem all that important but that you have to memorize anyway. If a new term crops up that you're unfamiliar with, check out the index to find out where else I cover the term. I always define technical terms the first time or two that I use them, but you may not be reading the book from beginning to end.

✔ After you've had a leisurely look at each chapter, go back and review the items that were new or particularly challenging. After you feel you've got a good handle on the information I've presented, set aside some cram time the night before or morning of your test. Finally, you'll be ready to take the test and pass it!

✔ Certain topics are much easier to learn if you're working with them hands-on. That's why I include labs wherever appropriate. Here's an example of a lab I use later in the book:

Lab 13-1   Creating Frames

1. **Open your text editor and type the following code to create a basic frameset page:**

```
<HTML><HEAD>
<TITLE>My Home Page</TITLE>
</HEAD>
<FRAMESET>
</FRAMESET>
</HTML>
```

2. **Create a folder on your desktop named** `myweb` **and save this document as** `default.htm` **inside it.**

3. **Leave** `default.htm` **open and create a standard new HTML document called** `top.htm` **and save it in the myweb folder.**

4. **In the body section of** `top.htm`**, type three words with two spaces between them like this:**

```
:<BODY>
Home  Products  FAQ
</BODY>
```

5. **Leave the two existing documents open and create another standard new HTML document called** `bottom.htm` **and save it in the myweb folder.**

6. **In the body section of the** `bottom.htm` **document, type some filler text like this:**

```
<BODY>
<P>Welcome to my home page.</P>
<P>Page content goes here.</P>
<P>Page content goes here.</P>
<P>Page content goes here.</P>
<P>Page content goes here.</P>
</BODY>
```

7. **In the** `default.htm` **document, in the** `<FRAMESET>` **tag, add the** `ROWS` **attribute to specify the number of rows in the frameset and the height of each.**

```
<FRAMESET ROWS="25%,*">
```

8. **Specify which pages will display in each frame by adding** `<FRAME>` **tags in between the** `<FRAMESET>` **tags.**

```
<FRAMESET ROWS="25%,*">
<FRAME SRC="top.htm">
<FRAME SRC="bottom.htm">
</FRAMESET>
```

9. **Save the changes to each page and open the** `default.htm` **page in your browser.**

Foolish Assumptions

This book isn't aimed at expert Web developers and network administrators. After all, if you fit in one of those two categories, you probably don't need to do much studying for the exam. I do, however, assume readers know certain things about computers and the Internet, including:

- You know your way around a PC or Mac. You should be comfortable enough with your computer that saving files and moving folders around should be second nature to you. You can use either a PC or a Mac for the labs in this book, but because most Web development is done on PCs, I focus more on PCs than on Macs.

- You're comfortable surfing the Web. You should have experience browsing Web pages and sending and receiving e-mail.

- You've at least attempted to make a Web page or two. Even if you've never coded a line of HTML in your life, the terminology of Web development shouldn't be entirely new to you. You'll have a much easier time coding a hyperlink, for example, if you know what a hyperlink is. It's okay if you've never created a navigation bar, but you should know what one is.

If you're comfortable with these topics, this book's for you!

How This Book Is Organized

I divided this book into parts, which I then organized by topic. Some topics are covered in more than one part. E-mail, for example, is covered in the first part of the book where I talk about how to use e-mail programs. In the Networking Fundamentals part of the book, I talk about how to set up a server to handle e-mail. If you're looking for information on a specific topic, check the headings in the Table of Contents or the index in the back of the book to see every place I mention that topic.

By design, this book enables you to get as much (or as little) information as you need at any particular moment. Maybe you're an HTML whiz, so you decide to skip the HTML chapters for the time being. When you're reading the section on connecting your Web page form to a database, however, you realize you don't remember how to create an HTML form. You just check the index or Table of Contents, and pop over to the pages that review just the information you need (or odds are, there will be a handy-dandy cross-reference telling you where to go).

Part I: The Basics

Part I answers any questions you may have about the makeup of the exam. It explains how many questions you'll have on each major topic and the format of the questions. It also offers an overview of the benefits of getting certified, and where to go to sign up for and take the exam.

Part II: Internet Fundamentals

Part II covers the history of the Internet and how it works. It explains how browsers work with Web pages and how DNS helps locate Web pages on the Internet. This part also explains how to perform several e-mail operations like attaching files and signatures to e-mails.

Part III: HTML Fundamentals

Part III takes you from the most basic HTML codes to creating tables and forms. It covers how to insert graphics into Web pages and how to create bulleted and numbered lists. There's also a chapter on other Web languages such as JavaScript that authors often use to add dynamic data and interesting effects to their Web pages.

Part IV: Networking Fundamentals

Part IV has everything you need to know about networks and servers. It explains the protocols networks use to accomplish tasks, and the server software you need to share Web pages and other system resources.

Part V: The Part of Tens

This section points you to additional resources that will help you study for the Foundations exam. I list ten Web sites that offer extra tips and tricks as well as additional sample tests and discussion areas for test-takers just like yourself.

Icons Used in This Book

To make your experience with the book easier, I use various icons in the margins of the book to indicate particular points of interest.

Whenever I give you a hint or a tip that relates the topic I'm covering to the real world, I mark it with this little Tip thingamabob — it's my way of sharing what I've figured out the hard way so you don't have to.

This icon is a friendly reminder or a marker for something that you want to make sure that you keep in mind for the exam.

Sometimes I feel obligated to give you some technical information, although it may not have much relevance to the exam. I mark that stuff with this geeky fellow so that you know it's just background information.

When I use the Instant Answer icon, be sure to pay close attention because the information here is, well, an instant answer to a question you're likely to see on the exam. Remember, though, that just because a paragraph has this icon beside it doesn't mean that nothing else in the section is on the test. For best results in any given area, knowing why answers are right is just as important as knowing the actual answers. For complete understanding, read everything.

When you see the Time Shaver icon, you know I'm giving you the fastest possible version of a topic so that you can retain the basics and move on to other topics.

Where to Go from Here

Now you're ready to use this book. Look over the Table of Contents and find something that catches your attention or a topic that you think can help you solve a problem. If you're not sure how much you really know about a certain topic, go to the chapter that covers that topic and take the Quick Assessment test. If you easily get all the questions right, you may be able to just skim that chapter for the time being. Or, flip the page, and start at the beginning with Chapter 1.

Part I
The Basics

"We sort of have our own way of mentally preparing our people to take the CIW Foundations exam."

In this part . . .

You've decided you want to become CIW certified to prove to everyone how much you know about the Web and networking. What's the first step? In this part of the book, I lay out all the basics about the test — the company that created it, where to take it, and how many questions you can expect on each of the main topics.

You find out the Foundations philosophy, how this book works to help you decide what to study, and what, if anything, to skip. This exam exists to help you prove your knowledge of the fundamentals of Web creation and networking. You'll be tested on a few items that you may not use in real life, but at least 90 percent of this book's content is relevant not only to the exam, but to real-world Web work as well.

The exam doesn't cover everything there is to know about creating Web pages and configuring networks. You're not going to get questions about right-clicking or double-clicking — the ProsoftTraining folks assume you know your way around a PC or Mac. The exam does cover fundamental topics that every successful Webmaster should know before delving any further into Web development.

Chapter 1

The CIW Certification Program

*I*f you think CIW stands for Creative, Infuriating Work, you've got an idea of what's in store for you. CIW actually stands for Certified Internet Webmaster, and successfully completing ProsoftTraining's CIW certification program enables you to say to the world, "I'm qualified to create your business' Web site." This career choice involves work that is often creative, sometimes infuriating, and always very rewarding.

No one can go through Prosoft's CIW program without first passing the Foundations exam. Typical CIW Foundations exam candidates have real-world, practical knowledge of the Web, the Internet, e-mail, and basic computer literacy, not to mention an interest in ramping up their careers to move into the exciting world of Webmastering.

But how do you know if this certification program is for you? This chapter tells you what you need to know about Prosoft and the CIW certification program. To get the scoop on what the Foundations exam covers, check out Chapter 2.

Is CIW Certification for You?

The Prosoft CIW certification program was created to give Web professionals the opportunity to prove their competence in various areas of Web development and design. The Foundations exam is designed for the entry-level Web professional who has a good basic understanding of Web and Internet technology, design, and administration.

After you pass the Foundations exam — and if you master the material from this book — you'll become a Certified Internet Webmaster Associate. What this means is that you have certifiable proof of specific skills and knowledge levels that employers are seeking in Web technicians. All CIW certifications are recognized by the International Webmasters Association (IWA) at www.iwanet.org and the Association of Internet Professionals (AIP) at www.association.org.

Other Webmaster certification programs are out there, but CIW certifications have become the most widely recognized in the industry. I believe there are two main reasons for this:

- ✔ CIW exams are platform neutral. Several software manufacturers have created certifications on their products, but their certifications don't have the industry-wide appeal of CIW certifications.

- ✔ CIW Web certifications have become the industry standard because of the various advanced certifications a candidate can move on to after passing the Foundations exam. Some certification programs offer a Web fundamentals exam and certification, but after that — poof — nothing. But the Foundations exam with CIW opens the door for you to increase and prove your knowledge in several areas — Web administration, enterprise development, application development, and advanced design.

What Is Prosoft?

Prosoft is a training company that began with a courseware library and instructor-led training. It was originally incorporated in Nevada in 1985. As the Web evolved, Prosoft increased the scope of its training network and created the first comprehensive, platform-neutral Webmaster certification program in 1996. Prosoft's CIW program is currently in its fourth generation and its global partners include IBM, Hewlett-Packard, New Horizons, and CompUSA, among others.

The idea of computer-related certification was nothing new when Prosoft introduced its program in 1996. One thing, however, differentiates Prosoft's program from many of the others out there. CIW certifications are based on specific job roles — a Web database administrator or network administrator, for example. Many other popular certification programs, including Microsoft's hugely popular MCSE (Microsoft Certified Systems Engineer certification) are designed to prove proficiency with specific computer technologies (guess which technologies MCSE covers), but they're not specifically targeted toward particular jobs one might hold in the computer industry.

Why Choose CIW Certification?

Why choose CIW certification over some of the others? Fair question. Certification offers a way to prove your knowledge and skill level to a current or prospective employer. Increasingly, companies are seeking employees who are already qualified. Proof of certification means you're ready to hit the ground running, reducing the learning curve you might otherwise face — and saving your employer the big headache of having to train you on the basics.

You may know people (I know I do) who bluffed their way into a position by stretching the truth a bit when it came to describing their Web skills. If those people end up with bosses who know even less about the specific technology than they do, they might be able to "fake it 'til they make it." But too many firms have been burned by blindly trusting a candidate's claims of technological proficiency, and they want some proof. That's what CIW certification gives you.

CIW has become the industry standard for Web certifications. It's recognized more widely in the Web arena than the others. The CIW program also offers many advanced certifications in key Web areas: enterprise development, Web administration, application development, Web design, and Web site management. So if you want to be certified, congratulations, you have chosen the right program.

What's in It for You?

You may be thinking, "What's in it for me?" Is it really worth your time to work your brain into a lather studying just to have to sit through the first exam you've taken in eons? I think it is. Here are some of the benefits of becoming CIW certified:

- ✔ **You can increase your marketability:** Having CIW certifications makes you more appealing to prospective employers. You may be able to command a higher salary because you won't need as much training after you're on board with your new company.

- ✔ **You have proof of your skills:** Being CIW certified proves to your employer and your peers that you have the skills that are necessary in your industry.

- ✔ **You have a leg up on the competition:** With CIW certifications, you've proven your skills, whereas others haven't. If you and another candidate have similar skills, the CIW certification may very well give you the advantage.

✔ **You get maximum achievement in minimum time:** Regardless of which Web technology you decide to focus on, you can learn the real-world skills needed for a job and prove yourself in that area in much less time than it would take to acquire similar knowledge in a traditional college environment.

✔ **You can increase your confidence in your abilities:** The job market can be a scary place, so you need every competitive edge you can get. When you prove yourself by passing your exam(s), you can interview for that job with confidence because you know you've got the right stuff!

Understanding the CIW Certification Program

The three main levels of certification in the CIW program are as follows:

✔ **Associate:** To achieve associate level certification, you need a passing score (75%) on the CIW Foundations exam. If you've already taken and passed the i-Net+ exam by CompTIA, you can skip the CIW Foundations exam and move on to the next level; just make sure you send Prosoft a copy of your i-Net+ certification.

✔ **Professional:** To become a CIW Professional, you need to pass one or more of the job role examinations:

- Server Administrator, exam #1DO-450.
- Web Languages, exams #1DO-435 and 1DO-437. (You need to pass both tests in this job role to become a CIW-certified Web languages professional.)
- Site Designer, exam #1DO-420.

You remain a CIW Professional after passing two or more job role examinations. You must pass all the exams that comprise a Master path to earn the certification of CIW Master.

✔ **Master:** A candidate becomes a CIW Master after passing all the necessary exams in one of four master certification paths (shown in Figure 1-1):

- **Master CIW Administrator:** This certification is awarded after you pass three job role exams: Server Administrator, Internetworking Professional, and Security Professional. If you're interested in becoming a network administrator or a network security specialist, this exam is for you.

- **Master CIW Enterprise Developer:** This is the most comprehensive CIW certification. You must pass three Internet job role exams: Application Developer, Database Specialist, and Enterprise Developer. Plus, you need to pass exams on four languages: JavaScript, Perl, Java Programming, and Object-Oriented Analysis. Choose this path if you want to get involved in Web-related programming and development.

- **Master CIW Designer:** This certification is awarded after you pass two Internet job role exams: Site Designer and E-Commerce Designer. If you want to be involved in the design and creation of Web pages, this certification is for you.

- **Master CIW Web Site Manager:** The newest Master CIW track, this certification is awarded after you pass two Internet job role exams: Site Designer and Server Administrator. Plus, you must pass two additional language exams, JavaScript and Perl Fundamentals. This certification may be a good choice if you want to have good general knowledge in all areas of Web design, development, and administration.

TIP

CIW program offerings continue to expand as Internet technology changes. To find out more about the CIW program, including any changes or updates, visit www.ciwcertified.com.

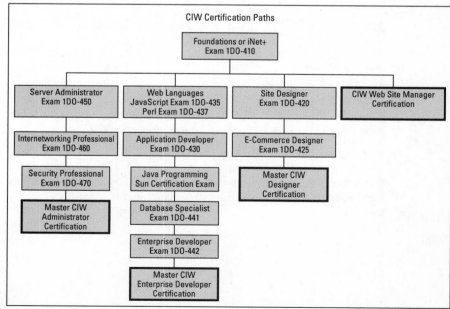

Figure 1-1:
CIW
certification
paths.

If you're already certified by Microsoft, Novell, or Intel

If you have already attained advanced networking certifications through programs offered by Microsoft, Novell, or Intel, you have another option when it comes to becoming CIW certified. The CIW i-Accelerate program enables candidates in this situation to take either accelerated exam #1D0-475 or #1DO-476 (depending on which certification you have). These exams cover server administration, internetworking, and security. After passing one of these exams, you'll be a Master CIW Administrator.

Taking CIW classes

Several authorized training centers offer classes to help you learn the material covered in the various CIW exams. If you've just started working in Web design, you may think about this option. Classes for each exam are usually 3–5 days long and, at the time of this writing, cost somewhere in the neighborhood of $800–$2,000, depending on class length and content. Check out www.ciwcertified.com for a list of authorized training partners in your area.

Introducing the CIW Foundations exam

This book gets you started in your quest to become CIW certified by helping you pass the Foundations exam. The Foundations exam covers three main areas:

- Internet Fundamentals
- Web Authoring (HTML) Fundamentals
- Network Fundamentals

For a complete rundown of the layout of the Foundations exam, how many questions to expect, and so forth, page ahead to Chapter 2.

Chapter 2

Getting to Know the CIW Foundations Exam

In This Chapter

▶ Taking a look at the format of the Foundations exam

▶ Preparing for the exam

▶ Scheduling and paying for the exam

*I*f you've decided to become CIW certified, the first major step you'll need to take is to study for and pass the CIW Foundations exam. This exam was created to test you on your fundamental knowledge of the Internet and how it works. You are also tested on the basics of Web page creation. After passing the Foundations exam, you can move on to one of the more specialized certifications in the path best suited for you:

- ✔ Administering networks
- ✔ Designing Web sites
- ✔ Writing Web-related programs and scripts
- ✔ Administering Web sites

How do you know if you're a good candidate for the Foundations exam? Well, according to ProsoftTraining, there aren't any prerequisites. Realistically, though, if you've just started browsing the Internet or are still struggling with sending standard e-mail, you probably need to get a little more familiar with Web technology before attempting to get CIW certified.

If you're comfortable with basic terminology — what a Web browser is, what a search engine is — and you've been at least dabbling in Web page creation, you'll pass the Foundations exam — as long as you study.

How long will it take you to prepare for the exam? Well, that's kind of like asking a woman how long it will take her to get ready. It depends. If you're already proficient with HTML (Hypertext Markup Language) and understand some fundamental networking components, studying for the exam shouldn't take more than a few days. But if you're not a guru yet, preparing for the exam may take a few weeks or even a month — depending on how much time you have on a daily basis — so that you can spend more time exploring the topics more fully and looking at some of the Web sites I point out to you throughout the book.

Prerequisites (And Where to Go for Help)

If you ask the good people at Prosoft, they'll tell you that there are no formal prerequisites for the Foundations exam, other than a basic understanding of Windows 95/98. But I've watched many students take this exam (most of them do very well, by the way), and the people who tend to do the best have already exposed themselves to some of the fundamental concepts:

- ✔ What is a Web page?
- ✔ What is a search engine?
- ✔ What is HTML?
- ✔ What is a network?

If some of these concepts are new to you, don't lose hope. You can still pass the Foundations exam, but you'll probably need to do a little reading beyond this book. Check out Chapters 22 and 23. Chapter 22 introduces you to some great Web sites to help you study. Chapter 23 gives you some ace studying tips. The CD that comes with this book also contains some great tools. Check out the appendix for more information.

If you need some more in-depth information, the following books, all published by Hungry Minds, Inc., may be useful to you:

- ✔ *Creating Web Pages,* 5th Edition, by Bud Smith and Arthur Bebak.
- ✔ *The Internet For Dummies Starter Kit,* 7th Edition, by John Levine, Carol Baroudi, and Margaret Levine Young. (This book includes a CD with Netscape Navigator and Internet Explorer, plus Eudora and Outlook Express, a couple of Web editors, and some graphics tools.)
- ✔ *HTML 4 For Dummies,* by Ed Tittel, Natanya Pitts, and Chelsea Valentine.
- ✔ *Networking For Dummies,* 5th Edition, by Doug Lowe.

Exam Objectives

The objectives of the Foundations exam are divided into three categories: Internet Fundamentals, Web Page Authoring Fundamentals, and Networking Fundamentals.

Internet Fundamentals

Table 2-1 gives you Prosoft's list of Internet Fundamentals objectives.

Table 2-1	Internet Fundamentals Objectives	
Objective	**Explanation**	**Check Out This Chapter**
Describe infrastructure required to support an Internet connection, including hardware and software components.	Know how Web servers and clients connect and interact.	Chapter 3
Explain important Internet communications protocols and their roles in delivering basic Internet services.	Understand how Transmission Control Protocol/Internet Protocol (TCP/IP) works and how SMTP, POP, and IMAP work together with e-mail.	Chapter 3
Explain the basic principles of the Domain Name System (DNS).	Be able to explain how DNS names are resolved to IP addresses.	Chapter 3
Describe how Web browsers can be used to access the World Wide Web and other computer resources.	You should be very comfortable using Microsoft Internet Explorer and Netscape Navigator to surf the Web and know how to customize browser settings like history and fonts.	Chapter 4
Explain how e-mail clients can be used to send simple messages and files to other Internet users.	Not only do you need to be familiar with the mechanics of writing, addressing, and sending an e-mail message, but you also should be able to describe how messages are transferred across the Internet and how to attach various types of files to an e-mail.	Chapter 5

(continued)

Table 2-1 *(continued)*

Objective	Explanation	Check Out This Chapter
Describe Internet services, including but not limited to news, FTP, Gopher, Telnet, and network performance utilities such as ping and trace route.	Know what all the standard network protocols do and when to use certain network utilities like ping and trace route.	Touched on in Chapter 3 and covered in detail in Chapters 18 and 19
Explain user customization features in Web browsers, including preferences, caching, and cookies.	This is really as easy as it sounds. If you know how to set these preferences on your home computer's Web browser, your life is golden.	Chapter 3
Describe security issues related to Web browsing and e-mail, including certificates and viruses.	Know the standard techniques Web authors use to keep content and payment data secure as well as how to protect your own system from viruses.	Chapter 7
Explain how to use different types of Web search engines effectively.	Know the various kinds of tactics search engines use (like spiders and directories), as well as the best search tactics for ferreting out the information you need (such as Boolean searching).	Chapter 4
Describe how to use the Web to obtain legal and international business information.	This is the business side of the Web — understanding copyrights, trademarks, and licensing.	Chapter 6
Describe issues in developing a corporate Web site, including but not limited to project management, testing, and legal issues.	Business aspects of Web development — understand the project management cycle and legal issues concerning e-commerce sites.	Chapter 6

Web Page Authoring Fundamentals

Some of the information you need to know about Web fundamentals you can memorize (such as HTML codes), and other information you need to know is a little more complicated, requiring you to come up with a process for completing specific tasks. Table 2-2 gives you the short version.

Table 2-2	Web Authoring Fundamentals Objectives	
Objective	*Explanation*	*Check Out This Chapter*
Explain how HTML files are formatted to maintain compatibility with older Web browsers.	Know the different versions of HTML including strict, transitional, and frameset as well as newer HTML variants such as DHTML and XHTML.	Chapter 9
Explain how to include images and graphical formatting in HTML files.	Know how to insert images, horizontal rules, and bulleted and numbered lists.	Chapter 10
Describe how to create a basic HTML form that accepts user input.	Create HTML forms that accept user input.	Chapter 12
Describe how to test and analyze Web site performance issues.	Understand how both server and client issues can affect Web page performance.	Chapter 9
Explain the features and appropriate use of XML.	You don't have to actually write XML, just understand why it's used and how.	Chapter 14

Networking Fundamentals

Some of the stuff you need to know about networking you may already be familiar with from working on the Internet. That seems logical because the Internet is just one big network. Table 2-3 shows you what you need to know about networking and where to find it.

Table 2-3	Networking Fundamentals Objectives	
Objective	*Explanation*	*Check Out This Chapter*
Describe networking and its role in the Internet, including protocols, packets, and the OSI reference model.	Know the down and dirty technical details about how servers process information.	Chapter 15

(continued)

Table 2-3 *(continued)*

Objective	Explanation	Check Out This Chapter
Explain the role of networking hardware, and configure common PC hardware for operation.	Know the standard hardware that networks use, such as cable types and network cards, and which networks use which.	Chapter 20
Discuss the relationship between IP addresses and domain names, including assignment of IP addresses within a subnet.	Know the rules for IP addressing including which addresses are valid and why.	Chapter 20
Describe the function and components of the Web server.	Know how servers process various types of data and which servers handle e-mail, transactions, file sharing, and so on.	Chapter 16
Discuss common Internet security issues, including user-level and enterprise-level concerns.	Know what the main categories of viruses are and the various steps to take in a hack attack. Know the common steps for protecting a network and an individual machine.	Chapter 21
Describe common performance issues affecting Internet servers and resources, including analysis and diagnosis.	Know how to troubleshoot network performance issues using ping, trace route, netstat, and other network utilities.	Chapter 19
Describe how to transmit text and binary files using popular Internet services, including the Web and e-mail.	Know how Multipurpose Internet Mail Extensions (MIME) types work; understand why Uucoding and BinHex are used.	Chapter 16

Other important objectives

For whatever reason, Prosoft doesn't include on its Web site some of the topics that are covered on the Foundations exam. This is an unfortunate fact because Prosoft does expect you to know these mystery objectives for the exam anyway. Table 2-4 lists the additional exam objectives you need to know, as well as where I cover them in this book.

Table 2-4	Additional Exam Objectives	
Objective	*Explanation*	*Check Out This Chapter*
Understand the purpose, security concerns, and key features of Web content that can be added with scripting and programming languages.	Know the difference between JScript, JavaScript, Java, VBScript, ActiveX components, and other dynamic content; know which of these scripting and programming languages can raise security concerns — and why.	Chapter 8
Explain the role of plug-ins in Web pages, as well as how plug-ins work.	Know which file types call for specific plug-in programs, and know the various modes that plug-in programs can run in.	Chapter 8
Explain how to incorporate graphic elements into Web pages.	Know the key features of the GIF, JPG, and PNG image formats, how to incorporate images and horizontal rules into HTML pages, and how to work with bulleted and numbered lists.	Chapter 11
Discuss the use of frames in Web sites.	Know how to create vertical and horizontal frames and how to link content in one frame to content in another frame.	Chapter 13
Explore the purpose and benefits of incorporating server-side content into Web sites.	Know the basics of incorporating server-side content into Web pages with scripting and programming languages. Know the pros and cons of using CGI, ASP, ColdFusion, SSJS, PHP, APIs, and Java servlets. Know the key features of standard database types.	Chapter 17
Explain how data is sent and received within standard networking reference models.	Know what happens in each step of the OSI/RM, and how those steps compare to the steps in the Internet Architecture Model.	Chapter 18
Describe the parts of a packet.	Know what's contained in the header, data, and trailer sections of a data packet.	Chapter 18

(continued)

Table 2-4 (continued)

Objective	Explanation	Check Out This Chapter
Discuss IP address classes, subnet masks, and routing protocols.	Know which IP addresses fall within which address classes; know the default subnet masks of each address class; know which protocols are used when routing a packet from one network to another.	Chapter 19

Getting the Lay of the Land: Exam Layout and Coverage

Unlike most exams you may have taken in high school and/or college, the Foundations exam is not a written exam (so just filling up one of those blue booklets won't get you anywhere). This test is a computer program that enables you to select the correct answer with a mouse. The good thing about taking a computer-based exam is that you get your score as soon as you're finished — it flashes on the screen, and the testing center gives you a print-out of your results. The results sheet shows how many questions you missed in each section, so in the (very) unlikely event you don't pass, you'll know which topics you need to work on.

How many questions, and how much time?

The Foundations exam has 70 questions — 60 scored questions covering three main areas of Internet-related technologies and 10 non-scored *beta* questions. (Beta questions are questions-to-be. Prosoft includes the questions to test them for use in future exams. Always thinking ahead.)

The beta questions are scattered randomly throughout the exam, so you won't know if a particular question will be scored or not. (See, I told you those Prosoft folks are always thinking ahead.)

You have 90 minutes to answer all the questions on the exam. You may skip a question and mark it to return to later. Ninety minutes may not seem like a lot of time to answer 70 questions, but if you're prepared, some of the questions will be easy enough for you to answer in just a few seconds.

Getting a breakdown of test-objective coverage

Table 2-5 lists the three main sections of the exam and what each section covers. It also shows how many questions to expect in each section of the exam.

Table 2-5	Foundations Exam Layout		
Area	**Number of Questions**	**Percentage of Test**	**What's Tested**
Internet Fundamentals	24	40%	History of the Internet and how it works; doing advanced searches in search engines; using e-mail; how FTP, Telnet, and Gopher work; e-commerce and security basics; plug-ins
Web Page Authoring Fundamentals	12	20%	HTML history and standards; creating HTML pages, tables, frames, and forms; good HTML coding practices
Networking Fundamentals	24	40%	Network architecture and standards; networking protocols; TCP/IP, Internet servers, server-side scripting and database connectivity, and security
Beta questions	10	Not scored	Scattered randomly throughout exam; the answers do not count toward your exam score

To pass the exam, you must get 75 percent of the questions right. That's 45 of 60 questions correct for you math whizzes.

Even though the section on Web page authoring (the HTML section) accounts for only 12 questions on the exam, knowledge of HTML is fundamental to creating and editing Web pages. Make sure you don't skimp on it!

Multiple-choice questions

All of the exam questions are multiple choice. You won't have to actually write any HTML code or create any part of a Web page. Each question has only one correct answer, but if you remember taking the SAT or some other standardized test, you probably remember all the dreaded possibilities: The correct answer may be "both A and B" or "both B and C" or "all of the above" or "A, B, and D, but not C." Arggh!

Out-tricking trick questions

As with many exams of this nature (exams constructed to torture innocent victims), the Foundations exam often includes two answers that are related closely enough to make you really think hard about which is correct. If you find yourself stuck between two answers, try to remember what Prosoft is looking for. Often, the wording of a question is a big tip-off, but here's another trick: Prosoft loves to ask questions that compare similar technologies and tools with each other. For example, you might get a question asking what is the most common type of program to use if you want to send a spreadsheet file to a co-worker in another city. The answer list includes both e-mail and FTP. Now you could use either of these methods to transfer the spreadsheet file, but the most *common* way to do it is to attach the file to an e-mail — see what I mean? If you've memorized the main similarities and differences between technologies or tools *before* you go into the exam, you should be able to sail through with no problem. (Throughout the book I supply comparisons between technologies.)

Of course, that advice won't be any help if you're drawing a blank in the middle of the exam. Sometimes you just can't remember stuff. If you're not sure which answer is correct, don't belabor it. Narrow your choice down to two answers, play rock-paper-scissors to pick one, and flag the question so you can come back to it later. It's always better to choose some answer rather than choosing none at all just in case you run out of time later. And even if you're just guessing, you may just guess right!

And here's something wacky to watch out for. Prosoft is really fond of using names and cities you don't know how to pronounce. Like Poughkeepsie. Or Pahrump. Or my personal favorite, Attapulgus. Don't worry about it. Just focus on what the question is asking. Pick out the key information in the scenario — the type of network, the number of users, the purpose of the search, whatever it is — and focus your brainpower on that.

Also, be sure to read each question carefully. A question may ask "which of these answers does NOT work in XYZ situation." Oh, the humanity.

Scenario questions

Some of the questions on the exam are presented in a scenario format. Although the answers are still in a multiple-choice format, scenario questions ask you what John or Sue, or some other fictitious person should do in a given situation. A typical scenario question may start like this: "Joe is using the AltaVista search engine to find sites about Paris, France. How should he word his search to get the most accurate results?"

Getting Your Tools Together

You're probably getting a little antsy, wondering what, other than your willing brain, you need to prepare for this exam. Well, you've got this book, so that's a good start. You also need a computer, which I assume you already own. If you're one of those highlighter types — you know who you are — have at it. Oh, and you'll want a notepad if you like to take copious notes. And that, my friends, is really about it.

Here is a bare-bones list of the tools you absolutely must have to study for and pass the exam:

> ✔ **A computer running either Windows 95 or later or Macintosh OS 9 or later.** The exam, just like the real Web design world, focuses primarily on Windows operating systems. Most of the information, however, will work just the same if you're a Mac user.
>
> Although UNIX and Linux are mentioned on the Foundations exam, the questions are written within the Windows framework. You're not required to know how to use either operating system.
>
> ✔ **A text reader program.** Both Windows and Macintosh operating systems come with text reader programs. Windows comes with Notepad and Macs come with SimpleText — either will do.
>
> ✔ **Internet access and either the Netscape Navigator or Internet Explorer Web browser.**

If you want to scratch beneath the surface a bit and explore some of the Foundations topics in depth, you will need additional tools. If you want to explore networking in depth, for example, you need a network with a server.

Signing Over Your Life: The Certification Agreement

Before you take your first CIW exam, you need to complete an online agreement with Prosoft called a CIW Certification Agreement. Even if you plan to take many CIW exams, you only have to complete the online form once, and it must be completed before you will be awarded a certificate that indicates you have passed any CIW exam.

You can find the CIW Certification Agreement at www.ciwcertified.com (just click the Certification Agreement link) either before or after you take an exam, but you won't receive a certificate until Prosoft has a record of your acceptance of its terms.

Read the legal mumbo jumbo, provide your name and address, and if you agree with the agreement, click Yes.

After you complete the online agreement, you'll receive a hard copy of it in the mail as well as hard copies of any certificates for any CIW exams you may have already taken and passed. You'll also receive future certificates in the mail.

Registering for the Exam

Two main testing organizations operate certified testing centers throughout the world. Prometric Thomson Learning operates over 4,000 Prometric testing centers around the world, and VUE Testing Services, the computer-based arm of NCS Pearson, operates testing centers throughout most of the world as well. In other words, these testing centers are the biggest and best in the business, so even if you live miles from nowhere, there's probably a testing center near you.

If you have taken other computer-based certification exams, you may already know of a VUE or Prometric testing center in your area. You've got an even bigger head start if you have memorized the test centers' phone numbers. Just pick up the phone and start dialing. If you're not quite that prepared, you can call Prometric at 800-380-EXAM (in North America) and VUE at 877-619-2096 in the Unites States and 877-619-2096 in Canada.

If you don't spend your time trolling the testing centers in your area, you can do what most people do and register online. To find a Prometric testing center and schedule your exam, go to www.2test.com. To schedule an exam at a VUE testing center, go to www.vue.com/ciw. Or, from the CIW certified home page, click the Exams link and look for the Prometric and VUE logos.

Follow the online instructions and be sure to have a credit card on hand — you need to pay upfront.

You can register up to 6 to 8 weeks before the exam, but you're probably cutting it too close if you try to register the day before the exam. Be smart and register a couple of weeks early so you have one less thing to worry about.

You may as well pick the testing center that's closest to you — the exam is the same whether you choose Prometric or VUE.

Prometric and VUE testing centers are located in several types of facilities, and, frankly, some are set up better than others. I prefer to take exams at centers where each testing computer is in its own little room. I've heard stories of some testing centers that have one large room with 10 or 12 testing cubicles. If you get stuck next to a person who continually hums or thinks out loud, it might interrupt your concentration, so you may want to find out the layout of the testing center upfront. Also, remember that you won't be able to leave the computer after you've started the exam.

The following sections answer some of your other registration questions.

How much does the exam cost?

The exam costs $125 U.S. and the equivalent dollar amount based on the exchange rate in other countries. You must pay for the exam *when you schedule your test date.* You can pay by credit card or check. If you pay by check, you'll have to wait until the check clears before your registration is confirmed and you're able to take the exam, so be sure to allow extra time.

What happens if I have to cancel or change my registration?

If you have to change your registration, just call the testing center at least 24 hours in advance. If you need to cancel your exam, call your testing center at least 24 hours in advance, and typically the center will mail you a refund within a few weeks.

What do I do the day of the exam?

Glad you asked. Here's a rundown of what you need to do on the big day:

- **Get there early.** Be prepared to get to your exam location 15 minutes or so in advance.

- **Bring ID.** In fact, bring *two* IDs. One must be a picture ID, such as a driver's license. The other can be a major credit card, a social security card, or a passport.

- **Don't bring anything else.** You can take nothing inside the exam room (not even a mobile phone, purse, or backpack) except your brain, and a blank tablet and a pencil you'll be handed when you check in to take your exam.

✔ **Use the tablet, Luke!** I recommend that you use the blank tablet to "brain dump" (that's a technical term, by the way) when you get inside the room. That's what the tablet's for.

You'll have to memorize several things that you might forget at the last minute when you're in the middle of taking the exam. I always recommend that you jot down any definitions or acronyms that are tricky or long as soon as you get inside your test booth. For example, I wrote down all the layers of the OSI reference model and all the protocols that reside at each layer. (If that just sounded like a foreign language, take it easy, I cover those topics in Chapter 18.)

✔ **Take the tutorial, even if you've taken a computer-based exam before.** After you're seated in front of the test computer, you'll have a chance to run through a tutorial that explains how to go from screen to screen during the exam and how to mark answers.

Take as much time as you want for this tutorial — the 90-minute timer doesn't begin until you begin taking the actual exam.

Part II
Internet Fundamentals

The 5th Wave   By Rich Tennant

THE SECRET ROOM AT EVERY INTERNET SERVICE PROVIDER

KNOCK FIRST

DISCONNECT

"I'll be right there. Let me just take care of this user. He's about halfway through a 3 hour download."

In this part . . .

Part II covers some information that you probably already know only if you studied it in college or read it in another (lower-quality) CIW study guide. You find out who invented the Internet and when, who's credited with creating HTML and why that was such a big deal, and how people found files on the Internet before search engines came along. Historical information like this, frankly, doesn't really help you much when you're struggling to get your company logo aligned properly on your Web page. But, history seems to be important to testing companies, so you have to play the game their way.

This part of the book covers the material that 40 percent of the exam questions come from. You can find Internet basics, such as what you need to know about surfing the Internet. You also find out what ProsoftTraining wants you to know about how search engines and Web browsers work. There are other sections on topics like e-commerce theory and copyright standards. Most test-takers find the fundamentals to be the easiest section of the exam. That does not, however, mean you should merely skim this section of the book. Because this content does count for almost half of your score, take the time to read it.

Chapter 3

Where the Internet Came From and How It Works

● ●

Exam Objectives

▶ Supporting an Internet connection — including hardware and software components

▶ Understanding important Internet communications protocols and their roles in delivering basic Internet services

▶ Knowing the basic principles of the Domain Name System (DNS)

▶ Accessing the World Wide Web and other computer resources through a Web browser

▶ Customizing features in Web browsers — including preferences and caching

● ●

*I*t's almost unbelievable that just a few years ago hardly anyone had heard of the Internet or the World Wide Web. Nowadays, I think it's safe to say that both of these technologies have had an incredible impact on our daily lives — even the lives of people who don't consider themselves to be very technical. And for those of us who think nothing of browsing the Web or surfing the Internet at least a thousand times a day, it's hard to imagine life without these technologies. The Internet, of course, didn't just spring up out of nowhere, and, contrary to what some believe, Al Gore didn't invent it.

For the Foundations exam, you need to know who did create the Internet and how it works. Although knowing the history of the Internet isn't crucial to your day-to-day interaction with it, the ProsoftTraining folks want you to know the key organizations who put it together and the general timeframe for some of the most important advances. In this chapter, I lay out this information as briefly as possible because I know you've got better things to do than memorize facts you won't need in real life. Much of the information in this chapter, however, is valuable info you'll probably use over and over.

Knowing common *protocols* is also important for the exam. A protocol is just a method of doing something. In computerese, a protocol is usually a way of transferring information from one place to another. This chapter gives you more specifics.

Quick Assessment

How the
Internet
works

1 The first global network of computers was called _____.

2 The language that's become the standard for creating Web pages is _____.

3 The protocol set that makes Internet connection possible is _____.

Client/server
model on
the Internet

4 Software that runs on a host computer and makes data available to users is _____ software.

5 The fastest analog modem transmits data at _____ in the United States.

6 Cable modems and DSL service are examples of _____ connections.

Internet
protocols

7 _____ is the protocol commonly used to upload Web pages.

8 _____ addresses are comprised of numbers placed in dotted quads.

9 _____ will soon be implemented to address the shortage of IP addresses.

10 The complete name of a top-level domain is called a _____.

Answers

1 *ARPANET.* Check out "History of the Internet."

2 *Hypertext Markup Language or HTML.* Read over "Then Came the Web."

3 *TCP/IP.* Review "Sending Information over the Internet."

4 *Server.* Look over "Understanding Clients and Servers on the Internet."

5 *56 Kbps.* Turn to "Dial-up connection speeds."

6 *Direct.* Check out "Direct connection speeds."

7 *File transfer protocol or FTP.* Review "Internet Protocols."

8 *Internet protocol or IP.* Take a look at "IP addresses."

9 *Internet protocol version 6 or IPv6.* See "Solving the IP addressing problem."

10 *Fully qualified domain name or FQDN.* Read "Fully qualified domain names (FQDNs)."

History of the Internet

Chances are, you know that a *network* consists of at least two computers hooked up so that they can share resources, such as printers and file storage resources. You probably also know that the larger a network is, the more complicated it is. Well, if you didn't, you do now. (Skip on over to Chapter 15 to brush up some more on networking basics.) And the Internet, well, the Internet is the mother of all networks. But I'm getting ahead of myself. . . .

The U.S. Department of Defense's Advanced Research Projects Agency (affectionately referred to as ARPA) is credited with creating the first global computer network, ARPANET. After its creation in 1968, it was renamed DARPANET for Defense Advanced Research Projects Agency. This huge network of computers enabled government and university personnel to research and work from any computer on a network.

This global computer network called ARPANET was a *huge* advance. One of the things that made it unique at the time was its use of multiple hosts. A *host* is a computer that stores information and makes it available to other computers. With multiple hosts storing and sharing information, a network is more dependable. If one of the hosts goes down, people can still access information from the other hosts.

In 1989, ARPANET was connected to the National Science Foundation (NSF) network, called NSFnet. The NSF added more supercomputers to the network and expanded access to more businesses, universities, and government installations. The NSF also expanded NSFnet to include many other networks, which resulted in the largest network of networks in existence: the Internet.

You may think that the Internet is old news, but believe it or not, you need to know ancient history for the Foundations exam. Know what ARPANET, DARPANET, and NSFnet stand for, when each of them was created, and what the difference between these three early networks is.

Then Came the Web

The Internet of the 1960s and 1970s was a lot different from the Internet you and I know today. Back then, there were no pictures or clickable words. You had to know the correct commands to type in to access the information you wanted. This all changed with the creation of HTML — Hypertext Markup Language.

In March of 1989, a researcher named Tim Berners-Lee was working at the Conseil Européenne pour la Recherche Nucléaire (CERN) or European Laboratory for Particle Physics. In an effort to allow fellow scientists to easily share information — no matter which operating system they were using — Berners-Lee created HTML — Hypertext Markup Language.

HTML is the standard authoring language people use to create Web pages. HTML made possible the addition of images, hypertext, and hyperlinks to Web pages. Hypertext connects Web pages and their content. Hypertext links make words *clickable* so that they can load other pages, images, or even multimedia files.

To steer the future of the Web, Tim Berners-Lee helped create the World Wide Web Consortium or W3C. The W3C is the organization that promotes standards and interoperability between Web browsers that read HTML and other Web technologies. The W3C suggests HTML improvements and tries to get the companies that make browsers to implement them.

People often use the terms "the Internet" and "the Web" to mean the same thing, but technically they're different. For the exam, you need to understand the difference between the Internet and the Web:

- ✔ The **Internet** is the actual network of computers spread out all over the world that are storing and sharing data.

- ✔ The **Web** is the collection of Web pages and programs that are stored on host computers.

Intranets

An *intranet* is a group of computers networked together, usually within the same building or office space. Only machines on that network can access the data stored on the network. Many companies set up Web servers within their network and post Web pages that are viewable only within that network. These are called intranet sites. Intranets provide a convenient way for computers running different operating systems — Windows, Macintosh, UNIX, and so on — to communicate because they all understand how to access Web pages.

Extranets

An *extranet* takes an intranet one step further. Not only can people within the organization look at data or Web pages stored on the network, but people outside of the network can access them as well — if they know the correct security codes or other access to log on to the internal network. An extranet is commonly used within companies who have employees who work from home or have clients that need to view private data on a continual basis. Because an external user logs on to an extranet, the information is more secure than if it were available on the Internet.

Sending Information over the Internet

The first time I got on the Internet (I won't tell you how many years ago that was), I thought it was just about as close to being real-life magic as I had ever seen. Well, the way the Internet works is a lot like the way magic tricks work — when you understand what's really going on, they don't seem so mysterious.

Here's a primer on some information technology terms you need to know for the exam:

✔ **Protocol:** Computers and networks use many different *protocols* (sets of rules) to transfer information. In a real-life analogy — if I wanted to travel from Paris, France, to Rome, Italy, I could take several "protocols" — the bus protocol or the plane protocol or maybe the train protocol. All would transfer me from Paris to Rome, some more quickly, others more cheaply, but all would do the job. Different methods of travel have different levels of security just like different protocols have different security arrangements. When computers transfer data, different protocols are used depending on the situation at hand.

Computers connected to the Internet transfer information via software that uses a set of protocols called *TCP/IP* — Transmission Control Protocol/Internet Protocol. I get into TCP/IP and lots of other network protocols in detail in Chapter 18, but for now, just remember that TCP/IP is what enables computers to transfer information over the Internet.

✔ **IP (Internet Protocol) Address:** Just as your house has an address, each Internet site has a numeric address called an IP address.

✔ **Router:** Just as in real life, if you drive from your house to the grocery store, you can probably take one of many different routes. When information is being sent from one computer to another, many routes could be taken as well. Because no stop signs or traffic cops guide traffic flow on the Internet, something called a *router* does the job. A router figures out the shortest, smoothest path between two points and guides data along that route.

✔ **Packet:** The data you send or retrieve — e-mails, Web pages, and so forth — aren't sent as complete documents or pages. Instead they're broken down into *packets*. Sending information in packets is kind of like sending a message one sentence at a time, except the Internet is very efficient at sending packets quickly. The good thing about sending data in packets is that if a problem crops up — maybe part of your message doesn't go through — the whole message doesn't have to be resent, only the missing or damaged packets.

Understanding Clients and Servers on the Internet

The software and protocols of the Internet were created using the *client/server model*. In the client/server model, networks are made up of both client programs and server programs that share the work of processing and distributing information. Say, for example, you're using a computer in your office that's hooked up to your company network. Maybe you're writing a letter using Microsoft Word. If Word is installed on your computer, you're using a *client application*. If, on the other hand, Word is installed on your company's server and you open and run it from there, you're using a *server application*.

The Internet uses the client/server model to split up the workload of transferring Web pages and e-mails between computers, like so:

1. The client software does its thing.

   To see Web pages on a computer, end users need browser software, such as Internet Explorer or Netscape Navigator, loaded on their machines. (Yes, I mean client software.) The browser software requests the information contained in a Web page, and then interprets that information and re-creates it on your computer.

2. The server software does its thing.

   To make this process work, a server program also has to be loaded on another computer that stores or hosts the Web page end users are seeking. When the client makes the request, the server sends the information back to the client. By using both clients and servers together, the process of downloading Web pages is much more efficient than if either one had to do all the work alone.

For a network of any size to work, three things have to be in place:

- **Network of computers:** The computers that are networked together and the hardware that connects them, such as network cards and cables.

- **Client software:** The programs that run on end-user computers.

- **Server software:** The software running on a host computer that makes files and other data available to client applications.

Clients and servers are able to communicate only if they speak the same language. Protocols are these languages. Several protocols can be used in various types of networks, but the clients and servers connected on any network must use the same protocol to be able to understand each other.

Push me, pull ya

When you type a Web address in the browser on a computer, the computer *pulls* this page onto your machine. Pull technology is very common on the Internet. Most Web pages and files just sit on a host computer waiting to be requested or pulled. The client request for information pulls the data from the server to the client.

Some programs use *push* technology. This type of program pushes information out to a machine whether it wants it or not. If you download a Web page that shows sports scores, your computer pulled that page to your machine. But if the scores on that page automatically update as you watch, the new scores are being pushed on to your machine. The server sends the information — pushes it — to the client without the client making a new request. Get it?

Here are two fairly common programs that use push technology that Prosoft wants you to know:

- ✔ Infogate (formerly PointCast) pushes customized sports scores, news, and weather information to your desktop or wireless device.

- ✔ Microsoft's Active Channel pushes custom information to your computer using Microsoft's proprietary *Channel Definition Format* (CDF).

Internet service providers

Internet service providers (ISPs) are companies that provide access to the Internet. AOL, EarthLink, and Sprint are examples of popular ISPs used in the United States. When you log on with your ISP and get on the Internet, you're using either a dial-up connection or a direct connection:

- ✔ **Dial-up connection:** Uses a regular modem to connect your computer to the Internet. Your ISP assigns your machine an IP address to be used during this session only. When you're finished online, you log off and break your Internet connection. In some areas, faster dial-up access is available by installing an *Integrated Services Digital Network* (ISDN) line, which is a digital phone line.

- ✔ **Direct connection:** Always on or always connected to the Internet. DSL and cable modems are popular examples. This type of connection is usually much faster and more convenient than a dial-up connection.

Dial-up connection speeds

Dial-up Internet access usually uses the analog modem that's built in to your computer. In this situation, the modem you're using determines how fast your connection speed is. In some areas, you can ask your phone company to install a digital phone line that supports ISDN. ISDN is still considered dial-up access, but connection speeds are at least a little or maybe even a lot faster than connection speeds over a regular, analog phone line. Connection speeds are measured in bits per second.

✔ A thousand bits per second are measured in *kilobits per second* or Kbps.

✔ A million bits per second are measured in *megabits per second* or Mbps.

✔ A billion bits per second are measured in *gigabits per second* or Gbps.

Eight bits of information make up a *byte*. When working with computers, some speeds or sizes (such as the amount of RAM in your computer) are measured in megabytes (MBs) or gigabytes (GBs). If you're trying to determine if a speed or size is megabits or megabytes, look at the size of the *b* in the acronym. A capitol *B* as in "128MB of RAM" stands for bytes. A small *b* as in "56 Mbps" stands for bits.

Table 3-1 compares common connection speeds for dial-up connections that you need to know for the exam.

Table 3-1	Dial-Up Connection Speeds
Speed	*Description*
14.4 Kbps	One of the slowest analog modems out there
28.8 Kbps	Moderately slow analog modem
33.6 Kbps	Moderate speed analog modem
56 Kbps	Highest speed analog modem available
64 Kbps	Standard ISDN speed with a digital modem on a digital line
128 Kbps	Speed achieved when two ISDN lines are used together

In some areas, especially rural areas in smaller towns, the fastest analog modem in the world won't increase your connection speed. Older phone lines can't handle 56 Kbps speeds, so even if your modem can transfer data at 56 Kbps, the phone line won't send it that fast.

Direct connection speeds

Direct or *always on* connections can be achieved in several ways. The three most popular methods are

- ✔ **Cable modem:** In areas where digital cable TV is available, cable Internet access is often available as well. Instead of using a regular analog modem, this type of connection utilizes a special digital cable modem usually provided by your cable company. The cable modem plugs in to a *network interface card* (NIC) that may have to be added to your computer as well.

- ✔ **Digital Subscriber Line (DSL):** In many communities, local phone companies offer customers DSL. DSL is available when the telephone switching office is updated with DSL-compatible equipment. This connection uses digital phone lines and must be set up by installers from your phone company. It uses a special DSL modem and usually plugs in to a network interface card or NIC.

- ✔ **Local area network (LAN):** In many business offices around the world, companies set up direct Internet connections over a LAN. A LAN router is used to connect the company's network to the Internet.

Table 3-2 compares common direct connection speeds. Know these speeds, especially for E1, T1, E3, and T3 for the exam.

Table 3-2		Direct Connection Speeds
Type	*Speed*	*Special Notes*
DSL	512 Kbps to 10 Mbps	
Cable	512 Kbps to 52 Mbps	
E1	2.048 Mbps	European version of T1
T1	1.544 Mbps	Often used in North America to connect corporate LANs to the Internet
E3	34.368 Mbps	European version of T3
T3	44.736 Mbps	Often used in North America to connect corporate LANs to the Internet; high speed but very expensive

Faster connections are available, but Prosoft doesn't include them in this section of the CIW Foundations exam.

Internet Protocols

A *protocol* is a set of rules that controls the way two or more computers swap data. The way various protocols work differs depending on their functions, just as the way a car or train work a little differently when it comes to transferring humans from place to place.

Different types of data call for different types of protocols just as different travel situations call for you to choose different means of transportation. (You wouldn't use a car to make a cross-oceanic trip, would you?) Table 3-3 is a primer on some of the most popular you need to know for the exam.

Table 3-3	Common Internet Protocols
Protocol	*Description*
Transmission Control Protocol/Internet Protocol (TCP/IP)	A suite of protocols that's the foundation of all Internet communication. Even when some programs are using other protocols (Web browsers use HTTP, for example) they're also using TCP/IP.
Serial Line Internet Protocol (SLIP)	Older protocol used with a dial-up connection. Widely replaced by PPP. SLIP allows only a single computer to use the dial-up line at a time.
Point-to-Point Protocol (PPP)	Commonly used with dial-up connections. Often used instead of SLIP because of its flexibility and security. PPP can allow multiple computers to share a single dial-up connection.
Hypertext Transfer Protocol (HTTP)	Used to transfer Web pages from servers to Web browsers. Supports hyperlinked text and images.
File Transfer Protocol (FTP)	Commonly used to publish Web pages. Publishing transfers pages, images, and folders to a server machine very efficiently. Also used to provide access to larger files on the Internet or within a company.
Simple Mail Transfer Protocol (SMTP)	Used by clients and mail servers to send e-mail. Paired with either POP or IMAP, which receive the e-mail.
Post Office Protocol (POP)	Used by client computers to request and receive e-mail.
Internet Messaging Access Protocol (IMAP)	Used by mail servers to manage access to stored e-mail. Used by clients to examine their e-mail on the server. Not as common as POP but more powerful. Allows sharing of mailboxes and access to multiple mail servers.

(continued)

Table 3-3 *(continued)*

Protocol	Description
Network News Transfer Protocol (NNTP)	Used by news servers to provide access to *newsgroups*— groups in which users exchange articles on a specific topic. Newsgroups were originally only part of a separate network called Usenet, which is now part of the regular Internet.
Telnet	Used with text-only or *shell* accounts. Very popular on the early Internet. Allows a user to log on to a remote network and allows users to access data *as if they were actually part of that remote network.* Still used to administer large networks.
Gopher	Older protocol that has been widely replaced by HTTP. Gopher was a *menu-based program* that allowed users to browse resources; considered the precursor to the modern Internet.
Wireless Application Protocol (WAP)	Used by many cell phones and *personal digital assistants* (PDAs) to browse Internet data.

Understanding Internet Addressing

The process of Internet addressing uses lots of geeky terms. The following sections explain some of the key terms and how they work together.

URLs

A *uniform resource locator* (URL) is often called a Web address because it goes in a Web browser's address bar and tells ISPs which protocol to use to access specific pages and files on the Internet. If a user tries to access a Web page, the URL usually begins with http://. (HTTP stands for Hypertext Transfer Protocol.) If the user is trying to access an FTP site, the URL begins with ftp://, which stands for File Transfer Protocol. (See "Internet Protocols" earlier in this chapter for more information about the protocols symbolized in URLs.)

IP addresses

When you type in a Web address like www.disney.com, how does your computer know where that Web site is stored? It looks up the 32-bit Internet Protocol (IP) address of the server based on its name. Just as houses on your street have addresses like 350 Main Street or 1115 Woodlake Drive, computers on the Internet have numeric addresses, too. Every computer on the Internet has an IP address. IP addresses are comprised of four numbers separated by periods — the infamous dots — like this:

```
212.021.65.101
```

The format for an IP address is called a *dotted quad* because it always contains four numbers separated by dots. The numbers in the dotted quads can range from 0 to 255.

There are some restrictions when it comes to IP addressing; I cover that topic thoroughly in Chapter 19.

Solving the IP addressing problem

When the creators of the Internet came up with the IP addressing system, they probably never dreamed we might actually run out of available addresses. But that's what we're facing at this point. Only so many number combinations can be created with this addressing format — about 4 billion — and with dozens or even hundreds of new Web sites going up every day, IP addresses are going fast.

A new protocol called Internet Protocol version 6 (IPv6) should help relieve the shortage of IP addresses. IPv6 uses eight numbers instead of four. IPv6 uses 128-bit numbers from the *hexadecimal* numbering system. The hexadecimal numbering system is a base 16 system that uses numbers 0–9 and letters A–F. Here's what an IPv6 address looks like:

```
1F00:A992:FF8B:C909:EE49:90DD:3733:4AAF
```

Because an IPv6 address uses eight numbers instead of four, and each number has four digits, IPv6 can support about 4 trillion numbers instead of the 4 billion currently supported. IPv6 is currently in heavy use in some parts of Asia, but it is being used only in experimental applications in the Americas. No one knows exactly when IPv6 will be fully implemented worldwide, but some experts expect to see it in place between 2010 and 2015.

Domain names

When you type in a URL to locate a personal or company home page, you're probably typing in a *domain name*. Domain names are the logical and (usually) easy-to-remember names people type in when they visit Internet sites. Unlike IP addresses, domain names are comprised of letters, numbers, hyphens, and underscores, separated by dots. Every domain name has a unique IP address. There are large databases that contain all the registered domain names and the numeric IP addresses they match up with. (See "Domain Name System" later in this chapter for more on matching IP addresses to domain names.)

If you know a company's IP address, you can type that in, but all those numbers are hard to remember. For example, to go to the CIW Web site, you could type in the IP address 63.72.51.85, but instead, you'd probably type www.ciwcertified.com, the company's *domain name*.

Domain names are much easier to remember than a bunch of numbers, so that's why we rely on them instead of those long, funky IP addresses. Domain names are broken down into three parts, or as Prosoft likes to call them, labels. The three standard parts of a domain name are shown in Figure 3-1. You should be able to identify these for the exam.

Figure 3-1:
Breaking
down
domain
names.

> ✔ **Domain category:** Prosoft calls the third section the *domain category.* Everyone else in the free world calls it the *top-level* domain. It indicates the category a site belongs in — educational, military, and so on (www.yourcompany.*com*). (More on this in "Domain categories" later in this chapter.)
>
> ✔ **Company name:** The second section, which the exam calls simply a *domain* or refers to as the *company name,* is commonly called the *second-level domain.* The domain name is the part of URLs that people are most likely to remember (www.*yourcompany*.com).
>
> ✔ **Server (host) name:** This is the name of the server machine the Web site is being hosted on. The name most Web servers use is www (*www.*your-company.com).

Domain categories

For the exam, you need to know that a top-level domain is the category the domain name belongs in. Most everyone is familiar with the three-letter `.com` category, which stands for a commercial or company site. You need to know the top-level domains in Tables 3-4 and 3-5 for the exam.

Table 3-4	Important Domain Categories to Remember
Domain	*Who It Belongs To*
`.com`	Commercial or company site
`.net`	Networking organization including ISPs
`.org`	Nonprofit organization
`.edu`	Educational institutions — usually universities
`.gov`	Government site
`.mil`	Military site
`.int`	International organization (rarely ever used)

Table 3-5	Important Country Code Domain Categories to Remember
Domain	*Who It Belongs To*
`.au`	Australia
`.ca`	Canada
`.ch`	Switzerland (Confederation Helvetique)
`.fr`	France
`.mx`	Mexico
`.uk`	United Kingdom
`.us`	United States

An entity that purchases a company name (otherwise known as a second-level domain) then has the ability to add subdomains in front of its purchased name. Usually a subdomain identifies a server within the organization, such as the WWW server. Subdomains can also identify departments or customers such as `www.sales.mycompany.com`.

The domain category (otherwise known as the *top-level domain,* or TLD) identifies the country of origin (refer to Table 3-5) and the location or type of domain within that country. Domains ending in `.tx.us` are located in Texas, USA. Domains ending in `.ac.uk` are academic institutions in the United Kingdom. Domains ending in `.co.jp` are commercial domains in Japan.

In real life, top-level domain categories don't mean as much as they used to. Years ago, one company registered all domain names and researched what type of site you were putting up to match it with the correct domain category. Now, most of the categories are on the honor system, so people and companies often register the `.com`, `.net`, and `.org` versions of each domain they register. Each country has the ability to implement its own rules on how the domains are organized.

Fully qualified domain names (FQDNs)

The complete domain name of an organization is called a *fully qualified domain name* (FQDN). A FQDN provides all the information necessary to find the computer that hosts that Web site. It always includes all three (or more, as the case may be) sections or labels of a domain name: the domain category, company name, and server name.

Registering domain names

Before you can use a domain name for your company Web site, you have to register the domain name you plan to use. Many organizations register domain names these days. I often use `www.register.com` to research and register domain names. On registration sites like this, you can research which domain names are available and register the one you like for a certain number of years. You can also pay for your domain and perform a WHOIS search of previously registered domains. A WHOIS search allows you to enter a domain name and find out to whom it's registered and for how long. The going rate to register domain names at the time of this writing is about $35 U.S. dollars a year.

Here are three companies involved with domain name registration you should know for the Foundations exam:

✔ **Network Solutions:** Until 1998, this was the only company allowed to register domain names. Now, many companies can do so. Network Solutions is now part of VeriSign.

✔ **The Internet's Network Information Center (InterNIC):** Prior to 1998, this cooperative organization coordinated domain name registration efforts of the U.S. government and Network Solutions.

> ✔ **Internet Corporation for Assigned Names and Numbers (ICANN):** After shared registration was introduced in 1998, ICANN was created to coordinate domain name registration among many registrars. ICANN decides which companies can act as registrars, though the process differs depending on which country you're in.

Virtual domains

Virtual domains allow two different IP addresses to reside on the same computer. For example, say you register the domain `www.boguscompanyurl.com`. You then choose a hosting company that has a server with a domain of `www.bogushosting.com`. Your address (and it's unique numeric IP address) can reside on the hosting company's machine through the use of virtual domains. Visitors can type in just `www.boguscompanyurl.com`, and they'll be routed to the correct location on the server machine. Another real-life example of a virtual domain in use is the Ask Jeeves search engine. You can type in either `www.askjeeves.com` or `www.ask.com`. Both take you to the same site; one of them is set up as a virtual domain.

Some hosting companies let individuals and businesses host their Web sites for free. The problem with this is that they don't set up virtual domains. For visitors to get to your Web site in the previous example, without the use of virtual domains, they'd have to type in

```
www.bogushosting.com/boguscompanyurl.com
```

That's a major pain, right? That's why any decent Web hosting company uses virtual domains — they help keep addresses short and easy to remember.

Domain Name System

Domain names are matched up or *resolved* to IP addresses using the *Domain Name System* (DNS). DNS is a giant collection of databases called *domain name servers* (also DNS) that match up the domain name you type with its numeric IP equivalent.

Large networking organizations like ISPs usually have their own domain name servers. Individual companies may also have their own domain name servers, especially if they utilize *intranet* Web sites. If the domain name server closest to the client cannot find an entry for the domain name requested in its own database, it asks other databases to resolve the domain name to an IP address.

Browser Settings and Customization

You thought it was bad enough that you had to memorize Internet history. Well, it gets worse. You also have to be able to regurgitate some of the basic stuff you do every day without even thinking. As you probably know, browser software enables computers to view Web pages and their content. Two of the most popular browsers (and, coincidentally, the two you need to know for the Foundations exam) are Microsoft Internet Explorer and Netscape Navigator. Browser software also allows you to customize the way you view and access Web pages.

For the exam, you don't need to know the exact steps to perform various tasks in each browser. In real life, you probably need to know how to customize various browser settings, but the exam doesn't ask hardly any program-specific information. If you need to know something specific about a program, I point it out.

Viewing Web page code

For the exam, all you need to know about viewing Web page code in browsers is that both popular browsers enable you to view the HTML (Hypertext Markup Language) code behind a Web page. In Internet Explorer, choose View➪Source. In Netscape Navigator, choose View➪Page Source.

Changing browser defaults

Being able to change the default font size of words on Web pages, is especially important for users with high-resolution monitors (like 1024x768 or higher) because high-resolution monitors pack pixels closer together and reduce the size of letters on the screen.

Whenever a user logs on to the Internet, a home page displays by default. Users can change the default home page to any page they like.

Users can turn on and off the image-loading feature in both Internet Explorer and Netscape Navigator. If a user accesses the Web with a slow dial-up connection, for example, turning off image loading speeds up page loading.

Caching pages

To save time, bandwidth, and effort, browsers usually *cache* or copy and store Web pages on the local hard drive for a certain amount of time. When a user types in a cached domain name or address into the address box in their browser, the browser displays a saved copy of the page instead of reloading the page from the Internet.

Users can change their browser's cache settings to save pages for as long as they like. To load the latest version of a cached page, just click Reload (in Netscape Navigator) or Refresh (in Internet Explorer).

Browser history

A browser's *history* folder keeps track of the pages users visit online. It also remembers the links users follow on each page, displaying clicked links in a different color.

By default, hyperlinked text is blue if you haven't clicked the link recently. After you have visited a page, any links to that same page display the link text in purple by default. You can set your browser history to remember pages for as long as you'd like, but you don't have to show off this handy skill for the exam.

Bookmarks and favorites

Users can easily recall Web pages that they have bookmarked or added to a list of favorites. To access or add to your list of bookmarked sites in Netscape, use the Bookmarks menu. To access or add to your list of favorite sites in Internet Explorer, choose the appropriate option from the Favorites menu. You can organize these sites however you'd like — creating folders and subfolders to place them in.

The only program-specific information you need to know for the exam is that although this feature is in both browsers, Netscape and Internet Explorer refer to it differently. Netscape uses the term *bookmark* and Internet Explorer uses the term *favorite*.

Prep Test

1 Until 1998, the only organization that could register domain names was

A ○ W3C
B ○ CERN
C ○ InterNIC
D ○ Network Solutions

2 If you have two registered domain names pointing to the same site, you are probably using _____.

A ○ TCP/IP
B ○ An intranet
C ○ A virtual domain
D ○ Hypertext

3 Which of the following must you have to access the Internet?

A ○ Modem
B ○ Operating system
C ○ Telephone line
D ○ Network

4 What system resolves domain names to IP addresses?

A ○ Domain Name System
B ○ Server/client system
C ○ Telnet system
D ○ Internet protocol system

5 A URL is comprised of

A ○ The company name plus the server name
B ○ The company name plus the domain category
C ○ The company IP address plus the domain name
D ○ The protocol used to access the page plus the full domain name

6 What protocol is commonly used on cell phones to access the Internet?

A ○ WAP
B ○ HTTP
C ○ FTP
D ○ TCP/IP

7 **What is the European equivalent of a T1 line?**

A ◯ T3

B ◯ Euro1

C ◯ PPP

D ◯ E1

8 **SMTP is commonly used with which two message protocols?**

A ◯ POP and PPP

B ◯ IMAP and NNTP

C ◯ POP and IMAP

D ◯ None of the above

9 **A domain name with** .ch **on the end of it means the company is**

A ◯ In Chechnya

B ◯ A chip-maker

C ◯ A commercial entity

D ◯ In Switzerland

10 **An _____ helps keep private information secure while allowing customers to log on and access their records.**

A ◯ Extranet

B ◯ Intranet

C ◯ Internet

D ◯ Excessnet

Answers

1 **C.** Network Solutions. The W3C coordinated Network Solutions registration with government efforts, but only Network Solutions actually registered domains. *See "Registering domain names."*

2 **C.** Virtual domain. Although TCP/IP is being used, that's not what enables two different Web addresses to point to the same Web site. *Review "Virtual domains."*

3 **B.** Operating system. All three of the other answers may be used, depending on how you're accessing the Internet. But the only one that is *always* used, or required, is an operating system. *Check out "Internet service providers."*

4 **A.** Domain Name System. The Domain Name System uses domain name servers to match up numeric IP addresses with domain names. *Look over "Domain Name System."*

5 **D.** The protocol used to access the page plus the full domain name. None of the other answers mention the protocol used to access the page. *See "URLs."*

6 **A.** WAP or Wireless Application Protocol is what cell phones and PDAs use to browse the Internet. *Review "Internet Protocols."*

7 **D.** E1. Remember, E1=T1 and E3=T3. *To review connections speeds, check out "Direct connection speeds."*

8 **C.** POP and IMAP. SMTP is the protocol commonly used to send e-mail, whereas both POP and IMAP retrieve and store e-mail. *Take a look at "Internet Protocols."*

9 **D.** In Switzerland. This was the tricky country code. The other country codes are pretty obvious. *Review "Domain categories."*

10 **A.** Extranet. An extranet allows remote users to log on to a company's network and access private information. *Review "Intranets" and "Extranets."*

Where the Internet Came From . . .

Chapter 4

The Search Begins

Exam Objectives

▶ Using different types of Web search engines effectively

▶ Searching the Internet

▶ Understanding Archie, Gopher, and Veronica

*W*ith literally millions of Web pages and Internet sites out there, the challenge becomes not finding pages that have the information that you want, but finding *only* the pages that have the information that you want. If you've been on the Web more than once or twice, I bet you're already familiar with the basics of using search engines.

Think of search engines as libraries. Most public libraries carry classics like *War and Peace* and *Catus Petasutus: The Cat in the Hat in Latin*. Some books, like the *Basque-English Dictionary* and *The Cambridge Encyclopedia of Human Paleopathology,* however, may not be available at every library branch. That's how search engines work. Many well-known, popular Web sites are listed in nearly every search engine's database. But you only catch the off-the-beaten-path stuff if you steer your Web browser off the beaten path.

In this chapter, I show you how you can use techniques (such as Boolean search terms) to find Internet resources that are actually about the topic you're researching. I also talk about finding newsgroups and about how people used to search back in the Stone Age of the Internet — 1990.

Quick Assessment

Basic and advanced search techniques

1 Search engines like AltaVista use _____ programs that crawl around the Web to find new sites.

2 _____ like AND, OR, and NOT help narrow search results.

3 The _____ search engine was originally designed to index the whole Internet.

4 _____ is a search engine that cross-references keywords that visitors type in.

Adding a Web site to a search engine

5 The _____ attribute in a meta tag contains words that search engines try to match up with visitor searches.

6 A search engine's _____ determines which order to return results in.

7 If you want your Web page to be unavailable to a search engine after a certain date, you can use a meta tag to specify that the page will _____.

8 _____ is a network of newsgroups that has been absorbed by the Internet.

Pre-Web search tools

9 _____ is a search tool used with Gopher.

10 _____ is a menu-based text-browsing tool.

Answers

1   *Spider.* Review "Understanding Search Engine Basics."

2   *Boolean operators.* Read over "Advanced Search Techniques: Going Boolean."

3   *AltaVista.* Review "A Few Search Engine Specifics."

4   *Excite or Lycos.* See "A Few Search Engine Specifics."

5   *Keyword.* Look over "Understanding the role of keywords and ranking in searches."

6   *Ranking system.* Check out "Understanding the role of keywords and ranking in searches."

7   *Expire.* See "Good search results = good meta tags."

8   *Usenet.* Look over "Finding newsgroups."

9   *Veronica.* Check out "Gopher and Veronica."

10   *Gopher.* Read "Gopher and Veronica."

Understanding Search Engine Basics

Search engines are programs that search through large databases of information on the Internet. The exact method each search engine uses to search for information varies, but there are three standard types of searches most search engines allow (in some form or fashion) that you need to know for the exam:

✔ **Static index/site map (often called directory searches):** Some search engines categorize all the Web sites in their databases into logical categories that you can search. To perform a search of a static index, you look through the major categories — usually listed on the search engine's home page — and then choose the subcategory that the information you're looking for fits into. It's much like searching through a list of folders on your hard drive. Yahoo! (www.yahoo.com) is one of the more popular search engines that allow directory (static index) searches. Figure 4-1 shows the categories listed on the Yahoo! home page.

Ursula User wants to find out about endangered birds. On the home page of her favorite search engine, links to about 20 categories are listed. She chooses the <u>Science</u> category and then must choose between all the subcategory links that appear: <u>Animals</u>, <u>Engineering</u>, <u>Meteorology</u>, and so on. She clicks the <u>Animals</u> link and then chooses <u>Birds</u>. About 25 subcategories are listed under Birds, and she chooses <u>Conservation and Research</u>. Behind the scenes, the search engine quietly sorts the resources that no longer match Ursula's request, slowly narrowing down the number of relevant resources to a manageable handful. Many e-commerce sites organize their products into a directory structure that works like static index (directory) searches.

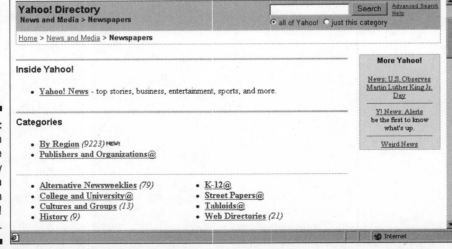

Figure 4-1:
You can search the Web by choosing a category on the Yahoo! home page.

✔ **Keyword searches:** Most every search engine out there allows keyword searches — you type in one or several words into a special field, and the search engine returns pages that contain the words you typed.

Ursula User logs on to a site like AltaVista (`www.altavista.com`) in search of information about endangered birds and types her search keywords into the text box. AltaVista quietly sifts through its indexes and displays the best results.

✔ **Full-text index:** This type of search allows users to type in longer phrases — entire sentences or paragraphs — and have the search engine return only pages that include that text. Because this type of search is more time-consuming, it's most commonly available within private company networks — law firm clerks can search though the firm's stored documents, for example. (For search engines to index the whole Internet this way wouldn't be practical, so this type of search isn't as commonly available as the other methods I mention.)

Ursula User remembers reading a Web page that mentions "the five most endangered species in North America." She types this entire phrase in the text box. Her search engine returns only pages that feature that entire phrase.

✔ **Meta searches:** When one search engine searches other search engines' databases and return results from several of them, this is called a meta search. One of the most popular meta search engines is Dogpile (`www.dogpile.com`).

Most search engines use a combination of tactics, with a heavier reliance on one method over others. For example, Yahoo! Search enables users to enter their own search terms at any point. (So Ursula could type *endangered birds* instead of clicking the links. Or she could narrow down her search to *birds* and then do a search for endangered birds from there.)

Basic Search Techniques

The first time you performed a search in a search engine, I bet you performed a basic search. If you're like most daily Internet users (and I suspect you are because you're studying for the Foundations exam), you probably type a word or phrase in the search engine field (for example, `scuba diving`) about 20 times a day. You may have also used quotes (for example, `"scuba diving"`). ProsoftTraining considers this a basic search, as well.

For the exam, you don't need to know much about basic searches. The main idea you need to know for this section is how placing quotes around search phrases affects your results.

No quotes, no exact matches

To understand how the use of quotation marks affects the results you may get when you perform a search, take a look at this example. If you were searching for information about chocolate almond ice cream, you might start by typing `chocolate almond ice cream`.

The search engine would return pages that contain all three words, *but not necessarily in that order*. In other words, you may end up with a page describing a chocolate candy bar with almonds and tutti-frutti ice cream. Now personally, I'd eat either one. But, if you have your heart set on chocolate almond ice cream, this might not be the best way to go.

Quotes give you WYSIWYG results

In the preceding section, I tell you that a search for chocolate almond ice cream might not give you results that match your yen. But if you use quotes around the phrase — `"chocolate almond ice cream"` — you're telling the search engine to look in its index of Web pages for this phrase *exactly as written*.

Advanced Search Techniques: Going Boolean

Basic searches are most effective when you're searching for easily distinguishable words or phrases. If you're searching for a company name, for example, you can just type it in quotes, and you should get relevant results. If you're researching the history of England, however, you may want to use some advanced search techniques.

Boolean operators allow visitors to get pretty specific when performing a search. These operators are words such as AND, OR, NOT LIKE, and NEAR. You can combine these words with other words and phrases to pinpoint which words must be included in the resulting Web pages and which words shouldn't be included. Say you want to find information about Paris, Kentucky, but you want to avoid getting a bunch of hits for Paris, France. You might type something like this: `Paris AND Kentucky NOT France`. This should help narrow your search results to pages about Paris, Kentucky, that have no mention of Paris, France. But you'll have to deal with Paris, Texas, all on your own.

Punctuation can affect your Boolean searches as well. Adding commas and quotation marks, for example, yields even better results in my ongoing quest to find out more about Paris, Kentucky: `"Paris, Kentucky" NOT "Paris, France"`.

You can narrow search results by using several symbols such as the plus (+) and minus (-) signs. The plus and minus signs are just like the Boolean words AND and NOT. Keep in mind, though, that not all search engines recognize all symbols or all Boolean words. Table 4-1 spells out the search engine operators you need to know for the exam.

Boolean operators are not case sensitive in most search engines. An exception to know for the exam is Lycos.

Table 4-1	Common Search Operators			
Operator	**How It Affects Results**	**Supported in AltaVista Advanced**	**Supported in Excite**	**Supported in Lycos Pro**
AND, &, +	Both words must be included	AND, &, +	AND, +	AND, &, +
OR, |	Either word must be included	Both OR and |	Only OR	Both OR and |
AND NOT, NOT, !, -	Word must be excluded	AND NOT, !, -	AND NOT, -	NOT, !, -
NEAR, ADJ (adjacent), FAR, ~, BEFORE	Describes the relationship between two keywords	NEAR and ~ (also means near)	N/a	NEAR, ADJ (adjacent), FAR, BEFORE
Quotes "..."	Specifies exact phrase to match	"..."	"..."	"..."
( ), < >, [ ], { } For example, Paris club AND (music OR band).	Groups phrases when using more than one operator	( )	( )	( ), < >, [ ], { }
*, $ For example, *spa* returns *dayspa* and *spas*.	Allows use of of wildcards or spelling variations	*	N/a	$
. (period) For example, Spa. = returns only pages with *spa*, not *space*.	Looks only for complete root word	N/a	N/a	.

A Few Search Engine Specifics

I'm sure that in real life you're probably comfortable with a couple of search engines and use them often. For the exam, though, the Prosoft folks have picked some search engines they really like, and they want you to know some of the unique features of each:

- **Yahoo!** (www.yahoo.com): Created by two college students at Stanford University, you can search within categories as well as perform keyword searches. Yahoo! is one of the oldest and most widely used search engines and also offers a people-searching feature.

- **AltaVista** (www.altavista.com): Prosoft wants you to know that you can use + and - signs only in advanced searches. (When you visit the AltaVista home page, click the <u>Advanced Search</u> link. Make sure you don't place spaces before or after the + or - signs.) Another key feature of the AltaVista advanced search feature is that it allows you to sort results by specific keywords or by date. AltaVista also enables you to search for images, and it uses automated programs *(spiders)* to validate links and make sure the content is current. This search engine was originally designed to index the whole Internet (can you say "biting off more than you can chew?").

- **Excite** (www.excite.com): Excite allows standard keyword searches, but unlike most other search engines, Excite cross-references your search words — it looks for other words that may have the same meaning as the words you typed in.

- **Lycos and Lycos Pro** (www.lycos.com): Carnegie Mellon University created these search engines. They offer standard keyword searches and use spiders to validate links.

Getting to Know the Technical Aspects of a Good Search

Even if you've performed a gazillion (hey, if *Forrest Gump* can say it, I can too) searches in your lifetime, you may not fully understand what a search engine is doing in the background while you're sitting there tapping your well-manicured nails. The following sections explain the key search engine principles you need to know for the exam.

Understanding the role of keywords and ranking in searches

When a search engine is reviewing a Web page, it makes a note of the most important *keywords,* the words and phrases that most aptly describe a site. Keywords are included in various places in the page — in the <HEAD> section of a document, for example — and help determine which Web pages are returned when a visitor performs a search.

For the Foundations exam, you just need to know the main function of keywords in a Web page. In real life, you may want to do some outside studying in order to understand the tricks of effectively using keywords in your Web site design. Of course, the goal is to get as many visitors to the site as possible, so if you need to unlock your understanding of keywords (Baaad pun. Sorry. Had to be done.), check out www.searchenginewatch.com or www.webmonkey.com. (You can also find more information about keywords in my discussion of meta tags later in this chapter.)

Keywords play a big role in determining how search engines *rank* pages. A search engine's ranking system determines which pages most closely match the keywords a user enters and which pages are returned in the first position and second position and so forth. The page that ranks number one is the closest match to the criteria the viewer typed in.

Becca wants to find information about antique porcelain dolls. She types dolls and antique and porcelain in the search engine's search field. Pages that include these three keywords repeatedly will rank higher than pages that only mention dolls once or twice.

Search engines determine ranking based on many factors, but the main three are

- ✔ **Whether there's an exact keyword match.** For example, *Model-T* is one of the search words, and *Model-T* appears on the Web page.

- ✔ **The order or combination of the keywords.** For example, *Model-T* appears in the same line of code as the word *speedster,* another of the user's search words.

- ✔ **How often the keywords are included in the page.** For example, the phrase *Model-T speedster* appears on the page 26 times. The word *car* appears eight times.

Good search results = good meta tags

Most popular search engines use *meta tags* to determine what a Web page is about. Meta tags are part of the HTML — Hypertext Markup Language —

code that makes up a Web page. (For a thorough explanation of HTML syntax, read Chapter 10.)

For the exam, you need to be familiar with meta tags and how search engines use them, though you don't need to know the exact syntax of the code examples I give you. Meta tags can tell search engines four main things:

- ✔ **Keywords:** The keywords list is a list of words and phrases inserted into a Web page's `<HEAD>` section that describe what that page (and often, the site as a whole) is about. (See the preceding section, "Understanding the role of keywords and ranking in searches.")

```
<META NAME="Keywords" CONTENT="jewelry, bracelets,
          rings">
```

- ✔ **Description:** This two to three sentence description of the Web site is sometimes called a condensed version of the site. I call it the *Reader's Digest* version.

```
<META NAME="Description" CONTENT="We sell fine jewelry">
```

- ✔ **Expiration:** This data tells a search engine when the page will start funking up the fridge. It's the day the information is expected to expire or be pulled down.

```
<META http-equiv="Expires" CONTENT="Mon, 24 February 2003
          08:00:00 EST">
```

- ✔ **Author:** This information is used to determine the next full moon. No. I can't fool you. If you're the site designer or manager, you're probably the author of the page. Your name goes here — not quite in lights, but Mom would be proud.

```
<META NAME="Author" CONTENT="Sharon Roark">
```

Finding Stuff Online

Most of the time, when I perform a search, I'm looking for information about a specific item such as printers, recipes, or flight information. There are, however, many other types of items you may want to search for, including people, graphics, newsgroups, and mailing lists.

Finding people

Regular search engines are great for finding information about general topics such as fishing or computers, but they're often somewhat limited when it comes to finding information about people. Sure, if you're searching for Mel Gibson, it's easy to find information — if not the man himself. But what if you're searching for an old friend you haven't seen in 20 years?

Lycos and Yahoo! are two of the many search engines that may help you track down your lost friend (and they're the two Prosoft wants you to know about). Sites like these build databases about people using several sources:

 ✔ They collect information from people who are online.

 ✔ They enable people to register their personal information so that they can be found.

 ✔ They use phone books and other public directories.

Finding mailing lists

A *mailing list* is a periodic e-mail distribution about a particular area of interest. If you want to keep up with advances in medicine, for example, you can sign up for many different mailing lists. For the Foundations exam, you just need to know a general definition of what a mailing list is, and that these two organizations help you find mailing lists on your chosen topics:

 ✔ **Liszt:** Recently renamed *Topica,* this site (at `www.liszt.com`) provides access to over 100,000 mailing lists.

 ✔ **Publicly Accessible Mailing Lists (PAML):** At `www.neosoft.com/cgi-bin/paml_search`, this is one of the oldest mailing list sites.

Finding newsgroups

Newsgroups are bulletin-board posting sites that focus on specific topics. All of them are related in some way to the original newsgroup network called *Usenet* (user network), which used to be a separate network. When you opt to join a newsgroup, all messages posted by members of the group are sent to you via e-mail. (The messages look just like e-mails, but, technically, they're newsgroup postings.)

You'll be amazed at how many newsgroups there are. The most popular newsgroup site is Google Groups at `groups.google.com` (formerly `www.deja.com`). There, you can search for newsgroups on topics ranging from aardvark farming to zip drives. For the exam, you just need to know what a newsgroup is — not the intricacies of how they work.

Searching Before the Web Came to Be

If you're up on your Internet history, you probably know that the Internet was around for years before the easy-to-use Web was invented. Before the Web came about, there were no easy-to-click search buttons and fields. To find information, you had to use Archie, Gopher, or Veronica.

In real life, you will probably rarely, if ever, use these three tools. Most every test candidate gets questions on these tools, however, so read on.

FTP and Archie

Archie enables you to search FTP (file transfer protocol) sites — sites that include directory lists of folders (for more on FTP, see Chapter 3). Figure 4-2 shows the GNU FTP site located at `www.gnu.org/order/ftp.html`. Obviously, you can click a link on an FTP site to see the information inside a specific folder.

Figure 4-2: The GNU FTP site.

But if you want to perform a search, you use Archie — a tool specifically designed to search FTP sites. For the exam, you need to know that Archie enables you to search FTP sites and that in order to perform a search, you have to know the name of an Archie server and the name of the file you're seeking. To use an Archie server, you type in *Archie* as the logon name.

Gopher and Veronica

Gopher is a tool that's been around since the early days of the Internet. It's not a search tool, but a way to browse files and folders stored on a server. And, like the other tools listed in this section, it's so old and outdated that you will rarely, if ever, use it in real life.

The key thing to remember about Gopher is that it's text-based (no images) and uses menus (lists of files) to show you what files are in which folders. It reminds me of a typical Windows 95 or 98 system in which you click a folder name and it expands to show you the files that are in that folder. The only difference is that Gopher doesn't use images or icons next to file and folder names.

When you want to search a Gopher site, you use Veronica, which stands for *Very Easy Rodent-Oriented Netwide Index to Computer Archives*. Veronica is a search tool created specifically to work on Gopher sites. Those are the only two things you need to know about Veronica for the exam.

Prep Test

1 **What does the** CONTENT **attribute in a meta tag specify?**

- **A** ○ A brief description of the Web site.
- **B** ○ Specific words and phrases that relate to the Web site.
- **C** ○ The <HEAD> section of the document.
- **D** ○ It depends on what the CONTENT attribute equals; it could specify Keywords, Description, Expiration, or Author.

2 **What meta tag attribute value offers a brief description of a Web site?**

- **A** ○ Description
- **B** ○ Keywords
- **C** ○ Boolean operators
- **D** ○ Content

3 **You're performing a search for information on planting violets. Which search string would return the most relevant results?**

- **A** ○ Planting OR violets
- **B** ○ Violets AND flowers
- **C** ○ Violets AND Planting
- **D** ○ Violets NOT Planting

4 **Which search engine features Boolean operators that are case sensitive?**

- **A** ○ Lycos
- **B** ○ Yahoo!
- **C** ○ AltaVista
- **D** ○ Excite

5 **You're performing a search for a gym that offers child care and either yoga or pilates classes. Which search string would return the most relevant results?**

- **A** ○ Gym AND childcare AND Yoga AND Pilates
- **B** ○ "Gym AND childcare" AND/OR (Yoga AND Pilates)
- **C** ○ Gym AND childcare OR Yoga AND Pilates
- **D** ○ Gym AND childcare AND (Yoga OR Pilates)

6 **Veronica stands for**

- **A** ○ Very Early Research of Network Internet Caching Algorithms
- **B** ○ Very Easy Rodent-Oriented Netwide Index to Computer Archives
- **C** ○ Valuable Electronic Research of Online Content Archives
- **D** ○ None of the above

7 Which of the following is not a type of search index?

   A ○ Content index
   B ○ Site index/Site map
   C ○ Keyword index
   D ○ Full-text index

8 Which search engine allows you to sort results by a field of your choice?

   A ○ Yahoo!
   B ○ Excite
   C ○ AltaVista
   D ○ Lycos

9 Search engines that help you find people on the Internet gather personal information by all of these methods except

   A ○ Tracing people who are online
   B ○ Having visitors register to have their information included
   C ○ Using public directories such as phone books
   D ○ Randomly calling people to ask if they want to be included

10 You're performing a search for a new shampoo you've heard about but can only remember that the first three letters of its name are G-r-o. Assuming the search engine you're using supports every operator, which of the following would you use to get the most relevant results?

   A ○ "Gro" shampoo
   B ○ "Gro shampoo"
   C ○ Gro* shampoo
   D ○ Gro. shampoo

Answers

1 **D.** It depends on what the CONTENT attribute equals; it could specify Keywords, Description, Expiration, or Author. *Review "Good search results = good meta tags."*

2 **A.** Description. Sometime the obvious answer is the correct answer. *Look over "Good search results = good meta tags."*

3 **C.** Violets AND Planting. None of the other answers would include both words in the results. *Check out "Advanced Search Techniques: Going Boolean."*

4 **A.** Lycos. *See "Advanced Search Techniques: Going Boolean."*

5 **D.** Gym AND childcare AND (Yoga OR Pilates). *Review "Advanced Search Techniques: Going Boolean."*

6 **B.** Very Easy Rodent-Oriented Netwide Index to Computer Archives. *See "Gopher and Veronica."*

7 **A.** Content index. *Look over "Understanding Search Engine Basics."*

8 **C.** AltaVista. *Take a look at "A Few Search Engine Specifics."*

9 **D.** Randomly calling people to ask if they want to be included. I guess they haven't thought of that yet. *Check out "Finding people."*

10 **C.** Gro* shampoo. By using Gro*, you're telling the search engine to look for the letters *Gro* with various combinations of letters after that. *See "Advanced Search Techniques: Going Boolean."*

Chapter 5

Getting the Most out of E-Mail

• •

Exam Objectives

▶ Sending simple messages and files to other Internet users with e-mail clients
▶ Attaching files to e-mail messages
▶ Practicing netiquette

• •

*E*lectronic mail, or e-mail, has become as commonplace to most of us as telephones were just a few years ago. Interestingly enough, the inventors of the Internet never dreamed e-mail would become such a popular method of communication. Of course, they didn't see how the Internet could possibly become a vehicle for business commerce either. (See Chapter 6 for more on e-commerce.)

E-mail was much different in the early days of the Internet. For one thing, there weren't any electronic greeting cards or pretty pictures included. This is going to sound like an imitation of my ol' granddaddy, but back in my day (when I first began using e-mail), you had to memorize often lengthy command lines and/or addresses to send a message. Also, because hardly anyone had a personal e-mail account, you could usually send messages only to others within your workplace.

In this chapter, I discuss some basic technologies and programs involved in sending and receiving e-mail. I also cover popular e-mail techniques, such as attaching files and adding custom signatures. If you're an old e-mail pro, most of this info may be yesterday's news. I encourage you, though, to scan through and pay attention to the sections on e-mail protocols and any other sections that may contain new terms.

Quick Assessment

Web browsers and the Internet

1 Messenger is the free e-mail program that comes with _____.

2 Outlook Express is the free e-mail program that comes with _____.

3 The easiest way to send a message to many people at once is to utilize a _____.

E-mail attachments

4 To send an image to someone via e-mail, you can _____ it to your message.

5 If you want to send a large file to someone, you can _____ the file to reduce its size.

6 If a file is larger than 2MB even after you compress it, you can still send it using the _____ protocol instead of e-mail.

7 If you want to add your phone number to the bottom of all outgoing e-mails, use a _____.

8 Typing in all capital letters implies you are _____ in an e-mail.

Netiquette

9 _____ is the set of guidelines that helps make e-mail easier to use and read.

10 Whenever an e-mail is sent, at least _____ e-mail protocols are used.

Answers

1   *Netscape.* Review "Popular E-Mail Programs."

2   *Internet Explorer.* Take a look at "Popular E-Mail Programs."

3   *Mailing list.* See "Mailing lists."

4   *Attach.* Read over "Getting attached."

5   *Compress or zip.* See "Getting attached."

6   *FTP (file transfer protocol).* Check out "Getting attached."

7   *Signature.* Take a peek at "Adding signatures."

8   *Shouting.* Review "Minding Your Manners."

9   *Netiquette.* Take a look at "Minding Your Manners."

10   *Two.* Check out "E-Mail Protocols."

Popular E-Mail Programs

Several companies make e-mail programs that are widely used. The only two programs you need to be somewhat familiar with for the exam are Microsoft Outlook Express, shown in Figure 5-1, and Netscape Messenger, shown in Figure 5-2. These are free programs that come with the Internet Explorer and Netscape Navigator browsers. They're not as powerful as full-blown e-mail programs like the full version of the Outlook program or Eudora, but then again they're free.

For the exam, you need to know only a little program-specific information:

✓ **Remember which of the freebie e-mail programs comes with which browser.** Outlook Express comes with Internet Explorer, and Netscape Messenger comes with Netscape Navigator.

✓ **Several e-mail programs, including Outlook (the full version of Outlook Express) allow you to download e-mail to be read while offline.** If you're using a program like this, you need to be online only while you're actually sending and receiving e-mails.

In real life, you may be e-mailing without a program. E-mailing without a program? How can that be? A lot of people these days use free, Web-based e-mail accounts. Yahoo! and Hotmail are two of the most popular Web-based services. With these types of services, you don't actually have a program downloaded to your system — you just pull up the appropriate Web page and e-mail over that company's server.

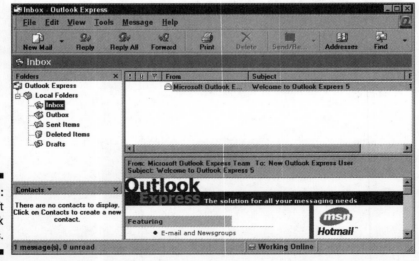

Figure 5-1: Microsoft Outlook Express.

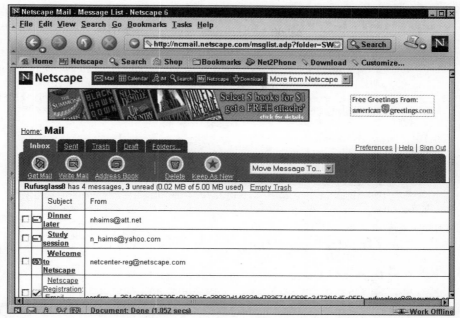

Figure 5-2:
Netscape
Messenger.

Working with E-Mail Addresses

Unless you've never sent an e-mail message before, you're familiar with the syntax of an e-mail address. The format of each address looks something like this:

```
you@company.com
```

Each part of the preceding address has a specific function. The next three sections explain what each part is called and what it does.

User name

The user name is the part of an e-mail address before the @ symbol. User names can contain any of the following characters in any combination:

- Letters
- Numbers
- Periods
- Underscores

If you see an address that appears to have a space, it's probably just an underscore, such as Sharon_Roark. (Or it could be a figment of your imagination.)

Companies often set up e-mail systems within their networks and come up with their own naming conventions. A user name your company assigns you identifies your account and the password needed to access it. The name may also identify your department like this:

```
you.sales_domestic2@company.com
```

The preceding address incorporates your name and department, as well as the fact that you work in domestic sales. The 2 means that you get to work the Alaskan seaboard in January — selling ice cubes. You lucky devil.

The @ symbol

The second part of an e-mail address is the @ symbol which means "at." This is the connection between your user name and the domain or company part of the name. In some e-mail programs, users can enter abbreviations of user names which don't appear to include the @ symbol. The symbol is still there, but the e-mail program is placing it in the address for you.

For example, I may have an address stored in my address book for Aunt Cynthia that looks like this: CmcMillan@goodisp.com. I can go into my address book and add the nickname Cynthia. After I set up the nickname, I can just type in my aunt's first name, and my e-mail program or service looks up her full address and gets the message to her. Now I don't have to remember her full e-mail address, just her first name (which shouldn't be that hard because I don't have 5,000 aunts). For more information on address books, see "Address books" later in the chapter.

In real life, people can often send e-mail to others in the same network without having to type in a full e-mail address. A server administrator can configure an e-mail server that may or may not include the use of nicknames (sometimes called aliases).

Domain name

The section of an e-mail address that comes after the @ symbol is the domain name. The domain name is usually the company or organization that created the e-mail address. Usually the company that issues you an e-mail address is also the company that runs your e-mail service.

Sending and Receiving E-Mail

If you've been using e-mail for a while, sending and receiving e-mail is probably second nature to you. Some of the more technical aspects of e-mail, however, you may have never considered. The following sections cover the key information you need to know for the exam.

You're not going to get program-specific test questions on how to perform the activities in the following sections (attaching files, adding signatures, and so on) However, you'll be far more prepared for the test if you know e-mail technology like it's the back of your hand. In real life, I recommend you use all the standard e-mail tools your e-mail program or service has to offer:

- ✔ Sending attachments
- ✔ Working with address books
- ✔ Creating and modifying mailing lists

Because every e-mail program or service differs in how to perform these tasks, I recommend you look in the help or options section of your e-mail interface to get some guidance.

Address books

Most every e-mail program or service contains an address book feature that stores e-mail addresses. Typically, you can also use the address book to store more detailed information about contacts, such as street addresses, phone numbers, and birthdays. If you switch e-mail programs at some point, most programs enable you to import your address book files from your old system to your new one. Figure 5-3 shows an address book in Netscape Messenger.

Mailing lists

Mailing lists are one of the features that have made e-mail such a big part of business commerce. Mailing lists make it easy to send a message to hundreds or thousands of people with just a click. Lots of people I know create mailing lists of all their friends who like to receive jokes so that they can forward any good ones with just a click. Figure 5-4 shows an address book with a mailing list (or group) called family.

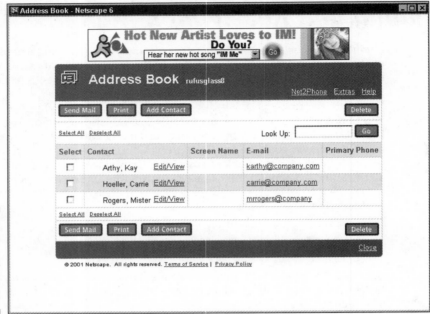

Figure 5-3:
The
Netscape
Messenger
address
book.

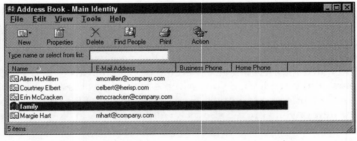

Figure 5-4:
A mailing
list in
Microsoft
Outlook
Express.

A major benefit of using mailing lists is that they're free. A company may spend hundreds or even thousands of dollars to send out a mass mailing of a paper flyer. After a company compiles the e-mail addresses of its customers, however, the marketing department can harass the customers at will through e-mail at no cost. Hooray for progress!

Getting attached

When you have a file you'd like to send someone, attaching it to an e-mail message can be the quickest way to go. You can attach most any type of file to e-mail — images, word processing documents, even Web pages.

Most e-mail programs let you know that a message has an attachment by putting a paper clip symbol beside the subject line or header of the message.

Watch out for the size of the attached files you send. Many commercial e-mail services don't let you send an attachment larger than 1.5 to 2MB. If you have a large file, the most convenient way to send it is to compress or zip it by using a program such as WinZip and then attach it to your message. If the file is still too large after compressing it, you may have to send it by FTP (file transfer protocol) — the best choice for sending files over 2MB in most cases. (For more information on FTP, see Chapters 3 and 16.)

Depending on the program being used, attachments may be automatically scanned with antivirus software before the files can be downloaded. Users can usually set up their systems to scan all outgoing messages as well. If you've had a problem with viruses in the past, this is the setup I would choose.

Adding signatures

E-mail signatures are lines of text automatically added to the bottom of every e-mail you send. Signatures are

- ✔ **Available in most commercial e-mail services and programs.**
- ✔ **Especially helpful in business environments.** You can let recipients know your phone number or position at a company, like the following signature:

```
Missy Mouse
Big Cheese
Happy Corporation
555-555-5555
```

- ✔ **Include whatever information you'd like.** Think about what information you'd like to see on e-mails that contacts send you.

Minding Your Manners

No, this next section isn't from the writings of Miss Manners. It's a section about minding your Internet manners. In every form of communication, certain practices work well whereas others are, well, less *appropriate*. If you're talking on the phone, for instance, nodding your head yes and no doesn't help the other person understand what you're saying. Okay, you may do it anyway, while also waving your hands and jumping around on one foot, because no one will see you anyway. Using certain techniques in e-mail can also help you get your message across more effectively.

Observing netiquette

Netiquette refers to the guidelines of common sense and politeness e-mailers should use. E-mail communication is easier for everyone if you keep common netiquette rules in mind. You won't get a lot of exam questions on this, but you still should be familiar with common guidelines:

- **Netiquette no-no:** Don't type with all capital letters — typing IN ALL CAPS implies you're SHOUTING! Also, check that your font choice, size, and color are easy to read. You know you have an annoying font problem if your friends start sending you their optometrist bills.

- **Miss Manners move:** When composing a subject line, use a brief, descriptive subject that accurately describes the content of the message.

- **Miss Manners move:** Try to be as error free as possible. Do a spell check. But don't rely completely on the spell checker feature in your e-mail program; read through the message to check the tone, spelling, and grammar yourself before sending out your message.

- **Netiquette no-no:** Don't put anything in an e-mail you'd be afraid for Mom to read. Remember that e-mails can easily be forwarded and printed and not always on purpose.

If you're angry or upset, wait a day before responding to a rude message. This isn't a testable topic, but it's also a good idea to avoid sending e-mails on any sensitive topics. Also, be sure to avoid sending very large e-mail attachments when possible — they take a long time to download and clog up company servers.

Respecting privacy

It's always a good idea to keep privacy in mind when you send e-mail. There are jerks out there that think nothing of trying to hack into your account and read your e-mail.

When ProsoftTraining talks about e-mail privacy, it's referring to the ability of your employer to read your e-mail.

In most countries, including the United States, any e-mail that was created or read on company time with company equipment is, legally, the company's possession. This means company bigwigs are within their rights to read any employee e-mail they'd like. Some companies make it a point to warn employees of this policy, but, even if they don't mention it, it's still the law.

In addition to the legal right company managers have to read your e-mail, another common privacy problem is company employees who know their way around a network and snoop into your account. Always remember — others may be able to read whatever e-mail you send — especially on a company network.

E-Mail Protocols

When you send e-mail, all you have to do is type in the address, type your message, and click Send. In the background, however, several protocols are at work. Internet protocols are covered thoroughly in Chapter 3, but Table 5-1 gives you a look at the e-mail protocols you need to know for the exam.

Table 5-1	E-Mail Protocols
Protocol	*Characteristics*
Simple Mail Transfer Protocol (SMTP)	Used by mail servers to send e-mail out. Used with either POP or IMAP, which receive or retrieve and store incoming e-mail. Usually requires a password to prevent unauthorized access.
Post Office Protocol (POP)	Used by mail servers in conjunction with SMTP to retrieve and store e-mail. Usually requires a password to prevent unauthorized access.
Internet Messaging Access Protocol (IMAP)	Used by mail servers in conjunction with SMTP to receive and store e-mail. Not as common as POP but more powerful. Allows sharing of mailboxes and access to multiple mail servers. Usually requires a password to prevent unauthorized access.

Two e-mail protocols are always at work — the one that concentrates on sending messages is always SMTP, and the one focused on retrieving them is either POP or IMAP. When you first install and configure a new e-mail program, you have to type in at least two addresses: your SMTP address and either a POP address or an IMAP address.

Many people get a question on the exam asking what do you need, at the very least, to send e-mail. Just remember that in order to send e-mail, you have to have an e-mail account, the e-mail address of the recipient, and a modem or network connection.

Prep Test

1 _____ is the protocol used to send e-mail messages.

- **A** ○ POP
- **B** ○ POP3
- **C** ○ SMTP
- **D** ○ IMAP

2 E-mail addresses cannot contain which of the following?

- **A** ○ Blank spaces
- **B** ○ Numbers
- **C** ○ Periods
- **D** ○ Letters

3 To prevent unauthorized access to an e-mail, the _____ e-mail protocol often requires a password.

- **A** ○ SMTP
- **B** ○ NNTP
- **C** ○ TCP/IP
- **D** ○ None of the above

4 If you're using an e-mail program like Microsoft Outlook, you need to be online

- **A** ○ Whenever you use any of the program's features
- **B** ○ To use the calendar features
- **C** ○ Only to read e-mail
- **D** ○ Only when sending and receiving e-mail

5 The easiest way for a business to keep a group of people informed about a certain topic is the use of

- **A** ○ Outlook Express
- **B** ○ Mailing lists
- **C** ○ Signatures
- **D** ○ Netscape Messenger

6 You want to send a large document (1.8MB) to a coworker who works in another office. The most efficient way to accomplish this is

- **A** ○ Compress the file and attach it to an e-mail
- **B** ○ Copy it to a disk and send it by courier
- **C** ○ Publish it to your company's Web site and notify the coworker via e-mail
- **D** ○ Create a newsgroup and post it as part of a message

7 You want to make sure all the business contacts you e-mail have your new office phone number. The easiest way to do this is by using

A ○ Newsgroups
B ○ Netiquette
C ○ Signatures
D ○ Attachments

8 The symbol most e-mail programs use to indicate an attachment is

A ○ A check mark
B ○ Stapler
C ○ Smiley face
D ○ Paper clip

9 Which one of these is not considered good netiquette?

A ○ Performing a spell check before sending out your message
B ○ Sending only messages you wouldn't be embarrassed for your boss to read
C ○ Typing messages in all capital letters
D ○ Explaining when you are joking because others can't see your facial expressions

10 In most cases, who legally owns the e-mail you send and receive at work?

A ○ Only you
B ○ You and the person(s) who sent it
C ○ The owners/management of the company
D ○ The owners/management, but only if you sign a legal release form

Answers

1 **C.** SMTP. SMTP is used with all e-mail. *Review "E-Mail Protocols."*

2 **A.** Blank spaces. If an e-mail address appears to contain a blank space, it's probably an underscore, as in `your_address`. *Read over "E-Mail Protocols."*

3 **A.** SMTP. All e-mail protocols usually require a password to prevent unauthorized access. *Check out "E-Mail Protocols."*

4 **D.** Only when sending and receiving e-mail. Most full e-mail programs allow users to perform many features offline, but you must be online to actually send and retrieve your messages. *Look over "Popular E-Mail Programs."*

5 **B.** Mailing lists. A and D are programs you could use, but the tool is mailing lists. *Review "Mailing lists."*

6 **A.** Compress the file and attach it to an e-mail. Unless the file is over 2MB, you normally attach it to an e-mail. You may be able to compress the file to get it under 2MB (or whatever file size limits your e-mail service places on you) and then attach it to your e-mail. *Read "Getting attached."*

7 **C.** Signatures. You can add your phone number, fax number, or any other information you want recipients to have to an e-mail signature. *Check out "Adding signatures."*

8 **D.** Paper clip. Although you don't need to know the specific steps involved with attaching a file in any specific program, the paper clip icon is so common to most e-mail programs that you should be familiar with it. *Take a look at "Getting attached."*

9 **C.** Typing messages in all capital letters. *Read over "Observing netiquette."*

10 **C.** The owners/management of the company. *Read "Respecting privacy."*

Chapter 6

Doing Business on the Web

• •

Exam Objectives

▶ Understanding security issues related to e-commerce

▶ Obtaining legal and international business information to use on the Web

▶ Developing a corporate Web site — including project management, testing, and legal issues

• •

*T*hese days it's easier to set up an online storefront than it is to install a new home stereo system. Because it's so easy to put an e-commerce site together, it's tempting to just hop online, set a site up, and go. But there's a lot more to creating an *effective* e-commerce site than posting pictures and prices of your company's products.

Security is a concern for everyone on the Internet, but particularly those doing business online — both merchants and customers. To make an online storefront successful, customers need to feel safe when supplying their personal and credit card information. This chapter covers the most common security measures used with e-commerce sites and which ones are appropriate in different situations. Online merchants must also be concerned with the legalities involved with Web sites. Even if you're not the one creating an e-commerce site, you still need to understand the legal issues behind trademarks, copyrights, and other licenses.

Planning and documenting your Web site's beginning-to-end development is also important for an effective Web site. In this chapter, I explain the standard project development life cycle and the fundamentals of project management. Not only are these topics helpful when it comes to creating a great Web site, but, as you may have guessed, they're on the exam as well.

Quick Assessment

Electronic commerce

1 The main elements of e-commerce are: _____, _____, and _____.

2 The _____ commerce model is conducted between a business entity and a consumer entity: low-volume, higher-price margins.

3 When e-commerce transactions use the _____ protocol, the credit card information is never seen by the merchant, only by its bank.

4 The _____ is a method of payment that can be used online and contains a microchip that holds up to 4MB of data.

Copyrights, licensing, and trademarks

5 An enterprise may acquire the rights to any domain that infringes upon one or more of its established _____.

6 Copyright protects _____ and _____ on the Internet.

7 _____ is the UN agency formed to protect intellectual property and enforce copyright laws worldwide.

Project management fundamentals

8 _____ occurs when changes in cost, schedule, or performance deviate from the initial expectations during a project.

9 The nonprofit membership organization that publishes standards and offers education regarding the project management profession is the _____.

10 The project cycle stage that involves inspecting and testing is the _____ stage.

Answers

1 *Communication; data management; security.* Read "What Is E-Commerce?"

2 *Business to Consumer (B2C).* Check out "Business-to-consumer (B2C)."

3 *SET (Secure Electronic Transaction).* Review "Using Secure Electronic Transaction (SET)."

4 *Smart card.* Check out "Using smart cards."

5 *Trademarks.* Take a look at "Trademarks."

6 *Expression; originality.* Look over "Copyrights."

7 *WIPO (World Intellectual Property Organization).* Review "Copyrights."

8 *Scope creep.* Read "Project management is fun-damental."

9 *PMI (Project Management Institute).* See "Project management is fun-damental."

10 *Pilot/parallel.* Look over "Understanding the project management cycle."

What Is E-Commerce?

Electronic commerce — otherwise known as *e-commerce* these days — is one of the key components of the modern Internet. Every year the number of people who do all or part of their shopping online increases dramatically — most notably during the holiday season. As more consumers depend on the Internet as a convenient shopping tool, more merchants are creating and expanding online storefronts. In fact, nowadays, companies that advertise on radio and television give out their Web addresses more often than they give out their phone numbers.

If you'd ask ten people to define e-commerce, you'd probably get ten different answers. ProsoftTraining defines e-commerce as the integration of communications, data management, and security capabilities to allow organizations to exchange information related to the sale of goods and services.

This definition may sound a bit convoluted, but I explain each of these terms throughout the chapter. I've included Prosoft's definition because you may encounter it word-for-word on the exam. It really just means e-commerce involves every aspect of selling products online from the Web site creation to the warehousing of products to the customer's information that you may store in a database.

The three main elements of e-commerce are

- ✔ **Communication:** The way buyers and sellers communicate; not only with the spoken language — phone calls, in-person conversations, and so on — but also common digital communications methods, such as e-mail and chat rooms.

- ✔ **Data management:** Defines the way data is exchanged and stored. This includes the databases set up to store information and the systems you have in place to allow others to access that information. A Web site that collects customer information and stores it in a database on a company server involves several aspects of data management — the database stores data and the Web site allows the transfer of data.

- ✔ **Security:** The method of keeping data safe from unauthorized parties. This is more important with e-commerce because the parties involved are often in different locations. If you buy some shoes at the local sporting goods store, only you and the clerk see your card number (and you can stare down the clerk to make sure he doesn't peek). Over the Internet, you have to put some security measures in place because your credit card number is traveling across phone lines all over the country and hackers can try to intercept it.

Benefits of e-commerce

If you're going to all this trouble to plan and create an e-commerce site, you might wonder, "What's in it for me?" The following list points out the benefits of e-commerce you need to know for the exam:

- ✔ **Sites are instantly available from any computer that has a connection to the Internet.** When you decide to open a traditional store, it can take months to build the structure and weeks to organize stock. With an online storefront, as long as you have pictures of the items you intend to sell, people can start shopping as soon as the site's up — they don't have to get into their cars and drive to you or get their hands on your catalog. And the e-commerce site is open 24/7 — hours most retailers can't match.

- ✔ **E-commerce technology offers easier access to new geographic markets.** You can reach potential customers all over the world. (Of course, if the good people of Russia don't know your business exists, then access isn't relevant, but that's another issue for the sales and marketing departments to handle.)

- ✔ **E-commerce technology reduces paperwork, errors, and therefore, overhead costs.** Web sites take paperless orders and usually have several steps of verification in place to reduce the number of errors. Many sites make customers type in their e-mail addresses twice and check all their address information before their order can be placed, which helps cut down on typos and other errors. Fewer problems mean less work, which saves money.

- ✔ **With back-end systems in place, you can streamline the ordering process.** Whether you're buying office supplies or wholesale goods that you plan to sell retail, ordering products on the Web can be much simpler for buyer and seller. (When I ordered a bedspread from JC Penney, for example, I didn't want to get dressed, get in my car, and drive across town just to see the limited inventory my local store had in stock. I just got on its Web site, where I could see pictures of nearly every bedspread it makes, and ordered in a snap!)

- ✔ **E-commerce technology helps you get all kinds of interesting information about your customers.** With the right software on a Web server, the Webmaster can track virtually any aspect of a Web site, including the number of visitors to a page, which pages they visit and in which order, the last site users visited before coming to your page, how long they stay on each page, and which browser and operating system visitors are using and much more than I can list here.

Identifying potential e-commerce problems

Just as there are great benefits to e-commerce, there are also some unique issues that are cause for concern. Here are the key e-commerce challenges you need to know for the exam:

- ✓ **Increased vulnerability to fraud.** Because buyers and sellers are in different locations, verifying data can be difficult — for both buyers and sellers.

- ✓ **Increased risk for copyright and trademark violations.** Copying other people's Web site content is easy, and catching violators is more difficult.

- ✓ **Increased taxation issues.** It's difficult for states to collect sales tax on goods sold over the Web. In most states, any business located in that state is supposed to collect sales tax and send it on to the state tax collection agency. It's often difficult to tell where a Web business is physically located, and some small online merchants aren't claiming income (do you notify the government if you sell your old dining room set online? What if you make a living buying used furniture and selling it online?) Because of these and other issues, tax agencies are constantly seeking new ways to enforce taxation laws on the Web.

  In addition to state taxes, which are the biggest tax issue in the United States, other countries may have unique tax structures that you need to consider if you're selling to international audiences.

- ✓ **Credibility concerns.** With a traditional storefront, a new business can help establish credibility with the appearance of the store. Because buyers on the Internet never see a physical storefront, it can be more difficult for buyers to distinguish legitimate businesses from fraudulent ones.

- ✓ **Multilanguage issues.** Many site owners want to sell their products in other countries. To do business in other countries, a site must be translated into the appropriate languages, which can be costly and time-consuming. One possible answer is to code text in *Unicode,* which many browsers can translate to the native language on a user's machine. (For more information about how Unicode works, go to www.unicode.org.)

- ✓ **International currency and shipping issues.** To sell in other countries, the Web site must be equipped to accept other currencies, and the business will need to have efficient international shipping methods in place.

Understanding Common E-Commerce Business Models

Starting any business (whether online or in the real world) is not an easy task. You have your choice of books that are devoted to creating successful online businesses. (A good one to read is *E-Commerce For Dummies* by Don Jones, Mark D. Scott, and Rick Villars; published by Hungry Minds, Inc.) But one thing that most successful e-commerce sites have in common is they effectively target their prime customers — things like how old they are, how much money they make, where they live, and so on.

Market demographics are just the beginning of the complicated process of building a Web business. Luckily, all you need to know are the basics. First question: With whom does your business do business? The following sections outline the options for you.

Business-to-business (B2B)

Just like it says, business-to-business (B2B) sales are conducted between two businesses. A good example of a B2B site is www.staples.com — it sells office supplies to people in offices.

For the exam, you need to know that the B2B sales model is characterized by selling high volumes with lower price margins. A company that sells a lot of an item (20,000 reams of printer paper, at $9 a ream, to one customer, for example) will make only a small profit per item, but the company will make a bundle for the whole sale.

Business-to-consumer (B2C)

The business-to-consumer (B2C) sales model involves businesses that target their sales efforts toward the public at large, otherwise known as consumers. A good example of a business-to-consumer site is the bookseller Amazon.com (www.amazon.com).

The B2C sales model is characterized by low-volume sales and higher price margins. B2C businesses typically don't sell as many units to one customer but make a larger profit on each product sold. Say you've got an online business that sells pianos. I guarantee you won't have very many customers repeatedly purchasing baby grands from your site. But a one-time sale can make you a tidy profit.

In real life, many companies sell both to other businesses and to consumers. If a company is courting both markets, you'll probably find certain pages of the site targeted towards consumers and certain pages targeted towards businesses.

Securing E-Commerce Transactions

In a traditional commerce environment (that is, in the bricks-and-mortar world), the buyer and seller are usually in the same location. The buyer can touch and try out products. When payment is made, the customer physically hands the merchant the source of payment, and the merchant hands the product to the customer, along with a receipt of the transaction, right there on the spot. For electronic commerce to succeed, safe methods of transferring product, customer, and payment information have to be in place.

When people speak of secure electronic transactions, they often focus on transmitting *payment* data securely. Although this is, of course, important, it's not the only type of data that people need to send securely. People may need to transfer legal documents or drug prescription information. This is where EDI (Electronic Data Interchange) comes in.

When two entities say they're using EDI, that just means they're using the same standards — which they've agreed upon in advance — to exchange information. Quite often, companies use EDI to exchange data they might otherwise have used paper for — invoices or bills of lading. The best example of EDI I can think of is the book you're holding in your hands. During the creation of the book, I'd e-mail each chapter (in the agreed-upon format) to the publishing company. The editors then sent their comments (usually just oodles of praise, of course) to me via e-mail too — I've never even met my project editor face to face.

There's no one technology or protocol used in EDI, it's just the term people use to describe the idea of exchanging data electronically. Even though EDI has been around since the early days of the Internet (you've probably submitted a school or work assignment over the Internet, haven't you?), it's only now coming into common use. Some people have been hesitant to use EDI for document exchange because they don't quite trust the Internet yet.

Some of the key features of EDI include the following:

- ✔ Handles large volumes of like transactions
- ✔ Works well in time-sensitive transactions
- ✔ Helps cut costs in tight-margin businesses

EDI sounds great, doesn't it? It is, but many businesses claim the cost to implement EDI is too high, although that perception is changing. Several industries — automotive, electronics, and retail to name a few — implemented EDI fairly widely years ago, but currently each industry tends to use its own version of EDI. One well-known organization that's been working for years to create common EDI standards is the Accredited Standards Committee (ASC) X12.

Keeping Online Payments Secure

I don't know about you, but I surfed the Web for just a few months before I made my first purchase online — a book on creating Web sites, wouldn't you know. Not everyone is as comfortable as I am, though, with purchasing products and services online — prospective buyers often have good reason to fear fraud or theft online. The risk of fraud on the Internet doesn't affect just buyers — sellers have to pay a price, too. Businesses that have experienced many fraudulent transactions have to pay credit card companies higher fees for every transaction they process. Also, the fees credit card companies charge for transactions online — where the credit card is not physically presented to the seller — are usually higher. Companies, of course, have to pass on these higher costs to buyers, so keeping transactions secure benefits everyone.

There are several protocols and technologies that can work alone or together to keep private information secure while it's traveling over the Internet. To explain the techno-geeky details of how each works, this book would have to be about three times its current size. For the exam, you just need to know a simple definition of each and their key abilities. And, lucky for you, I give you all that information in the next few sections.

Using Secure Sockets Layer (SSL)

The standard and most commonly used security protocol on the Internet is called Secure Sockets Layer (SSL). SSL scrambles up (encrypts) data going to or coming from a Web server, making it unreadable to all those evil hackers lurking in the background. When companies use SSL to secure a transaction, a little padlock usually appears in the status bar. The padlock is what many buyers look for to let them know that the page is secure and that any sensitive data they submit from that page (such as credit card numbers or social security numbers) will be transmitted securely. (For more details on how SSL works, see Chapters 7 and 21.)

Using Secure Electronic Transaction (SET)

Secure Electronic Transaction (SET) is a method of exchanging secure information that combines SSL and digital certificates. (Both are covered in Chapters 7 and 21.) MasterCard created the SET standard originally, but now most other credit card companies and financial institutions use it.

For the exam, keep in mind the connection between credit card companies and SET. Other key features of SET you need to know for the exam include the following:

✔ **SET offers enhanced identification.** All sensitive information involved in a transaction is encrypted and signed with a digital certificate that verifies the identities of the parties sending and receiving information. Digital certificates are covered in detail in Chapter 7.

✔ **Merchants never see credit card numbers.** All information is sent securely to the merchant's bank, reducing the chance of credit card abuse or carelessness by merchants and their employees.

✔ **SET was created specifically for financial transactions.** The SET protocol includes *payment gateways* — software that not only connects merchants to the merchants' banks but also supports credit card transactions such as returns and credits.

If you'd like to find out more about SET for real-life use, visit www.setco.org.

Accepting Online Payment

The last time you purchased something online, you probably used a credit card. But there are several methods consumers can use to pay for their purchases online, such as e-cash, digital cash, and smart cards. As technology becomes more advanced, the methods abound. In the following sections, I discuss the methods of online payment Prosoft expects you to know for the exam.

Passing the buck (e-cash)

When I first heard about accepting cash online, I had this vision of shoving dollar bills (face up) into a slot in my monitor the way I do when I'm trying desperately to get myself a cold, carbonated, sugar-free beverage. Boy, was I off track! Merchants can accept cash online by using *e-cash*.

E-cash (electronic cash) works a lot like a checking account. The first thing you need to do is set up an e-cash account that establishes your e-cash spending limit. When you purchase something from a site that accepts e-cash, you enter your account number, and the amount of the purchase is deducted from your account.

There are several reputable online companies that buyers and sellers can use to establish e-cash accounts. Some of the most popular are DigiCash (www.digicash.com), CyberCash (www.cybercash.com), and NetCash (www.netcash.com).

E-cash is still an evolving technology, and its main drawback is that it's a bit cumbersome. For example, in addition to the special account consumers set up to send e-cash to a merchant, merchants also have to set up special accounts with e-cash vendors. The e-cash vendor then processes the e-cash payments. There are merchants out there that accept e-cash payments, but you have to search for them.

Just digital checking in

Digital checks work much like e-cash. This method of payment also requires buyers to have a special account called a *digital checkbook* set up with an online checking account company such as CheckFree (`www.checkfree.com`). When you use a digital check to purchase something online, you digitally sign the check with a digital certificate issued by the service that created your digital checking account. The service guarantees the check's validity to the merchant and electronically transfers the funds to the merchant's bank. I encounter a few merchants that accept e-checks (more than accept e-cash), but most merchants that accept electronic payment prefer credit cards, which are covered in the next section.

Using credit cards

Credit card transactions are by far the most popular method of online payment. One reason is that buyers and sellers who are already using credit cards for in-person transactions don't necessarily have to set up an additional account to use them online. Also, credit cards already use electronic verification (usually over a phone line), so the credit card payment model works well in an electronic-commerce environment.

If merchants want to accept online credit card payments, they need to set up a secure method of accepting customers' credit card numbers. Merchants typically use SSL and/or SET. If merchants prefer not to take on the responsibility of keeping credit card numbers secure during online data transfer, they can outsource it to one of many online companies that specialize in performing online credit card processing for companies. One such company is CyberCash (`www.cybercash.com`).

Using smart cards

Smart cards are looming on the horizon. They work much like traditional credit cards, but they include a microchip that can hold a lot more information than the magnetic strip that standard credit cards use. This chip can hold small security programs to help cut down on fraud. To use a smart card for payment, a machine has to be equipped with a smart card reader — something fairly rare in the United States at this point. Smart cards are used in the U.S., but more often they're used as tools to permit or deny access to some geographic area — such as the swipe cards many people have to use to enter a secure work area.

The pros and cons of smart cards are

- **Pros:** Smart cards offer better security than traditional credit cards because they can store a lot more information — up to 100 times more. This means they can perform more thorough authentication than a traditional card — making your transactions more secure. If a regular credit card is stolen, a thief can often purchase items long after the card has been reported stolen — especially at small shops that don't use an electronic machine that checks to see if it's a valid card. Because a smart card has to be processed electronically, no purchases should be able to go through on a stolen card (at least in theory); the smart card will always be validated with every purchase.

- **Cons:** Smart cards are not widely used for payments at this point — mostly because they're expensive. As the technology catches on and is used more widely, the cost will go down, but at this writing, the cost to make a smart card is about ten dollars. In comparison, a standard ATM card costs about ten cents to create.

A good site with links to pages that accept various types of payments is `ganges.cs.tcd.ie/mepeirce/Project/oninternet.html`.

Keep Your Hands Off My Brains: Intellectual Property 101

Doing business online requires a complete transition in the way you think about the law. Any decent-sized online business worth its salt has a legal department that is able to maneuver through the miasma of issues that the Internet gave rise to. I'm talking about intellectual property and copyrights, trademarks and branding, and more. Good thing we have about a million lawyers for every CIW-certified professional — we can let those schlumps handle the hard stuff. As long as you know the information in these sections (and ask a qualified expert for help when you're out of your element), you'll be okay for the Foundations exam and for your future career online.

If I'm going to talk about copyrights, trademarks, and the like, you have to first understand intellectual property. The term reminds me of an old Igor-type character guarding brains in jars in a laboratory. Alas, that's completely wrong. *Intellectual property* is a person's (or company's) legal ownership of a creative work or innovation.

The Internet makes it much easier for people to (knowingly or unknowingly) violate intellectual property laws for several reasons. First of all, it's so easy for people to copy text, music, photos, and the like. Maybe someone sees a neat picture that would look great on the church newsletter — he right-clicks on it, saves it, and *voilà*, it's on the church newsletter. Chances are this person had not intention of breaking the law, but he did.

Another reason intellectual property laws are frequently broken on the Internet is that every country has its own laws. What's legal in one country can get you thrown in the pokey in another, so the waters get pretty muddy. For the exam, you just need to know the definition of trademark, copyright, licensing, and some key features of each, which I cover in the following sections.

The idea of intellectual property is pretty easy to understand if you boil it down to the basics — yeah, I mean money. Anything that can be bought and sold can be owned. But sometimes intellectual property can get a little on the ethereal side. That's why it's best to turn to legal experts whenever you have a question.

Trademarks

A *trademark* can be any word or words, package design, or device that distinguishes one product from another. Yahoo! and Coca-Cola are both trademarks. Trademarks are very important to companies that do business online because the Internet is such a visual medium — all pictures of product packages and logos help uniquely identify products. To trademark something in the United States, contact the U.S. Patent and Trademark Office at `www.uspto.gov`. International trademarks are protected through the World Intellectual Property Organization (`www.wipo.org`).

Copyrights

To protect the data on Web sites from theft, businesses can copyright text and images. In fact, any tangible work can be copyrighted: literary works (including computer programs), musical works, graphics and other visual works, as well as other audio works.

The two main elements that factor into copyright are

- **Expression:** A work must be fixed in a tangible medium of expression, which means you have to be able to store it in some medium that can be reproduced. This would, of course, cover all print materials, but also all video or audio — anything that can be reproduced in some fashion.

> ✔ **Originality:** The work must be original. The legal technicalities can get a little blurry when it comes to how much one work can resemble another before it ceases to be original (but that's what keeps intellectual property lawyers in business).

Though there are different interpretations of copyright laws on the Internet, you want to concentrate on the interpretation the Prosoft folks offer. They say that although many people mistakenly believe some type of "international copyright" automatically exists, that's just not the case.

In real life, you can place a copyright symbol on anything you create. To strengthen your copyright protection, you register the copyright with the copyright authority in the country where you reside. In the United States, you contact the Library of Congress Copyright office. A good Web site that explains more about copyright is www.bitlaw.com/copyright/obtaining.html.

There are a couple of organizations involved in copyright that you should know about for the exam:

> ✔ **Information Infrastructure Task Force (IITF):** Works to understand and codify copyright and intellectual property laws as they relate to the Internet. For more information on the IITF, visit iitf.doc.gov.

> ✔ **World Intellectual Property Organization (WIPO):** A United Nations agency formed to protect intellectual property rights around the globe. It consists of a conglomerate of countries that agree to support each other's copyrighted materials. For more information on WIPO, visit www.wipo.org.

Obtaining Permission to Use Material

You can't sit down and draw a picture of Mickey Mouse, transfer it onto a T-shirt, and sell the T-shirt without infringing on the Walt Disney Corporation's intellectual property rights. But if you work for a company that's in the T-shirt business, you could use a bona fide image of Mickey Mouse. All you need is permission and a license agreement. And maybe you need to fork over some dough.

Businesses and individuals who want to use copyrighted or trademarked material must get permission to do so from the copyright or trademark holder. Often, a license agreement is also required. License agreements are similar to contracts — they set the terms of use of that material. (By the way, Disney's notoriously strict about its *terms of use*.) Licenses typically specify the payment arrangements for use of the work and how the work can be used.

Many major companies, especially those with a large online presence, like Microsoft, make their terms of use available from their Web sites. According to the Microsoft site, I have Microsoft's permission to use the image in Figure 6-1, but according to the copyright material at the front of this book, you don't have permission to photocopy this screen shot and give a copy of it to all of your friends. So don't do it!

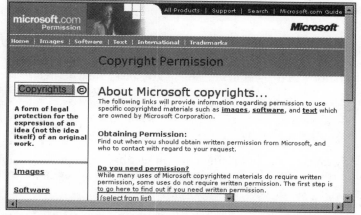

Figure 6-1:
A copy
of the
Microsoft
copyright
permission
agreement.

Unless you're an attorney, you shouldn't sign a license agreement without having it reviewed by someone with a background in intellectual property law.

Knowing Your Legal Precedents

For the exam, you should be familiar with three precedent-setting cases concerning copyright law on the Internet:

- ✔ **Sega Enterprises Ltd. vs. MAPHIA:** Sega brought a lawsuit against MAPHIA, charging that MAPHIA downloaded copies of a copyrighted Sega game and posted the copies onto a bulletin board system (BBS). Sega won.

- ✔ **Playboy Enterprises vs. Frena:** Playboy brought suit against George Frena for copying pictures from Playboy and posting them to a BBS. Although Frena claimed he didn't know he had broken copyright laws, the court ruled that his ignorance of the law didn't matter. Playboy won.

- ✔ **Recording Industry Association of America (RIAA) vs. Napster:** This suit was filed by RIAA to prevent Napster from enabling people to distribute copyrighted MP3 music files over the Internet. RIAA won.

Planning a Successful Web Site

When I look back on the first Web site I created, all I can think is, "What a mess!" I made the same major mistake a lot of new Web authors make — I didn't spend adequate time planning the site. This is particularly important if you plan on implementing an e-commerce site. This section explores the key steps in planning and developing an e-commerce site.

Project management is fun-damental

The principles of project management are the same whether you're building a house or creating a Web site. You probably already have a definition in your head for the term *project*. Prosoft defines the concept as "a temporary effort to create a unique product." That sounds simple enough, right? And the pyramids were built overnight.

For the exam, you need to know that project management is a combination of techniques, practices, and principles that help you manage the three main elements of project management:

- ✔ **Costs:** The costs of every aspect of a project including software, hardware, labor, and all tangible materials.

- ✔ **Project schedule:** The schedule for every aspect of the project including the project's interim and final deadlines to outside contractors' schedules.

- ✔ **Performance risks:** Things that could change either the project's cost or schedule. This could include the threat of a labor strike, the weather, or the inability to hire enough qualified people to work on the project.

Even if you're creating a site that contains only three pages, following the basic tenets of project management — establishing starting and ending dates, a budget, and project objectives — will help you succeed.

In real life, you could spend months studying and learning how to manage large projects. For this exam, you need to know the following terms:

- ✔ **Scope:** The range or size of a project.

- ✔ **Scope creep:** The tendency of a project's scope to increase as the project wears on. (For example, say you want to implement a simple directory of inventory items. If you find yourself creating a sophisticated, superpowered, lean, mean search machine, you've been victimized by scope creep.) Any changes in the project's budget, schedule, or performance can add to scope creep.

- ✔ **Scope matrix document:** A spreadsheet or table that lays out project scope in tables to organize the project's structure.

- ✔ **Business requirements document:** A report that spells out the customer's or company's needs as they relate to the project. It includes project details like goals, features, budgets, and deadlines.

- ✔ **Online cataloging:** An online catalog of data on company products. An online catalog results in a fully searchable inline index.

- ✔ **Technical architecture document:** A report that details the design and specifications for the project.

- ✔ **Project Management Institute (PMI):** Nonprofit organization that publishes standards and teaches project management principles.

- ✔ **International Organization for Standardization (ISO) 9000 series:** ISO is comprised of standards groups from over 120 countries. It develops technical specifications and offers certification in project management and quality-management systems.

Understanding the project management cycle

There are five steps in the project management cycle that you need to know for the exam:

1. **Business process/functionality design:** Management picks a project team and determines an appropriate and feasible development process. The *business requirements document* and the *scope matrix document* are created.

2. **Technology/architecture design:** Plan the project's design and determine the necessary resources. All team members are involved. This step includes the creation of the *technical architecture document.*

3. **Implementation/development:** Develop the project according to the project plan. This involves securing resources and keeping the project on track.

4. **Pilot/parallel:** Test and inspect the project. For a Web site, this would include a pre-launch of the site — testing it on a server that's not fully live.

5. **Cutover/live:** Launch the product. Launching should involve analyzing the project's success.

Putting Your Site Together

When you plan your e-commerce Web site, even if you're not following the formal project management steps I discuss in "Understanding the project-management cycle" earlier in this chapter, there's one step you won't be able to miss — putting the site together. You can plan and scheme all day long, but if you don't actually take the time to create the pages and features of the site, all your work's been for nothing.

In this section, I tell you about your site-creation options.

Creating your site in-house

If you decide to create an e-commerce site in-house, you (or someone in your office) develop and maintain every aspect of the site. The company also sets up the secure payment processes and 24-hour monitoring. Some of the pros and cons of in-house solutions are as follows:

- **Pro:** Not only do you have total control of the site's appearance and functionality (Hello, Control Freak!) but you'll also have an easier time integrating the new systems and software with existing back-end systems and/or data because you already know how your existing systems are set up. (You might have to spend all kinds of time with outside contractors to teach them how your mainframe/networks and databases are configured.)

- **Con:** Taking on in-house deployment of an e-commerce site can be very expensive, though the costs are decreasing every day. This is primarily because more vendors are creating more capable software that costs less than it would to have your own people do all the programming from scratch. Also, more people are learning how to do the kind of programming an e-commerce site needs, so you're not stuck shelling out big bucks to hire a capable Web programmer.

Choosing a third-party solution

Third-party solutions have become very popular with small- and medium size businesses for creating online storefronts. You may decide to purchase software, which you load onto your computer to create a site, or you may build the site using the software that resides on the vendor's site. Either way, you'll create your storefront.

If you're considering building a storefront with software that resides on the vendor's site, keep in mind that you will face limitations. I always say the easier the procedure, the less control you get, and that's the case here, too. It will take a little more time to develop a site with a program you've downloaded to your computer, but you'll get a lot more control and flexibility in the long run.

Prep Test

1 Which of the following is not a primary element of electronic commerce?

A ○ Communication

B ○ Data management

C ○ Security

D ○ Planning

2 Which of the following e-commerce payment methods enhances authentication and is capable of storing and updating passwords and other sensitive information?

A ○ Check model

B ○ Smart card model

C ○ Cash model

D ○ Credit model

3 What is the relationship between IITF and WIPO?

A ○ Both are authentication standards for e-commerce transactions between nations.

B ○ Both are organizations concerned with protecting intellectual property.

C ○ IITF is for the marketing industry, and WIPO is for the financial industry.

D ○ There is no relationship between the two.

4 What is the order of the five stages of a project cycle?
1 Pilot/parallel
2 Technology/architecture design
3 Cutover/live
4 Business process/function design
5 Implementation/development

A ○ 1, 3, 5, 2, 4

B ○ 5, 2, 4, 1, 3

C ○ 4, 2, 5, 1, 3

D ○ 4, 5, 2, 3, 1

5 Select the standardized interorganization exchange of documents in electronic form directly between participating computers:

A ○ PNG

B ○ OSPF

C ○ EDI

D ○ None of the above

6 **Which of the following is the worldwide grouping of national standards bodies from more than 120 countries?**

A ○ W3C

B ○ ISO

C ○ SSL

D ○ Internic

7 **Which describes the primary benefits of SET?**

A ○ Protects expression and originality

B ○ Enables easy and inexpensive communication, reduces the amount of data capture, and ensures fast handling of cash flow

C ○ Provides enhanced identification, protects credit card information from the vendor, encrypts all sensitive information between parties, and facilitates financial transactions

D ○ Allows data encapsulation for efficient transfer of information over wireless networks

8 **The business to business e-commerce model is characterized by _____.**

A ○ Low volume, low profit

B ○ High volume, high profit

C ○ High volume, low profit

D ○ Low volume, high profit

9 **What is the name of the project management report that contains the design and format specifications of a Web project?**

A ○ Scope matrix document

B ○ Technical architecture document

C ○ Business requirements document

D ○ RFC report

10 **At which stage in the project management cycle should you create your business requirements document?**

A ○ Stage 1. Business process/functionality design

B ○ Stage 2. Technology/architecture design

C ○ Stage 3. Implementation/development

D ○ Stage 4. Pilot/parallel

Answers

1 **D.** Planning. *Check out "What Is E-Commerce?"*

2 **B.** A smart card is a small electronic device about the size of a credit card that contains electronic memory. *Read over "Using smart cards."*

3 **B.** The IITF and the WIPO are organizations dedicated to protecting intellectual property rights. *Look over "Copyrights."*

4 **C.** Business process/function design, Technology/architecture design, Implementation/development, Pilot/parallel, Cutover/live. *Read "Understanding the project management cycle."*

5 **C.** EDI (Electronic Data Interchange) is a mechanism for companies to buy, sell, and trade information. *Review "Securing E-Commerce Transactions."*

6 **B.** The ISO (International Organization for Standardization) has defined a number of important computer standards. *See "Project management is fun-damental."*

7 **C.** SET (Secure Electronic Transaction) is the standard that enables secure credit card transactions on the Internet. *Read "Using Secure Electronic Transaction (SEC)."*

8 **C.** High volume, low profit. *Review "Understanding Common E-Commerce Business Models."*

9 **B.** A technical architecture document contains the design and format specifications of a Web project. *Review "Project management is fun-damental."*

10 **A.** Stage 1. Business process/functionality design. *Look over "Understanding the project management cycle."*

Chapter 7

Dealing with Security Issues

• •

Exam Objectives

▶ Protecting your computer using antivirus programs and digital certificates

▶ Understanding how Web cookies work

▶ Assessing the risk of sending data over the Web

▶ Configuring security settings in your browser

• •

*W*hen you go to the amusement park, you can always find all kinds of fun things to do, interesting things to see, and fun people to watch. The drawback of amusement parks (besides the heartburn you may get from all the cotton candy and cheese fries) is that they can be dangerous. You might get a pain in your neck from one of the rides, for starters. Then you have to deal with all the people. By the end of the day, you're probably as sick of bumping into strange people in the crowds as I am. Come to think of it, your local amusement park sounds a whole lot like the Web.

Some people surf the Web for years without a single mishap. Others (like my sister-in-law) seem to infect her computer with every Internet virus that comes down the pike. You can take some steps, though, to minimize your risk in both environments.

In this chapter, I focus primarily on protecting you and other users from possible virus attacks, theft of personal information, and plain nosy people. I'd like to tell you that this information will keep you safe from everything, but unfortunately I can't, because it won't. What this chapter does do, however, is help protect you from the most common types of attacks — like the way a home security system *usually* keeps out typical burglars. (By the way, another important benefit of knowing this information is that it will help you pass the Foundations exam!)

Because many Web developers work in a networked environment, no discussion of security would be complete without mentioning network security. I touch upon the primary network security tools, such as firewalls and proxy servers, in this chapter. For a more thorough look at network security, check out Chapter 21.

Quick Assessment

Viruses and cookies

1 The _____ virus affected Windows 95/98 machines and caused over $250 million in damage in Korea.

2 A _____ is a small text file often created by a Web server that resides on a client's computer.

3 Cookies are often written in the _____ language when they are embedded into Web pages.

Sending secure data over the Web

4 Data can be exchanged securely over a public network using a URL that begins with _____.

5 A _____ appears in the status bar of a browser to indicate you are visiting a secure site.

6 A _____ encrypts or scrambles information so it can't be read by unauthorized users.

7 Common encryption levels in the U.S. are _____ and _____.

8 Requiring a username and password is a feature of both _____ and _____ authentication.

Proxy servers and firewalls

9 A _____ improves performance of a network by caching and filtering.

10 A _____ acts as a filter to prevent unauthorized users from accessing a network.

Answers

1 *Chernobyl (CIH).* Review "Defining viruses."

2 *Cookie.* Check out "Crumbling Up the Cookies."

3 *JavaScript.* Look over "How cookies work."

4 *HTTPS (Hypertext Transfer Protocol Secure).* See "Putting the S in HTTP."

5 *Padlock.* Read over "Putting the S in HTTP."

6 *Key.* Take a look at "Introducing encryption."

7 *40-bit and 128-bit.* Read "Introducing encryption."

8 *Basic and Secure.* Check out "Using other authentication tools."

9 *Proxy server.* Review "Introducing proxy servers."

10 *Firewall.* See "Introducing firewalls."

Keeping Your Computer Safe and Sound

I can remember a time when offices and stores ran completely without computers. (I hand-wrote orders on pads to take orders at McDonald's, if you can believe that.) These days, though, nearly every office I know of depends on these machines more than they'd like to. Most decent computers run fine most of the time, but what happens if a virus strikes your computer? In the last two weeks, viruses hit three people I know, and their machines were out of commission for days or weeks while they waited for a technician to get to them.

Want to know one thing all three of these people had in common? No antivirus software. They kept meaning to install a good antivirus program, but never got around to it. If you're accessing the Internet with a computer that's not already protected by network security, you must have some antivirus software installed on your system to protect you, or you're a sitting duck.

Defining viruses

A *virus* is a program that's been placed inside a file and is designed to do damage to computers and networks when the file is opened and the program is set in motion. Viruses can be spread many ways — over a network or on disks that are shared — but modern viruses are usually transmitted through executable (.exe) files and sent in e-mail. (An executable file is a file that, when opened, automatically starts running without you having to do a thing.) Although most viruses cause relatively minor damage, such as corrupting a file so that the data in it is lost, some viruses have caused major damage. A couple of viruses you may see mentioned on the exam are:

- **Chernobyl (CIH):** Virus in executable files that infected Windows 95/98 and Windows NT files wiping out the data completely. It affected over 1 million computers in Korea and caused more than $250 million in damage.

- **VBS Love Letter:** Virus that overwrote certain types of Windows files (.vbs, .gif, and .ini) replacing their content with a virus code.

If you access the Internet from a computer that's attached to a network, the IT or server administrator has probably protected the network and all the machines in it. Most network administrators protect company networks with a *firewall* and/or *proxy server*. I cover both firewalls and proxy servers later in this chapter in the section "Securing Networks" and later in the book in Chapter 21.

Detecting viruses

Most viruses are embedded in executable files (files with an `.exe` extension). Executable files are essentially tiny programs that execute automatically, so they're perfect hiding places for viruses.

Even if you know better than to open unfamiliar executable files, a virus can still hit you. Many popular programs, such as Microsoft Word and Excel, support mini-programs called macros that are much harder to detect. The only way to keep out nearly all viruses is to install good antivirus software before you get hit.

Although the technical inner-workings of antivirus software packages are beyond the scope of this book, you may benefit from knowing some of the key features of typical antivirus programs:

✔ **They look for virus *fingerprints* — telltale signs a virus has been doing its dirty work on a system.** Antivirus programs contain information about known viruses and ways to prevent or remedy them.

✔ **They can scan your hard drive periodically in the background.** Antivirus programs usually allow users to configure the program to scan a computer's hard drive on a regular basis so the user doesn't have to remember to do it.

✔ **They can scan specific items upon request.** Users can have the software scan specific files/folders at any given time. If a user suspects he has a disk with an infected file, for example, he can scan all the disk's contents before any of its files are opened and possibly prevent an infection.

This won't be on the test, but if you're looking for a good antivirus program, you can't go wrong with either Norton Antivirus from Symantec (`www.symantec.com`) or McAfee (`www.mcafee.com`). Just make sure you return to the site you downloaded from every month or two to get updates.

Cleaning up viruses

If you've been unlucky enough to have your computer infected with a virus, you have to clean up the system. Often, just installing an antivirus program will wipe out any existing viruses. If that doesn't work, you may have to resort to taking your machine to your local computer repair shop. Professional computer repair technicians can attempt to rid your system of the virus by targeting the files that have been infected and try to repair or replace them. If the virus attack is too brutal (it's infected too many files too severely), the technician may have to reformat your hard drive — wipe out all the data on your hard drive and reinstall all your programs. (And that's just as much fun as it sounds, believe me.)

Crumbling Up the Cookies

Have you ever visited a site that seemed to remember you from your last visit? Such sites have messages on-screen that say things like "Welcome back, Sharon! You haven't visited us since April 2." Sites like Yahoo!, AltaVista, and other Web portals enable you to customize settings so that you can see content that suits your interests. And many online retail sites, such as Amazon and Travelocity, let you set up user accounts that remember what kinds of products you like to buy and what kind of adventure vacations you like to take. They also remember your shipping address, how you usually pay for products and services, and other preferences. How do Web sites perform these magic feats? Cookies! Not the kind you eat, the kind you program.

How cookies work

Cookies are created with code that's embedded in Web pages and run by the client browser. They're often created in the JavaScript language, although you can create them with other scripting and programming languages. (For more information on scripting and programming languages, see Chapters 8 and 14.)

One way cookies are used is to create a sense of interaction between a user and a Web site. For example, for a page to display a message that says, "Welcome back, (name). You haven't visited since (date)," the process works like this:

1. A user logs on to the Internet and visits a Web site that uses cookies.

2. When the user arrives at the Web site's home page, a script prompts the user's Web browser to look for specific information.

   One of the key areas cookies may examine is the profile information that's usually created when you install programs on your computer. Remember how programs almost always ask for your name, your company's name, e-mail address, and other personal information? That data is stored on your system as profile information, and cookies can read it easily. Cookies can also read system information, such as which operating system you're using, which browser program and version you're using, your screen resolution, and the date you visited their page(s).

3. The script copies the information it receives into a text file.

4. The cookie stores the text file on the user's machine.

5. The next time the user logs on to the site, a new embedded command is executed. This command looks for the stored text files (the cookies) that it gathered from the user on his or her previous visit.

6. The script retrieves the cookies and plugs the data from them into the appropriate places on the Web page.

Why businesses use cookies

Businesses use cookies for these main reasons:

✔ **To customize page content for visitors.** Pages can be customized with visitors' names and the date they last visited, and sites can use cookies to customize advertising based on the products visitors browsed for or purchased during their last visit. When cookies are used this way, they're often connected to a database on the Web site's server that dynamically updates the page you see. (The bookseller Amazon (www.amazon.com) uses a similar feature to customize the products you see featured on their home page.)

✔ **To collect information for marketing purposes.** Although many cookies stay on users' computers, they can also be used to collect important *aggregate* information that the Web site uses (or allows other companies to use) to figure out the characteristics of its typical customers so that it can market to them more effectively.

Aggregate means collection. In other words, information collected by cookies doesn't identify individual users. It might be used to tell a Web site that 64,000 visitors to the site also visited another site, or that the majority of visitors come to the site between 9:00 p.m. and midnight Eastern time.

✔ **To make Web sites more user friendly.** Some sites require users to log on before you can access its data. Web-based e-mail providers like Hotmail and Yahoo! mail work like this. During logon, some user information is stored in a cookie on individual hard drives so that users don't have to re-enter their log on information again if they want to check their e-mail again a short time — maybe an hour — later. E-commerce sites also use cookies to carry your ordering information from one screen to another.

Why people fear cookies

Cookies have gotten a bad reputation because the data they collect is sometimes shared with other companies. But the text files that are placed on your computer are, by themselves, harmless. The concern comes in when a site uses cookies to gather personal data about you — your e-mail address, street address, phone number — and sells that data to a direct marketing company. (Direct marketing companies are the companies that flood your inbox with offers for you to buy everything imaginable.)

Because companies can use cookies to invade your privacy, most reputable sites contain privacy policies that specify whether they use cookies, what type of data they're collecting, and what other companies (if any) they're going to share this data with. In real life use, privacy policies can help visitors feel more comfortable doing business with your company, especially if your company is new to them.

Another option many reputable sites employ is the use of (per) session cookies. These cookies can store personal information or information about what you're purchasing, but they expire (become unusable) after your Internet session ends. Your private information won't be accessible to others who have access to your computer.

This chapter just nibbles around the edges of the subject of cookies (another bad pun, I know). For more information on how to use cookies in your real-life Web sites, you can visit www.cookiecentral.com for Web cookies or www.cookierecipe.com for the kind you eat.

Monitoring your cookies

Cookies have become a standard on the Internet, but because they are run on Web browsers, both Netscape Navigator and Internet Explorer can be customized to control how cookies are used — at least to some extent. To access the cookie controls

- ✔ In Navigator, choose Edit⇨Preferences and click the Advanced category from the choices on the left.

- ✔ In Internet Explorer 5.0, choose Tools⇨Internet Options and select the Security tab. (If you're using another version of Explorer, your cookie controls may be in another location. Look up cookies in Help to find out where they're controlled in your browser.)

Both browsers allow you to select these options:

- ✔ **Allow all cookies to be loaded onto your system.** This is the default setting.

- ✔ **Allow no cookies to be loaded onto your system.** Users who choose this option can't use many popular Web sites like Yahoo! and Hotmail.

- ✔ **Ask you before any cookie is loaded onto your system.** If users choose this option, they will respond to dialog boxes that question whether they want to accept a cookie every few seconds. What a pain.

In addition to the three options listed previously, each browser offers one additional option the other browser doesn't:

- Netscape offers the option of enabling only cookies that are sent back to the original server. This helps prevent cookies created by one company from being sent to another (possibly direct marketing companies).

- Explorer offers the option of allowing only (per) session cookies. Session cookies *expire* after your current Internet session. They only exist while you're still on the Internet this visit. Web site developers can make cookies *expire* (stop working) whenever they want: today, next month, never, and so on.

Secure Transactions and Encryption

Most everyone wants to keep his or her personal information out of the public eye. That's one reason you probably don't go walking around with your social security number, mother's maiden name, and date of birth tattooed onto your forehead. (Another reason is that this information is much more stylishly worn tattooed on your forearm.) When you make a purchase online, you can't get around supplying some personal information (especially your credit card number and expiration date) to Web sites. To help ensure that this (and other) data is protected from people who shouldn't see it, companies employ several methods of securing this data. (See Chapter 21 for more information on transferring data securely.)

Putting the S in HTTP

The most common Web transport protocol is Hypertext Transfer Protocol (HTTP). The problem with HTTP is that it doesn't have the advanced security measures that ensure secure transfer of data. Also supported by Web browsers is Hypertext Transfer Protocol Secure (HTTPS), which was created to securely transfer the private data that users enter on a Web page back to the company's server.

You may use HTTPS every day, but you probably don't notice it. Next time you're online, look in the address bar when you're visiting a secured site. (See Figure 7-1.)

Whether you're using Internet Explorer or Netscape Navigator, a padlock is the universal sign of a secured site.

In Microsoft Internet Explorer, a padlock appears in the lower-right corner of the status bar only when you are visiting a secured page. (See Figure 7-2.)

By default, when users enter or leave a secure site, Netscape Navigator and Internet Explorer alert them with a dialog box similar to the one shown in Figure 7-3.

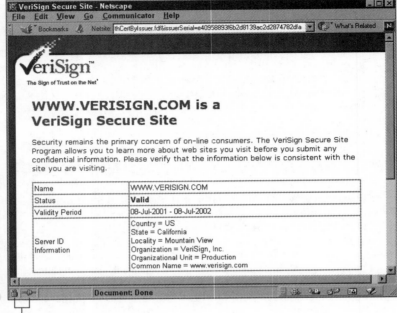

Figure 7-1:
You're looking at a secured page loaded in Netscape Navigator.

Netscape's padlock

Figure 7-2:
A secured page loaded in Microsoft Internet Explorer.

Internet Explorer's padlock

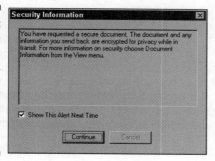

Figure 7-3:
You receive
a warning
dialog box
when
entering or
leaving a
secured
site.

Introducing encryption

Encryption is used with several security tools to prevent theft of information sent over the Internet. Encryption scrambles or encodes data as it is being sent so that even if someone intercepts the data along its route, the data isn't readable.

To open an encrypted message, users require a key. Only the person(s) with the correct key can decode the message. A *key* is a math algorithm that encodes or decodes a message. Some encryption software encrypts and decrypts with the same key; other software uses different keys for each. For a more detailed explanation of how encryption keys work, see Chapter 21.

Encryption levels can vary from software to software and from country to country. In the United States, most commercial encryption is either 40-bit or 128-bit. The more bits, the more secure the encryption. Make sure your browser supports the higher, 128-bit encryption. To check, choose Help➪About (browser name).

Depending on which version of which browser you're using, the encryption may be referred to as *cipher strength* as in `Cipher strength: 40-bit.` If you're using a browser that only supports 40-bit encryption, you may want to think about downloading the 128-bit version to increase security. For more information on how encryption varies from country to country, look at Chapter 21.

Digital certificates

A digital certificate is a digital ID issued by an agency that has authenticated the identity of an individual or company on the Web. Digital certificates work kind of like drivers licenses. The certificate is digitally signed by the certificate's creator to authenticate a user's identity. Certificates can be issued by a third party, such as VeriSign, or a company may have its own certificate server that creates certificates for users within the company's network.

VeriSign (www.verisign.com) is one of the most popular and trusted *certifying agencies* (companies that offer digital certificates) on the Web. It offers several types of digital certificates and often allows you to download a free 30-day trial.

When digital certificates were first introduced, they were most commonly used by software manufacturers. For example, online shoppers could check out the company and make sure that it was on the level. Now, other businesses are starting to use them to exchange legally binding documents electronically — and securely. The certificates validate that no one has tampered with a file after it was created and sent.

Using other authentication tools

Computers use technology to authenticate and verify the identity of a person who uses it to try to log on to a computer or network. Whether your computer is networked or not, for example, you may have to type in a user name and password before you can check your e-mail.

Some authentication technology requires users to log on to every program or interface that they want to use. For individual workstation computers and network servers to verify the information supplied back and forth with each other, both the workstation and the server need to use the same type of authentication technology.

The following list includes the four types of authentication technology you may be asked about on the exam:

- ✔ **Anonymous:** Requires no user name or password. Everyone can access this site. Most public Web sites use this type of authentication — you can peruse pages and browse through product catalogs without having to provide any user name or password.

- ✔ **Basic:** Requires a user name and password, but they are sent as plain text. If someone intercepts the data while en route, he or she can read it. Not many Web sites use this type of authentication because it's somewhat dangerous. Users may be led to believe the Web site and any data they provide to the Web site is secure because they're prompted for a user name and password. But a hacker can easily intercept the name and password and because it's not encrypted, the hacker can read and use any data the user typed in.

- ✔ **Secure:** Requires a user name and password that are encrypted to prevent unauthorized access. (I discuss encryption earlier in this chapter in the "Introducing encryption" section.) Secure authentication is common because it protects the user's name and password while they're being transmitted over the network.

  ✔ **Digital certificates:** Requires you (or your computer) to have a verified user certificate to access a site. (I discuss digital certificates earlier in this chapter in the "Digital certificates" section.) The process may appear to occur seamlessly — your browser can accept a certificate without checking with you first. The server and your computer communicate behind the scenes to verify that you're allowed to access a site.

Securing Networks

Most networks have access to the mother of all networks — the Internet. Nowadays, most companies have entire local area networks (with individual workstations for each employee) that need to be protected from the perils that lurk in the larger network of networks.

The security issues faced by local area networks (LANs) are somewhat unique. For example, top-secret company information can be very valuable in the wrong hands. Also, networks are usually at a higher risk of being infiltrated or attacked by viruses than a computer of a home user's machine. In Chapter 21, I discuss network security in much more detail. For the Internet Fundamentals portion of the exam, however, you need to know about just two network security tools: proxy servers and firewalls.

Introducing proxy servers

A proxy server is software that acts as a connection point between a local area network (LAN) and the Internet. Proxy servers work kind of like a two-sided funnel: All network traffic must go through the proxy server to access the Internet and all Internet traffic must go through the proxy server to access any computer in that network.

There are four main points you need to know about proxy servers:

  ✔ **Proxy servers can cache Web pages.** Say everyone in your office is investing with XYZ Online Investment Company. (It offers you super-cheap trading if everyone in the company signed up.) If employees frequently check on their stocks, the company's Web server must download the XYZ Investment page maybe 50 to 100 times a day — that's a lot of traffic. If the company instead uses a proxy server to access the Internet, the proxy server can be set up to cache, or save this page in advance, first thing every morning. This cuts down on network traffic and decreases the time it takes to download the XYZ Investment page, because it's already saved on the network.

✔ **Proxy servers can act as firewalls.** A *firewall* is a set of programs (and sometimes hardware) that helps restrict access to a network by outside users. Along the same lines, a proxy server firewall can also target specific file types and prevent them from passing from the Internet to the network and vice-versa. Executable files, for example, are often used to embed viruses, so a network administrator may decide to forbid executable files from entering or exiting the network. Companies often install a proxy server in addition to a regular (non-proxy-server) firewall. Firewalls perform several other functions, which I discuss in the "Introducing firewalls" section later in this chapter. (For a more thorough examination of proxy servers and firewalls, see Chapter 21.)

✔ **Proxy servers mask IP addresses.** If an outside user can find the Internet Protocol (IP) address of a computer inside a network, the whole network becomes vulnerable to attack. Proxy servers hide or mask the IP addresses of all the machines inside the network, helping to prevent unauthorized access. (For more information on IP addresses, see Chapters 3 and 19.)

✔ **Proxy servers require special configuration.** Every client program that you want to use to access the Internet from your LAN must be configured to go through the proxy server, if that's the sole point of Internet access. Most programs that typically require Internet access, such as browsers and e-mail programs, include a screen where you can type in the address of your proxy server. (The network administrator(s) usually supplies this address.)

Introducing firewalls

Firewalls act as filters between two networks — often between a LAN and the Internet. A firewall can combine software, hardware, and other network settings. Network administrators can modify the settings of a firewall to restrict which Web addresses employees can access and restrict external access to a network only to authorized users or to no external users. Firewalls are often a first line of defense for network administrators trying to protect their networks.

Both firewalls and proxy servers perform some filtering. Although the functions of the two do sometimes overlap, companies often use both. Administrators typically install a proxy server to cut down on network traffic (caching), mask IP addresses, and filter out specific file types and sizes. Although firewalls can perform some of these same functions, the primary focus of a firewall is usually different.

The filtering that a firewall performs concentrates on examining the source and destination IP addresses of packets in order to determine if the parties involved have proper authorization to complete the action. (For more information on packets, see Chapter 18.) To simplify this a little, remember that a proxy server examines the content of a file; a firewall examines the source and destination addresses. (Firewalls perform several other security functions not listed in this chapter. For more information on firewalls and security, see Chapter 21.)

Prep Test

1 **A program designed to do damage to computers or networks is called a**

A ○ Cookie

B ○ Viper

C ○ Virus

D ○ Proxy

2 **Yvonne receives an e-mail attachment from an unknown sender with a** .doc **file extension. She has been warned about the danger of opening attachments with the** .exe **file extension. Why should she beware of the** .doc **extension as well?**

A ○ .doc files cannot be attached to e-mail.

B ○ Viruses are often written to perform a series of actions, or macros, which can be contained in a variety of file formats.

C ○ The .doc file format is only compatible with computers manufactured before 1998 and will immediately crash any newer computer.

D ○ She should not beware because the .doc file format can never cause problems on any computer.

3 **Which statement is correct regarding cookies?**

A ○ When a server creates a cookie about you, it will always be able to access your e-mail settings, even if you didn't provide them.

B ○ Cookies can be used to read encrypted messages.

C ○ It is possible to configure your browser so that you receive an alert when a server attempts to give you a cookie.

D ○ Cookies never contain information about you and your preferences.

4 **Which browser application offers you the option of accepting only (per) session cookies?**

A ○ Netscape

B ○ Internet Explorer

C ○ Both

D ○ Neither

5 **"Applications used for scrambling information using mathematical algorithms" best defines:**

A ○ Virus scanning and removal

B ○ Firewalls

C ○ Encryption

D ○ None of the above

6 Which of the following is not true regarding digital certificates?

   A ○ They can be used to exchange legally binding documents securely.

   B ○ They must be created by the company that is sending the secure information.

   C ○ They are digital IDs that verify the identity of the sender.

   D ○ They can be created by a third party company.

7 What type of server can be set up on a network to create a firewall between client workstations and the Internet?

   A ○ E-commerce

   B ○ Certificate

   C ○ Proxy

   D ○ Cookie

8 What network solution serves the purpose of isolating information from intruders?

   A ○ Certificate

   B ○ Private key

   C ○ Authentication

   D ○ Firewall

9 A proxy server

   A ○ Increases network security and decreases network performance.

   B ○ Decreases network security and increases network performance.

   C ○ Increases network security and increases network performance.

   D ○ Increases network security and does not affect network performance.

10 The components of a firewall include

   A ○ Hardware

   B ○ Software

   C ○ Both A and B

   D ○ Neither A nor B

Answers

1 **C.** Virus. Viruses are specifically created to do damage to computers or networks. *Review "Defining viruses."*

2 **B.** Viruses are often written to perform a series of actions, or macros, which can be contained in a variety of file formats including `.doc`, `.xls`, and `.gif`. *Review "Detecting viruses."*

3 **C.** It is possible to configure your browser to specify that you be alerted when a server attempts to give you a cookie. Although cookies may contain information stored in your profile information, such as an e-mail address, they usually contain information you enter in form fields or track which pages you've been visiting. *See "Monitoring your cookies."*

4 **B.** Internet Explorer offers you the option of accepting only (per) session cookies. *Check out "Monitoring your cookies."*

5 **C.** Encryption. Encryption uses math algorithms to scramble or encrypt data to prevent unauthorized users from accessing it. *Review "Introducing encryption."*

6 **B.** They must be created by the company that is sending the secure information. Digital certificates can be created by the company that is sending the secure information or by a third party company, such as VeriSign. *See "Digital certificates."*

7 **C.** Proxy. Remember, one of the functions of proxy servers is the ability to act as a firewall. *See "Introducing proxy servers."*

8 **D.** Firewall. Firewalls are usually the first line of defense when it comes to keeping intruders out of your network. *Review "Introducing firewalls."*

9 **C.** Increases network security and increases network performance. *See "Introducing proxy servers."*

10 **C.** Both hardware and software. A firewall can consist of hardware, software, and other internal network settings. *Review "Introducing firewalls."*

Chapter 8

Handling Dynamic Web Content

Exam Objectives

▶ Including various programmed objects in Web pages

▶ Working with multimedia and other file formats

▶ Identifying which plug-ins and viewers to use in certain circumstances

• •

*T*he Web has come a long way from the text-based data-sharing tool it used to be. When HTML came about, the appearance and function of the Web changed. Today, authors can use even more advanced tools to add pizzazz to their pages, but the bulk of the code that creates Web pages is still good old HTML.

HTML allows you to create hyperlinks, place images on pages, and change the color of text and page backgrounds. But what if you want something more exciting or interactive? Dynamic content to the rescue!

In this chapter, I talk about popular tools that help you add sounds, animation, and interaction to Web pages. In real life, I recommend that you use these features sparingly because many Web authors go overboard, making their sites more irritating than cutting edge.

Used correctly, these features can add that extra touch that makes your site look more professional. Keep in mind that advanced Web features do have drawbacks — the main one being that not all visitors can access them — so know your audience before you decide to incorporate them.

Quick Assessment

Multimedia on the Web

1 JavaScript, Java, and DHTML are three methods used to create _____ Web content.

2 A(n) _____ is an element on a Web page that contains data and procedures for how that item will react when activated.

3 _____ is an object-oriented programming language developed by Sun Microsystems that's based on the C++ programming language.

4 Mini-programs for the Web written in Java are called _____.

5 _____ controls can do nearly all the same things that Java applets can.

Types of browser plug-ins and viewers

6 The _____ plug-in mode doesn't appear as a separate window — it works as part of the page.

7 _____ is a three-dimensional authoring language that allows visitors to interact with objects in real time.

8 _____ is a cross-platform file format for saving large text documents that download quickly yet retain their original formatting.

9 A(n) _____ is a scaled-down version of a program that allows visitors access to files, such as PowerPoint presentations, that they could normally see only if they had a full version of the program installed.

10 The _____ file format compresses audio files to about one-twelfth of their original size.

Answers

1 *Dynamic.* See "What Is Dynamic Web Content?"

2 *Object.* Review "I Object!"

3 *Java.* Check out "Care for some Java?"

4 *Applets.* Read over "Care for some Java?"

5 *ActiveX.* Look over "Staying ActiveX."

6 *Embedded.* Take a look at "A Few Good Plug-ins."

7 *Virtual Reality Modeling Language (VRML).* See "Virtual Reality Modeling Language (VRML)."

8 *PDF.* See "A Room with a Viewer."

9 *Viewer.* Check out "A Room with a Viewer."

10 *MP3.* Review "Incorporating Miscellaneous File Formats."

What Is Dynamic Web Content?

Dynamic means constantly changing. *Interactive* describes content that responds to user actions. Dynamic and interactive Web items are comprised of programming and/or coding that do things that regular HTML can't do. You can create dynamic Web content with a scripting language like JavaScript, a programming language like Java, or a newer HTML standard called *dynamic HTML* (DHTML). Each tool has its pros and cons. Some tools can accomplish relatively simple effects like making text appear to "fly" across the screen, and some can create extremely complex effects like interactive games.

You could spend months studying any of the tools I cover in this chapter. If you're so inclined, go for it! I recommend any of these books (all of which are published by Hungry Minds, Inc.) to get you going:

- *JavaScript For Dummies,* 3rd Edition, by Emily Vander Veer
- *Java 2 For Dummies,* by Barry Burd
- *C For Dummies,* Volumes One and Two, by Dan Gookin
- *C++ For Dummies,* 4th Edition, by Stephen Randy Davis
- *Flash 5 For Dummies,* by Gurdy Leete and Ellen Finkelstein

The reality is that many Web authors get started with dynamic content knowing only the basics. They get help from great Web sites that offer free dynamic content that you can copy or download. On the CD that comes with this book, I list several sites that offer free dynamic effects created with various techniques.

If you plan to advance your certification beyond the Foundations level, you'll need to have a working knowledge of the languages and scripts I describe in this chapter. For the Foundations exam, however, you don't need to know much about specific programming code or scripts — just a little bit of JavaScript code. Chapter 14 covers the JavaScript code you need to know for the exam.

I Object!

If you're going to work with multimedia on the Web, you need to understand the idea of an *object*. Though you can use a variety of programming or scripting languages to create dynamic content, one feature that these languages have in common is that they use objects. ProsoftTraining defines an object as an element on a Web page that contains data and procedures for how that item will react when activated.

That sounds simple, right? Just think of objects as the elements you combine to create an effect. If you were building a house, you'd use a variety of objects. The principle is the same when you create a Web effect. Standard objects can be combined differently to create different effects. These predefined objects also have predefined relationships. For example, a document object already knows it's inside the window object, and a form object knows it's inside the document object. Get it?

We Interrupt Your Regular Programming

You're probably aware that nearly all Web pages are created with one common language — Hypertext Markup Language (HTML). When it comes to adding multimedia and other special effects, however, you can choose from a variety of languages.

Most popular programming languages these days are *object-oriented* — probably because object-oriented languages are easier to work with than languages that aren't oriented. Object-oriented languages use predefined objects to cut down on the amount of programming that has to be included. If a language already contains a definition of standard objects such as the document or the taskbar, you don't have to spend time defining them every time you want to do some programming. All the programming languages I discuss in the following sections are object-oriented — except for C.

Prosoft just wants you to know a little history about the most popular programming languages and a key feature or two of each.

Oh say can you C

C is an older programming language used primarily to create operating systems such as UNIX. Because C is not object-oriented, it's more difficult to program in, and has largely been replaced by C++.

Two if by C++

C++ is a superset of the C programming language. Even though C++ and C have similar names, they use completely different programming concepts. C++ is a very powerful programming language and is often considered the best choice for creating complex programs such as operating systems. Another reason C++ is popular is that several vendors make tools to help make developing in C++ easier.

Care for some Java?

Java is a programming language that has become very popular with Web programmers. It is an object-oriented programming language created by Sun Microsystems and based on the C++ programming language.

Another key feature of Java is that it's *cross-platform,* which means that it can work on any operating system. When Java first came out, its cross-platform ability was a huge advance over existing programming languages like C or COBOL.

As with many programming languages, you can create just about any type of program you'd like with Java.

Java applets

Java *applets* are miniature Java-created programs that are embedded in Web pages. The browser software on the client machine interprets and runs the applet. If you want to create a complex program, such as a word processing or spreadsheet program, you can use Java, but this type of program would be far too large to embed in a Web page. Java applets are smaller and less complex than full-blown programs, but they can create many types of effects on Web pages including:

- **Interactive items:** Applets can provide interactive objects, such as an image that produces a ripple effect when the user positions the mouse over it, or an object that follows or "trails" the mouse around the screen.

- **Animation:** Applets can add video, text effects, and other movement on the screen.

- **Sound:** Applets can add background music or sound effects that play constantly or only when prompted by the user.

- **Real-time data feeds:** Applets can establish live connections to a server, enabling users to "chat" in real time. They can also send data to a client to update items such as a clock or a stock ticker.

Like other programs, programs created in Java can run independent of a browser, if they're created to play that way. Java applets, however, need special consideration. Applets will play only in browsers that are Java-enabled, meaning the browser must include the Java virtual machine.

The Java virtual machine is some extra code — similar to a plug-in — that knows how to interpret and run the applet. By default, the 4.0 and later versions of Netscape Navigator automatically include the Java virtual machine. Internet Explorer versions 4.0 through 5.0 and Windows 2000 and Me include it, too, but Microsoft stopped including Java virtual machine in later versions of its browsers and operating systems. You can, however, download the JVM (sometimes referred to by Microsoft as just the *virtual machine*) from the Microsoft Web site at `www.microsoft.com/java`.

Staying ActiveX

ActiveX is Microsoft's answer to Java. It's an open set of technologies that activate components within Web pages and Microsoft programs. An *open set* means there's not one specified program or technology used to make ActiveX components or controls — they can be made in nearly any programming language, though they're usually created in Visual Basic or C++. You can do nearly all the same types of things with ActiveX as you can with Java applets, but unlike Java applets, ActiveX controls aren't cross-platform. One common reason developers may opt for ActiveX over Java applets is because they already know the Visual Basic or C++ language and they don't have to take the time to learn Java.

To fully explain how ActiveX works, I'd have to spend several pages discussing programming theory, and frankly, that's way beyond the scope of the Foundations exam. If you just remember a few key features of ActiveX, you'll do fine on the test:

- ✔ ActiveX is capable of roughly the same things as Java. That includes incorporating sound, video, animation, and 3-D virtual reality.
- ✔ ActiveX was created by Microsoft but later turned over to an organization called The Open Group.
- ✔ ActiveX isn't just one technology but a set of several technologies using the same standard to allow objects to work together.

In real life, ActiveX isn't used in Web pages nearly as much as Java applets are because it isn't fully supported in Netscape Navigator and it can open up security issues that Java doesn't.

Studying Your Script

Scripting languages are like programming languages in that they can add special effects and interactivity to Web pages. Unlike programming languages, scripting languages are *event-driven*. This means scripts run only in response to a triggering event such as a user moving a mouse over a graphic or clicking a button.

On the other hand, with a programming language like C++ or Java, you can create independent programs — instead of being prompted to run by user events, they can make events happen. An antivirus program, for example, can be configured to run at regular intervals — every week or every month — without the user having to interact with the antivirus program each time.

Another difference between programming languages and scripting languages is that you include the scripting code within the HTML code when you create a Web page. Programming code may be referenced in the HTML code, but the bulk of the code resides outside of the Web page — sometimes in the same folder, but not visible when viewing the source code of the page.

Scripting languages such as JavaScript and VBScript (both covered in the following sections) allow you to create lots of common effects — rollover buttons, (annoying) pop-up windows, and scrolling messages in a taskbar. Even though you could create any of these same effects in a programming language like Java, it's easier to create them in scripting languages, and effects created by scripts often require less download time.

JavaScript versus Java

Although they have similar names, Java and JavaScript are completely different. JavaScript was created by Netscape as the first scripting language designed specifically for Web content. It's derived from *LiveScript,* an earlier language Netscape released. Java, as you may have read earlier in this chapter, was created by Sun Microsystems. Another key difference between Java and JavaScript is that Java is object-oriented and JavaScript is object-*based.* An object-based language uses predefined objects (just as an object-oriented language does), but an object-based language can't do as many things with the objects — it can't take full advantage of every object.

Table 8-1 details the differences between JavaScript and Java.

Table 8-1	**Comparing JavaScript to Java**	
Feature	*JavaScript*	*Java*
Use of objects	Object-based	Object-oriented
Independence	Must be embedded or linked to HTML code	Can run independent of HTML or a browser
Prompted to run by	Must be triggered by an event; considered event-driven	Can run without any prompting

Feature	JavaScript	Java
Special programs needed to run it	No special plug-ins needed, though it works better in later versions of browsers	Applets created in Java must be run in a Java-enabled browser — one that includes the Java virtual machine
Created by	Netscape	Sun Microsystems
Based on/derived from	LiveScript	C++

JScript

JScript is Microsoft's version of JavaScript. Back in the mid '90s, Netscape came out with JavaScript. Microsoft thought it was cool and wanted to program its browser, Internet Explorer, to read JavaScript as well. But because Microsoft didn't have Netscape's license to copy the exact same programming code, Microsoft came up with its own, similar version of JavaScript called JScript. Although the bulk of the codes written in JavaScript and JScript work the same in both browsers, some codes written in one don't work in the other. Because JScript is just another version of JavaScript, you can do the same types of things in each — scrolling messages and pop-up windows, for example.

VBScript

Visual Basic Script (VBScript) is another Microsoft answer to JavaScript. VBScript is derived from the Microsoft programming language Visual Basic. Visual Basic is a popular object-oriented programming language that's used to create Windows applications. It's based on a version of an older programming language called BASIC.

VBScript can work with two main types of objects:

✔ **Standard HTML objects:** For example, standard fields found in an HTML form — text fields, drop-down fields, and so on.

✔ **ActiveX controls or objects:** ActiveX controls are more flexible and powerful than standard HTML objects. ActiveX is discussed earlier in this chapter.

Dealing with Web Technology Security Issues

As a rule, the more powerful a Web technology is, the more dangerous it can be. That's true of the advanced Web tools discussed in this chapter. Both Java applets and ActiveX objects are downloaded to and run on the client machine. Although both can be used to create wonderfully interactive content, both can also be used to create malicious objects that can damage data and/or files stored on a visitor's machine.

Security problems with Java applets are rare. ActiveX controls, however, can be very dangerous because ActiveX can interact with the system files of Microsoft operating systems. If a developer has a malicious bent, he or she can easily create ActiveX code that wipes out or alters system files, which can seriously compromise or even ruin your system.

Most Java applets and ActiveX controls are safe; usually if an author includes destructive ones on a page, they're only there to be used as an example, and a warning is posted on that page to inform visitors.

If you want to decrease your risk of downloading destructive content, you can change your browser's settings. Both Netscape and Internet Explorer include options that allow you to control whether your computer will accept ActiveX and Java objects. (For more information on disabling ActiveX content in your browser, look in your browser's help menu under ActiveX.)

If you disable all dynamic content, pages that include this type of content may still load, but you'll see only the portions of the pages that don't contain active content. Depending on how the page is constructed, an empty hole may appear on the page where the active content would have loaded, but you won't see any error messages or other evidence of the missing content.

A Few Good Plug-ins

Plug-ins are miniature programs you can add to your browser so it can read certain types of files. You need to have plug-ins to be able to access most types of audio and video files in a Web page. Plug-ins are kind of like the different components that make up a stereo — a CD player, a cassette player, and a record player, for example. All three play music, but the recording format of the music determines which device can play it properly.

Here's how it works:

1. When a browser retrieves a Web page that contains certain types of multimedia files, the browser determines which, if any, of the programs or plug-ins you have loaded know how to read that file.

2. The browser then launches that file with the appropriate program.

3. If a multimedia file is very large, the plug-in may retrieve only a small part of the file at first and let the rest continue to load in your machine's *disk cache*. (Disk cache is a storage area on your hard drive that's used to temporarily store data.)

4. The plug-in continues to retrieve the remaining data from your disk cache as it continues to play the file.

   This method of allowing the beginning of a file to start playing while the rest of the file continues to download is called *streaming media*.

You need to know three plug-in modes for the exam:

- **Full-screen:** The plug-in completely fills the browser window. This is the typical mode Adobe Acrobat Reader opens in.

- **Embedded:** The plug-in works as part of the page — it doesn't appear in a separate window. Most Flash/Shockwave content opens in this mode, where it appears as part of the page, like an image would. To see Flash content embedded in a page, go to www.flashkit.com.

- **Hidden:** The plug-in runs in the background; it's hidden from view. Several music file plug-ins run in this mode — they play the music files, but you don't see them run. To see an example of hidden plug-in use, visit www.keytrax.com.

Installing plug-ins

Some people, as soon as they buy a new computer, search all around the Web to find every plug-in imaginable to download. I think that's unnecessary. Many new computers come with common plug-ins like Adobe Acrobat Reader already loaded. Chances are, you won't need to download every plug-in that exists.

I wait to download most plug-ins until I'm prompted to download them on a Web site. If you visit a Web site that asks you to install a plug-in, that's an indication there's content on that page that needs a certain plug-in to run.

If you decide you want to install a plug-in, you can install it one of two ways:

- ✔ **Offline:** In this type of installation, you download the appropriate plug-in while online, but you don't have to remain online to install it.

- ✔ **Online:** In this type of installation, you must remain online throughout the download/installation process.

If you include files in your Web site that require a plug-in to run, it's a good idea to provide a link to a site where the visitor can download the needed plug-in.

Macromedia Shockwave and Flash

Shockwave is a group of multimedia players created by Macromedia (www.macromedia.com) that can play animation, sounds, and streaming media. When you download the Shockwave player, the Flash player may be included as well, though you can download them separately. The Flash player allows you to play files created in the very popular Flash program. Flash allows developers to create very complex animations — even video games — with short download times because Flash files are very small. You can read more about how to incorporate Shockwave and Flash content into your Web sites at www.macromedia.com.

RealNetworks RealPlayer

RealNetworks created the *streaming* media format. It first released the RealAudio plug-in, which played high-quality streaming and non-streaming audio. Then it released RealVideo, which played streaming and non-streaming video. Nowadays, it has a combination audio/video plug-in called RealPlayer. You can read more about it at www.realplayer.com.

Apple QuickTime

QuickTime (www.quicktime.com) is an audio/video file format from Apple for the Macintosh operating system. QuickTime supports a feature called fast-start, which is Apple's equivalent to streaming audio and video.

You need to know two main types of QuickTime files for the exam:

- ✔ **QuickTime Movie (MOV):** This format combines video and sound into one file. QuickTime Movie files can end in .mov, .moov, or .qt.
- ✔ **QuickTime Virtual Reality (QTVR):** QTVR is a 3-D virtual reality format. It can take 2-D photos and expand them into 3-D so items can be displayed and rotated 360 degrees.

To find out more about Apple QuickTime formats, go to www.apple.com/ quicktime.

Windows Media Player

Windows Media Player can play both streaming audio and video, and it can play FM-quality audio. Media Player comes automatically installed on all new Windows-based computers. A version for Macintosh computers is also available. To find out more, visit www.microsoft.com/windows/ windowsmedia.

Virtual Reality Modeling Language (VRML)

Virtual Reality Modeling Language (VRML) isn't a media player or plug-in; it's a three-dimensional authoring language that enables developers to create 3-D objects with lifelike animation. VRML allows visitors to interact in real time with text, images, animation, sound, and video. When I think of VRML, I think of a 3-D picture of a house that I can click to turn any direction, zoom in, zoom out, and handle as if I had a small model of that house right in my hands.

Several viewers are available for VRML. One that works in both Windows and Macintosh environments is Cosmo Player, which is available at www.cai.com/ cosmo.

Although VRML was an important early development in 3-D modeling, it creates large file sizes (and you know what that means — looong download times). Both Macromedia (www.macromedia.com) and Adobe (www.adobe. com) offer 3-D modeling products that create smaller files and are becoming popular.

A Room with a Viewer

A *viewer* is a scaled-down version of a program that enables the user to view or print a file from that program, even if the user doesn't have that program installed. Viewers are like plug-ins, except they usually allow a user to view a document outside of the browser if desired. Two viewers you need to know about for the exam are

- ✔ **Adobe Acrobat Reader:** This viewer allows visitors to view and print files that are in a PDF format. *PDF* (Portable Document Format) is a format created by Adobe Systems, Inc. PDF files are highly compressed. PDF is the format of choice on the Web for large text documents and other large files because they download quickly and can be viewed on any operating system, as long as the visitor has the Acrobat Reader installed. You can download Adobe Acrobat Reader from `www.adobe.com`.

- ✔ **PowerPoint viewer:** This viewer allows PowerPoint slide shows to be viewed on machines that don't have PowerPoint installed or have a different version of PowerPoint installed. The PowerPoint viewer is available at `office.microsoft.com/Downloads/`. Viewers are also available for the other Microsoft Office programs on the Microsoft Web site.

Incorporating Miscellaneous File Formats

Many file formats can be included in Web sites. In fact, you can link to any type of file from a Web page — Microsoft Word files, Corel WordPerfect files, Excel spreadsheets — whatever you like. The catch is the computer the visitor is using must have a program installed that knows how to read the file type you're downloading. For example, if you're sharing an Excel spreadsheet and you know everyone you're sharing it with has Excel installed, you can just leave it in its original format and link to it from a Web page.

Unless the users who are viewing your file have a program installed on their machines that knows how to read the file, the program won't open. (That's when you get that annoying box that says "Which program would you like to use to open this file?" Most common file types used in Web pages — `.html`, `.gif`, `.jpg` — can be displayed by browsers. But some file types — audio and video files, for example — need plug-in programs to run.

Here's a list of some common file formats in Web sites:

- ✔ **Audio Video Interleave (AVI):** Standard video file format for Microsoft Windows. AVI files are also supported in the Netscape browser via LiveVideo. Both major browsers allow visitors to instantly view AVI files embedded in Web pages.

- ✔ **Moving Picture Experts Group (MPEG):** Standard, high-quality compression format for digital audio and video files. Different versions of MPEG exist, from MPEG-1, which works well with video CDs, to MPEG-3, which was created for High Definition Television (HDTV). Videos and sound saved in MPEG format don't work very well over slow Internet connections.

- ✔ **MPEG-1 Audio Layer-3 (MP3):** Standard for compressing audio files that uses the MPEG-1 standard. MP3 compresses audio files to one-twelfth of their original size. Many MP3 players are available on the Internet — Windows 98 and later versions include an MP3 player.

- ✔ **AIFF, AU, MIDI, and WAV files:** Standard audio file formats supported by both major browsers. These formats are good for reaching a large audience, but aren't compressed as well or with as high-quality sound as MP3.

- ✔ **Encapsulated PostScript (EPS):** Standard file format used to import and export graphics between programs and between operating systems. Although saved with a .eps extension, these files are viewed in different formats because EPS is often used as a temporary format. It keeps all the bitmap information about the graphic while being transferred. On Windows machines, EPS files are commonly previewed as TIFF files. On Macintosh machines, files are commonly previewed as PICT files.

- ✔ **Tagged Image File Format (TIFF):** Graphics format used primarily for print that was developed by Aldus Corporation (now part of Adobe). TIFF supports grayscale, 8-bit, 24-bit, and monochrome formats.

- ✔ **Rich Text Format (RTF):** Portable format created by Microsoft that allows users to save and share text files across across applications retaining original formatting and graphics. RTF files can be viewed on nearly any operating system including Windows, Macintosh, Linux, and UNIX.

Prep Test

1 Scripting languages and programming that create dynamic Web content all center around the use of

- **A** ○ Cookies
- **B** ○ Applets
- **C** ○ Objects
- **D** ○ Beans

2 Which of the following is platform-independent, meaning it can run on any system?

- **A** ○ Java
- **B** ○ JScript
- **C** ○ VBScript
- **D** ○ ActiveX

3 Which programming language was used to create operating systems such as UNIX?

- **A** ○ ActiveX
- **B** ○ C
- **C** ○ JavaScript
- **D** ○ Shockwave

4 Which of the following is true about JavaScript?

- **A** ○ It was developed by Microsoft.
- **B** ○ It always functions exactly the same in all browsers.
- **C** ○ Its code is contained entirely within or linked to the HTML code of the Web page.
- **D** ○ It has replaced Java as the programmers' choice for building stand-alone applications.

5 Which of the following was not developed by Microsoft?

- **A** ○ JScript
- **B** ○ VBScript
- **C** ○ ActiveX
- **D** ○ Java

6 **Which of the following is not a common plug-in mode?**

A ○ Hidden

B ○ Full-screen

C ○ Embedded

D ○ Anonymous

7 **Which of the following statements is not true regarding plug-ins?**

A ○ Nearly all audio and video files require plug-ins to play in a Web page.

B ○ Plug-ins may be installed online or offline.

C ○ Plug-ins can be prompted to run by a browser.

D ○ Every plug-in a user may need comes already installed on new systems.

8 **The Flash Player plug-in can be included with which of the following?**

A ○ QuickTime

B ○ RealPlayer

C ○ Shockwave

D ○ Adobe Acrobat Reader

9 **Which of the following file formats can be delivered as streaming media?**

A ○ RealAudio (.ra)

B ○ WAV files (.wav)

C ○ Rich text (.rtf)

D ○ MPEG-1 Audio Layer-3 (.mp3)

10 **Which of the following was developed by Apple?**

A ○ Shockwave

B ○ QuickTime

C ○ Windows Media Player

D ○ RealPlayer

Answers

1 **C.** Objects. Objects are predefined bits of code. *See "I Object!"*

2 **A.** Java. One reason Java is so popular is that it was one of the first programs that could run on any system. Review *"Care for some Java?"*

3 **B.** C. Although C isn't as commonly used now as it was years ago, it is a powerful language. *Check out "Oh say can you C."*

4 **C.** Its code is contained entirely within or linked to the HTML code of the Web page. *Read "Studying Your Script."*

5 **D.** Java. Java was developed by Sun Microsystems. *See "Care for some Java?"*

6 **D.** Anonymous. Plug-in files can be viewed while they play in either full-screen or embedded mode or may play in the background in hidden mode. *Look over "A Few Good Plug-ins."*

7 **D.** Every plug-in a user may need comes already installed on new systems. Though several popular plug-ins (like Macromedia Shockwave/Flash) do come already installed on new computers, many others aren't. *Review "Installing plug-ins."*

8 **C.** Shockwave. *Take a look at "Macromedia Shockwave and Flash."*

9 **A.** RealAudio (.ra). None of the other three support streaming media. *See "RealNetworks RealPlayer."*

10 **B.** QuickTime. *Check out "Apple QuickTime."*

Part III
HTML Fundamentals

The 5th Wave   By Rich Tennant

"Give him air! Give him air! He'll be okay. He's just been exposed to some raw HTML code. It must have accidently flashed across his screen from the server."

In this part . . .

Part III covers information that comprises 20 percent of the exam. The bulk of this part is about coding HTML, but it touches on some other markup languages, too. You don't need to know a great deal about coding in other languages, but you do need to know standard HTML very well (how the tags you use define sections of a document, and how the tags you use apply various types of formatting — as well as all of its different flavors). For example, you should be aware of the purpose of several languages related to HTML, such as XML and XHTML. And even though you need to know only a tiny bit of actual JavaScript code — just enough to recognize code that creates a pop-up message box or that puts text on a Web page — you should have a solid understanding of how to incorporate JavaScript into an HTML document.

The chapters in Part III show you how to put together a table with various row and column configurations and how to place data or graphics in its cells. You get the short course in creating form fields, numbered lists, and bulleted lists.

Because you don't have to actually type any HTML code during the exam, you may be inclined to just read this information and not practice using it. I've included a few labs in some of the chapters in this section, but I strongly encourage you to create pages in HTML using all the tags in the book before you take the exam. Practicing helps embed tags in your memory so that you have one less thing you have to worry about at test time.

Chapter 9

Before You Work with HTML

- -

Exam Objectives

▶ Identifying front-end and back-end Web design issues

▶ Testing and analyzing Web site performance issues

▶ Formatting HTML files to maintain compatibility with older Web browsers

▶ Recognizing the benefits and drawbacks of hand-coding HTML pages and using a GUI editor

- -

*P*lenty of people out there can create Web pages in programs that write HTML code for them. You can use programs like Microsoft FrontPage and Macromedia Dreamweaver to put together pages even if you don't know a bit of code. But to control your Web page design and function as much as possible, you need to know HTML. Knowing HTML is kind of like knowing how to do math without a calculator. I see a lot of kids today who can't seem to perform even simple calculations unless they have a calculator. The problem is, a calculator isn't always handy when you want to figure out how much to tip a waiter.

The same principle is at work when it comes to using HTML. Although you'll probably use an editor like FrontPage or Dreamweaver much of the time, you may occasionally want to add a feature to a page that your program doesn't include. If you decide to add advanced features to your Web, such as database connectivity or JavaScript (which I cover in Chapters 8, 14, and 17), you'll have to manually alter your code.

The process of creating Web pages is often called *Web page authoring*. In this chapter, I cover some of the marketing concepts and terms good Web authors remember when planning Web sites. I also introduce you to HTML — where it came from and several variations of it.

Quick Assessment

Front- and back-end issues

1 Server-oriented issues that must be addressed in the planning phase are considered _____ issues.

2 When designing Web pages, it is important to remember that a sizeable group of users are still dialing up with _____ Kbps (kilobits per second) connection speed.

3 Calculating approximate _____ times for Web pages assists in the development of successful Web sites.

4 If a Web server is not able to find a file that matches the URL, the browser will display a(n) _____ message.

5 _____ is the reinforcement of a company's image throughout its marketing strategy.

Web browsers and standards

6 _____ is the man credited with creating HTML and the World Wide Web.

7 HTML version _____ is the current version, released in December 1999.

8 _____ is the flavor of HTML 4.01 that is required for Web pages using frames.

Text and GUI editors

9 The _____ method of Web authoring provides the most control over page content and display.

10 Web authoring software, such as Macromedia Dreamweaver and Microsoft FrontPage, are often referred to as _____ editors.

Answers

1 *Back-end.* Review "Back-end issues."

2 *28.8.* Check out "Estimating download times."

3 *Download.* See "Estimating download times."

4 *"Page Not Found" error or http 404 error.* See "Where nobody knows your page's name."

5 *Branding.* Look over "Marketing 101."

6 *Tim Berners-Lee.* Check out "Making Your Mark-Up: A Little History Lesson."

7 *4.01.* Review "HTML versions 4.0 and 4.01."

8 *Frameset.* Take a look at "HTML version 4.01: Knowing the difference."

9 *Hand-coding.* See "To Hand-Code or Not to Hand-Code."

10 *GUI.* Look over "GUI editors."

Planning the Content and Design of a Web Site

You may have heard that old adage, "If you fail to plan, then you plan to fail." That saying holds true in the case of Web design. You can't create a highly functional, attractive Web site without spending some time planning the content and the layout of each page. The issues you need to keep in mind when planning your sites fall into two main categories: front-end and back-end.

Front-end issues

The front-end of a Web site is the part the viewer sees. Front-end issues are those that concern the people who actually see and use the Web pages — and not to mention all the content on those pages.

To make the front-end of your site easier to access, maneuver, manipulate, and utilize, try the following techniques:

✔ **Keep download times short.** The content of your page, especially the number and size of the graphics you include, is the primary factor that determines how long your pages take to load. (For information on how to calculate the download time of a Web page, see the section in this chapter "Estimating download times.")

✔ **Make navigation easy for beginners and avoid dead ends.** It should be easy for visitors to figure out how to get to any page from any page in your Web site. Don't link to a page in your site that doesn't offer links back to other pages in your site — that's called a dead end.

✔ **Use eye-catching graphics but use them sparingly to prevent long download times.** Even though you don't want to overload your site with graphics (the download time will be horrible), you still need to use at least a few eye-catching graphics to enhance your site's appearance. (Think of how boring most Web pages would be if they contained no graphics at all.)

✔ **Keep page content up to date.** A big tip-off to readers that you haven't been paying attention to your Web site is content that's obviously out of date. (What if you opened a page with a headline reading, "Elvis Presley drafted into the military"?)

✔ **Use tables and forms when appropriate.** Tables and forms are great ways to organize information on your Web pages and can make them easier for users to interact with as well. (For more information on tables and forms, see Chapter 12.)

✔ **Use text links.** Even if you use buttons for your main navigation, use hyperlinked text going to the same locations to make your site viewable to those browsing with image loading turned off.

You won't be tested on this, but typically you should try to keep the downloading time of your home page to 10 to 12 seconds or less. Pages linked to your home page can take a little longer, maybe 20 to 25 seconds.

Back-end issues

It can be very frustrating to spend hours upon hours incorporating all the techniques to keep your page sizes small and your download times short only to find it still takes way too long for your pages to load. What's the problem? Well, if the problem's not your page design, it must be a server-oriented or *back-end* issue.

I'm with the bandwidth

One of the most problematic back-end issues is limited bandwidth. *Bandwidth* refers to the transfer rate of a network and affects the amount of information that can pass through a network connection at a given time. If your server is connected to the Internet via a line that doesn't offer enough bandwidth, your site will take a while to download, regardless of how well you've designed your pages. For more information on connection speeds, see Chapter 3.

Estimating download times

Most Web authoring programs provide you with an estimate of the time each page takes to load on your Web site. You really should know how to calculate the approximate download time for a page without having to rely on a Web authoring programs. Besides being a good idea, it's on the exam. To calculate the download time of a Web page, see Lab 9-1.

Lab 9-1   Calculating the Download Time of a Web Page

1. **Add the file sizes of your HTML file and all other files, such as images that are included in that page.**

   For this example, say I have 10 files associated with a page and they add up to 100 kilobytes (K).

2. **Determine the connection speed you're using.**

   Although you may have a high-speed connection, a sizable number of visitors to your Web page are still using dial-up connections with 28.8 Kbps (kilobits per second) speed. For this example, I use 28.8.

3. **Convert the file size and the connection speed to a common unit of measure.**

1 byte = 8 bits. The connection speed is already defined in bits (28.8 kilobits = 28,800 bits), so I've just got to convert the file size from bytes to bits. I take my file size of 100K, which stands for 100-thousand (kilo = 1,000) bytes, and change it to display as 100,000. Because 8 bits are in a byte, I multiply 100,000 by 8 to get 800,000 bits.

4. **Divide the file size by the connection speed.**

So, I divide 800,000 by 28,800. The zeros at the end cancel out and I get 27.7, which I round up to 28 seconds. Looks like I need to cut something out to get closer to my 10- to 12-second goal.

The preceding steps are the technically correct method of calculating download times. To get the same result with fewer steps, here's how I estimate download times.

1. **Total the sizes of all the files connected to your page and multiply that number by 8.**

Using the same example from the preceding steps, I multiply 100 by 8 to come up with 800.

2. **Divide this number by your connection speed.**

I divide 800 by 28.8 to get 27.7 that I round up to 28 seconds.

Doesn't that seem easier?

For the exam, it doesn't matter which way you calculate a page's download time, as long as you come up with the correct answer. Make sure you know at least one method.

Where nobody knows your page's name

A fairly common back-end error a Web server might generate is the "HTTP 404 — File Not Found" error. This kind of message indicates that the Web page's host server is functioning but, for whatever reason, it can't find a page that matches the address the user typed in.

A 404 error can occur if someone has renamed or moved the file, or if the user made a mistake and just happened to type in the wrong URL. I get this error message frequently when I'm trying to access older Web sites. If a site's been up for a long time, there's a decent chance that somewhere along the line the site has been moved, renamed, or no longer exists.

Marketing 101

When planning the content and design of your Web site, you can't just focus on what looks good on the page. You have to tailor your content a bit so search engines can find you. Professionals use many tricks to tweak a Web page's content to help improve its ability to be found by search engines. In fact, you could fill an entire book (and many people have) with information about Web site marketing. There's a good one called *Internet Marketing For Dummies,* by Bud Smith and Frank Catalano (published by Hungry Minds Inc.), if you're interested in finding out more. Because I don't have 30 chapters to devote to marketing, I'm going to concentrate on the key terms and concepts you need to know for the Foundations exam (because that's probably why you're reading this book).

The marketing concepts you need to know for the exam are

- ✔ **Market intelligence** requires gathering information and obtaining knowledge of a whole *industry sector* or *niche market* from a number of companies and sources. (Gathering information in this fashion is also called *secondary market research.*)

   When you gather market intelligence, you're studying not just your competitors' Web sites, but also the customer demographics, advertisers, and the rest of the industry. Recently, I designed a Web site for a plastic surgeon. One of the first steps I took was to study other plastic surgeons' Web sites. But I also gathered other market intelligence by looking at studies that indicated what percentage of a plastic surgeon's clientele was referred by Web sites and which procedures prospective patients are more likely to want more information about.

- ✔ **Mind share** is the name-recognition that results from a combination of easily recognized company names, brands, logos, slogans, and commercial phrases. Mind share usually leads to market share, and in business terms, that's a very good thing.

   Mind share is the stuff that marketing managers dream of, and successfully snaring mind share is the result of a concerted and well-crafted marketing campaign. An example of a company that has achieved strong mind share is Coca-Cola. Its name recognition is extremely high, and throughout the years, the company has used easily remembered catch phrases like, "Have a Coke and a smile."

- ✔ **Branding** consists of reinforcing a company's look and image throughout all facets of its marketing campaign. Many large companies use Web sites mainly to help reinforce companies' brands. Designers that put their logos all over their clothes and on all their marketing materials are using branding.

✔ **Branding standards** are the rules that all facets of a marketing campaign follow to tie them together — the color choices and logo placement, for example. This also includes the company's rules about which products or materials are eligible to carry the company's logo. (Coca-Cola, for example, probably wouldn't put its logo on a bottle of fruit juice, and the overuse of the logo would dilute the impact it has on customers.)

Making Your Mark-Up: A Little History Lesson

HTML stands for Hypertext Markup Language. Some people think that they're programming whenever coding is involved, but that's incorrect. A markup language is different from a programming language. Most markup languages, especially HTML, control only how an item is positioned on a page and some of that item's formatting. They specify the color of text, the alignment of an image, and things like that.

The first markup language was the IBM-created *Generalized Markup Language* (GML). GML evolved into *Standard Generalized Markup Language* (SGML), which became the mother of all markup languages. Everything that's come since has been based on SGML. Both GML and SGML allowed authors to lay out or *markup* pages, but these languages were hard for the average person to use. HTML is a simplified application of SGML.

HTML was created to standardize the look and feel of information on the Internet, regardless of what kind of computers, operating systems, and settings users might have on their machines. With the arrival of HTML came Web browser software. The readability of the browser interface and the usability of *hyperlinks* were major driving forces behind the explosive growth of the Internet. (For more information on the history of the Internet, see Chapter 3.)

If you just put together a bunch of HTML code and asked visitors to look at it, they probably wouldn't understand what the heck you were trying to say. When visitors look at Web pages, they see their browser software's interpretation of the code. Interpreting software (also called *user-agents*) reads the HTML and renders a page that looks however the HTML says it should look. Browsers aren't the only types of programs that can interpret HTML. Many e-mail programs and other business applications can now read and render HTML on your screen.

As the HTML Turns: Standards and Versions Galore

HTML has evolved since it was originally created. Newer HTML codes or *tags* have been created to enable Web pages to do more exciting things. The World Wide Web Consortium (W3C) recommends changes, but it's up to the companies who make the browser software to decide when to program their browsers to understand new HTML tags and other new technology.

"Doesn't this delay cause problems?" you ask. Why yes, it does. This is why approximately 39.3 percent of Web authors (the people who create Web pages) have bald spots in the back of their heads from pulling their hair out!

The various versions of HTML have specific, documented variations that you need to know for the exam — these are covered in the following sections. If you're completely new to HTML, you may want to look over Chapter 10 to familiarize yourself with HTML structure before you attempt to learn about different versions of HTML.

HTML version 3.2

The earlier version of HTML is version 3.2. HTML 3.2 is still widely used because most older and newer browsers can recognize the HTML code. It's up to the good people at Netscape and Microsoft to program their browser software so that it can read new tags, and the two companies don't always agree on how to interpret them. Many Web authors, especially those new to HTML coding, think HTML version 3.2 relieves Web authors of having to memorize which new tags are read by which versions of which browsers — HTML 3.2 code is almost universally interpreted correctly.

HTML versions 4.0 and 4.01

HTML version 4.01 is the version referenced in the latest W3C Recommendation, released in December of 1999. HTML 4.01 contains minor modifications to HTML 4.0, and both versions are often referred to interchangeably.

The biggest drawback of using HTML 4.01 is that users must upgrade to a later version of a browser in order to view the newer HTML tags as they were intended. And even if visitors do have a later version browser, that doesn't guarantee it will render the Web page the way the author intended.

HTML 4.01 supports several new features that many authors like, including Cascading Style Sheets (CSS) and multiple language interpretation. *Cascading Style Sheets* are comprised of newer HTML codes that help Web authors reduce the amount of formatting codes necessary to design Web sites. I cover Cascading Style Sheets in more detail in Chapter 14. Multiple language support enables a browser to work with languages that read left-to-right, like English or Greek, and right-to-left, like Hebrew or Arabic.

HTML version 4.01: Knowing the difference

If the different versions of HTML weren't confusing enough, there are three distinct variations or flavors of HTML 4.01 to know as well. You're almost certain to get test questions on these:

- ✔ **Transitional:** Allows formatting of fonts, colors, and so on, using either CSS or the more traditional formatting methods of earlier HTML versions. Authors can choose to format certain features with older formatting tags and other features with CSS. (Just because transitional HTML allows the use of CSS, that doesn't mean older browsers understand it. If a browser doesn't understand the CSS in a page, it just renders the page the best it can — the page may look okay or the alignment and other formatting might be way off.)

- ✔ **Strict:** Requires author to use CSS only for formatting.

- ✔ **Frameset:** Required version for Web pages that use frames. Frames allow multiple pages to display on the screen at one time, giving the appearance of being parts of one page. (I discuss frames in depth in Chapter 13.)

DTDs: Document Type Definition statements

When you create a Web page using one of the flavors of HTML 4.01, you must specify which flavor you're using in a DTD statement. A *DTD* (Document Type Definition) statement goes at the very beginning of an HTML document and specifies which version of HTML you're using and, if you're using HTML 4.01, which flavor. Optionally, you can include the W3C's Web address. (If you're interested in finding out more about HTML standards than you need to know for the exam, visit the W3C Web site at www.w3c.org.)

The following example describes a document created in HTML version 4.01, transitional version. The word PUBLIC means it's a nonproprietary version and the EN at the end specifies the language in this page is English.

```
<!DOCTYPE HTML PUBLIC "-//W3C//DTD HTML 4.01
         Transitional//EN">
```

Shhh. Don't tell anyone, but in real life, authors sometimes leave out the DTD statement and the page works just fine. This is an acceptable choice if you're not including some of the more advanced HTML 4.01 features in your page. But it's not acceptable if the CIW Foundations exam asks you if it is.

You won't have to write DTD statements for the exam, but you should be able to tell by looking at a Web page which version of HTML the Web author used, and, if it's HTML 4.01, which flavor.

Home Sweet Home Page

Have you ever noticed that the home pages of most Web sites are named `default.htm` or `index.htm`? Well, it's not just a coincidence — there's a good reason you need to name the home page of your Web site something special.

When users type in a Web address, such as `www.hungryminds.com`, their Internet Service Provider (ISP) takes their browser to the server computer that hosts that Web site. At that point (unbeknownst to users), the browsers are taken to a folder that contains all the Web pages in that site. But what if 100 pages are in the folder? What determines which of the pages a browser should pull up to display for those patiently waiting users?

The Web site's server software determines the first page you look at. Web servers are programmed to look for special file names that denote which page is the home page of a Web. `Default.htm`, `Index.htm`, and `Welcome.htm` are standard choices, although the server administrator can program the server to look for whatever name he chooses.

If the home page is not an HTML page, the extension at the end of the file name reflects that. For example, if the page is an Active Server Page, it might be named `default.asp`. (I cover Active Server Pages in Chapter 17).

The sample home page names in the previous paragraphs have three-letter file extensions like `.htm` and `.asp`. Windows operating systems use three-letter file extensions. Other operating systems such as UNIX, use four-letter extensions. A page named `default.html` is the same type of page as one named `default.htm`, regardless of how many letters display at the end. The only difference is which operating system an author or server is using.

To Hand-Code or Not to Hand-Code

Almost every Web page on the Internet is created, at least partially, with HTML code. That doesn't mean, however, that you have to write the code manually (or hand-code it). As you may know, in software land, you can find several Web-authoring programs that do the often tedious work of coding HTML for you. The question is: Should you hand-code your Web pages or use a Web-authoring program that writes HTML for you? Depends.

Hand-coding

If you decide to hand-code pages, you'll probably use a text-editor program like Notepad for the Windows operating system or SimpleText in the Macintosh operating system. *Text editor programs* are like extremely pared-down versions of word-processing programs. They allow only the most basic formatting, such as font changes and spacing, but this makes them perfect for writing code.

There are several reasons to hand-code a Web document:

- ✔ **Hand-coding gives you more control over a page's content and display.**

- ✔ **No Web authoring program includes every Web feature in existence.** If you know how to write HTML, you can add other features manually.

  If you want to add advanced features to pages, such as scripting or database connectivity, you have to write at least some code by hand.

GUI editors

Web authoring programs like Microsoft FrontPage and Macromedia Dreamweaver are often referred to as GUI (Graphical User Interface) editors, which feature graphical items, such as menus and buttons, for you to use. Without this interface, you'd have to write code for every document you create. That sounds like fun, doesn't it?

GUI editors offer several benefits over hand-coding:

- ✔ **Create Web pages more quickly.** No matter how fast and accurate a typist you are, there's no way you can create a complex Web page as quickly by hand-coding as you can with a GUI editor.

- ✔ **Easier to use.** You don't have to know a bit of HTML to create a Web site in most GUI editors. (But as I've mentioned throughout this chapter, it's still a good idea to know HTML.)

- ✔ **Document information is readily available.** Most GUI editors will calculate your page's download time for you. They also calculate other summary information, such as the number of pages in your site or a summary of browser compatibility issues within your site.

Prep Test

1 **Which of the following is not an example of a front-end issue in Web planning?**

  A ○ Regular content updates

  B ○ Maintaining an active connection between the database server and the Web server

  C ○ Providing text links to aid site navigation

  D ○ Keeping download times short by using small image files

2 **What is the main reason Web pages take too long to download?**

  A ○ Outdated or incompatible video card on user's computer

  B ○ Too many paragraph breaks

  C ○ No meta tags

  D ○ Too many graphics and large graphics files

3 **The transfer rate of a network is often called**

  A ○ Hypertext

  B ○ Bandwidth

  C ○ Markup

  D ○ Traffic

4 **The approximate download time for a 50K (kilobyte) Web page over a 28.8 Kbps (kilobits per second) connection is**

  A ○ 14 seconds

  B ○ 20 seconds

  C ○ 7 seconds

  D ○ 28 seconds

5 `"HTTP 404 - File Not Found"` **most likely indicates which of the following?**

  A ○ The end user's Internet session has been terminated, and the user has to shut down and reboot the computer.

  B ○ The user is entering a password-protected area and must contact the Webmaster.

  C ○ The server is down and not responding.

  D ○ The server is functioning, but the requested Web page could not be located.

6 **HTML is a simplified application of which language?**

A ○ XML

B ○ SNL

C ○ SGML

D ○ CSS

7 **Which group recommends changes to HTML standards?**

A ○ W3C

B ○ WIPO

C ○ UFO

D ○ GML

8 **The strict flavor of HTML version 4.01**

A ○ Requires the author to use frames.

B ○ Is only supported by older browsers.

C ○ Is required to view secure Web pages.

D ○ Requires the author to use CSS only for formatting.

9 **In what part of the page must a Web author specify which flavor of HTML 4.01 is being used?**

A ○ BODY

B ○ DTD

C ○ ISP

D ○ CGI

10 **The rules that govern a company's use of colors, logos, and such in all their marketing materials are referred to as**

A ○ Branding standards

B ○ Mind share

C ○ Best practices

D ○ Mark-up

Answers

1 **B.** Maintaining an active connection between the database server and the Web server. Anything involving server connection is considered a back-end issue. *See "Front-end issues."*

2 **D.** Too many graphics and large graphics files. Although slow server connections can cause long download times, graphics are usually at fault. *Read "Front-end issues."*

3 **B.** Bandwidth. Bandwidth describes how much data can pass through a network at a given time. *Take a look at "I'm with the bandwidth."*

4 **A.** 14 seconds. Multiply 50 by 8 (50 x 8 = 400) and divide that by the connection speed of 28.8 (400/28.8 = 13.8) and round the result, 13.8 up to a whole number, 14. *Review "Estimating download times."*

5 **D.** The server is functioning, but the requested Web page could not be located. *See "Where nobody knows your page's name."*

6 **C.** SGML (Standard Generalized Markup Language). SGML is the grandfather of all the popular Web markup languages — HTML, XML, among others. *Check out "Making Your Mark-Up: A Little History Lesson."*

7 **A.** W3C (World Wide Web Consortium). Although it's up to the makers of browser software to enable their browsers to read new HTML codes, the W3C recommends standards for them to follow. *Look over "As the HTML Turns: Standards and Versions Galore."*

8 **D.** Requires the author to use CSS (Cascading Style Sheets) only for formatting. *Read "HTML versions 4.0 and 4.01."*

9 **B.** DTD (Document Type Definition). The DTD, when used, goes at the very beginning of a page of code and contains any HTML version information. *See "DTDs: Document Type Definition statements."*

10 **A.** Branding standards. Branding standards ensure the use and placement of company logos and colors are consistent with a company's established rules. *Check out "Marketing 101."*

Chapter 10

Putting Together HTML Pages

Exam Objectives

▶ Understanding the syntax of standard HTML tags

▶ Explaining HTML document structure

▶ Describing text formatting methods

▶ Creating hyperlinks

· ·

*T*he test has 15 multiple-choice HTML questions, each with only one correct answer. So, what do you need to do to prepare? Well, for starters, you can memorize the tags I set forth in this chapter. You thought your days of memorizing and regurgitating stuff for a test were behind you, didn't you? The good news is that unlike in college, you'll actually *use* the tags you have to memorize for the Foundations test in real life. In this chapter, I discuss how to begin coding HTML pages. I also cover some out-dated codes that you may get questions about on the exam.

In the real world, you probably won't be *hand-coding* pages (geek-speak for designing an entire page by painstakingly typing HTML tags), but when you start putting advanced Web features such as database-connectivity and JavaScript into your pages (which I describe in Chapters 8, 14, and 17), you have to be able to manually add them to your code.

Even if you're already pretty familiar with HTML, I encourage you to at least scan the next few chapters. I know of at least two people who have been coding HTML for some time but failed the Foundations exam on their first attempt — primarily because they missed so many HTML questions. The sad truth is that sometimes knowing what the guys and gals at ProsoftTraining want you to know is more important than having the real-world knowledge you probably already put to use every day. They're the ones testing you so you have to play the game their way.

Quick Assessment

1   Tags that need to be opened and closed are called _____ tags.

2   The _____ must be specified at the beginning of the document when using HTML 4.0.

3   The tag that tells the browser which language you are writing is _____.

4   Text and graphics that display on a page are inserted in the _____ section.

5   A code that specifies a certain property of the HTML element is a(n) _____.

6   Two categories of formatting tags are _____ and _____.

7   Text-level formatting is also referred to as _____-level formatting.

8   Tags that are no longer in common use are considered _____.

9   A tag that is always preceded and followed by a line break is a(n) _____ element.

10   To link from one page to another you create a(n) _____.

Answers

1   *Container.* Look over "The Basics: Containers and Empty Tags."

2   *Document type definition or* `<!DOCTYPE HTML PUBLIC "-//W3C//DTD HTML 4.0 Transitional//EN">`. See "What's up, DOCTYPE?"

3   `<HTML>`. See "What's up, DOCTYPE?"

4   `<BODY>`. Review "Body of work."

5   *Attribute.* Check out "Body of work."

6   *Paragraph-level and block-level.* See "Formatting Your Documents."

7   *Paragraph.* Look over "Paragraph-level formatting: Bold, italic, and underline" and "Paragraph-level formatting: Font elements versus phrase elements."

8   *Deprecated.* See "Block-level formatting."

9   *Block-level.* See "Block-level formatting."

10 *Hyperlink.* Refer to "Unchaining your links."

On Your Markup, Get Set, Go: Markup Tags

The codes you use to create an HTML page are referred to as *markup tags* (or *tags* for short). Markup tags are the codes the interpreting software (otherwise known as a browser — usually Internet Explorer or Netscape Navigator) use to display a Web page the way its author intended it to look.

For the Foundations exam, you need to know three key things about HTML tags:

- ✔ **What each tag does:** Each tag has a specific function. Read on to get information about the most important tags you'll see on the test. Later in this chapter, I present these tags in the order you'd see them on-screen.

- ✔ **When to use a tag:** You can't get away with memorizing all the tags and sail through the Foundations exam. You need to be able to identify which tag should be used to achieve specific effects.

- ✔ **The proper syntax of the code you should use:** When you use HTML, one missed backslash can mess up your Web page (not to mention ruin your day). The Foundations exam tests you on your ability to put the code together in the right order to achieve the right effect.

HTML is not case sensitive, but it's considered good coding practice to put all your codes in caps so you can easily differentiate them from other types of code or text that appear on the page. You can code your real-life pages however you want, but, in the unlikely event you get an exam question on this, assume all codes should be in caps.

The Basics: Containers and Empty Tags

Before you can get very far in your understanding of HTML, you have to know what containers and empty tags are. Markup tags are usually, but not always, encased by greater than and less than symbols, like this:

```
<tag goes here>
```

Most tags come in pairs — you insert the tag once before some content and you insert the tag again after the page content, but you put a forward slash (/) at the beginning of it, just inside the less than bracket (<). Think about working in a word processing program. When you begin typing some text that you want to appear bold, you click the B button on the toolbar. When you want to stop the bold effect, you click the B button again to end it. Inserting container tags is similar. The following code produces text that appears bold — it's encased in opening and closing bold `<B>` tags:

```
<B>This text is bold.</B.>
```

Empty tags don't come in pairs — there's an opening tag before some content, but no closing tag. The line break tag, `<BR>`, for example, is used just once like this:

```
<BR>This text is on a line below any text above.
```

As a rule, a tag needs to be closed if there is a starting and ending point to its effect. You insert the `<B>` tag where you want the bold effect to start, and close it with the `</B>` tag where you want the bold effect to stop. You don't close a line break with the `<BR>` tag, however, because there's not a starting point to the breaking of the line or an ending point. The line is either broken or it isn't.

The number of spaces between tags (`<B>space..space</B>`) usually doesn't matter. If you want to spread out the code so that you can read it more easily, that won't affect how the page displays for Joe Schmoe of Peoria, Illinois, when he logs on to the Web site.

If your HTML's a little rusty, you may need to seek answers from a book that focuses on HTML, like *HTML 4 For Dummies,* by Ed Tittel, Natanya Pitts, and Chelsea Valentine (published by Hungry Minds, Inc.).

Understanding Document Structure

The best way to get a handle on the most important HTML tags to know for the test is to look at them in the order you would type them in an HTML document if you were hand-coding a Web page from scratch. That's not to say that the questions on the Foundations exam will be listed in such a convenient order. (They won't.) But you should have a system to your studying, and I find this system to be the simplest and most logical one. You can quiz yourself alphabetically or by function. The world is your oyster. Just get a system that makes you happy and stick with it.

What's up, DOCTYPE?

The first shred of code you normally insert on a document is the `<!DOCTYPE>` tag. The `<!DOCTYPE>` tag lets browsers know which version (or *flavor,* as they like to say on the exam) has been used to create a Web page. (The versions of HTML are covered in depth in Chapter 9.) Here's what the `<!DOCTYPE>` tag looks like in practice:

```
<!DOCTYPE HTML PUBLIC "-//W3C//DTD HTML 4.0
Transitional//EN">
```

In this example, I'm declaring that I'm using HTML, it's a public (non-proprietary) version, and I'm using transitional HTML 4.0.

In real life, authors don't always use the `<!DOCTYPE>` tag at the beginning of all HTML documents — sometimes they use the `<HTML>` tag instead. The `<HTML>` tag announces to the browser, "Hey, I'm writing some HTML code now." Because the `<HTML>` tag is a container tag, it always needs to be closed, like this:

```
<HTML>All other HTML tags go here.</HTML>
```

If you opt to start your page with the `<!DOCTYPE>` tag instead of the `<HTML>` tag, you still place a closing `</HTML>` tag at the very end of the document.

Don't lose your <HEAD> tag

The `<HEAD>` tag typically follows the `<HTML>` tag (or the `<!DOCTYPE>` tag, if that's what you're using). The `<HEAD>` tag defines the head section in your document where you store data that needs to stay with the document but doesn't necessarily display on the actual Web page. This data includes the page title, which displays in the colored title bar at the top of your browser window (and which I discuss in the following section). You also place data for search engines to read in the head section. (Check out Chapter 4 for a more thorough explanation of how to place search engine–related data in your document.) You can think of the `<HEAD>` section as the introductory section of your page — here's how it looks:

```
<HEAD>Title and search engine data goes here.</HEAD>
```

Page title

The `<TITLE>` tag creates a Web page's title; it displays in the colored (often blue) bar at the top of a browser window. The `<TITLE>` tag goes inside the `<HEAD>` section of the document. Technically, you could omit the `<TITLE>` tag from a page, but, in reality, you should always include one to keep your page recognizable to visitors and search engines alike. Titles of Web pages can be anything from *My Home Page* to *XYZ Company Product Line* — they usually describe what the page is about and look like this:

```
<HEAD>
<TITLE>Sharon's Cool Home Page</TITLE>
</HEAD>
```

Body of work

The body section of the document follows the `<HEAD>` section and is the section where you put most of the content you want to display on your Web page. That includes all the text, graphics, and links that make up your page. Whatever content you put in between the opening and closing `<BODY>` tags displays on the Web page. Here's what the `<BODY>` tag looks like in practice:

```
</HEAD>
<BODY>This text appears on the Web page.</BODY>
```

The `<BODY>` tag may contain a number of *attributes* — descriptive properties of a tag. Using attributes, you can designate the color of the page background or specify that you want a particular image to appear on the background of the page. Attributes are found in many tags and usually equal something (hold a value), such as:

```
<BODY BGCOLOR="#FFFFFF">...</BODY>
```

In this example, I specify the background color is white by using `<BGCOLOR="#FFFFFF">`. The `#FFFFFF` is a numeric color code that the browser interprets. (For more information on color codes, refer to Chapter 11.)

To insert an image in the background of a page, you use the `BACKGROUND` attribute in the `<BODY>` tag like this:

```
<BODY BACKGROUND="myimage.gif">
```

Formatting Your Documents

When I talk about formatting in this section, I'm referring to the ability to change colors, fonts, and other standard text effects such as bold and italics. For this part of the exam, make sure that you know the difference between the two main types of formatting: paragraph-level and block-level. In the next few sections, I explain the difference between paragraph-level and block-level formatting and introduce you to the most common tags in each category.

Paragraph-level formatting: Bold, italic, and underline

In most of the popular word processing programs in use today, you'll notice a formatting toolbar with B, I, and, U buttons. These buttons bold, italicize, and underline text — the same types of effects you apply to text in HTML documents. The following example shows text to which I've applied bold ⟨B⟩, italic ⟨I⟩, and underline ⟨U⟩ effects.

```
<B><I><U>This text appears bold, underlined, and
          italicized</U></I></B>
```

On a Web page, all the text in this line would be boldfaced, underlined, and italicized. Because each of these tags is a container tag, I closed each one to end the bold, italics, or underlining effect. The opening and closing tags are *nested* around the text — the tag that is opened immediately before the text is closed immediately after the text; the tag opened first in this sequence is closed last. In reality, you can sometimes change the order of these tags and have them still work correctly, but for the exam, you need to know that multiple tags should be nested around the content they affect.

In real life, it's best to avoid underlining text that isn't meant to be hyperlinked. Underlining text confuses visitors because most will assume underlined text is hyperlinked text.

Paragraph-level formatting: Font elements versus phrase elements

If you want to apply bold or italics effects to text, you usually use the ⟨B⟩ (boldface) and ⟨I⟩ (italics) tags, otherwise known as *font elements*. Two other tags exist, however, that produce nearly identical results:

- ⟨STRONG⟩, which is like bold
- ⟨EM⟩ (for emphasis), which mimics italic

These two tags are examples of *phrase elements*. You may be asked questions about phrase elements on the exam, but will rarely (if ever) use them in your pages. (Why would you if you already have shorter and easier to remember tags like ⟨B⟩ and ⟨I⟩?)

There actually is a difference between the way that font elements and phrase elements work — at least in some situations. Some software — such as software that reads page text to visually impaired visitors — will make the appropriate inflection when reading a phrase element. (Bold text might be read louder, for example.) Whether you use <B> (a font element) or <STRONG> (a phrase element) to make something bold, the text appears bold on the Web page. Same thing with <I> and <EM> for italics. The key difference between the two is how text reader programs might interpret them.

Block-level formatting

Block-level formatting affects an entire paragraph or *block* of text. A good example is the <P> (paragraph) tag. This tag is often used as a spacer to break the current line and insert a blank line. Because the <P> tag (which, like the <BR> tag is an empty tag), can't affect just one word out of several in a sentence, it's a block-level element.

Table 10-1 lists the block-level formatting elements you need to know for the exam.

Table 10-1	Block-Level Formatting Tags
Tag	*What It Does*
 	Breaks a line
<P>	Breaks a line and puts a blank line after
<BLOCKQUOTE>...</BLOCKQUOTE>	Indents a paragraph
<CENTER>...</CENTER>	Centers a paragraph
<H1>...</H1> up to <H6>...</H6>	Formats a paragraph as a heading

Many block-level elements, including <P>, <BLOCKQUOTE>, <CENTER>, and <H1> through <H6> force line breaks before and after their insertion — whatever text you place inside these tags will be placed a line below any text above it, and any text after it will be forced to a line below.

The <CENTER> tag, described in Table 10-1, is one of several tags that is *deprecated* in HTML. This means that it is outdated and its use is discouraged. You may get a question concerning deprecated tags on the exam. You shouldn't need to know all the deprecated tags in existence, just what deprecated means.

Heads up!

Headings, not to be confused with the head section of the document, allow you to segment and emphasize sections of a page. You use them to encase a heading within one of the six available heading tags to make it stand out by making text bold and changing its size. Heading one, <H1>...</H1>, is the largest of the six, whereas heading six, <H6>...</H6>, is the smallest. Although you can change the size of the text and make it bold so it looks about the same as if you applied the heading tag, search engines make special note of the heading tags and use their content to help determine what your page is about. Here's an example of a heading tag:

```
<H1> Reasons I love HTML.</H1>
```

In <Pre>-historic times

You usually can't just hit the enter key in your code to break a line — a line break will be visible in your code but will be ignored when a browser renders the page. Instead, you insert one of the line breaking codes, such as <P> or <BR>. The exception to this rule is the <PRE> tag. That's right, whatever spaces or returns you key in will show on the page. Well, why don't you just put everything inside <PRE> tags and not worry about <P> and <BR> tags? Good question. The main reason is you have limited formatting ability within <PRE> tags, so you usually avoid them.

Because <PRE> tags force a browser to display any spaces or returns you insert in your code, you can actually create tables of information with them. HTML tables are typically a better choice for displaying tabular data, but if you're in a hurry, you can use the <PRE> tag. Here's an example:

```
<PRE>   Name of Student                     Test Score
        Becca Roark..................... 98
        Ryan Robert..................... 90
        Marcia Hart..................... 100
</PRE>
```

A font of knowledge

You can specify fonts with the <FONT> tag. This tag tells the browser which font to use when displaying your text. If you don't specify a font, your page will render using the default font on the user's browser, which may be very different from the font you chose. Typically, you specify the font size as well as the font face. Here's an example of how you'd code a line of text to be in 12 point Arial font:

```
<FONT FACE="Arial" SIZE="3">This is some text on the
            page.</FONT>
```

In the preceding example, the SIZE="3" attribute makes the letters 3 pixels thick, which is the equivalent of a 12 point font. Table 10-2 shows the font tags and attributes you should know for the exam.

Table 10-2	Font Tags and What They Do
Tag	**What It Does**
`<FONT FACE="Fontname">...</FONT>`	Specifies font name
`<FONT SIZE="?">...</FONT>`	Specifies font size in pixel thickness of letters
`<FONT COLOR="#FFCC99"`	Specifies font color in hexadecimal color codes

Unchaining your links

You're no doubt familiar with hyperlinked or clickable words and images from having surfed the Web. Linking one page to another, an image to a page, or a word on a page to another part of that same page (among other hyperlinking possibilities) is really pretty easy, which is a good thing because you need to be able to recognize linking code for the Foundations exam. Lab 10-1 walks you through the process of creating a hyperlink.

Lab 10-1   Creating an HTML Page with Hyperlinks

1. **Create a new folder, name it MyWeb, and save it to your desktop.**

2. **Open a blank Notepad document and type the following code to lay the basic foundation for an HTML page:**

```
<HTML>
<HEAD>
<TITLE>HTML Home Page
</TITLE>
</HEAD>
<BODY>
</BODY>
</HTML>
```

3. **Save this document to the MyWeb folder as** `default.htm`.

   Make sure to type **.htm** so the document is saved as a Web page.

4. **Between the body tags, type this text:**

```
<BODY>This is my HTML home page.
<BR>
To see an HTML tutorial. click here.
</BODY>
```

5. **Save your changes.**

6. **Leave the current document open and start Notepad a second time to create a new document.**

   Both your default document and a blank new one are now open.

7. **On the blank new page, type the same basic page you typed in Step 2, but change the title to *HTML Tutorial* like this:**

```
<HTML>
<HEAD>
<TITLE>HTML Tutorial
</TITLE>
</HEAD>
<BODY>
</BODY>
</HTML>
```

8. **Save this page in the MyWeb folder as** `tutorial.htm`.

   Notice that you didn't have to put a file path when referring to the tutorial page. If you link to another page within the same folder, the browser automatically searches there first.

9. **To create a hyperlink from the default page to the tutorial page, you type the needed code around the word *here* in the default document, so *here* becomes the hyperlinked word:**

```
<BR>
To see an HTML tutorial, click
<A HREF="Tutorial.htm">here</A>
</BODY>
```

10. **Save your changes.**

11. **Launch your browser. Choose File⇨Open and browse for the default page.**

    With the default page pulled into the browser, the word *here* is underlined in blue. When you click the new hyperlink, the tutorial page you created appears.

    If the tutorial page doesn't appear, check your syntax.

Linking to outside pages

In Lab 10-1, I asked you to save your second document (`tutorial.htm`) in the same folder as the `default.htm` page to make the linking easier. If you link two pages that aren't saved in the same folder, you have to tell browsers where to look by typing in the file path of the page to which you're linking.

If you have several folders saved within one main folder (which is usually the case in larger Web sites), you don't have to type the complete file path. You can just specify which subfolder to look in by putting a forward slash in front of the folder name, like this:

```
<A HREF="/MyFolder/schedule.htm">schedule</A>
```

To link to a page outside your Web, you enter the full file path:

```
<A HREF="http://www.wildcats.com">Click Me</A>
```

Linking within a Web page

If you want to link to another location within the same page, you first have to mark a location in the page to link to. You mark this location — also called a target — by giving it an *anchor name*. If you want to link from the bottom of the default page to the top, for example, mark the first word on the page as the target as in the following example:

```
<A NAME="top">This</A> is the HTML home page.
```

Then you create a link to the top from the bottom of the page like this:

```
To see an HTML tutorial, click
<A HREF="Tutorial.htm">here</A>.
<A HREF="#top">Page</A>
```

It doesn't matter what you name the target location; call it something that makes sense to you. Keep in mind when naming targets that although HTML isn't, as a rule, case sensitive, anchor names are. Inside a paragraph about boats, for example, you might create a named anchor called `boats`; if you spell *boats* with all lowercase letters when you name it, you can't try to link to the target by typing uppercase *BOATS*.

Even though you put text inside the anchor tags, the text is invisible when you view it in the browser. This link isn't very impressive at this point because the bottom and top of the page are both visible within one screen because the page is so small. If you add a few more elements to lengthen the page, you'll see that clicking the link moves the page, and you'll think you're super cool!

Make sure that you know how to recognize all aspects of linking code, especially how to name a location within a page you're linking to. You'll most likely get a question like this on the exam: "If you want to link the bottom of a page to the table of contents section near the top, what would you do?" The answer would look something like this:

```
<A NAME="Table of Contents">Table of Contents
Section </A>
```

Then create the link to it like this:

```
Click <A HREF="#Table of Contents">here</A> to
go to the Table of Contents.
```

Linking to images

In addition to creating text hyperlinks, you can also create image hyperlinks (or *hypermedia* links). (I cover images in more detail in Chapter 11.) Just substitute the image source code for the page name as in this example:

```
<A HREF="NewPage.htm"><IMGSRC="Imagename.gif"></A>
```

Prep Test

1 **HTML tags that come in pairs are called**

- **A** ○ Empty tags
- **B** ○ Double tags
- **C** ○ Nested tags
- **D** ○ Container tags

2 **Which of the following tags is an empty tag?**

- **A** ○ `<HTML>`
- **B** ○ `<BR>`
- **C** ○ `<B>`
- **D** ○ `<U>`

3 **Which statement is true regarding the** `<!DOCTYPE>` **tag?**

- **A** ○ It creates the main section of the HTML document.
- **B** ○ It goes at the very end of an HTML document.
- **C** ○ It specifies which version of HTML the page has been coded.
- **D** ○ It specifies the height and width of an HTML page.

4 **Codes that contain descriptive properties of a tag are called**

- **A** ○ Specifications
- **B** ○ Anchor names
- **C** ○ Block-level elements
- **D** ○ Attributes

5 **Duncan wants to create a Web page with an image named** `clouds.jgp` **in the background. Which of the following code sequences should he use?**

- **A** ○ `<BODY BG="clouds.jpg">`
- **B** ○ `<BODY SRC= "clouds.jpg">`
- **C** ○ `<BODY BACKGROUND="clouds.jpg">`
- **D** ○ `<BODY IMAGE= <"clouds.jpg">`

6 **Joel wants to make some text on a page appear bold and italicized. Which of the following should he type?**

- **A** ○ `<BLD><ITL>Welcome to my home page.</BLD></ITL>`
- **B** ○ `<B><I>Welcome to my home page. <B><I>`
- **C** ○ `<B><I>"Welcome to my home page." </B></I>`
- **D** ○ `<B><I>Welcome to my home page.</I></B>`

7 HTML tags that can specify the way text is interpreted by text reader programs are called

A ○ Block-level elements

B ○ Phrase elements

C ○ Font elements

D ○ Paragraph-level elements

8 Which phrase best describes formatting that can affect an entire page or as little as one word?

A ○ Markup elements

B ○ Paragraph-level elements

C ○ Block-level elements

D ○ Container tags

9 The section of the document that holds the page title and search engine information is the

A ○ `<HEAD>`

B ○ `<BODY>`

C ○ `<P>`

D ○ `<!DOCTYPE>`

10 Susan wants to make the word *Books* a hyperlink to the Hungry Minds Web site. Which of the following should she type?

A ○ `<A HREF="http://www.hungryminds.com">Books</A>`

B ○ `<A LINK="http://www.hungryminds.com">Books</A>`

C ○ `<A HREF=http:\\www.hungryminds.com>Books</A>`

D ○ `<A HREF=<http://www.hungryminds.com>Books</A>`

Answers

1 **D.** Container tags. Container tags come in pairs; empty tags are used alone. *See "The Basics: Containers and Empty Tags."*

2 **B.** `<BR>`. The `<BR>` tag and the `<P>` tag are empty tags; they don't need to be closed. *See "The Basics: Containers and Empty Tags."*

3 **C.** It specifies which version of HTML in which the page has been coded. The `<!DOCTYPE>` tag can also specify which language the Web page is based in. *See "What's up, DOCTYPE?"*

4 **D.** Attributes. Attributes are descriptive properties of an HTML tag. An attribute can describe, for example, which color you see in the background of a page. *See "Body of work."*

5 **C.** `<BODY BACKGROUND="clouds.jpg">`. The attribute in the `<BODY>` tag which specifies a background image is `BACKGROUND`. *See "Body of work."*

6 **D.** `<B><I>Welcome to my home page.</I></B>`. When multiple formatting tags are used, they should be nested around the items they affect. *See "Paragraph-level formatting: Bold, italic, and underline."*

7 **B.** Phrase elements. Phrase elements apply formatting that looks much the same as the formatting applied by font elements, but phrase elements can specify the way text is interpreted by text reader programs. *See "Paragraph-level formatting: Font elements versus phrase elements."*

8 **B.** Paragraph-level elements. Paragraph-level elements can affect as little as a word (or even a letter) of text, whereas block-level elements always affect at least an entire paragraph. *See "Formatting Your Documents."*

9 **A.** `<HEAD>`. The head section of the document can hold the page title and page summary information that search engines read. *See "Don't lose your <HEAD> tag."*

10 **A.** `<A HREF="http://www.hungryminds.com">Books</A>`. *See "Unchaining your links."*

Chapter 11

Incorporating Graphic Elements into Web Pages

Exam Objectives

▶ Including images and graphical formatting in HTML files

▶ Working with colors in the Web environment

▶ Utilizing special objects and characters

*I*nserting graphic elements into a Web page is a fundamental part of improving the page's appearance. Although the Internet was created back in 1968, it didn't really take off until the early 1990s. One major reason for the surge in popularity at that time was the creation of ways to easily incorporate graphic elements into pages. Look at almost any Web site in existence today, and you find a combination of pictures, logos, clipart, and other special symbols that not only improve the look of a page, but also make it easier to read, if used correctly.

For the Foundations exam, you should concentrate on the technical aspects of placing graphics and colors in your Web pages. In reality, of course, you need to consider many other things when choosing or creating images to incorporate in your Web sites, such as which colors communicate various sentiments (red is the color of aggression, for example) and a whole host of other considerations that graphic design professionals get paid a lot of money to worry about.

In this chapter, I talk about the three main image formats you use on the Web and the pros and cons of each. I also cover how to set background and text colors, as well as how to ensure your colors appear consistently in various browsers. I also show you how to separate sections of your page by using horizontal rules, and how to incorporate characters, such as copyright and trademark symbols.

Quick Assessment

Incorporating images into pages

1 The _____ image format supports only 256 colors.

2 When an image "fades in" as it appears on a page, it's _____.

3 The best format to save most photographs in is_____.

4 To center an image on a page, the preferred HTML code is_____.

5 The _____ attribute enables you to attach text to a graphic that pops up when your move your mouse over it.

6 A horizontal rule is a _____ on your page.

Specifying colors in HTML

7 If you see a page background color code of "#00FF00", the page is _____.

8 To ensure your text colors look the same in both Internet Explorer and Netscape, choose colors that are _____.

9 RGB stands for _____, _____ and _____.

10 The code "<" would render the _____ symbol on your page.

Answers

1   *GIF.* See "Choosing the Right Image Format."

2   *Interlaced or progressive.* Review "Choosing the Right Image Format."

3   *JPEG.* Also covered in "Choosing the Right Image Format."

4   *<DIV ALIGN="center">.* Check out "Understanding Image Attributes."

5   *ALT.* See "Understanding Image Attributes."

6   *Line.* Review "Working with Horizontal Rules."

7   *Green.* Look over "Color My World: The Joys of Hexadecimal Codes."

8   *Web-safe.* Check out "Color My World: The Joys of Hexadecimal Codes."

9   *Red, Green, Blue.* See "Color My World: The Joys of Hexadecimal Codes."

10 *<, the less than symbol.* Refer to "Adding Special Characters."

Adding Images to Your Page

I want to caution you about using too many images. Although graphics can phenomenally enhance a page, pages that use too many graphics or whose graphics files are very large take too long to load. You're not going to get hit with questions about specific graphics file sizes on the exam, but you still need to remember this basic principle.

In real life, I try to keep all images in my Web pages under 20K. A good image-editing program, such as Adobe PhotoShop or Macromedia Fireworks, contains several tools to help you compress and slice images to reduce file sizes.

You add an image to your page with the `<IMG>` (image) tag. Inside the image tag, you place the `<IMG SRC="filename.ext">` (source) attribute; *filename.ext* is where you put the name of the image. If you want to include a gif image file named `cow.gif` on the page, here's what the code looks like:

```
<IMG SRC="cow.gif">
```

When you refer to a file name in your code, you must do two things: Put the file name in quotes, and put the file extension at the end of the file name.

Choosing the Right Image Format

When it comes to saving images for Web pages, you have three formats to choose from: JPEG, GIF, and PNG, with JPEG and GIF being the most popular.

Here's a list of the key features of each format:

- ✔ **JPEG (Joint Photographic Experts Group):** JPEG is the image format most commonly used for photographic images on the Web because it enables you to dramatically reduce file sizes of true-color, 24-bit graphics. JPEG is also great for photos because it can use up to 16 million colors in a file.

  It's not the best choice for line-art or clip-art files, however, because of its *lossy* compression. When you reduce a file size using lossy compression, part of the image information is actually lost: If a very colorful photograph is missing a few colors, you probably won't even notice it. But if you use a clip-art image with only six colors in it to begin with, you can't really afford to lose any colors.

- ✔ **GIF (Graphics Interchange Format):** Created by the geeks at CompuServe, GIF is the image format most commonly used for line art or clip-art files. When you compress a file using GIF, you're limited to 256 colors, so it's not a great choice for photos. Unlike JPEG, GIF compression is *lossless,* meaning that an image doesn't lose any of its image code when it's compressed. Other features of the GIF format include the ability to animate your images and the ability to make one of the colors in the image transparent.

There are two versions of GIF: GIF 87 and GIF 89a. GIF 89a is a later release that supports some of the most popular features of GIF — interlacing, transparency, and animation. I talk more about these features later in this chapter.

If you get a question asking how many colors can be in a GIF image, either 255 or 256 would be considered correct. There's a discrepancy about how to count the colors — even among professionals — so that's why you see both figures tossed around. The ProsoftTraining people know about this, and they aren't known for trying to trick people with this issue.

✔ **PNG (Portable Network Graphic):** Independent developers created the PNG format as a replacement for the GIF format. Some developers who wanted a little more freedom got together and created the PNG format for open use on the Web. Although you usually use PNG for the same types of images you would use GIF for — line art and clip art — PNG still isn't as popular a format as GIF. The main reason? Only newer browsers (versions 4.0 and later, to be exact) recognize the PNG format. PNG does have some advantages over GIF: It supports 16 million colors and allows you to make up to 254 colors transparent in an image whereas GIF allows only one color transparency.

The bottom line? If you want to put your company logo on the Web site and have to choose between saving the file as a GIF, which any browser can read, or saving it as a PNG, which some browsers can't read, most people would choose to save the file as a GIF.

Understanding the Different Image Format Features

The Foundations exam expects you to know how to choose the right file format based on a few key features.

✔ **Interlacing:** *Interlacing* is a feature that enables browsers to load images in several passes. In the first pass, the interlaced image loads on the Web page at its full size, but is somewhat blurry or very pixilated. The picture sharpens as the remaining pixels are loaded in the next three passes. Although only the GIF format supports interlacing, a similar feature, called *progressive* passes, is sometimes available for JPEGs (depending on the program you're using). Interlacing allows visitors to get an idea of what an image looks like before it fully loads. You can apply interlacing to an image in image-editing programs, such as Adobe Photoshop or Macromedia Fireworks.

✔ **Transparency:** When a browser renders a graphic on the screen, it always puts it in a rectangular shape. Even if you have a picture of, say, an egg, the picture appears within a rectangle. Now a big square behind your egg doesn't look that great, so you want to hide it. How? By making all the pixels in the background square magically disappear! Okay, so it's not magic. I'm just talking about the *transparency* feature available in the GIF and PNG formats.

You can use an image-editing program like PhotoShop or Paint Shop Pro to specify which color in a particular image you want to make invisible. The trick with the transparency feature is that if you make a color transparent, you make *every* pixel in the image of the same color transparent, too. Maybe you have a clip-art image of a dog against a white background, and you want to make the white background transparent. If the whites of the dog's eyes are the exact same shade of white, they become transparent too. In real life you can avoid this by changing the shade of white in the dog's eyes to a slightly different shade of white.

✔ **Animation:** Animated GIF files are all over the Web and you can find a bunch of programs out there to help you animate GIF files. These programs help you place a series of *frames* together which, when played, give the illusion of movement. You know how with old-fashioned cartoons (like Bugs Bunny) the artist draws each frame of movement on a separate piece of paper? When you flip through the images, the cartoon character appears to be moving. That's how GIF animation works. Photoshop and Fireworks are just two of the many image-editing programs that help you create animated GIFs.

On the exam, you'll get a question or two about the features of image formats. If you know the information in Table 11-1, you'll ace them!

Table 11-1		Comparing GIF, JPEG, and PNG	
Format	*# of Colors*	*Transparency?*	*Other Features*
GIF	256	1-color transparency	Can be animated; supports interlacing
JPEG	16 million	No transparency	Lossy compression
PNG	16 million	254-color transparency	Created independently

Understanding Image Attributes

Attributes are descriptive codes you add into an HTML tag to set the tag's properties. When you're working with images, you can use attributes to specify images' height and width, create borders around images, or attach alternate text to images (*alternate text* is text that appears on-screen when you move your mouse over the image). I show you the image attributes you need to know for the exam in this section.

Changing height and width

You can set the height and width of an image by using two attributes called — are you ready for this — the HEIGHT and WIDTH attributes. These attributes specify image height and width in pixels (or, rarely, percents). If you don't add either attribute to your code, the image will display on-screen the same size it was when you originally saved it. Images that are a fixed size may appear to change in size when viewed on computers with different screen resolutions. An image that's 50 pixels wide, for example, is always 50 pixels wide, but it appears smaller on a screen with a high resolution. The higher the screen resolution, the more pixels that are packed together in less space, so 50 pixels appears larger on 640x480 resolution monitor than on a 1024x768 resolution monitor.

You can set both of these attributes or only one. If you specify only one, the other automatically changes to keep the image proportionate. For example, if you have an image that starts out as 100x100 pixels and you set the height to be 80 (HEIGHT= "80"), the width would also adjust to 80 even if you didn't put a width attribute in the code. Here's how you insert a GIF image named cow.gif that you want to be 80 pixels tall and 100 pixels wide:

```
<IMG SRC="cow.gif" HEIGHT="80" WIDTH="100">
```

 If you start out with a large image and code the height and width smaller, you're only changing how large the image appears on your page. To actually reduce the file size and speed up load time, you need to resize it in an image-editing program.

 Although you can specify an image's height or width in percents, it's not usually a good idea (at least with the image formats currently in use). You could specify that an image should be 50 percent of the width of a page (WIDTH=50%). With this setting, the image increases or decreases in size for various monitor resolutions and always remains 50 percent of the screen width. When you increase an image's size very much, however, it becomes pixilated or grainy.

Adding and modifying borders

The BORDER attribute enables you to place a border around an image and adjust the border's width. Borders are measured in pixel thickness. Here's what the code looks like to place a border that's 2 pixels thick around an image named cow.gif.

```
<IMG SRC="cow.gif" BORDER="2">
```

Including alternate text

The alternate text attribute (usually called ALT TEXT) allows you to add some text to an image. This text pops up in a box when you hover over the image with your mouse (kind of like ToolTip text that pops up over the toolbar buttons in a Microsoft program). Search engines sometimes read ALT TEXT to determine the topic of your page and produce more accurate results. One of the most important uses of the ALT TEXT attribute is to identify an image to programs used by visually impaired visitors. Here's how you code one:

```
<IMG SRC="lion.jpg" ALT="Picture of a lion.">
```

Adjusting image alignment

After you place an image on a page, the next big question is, "How do I get this thing where I want it?" In real life, you usually use tables (covered in Chapter 12) to position images. The Prosoft folks, however, like for you to know some other image alignment codes, so make sure you know the attributes in Table 11-2 that specify how the image interacts with nearby text.

Table 11-2	Image Alignment Attributes
Attribute	**What It Does**
ALIGN="Right"	Places the image to the right of neighboring text. The top of the image lines up with the first line of text.
ALIGN="Top"	The top of the image lines up with the first line of text.
ALIGN="Middle"	Aligns the middle of the image with the baseline of the text.
ALIGN="Bottom"	Aligns the bottom of the image with the bottom of the text. This is the default alignment.
HSPACE="2"	Specifies how many pixels of empty space surround the image to the left and right.
VSPACE="3"	Specifies how many pixels of empty space surround the image on the top and bottom.

These alignment attributes aren't used often because they don't give you the flexibility you usually want in a page. You can use another pretty common method — outside of using tables — to center an image on a page. This method involves using the <DIV> (division) tag with an alignment attribute of center (ALIGN="center"). The <DIV> tag sections off an area in your document so that you can specify an alignment for that entire section. Here's how that looks:

```
<DIV ALIGN="center"><IMG SRC="lion.jpg"></DIV>
```

A centered lion graphic with the ALT TEXT attribute, a 2-pixel thick border, and a height and width of 100 pixels looks like this:

```
<DIV ALIGN="center"><IMG SRC="lion.jpg" ALT="Picture of a
        lion." BORDER="2" HEIGHT="100" WIDTH="100"></DIV>
```

Working with Horizontal Rules

The horizontal rule tag <HR> creates lines that visually separate sections of a page. You can specify the end-to-end width of the line in either pixels or as a percentage of the width of a page. You can specify the thickness or size of the line in either pixels or percents as well.

By default, a horizontal rule appears three-dimensional. If you're having a hard time picturing what I mean, either whip out your GUI editor or hand-code a horizontal rule with the codes I show you in this chapter. (I'd show you a picture of a horizontal rule with a three-dimensional look, but when I reproduce a screenshot of it in the book, it's not very clear.)

Test-takers often get at least one question on horizontal rule attributes, so take a good look at the Table 11-3 and commit the codes to memory.

Table 11-3	Horizontal Rule Tag and Its Attributes
Tag or Attribute	*What It Does*
<HR>	With no attributes added, creates a centered line that spans 100 percent of the width of a page.
ALIGN="center", "left", or "right"	Aligns the line on the page.
SIZE="2"	Specifies the thickness of the line in pixels.

(continued)

Table 11-3 *(continued)*

Tag or Attribute	What It Does
`WIDTH="100"` or `"100%"`	Specifies the end-to-end width of the line in either pixels or percents.
`NOSHADE`	Removes the 3-D effect from a line. One of the few attributes that is used alone; it holds no value.

Color My World: The Joys of Hexadecimal Codes

Web pages would look pretty dreary if the only colors they displayed were black and white. Fortunately for happy Internet surfers everywhere, you can make text, links, and backgrounds nearly any color you can dream of. To get started with coloring, you should first be familiar with the way computers handle colors.

Computers utilize a combination of just three colors — red, green, and blue (RGB) — to render colors on the screen. They combine varying amounts of each color to create all the other colors under the rainbow.

Cracking hexadecimal color codes

Life would be simple if you could just use a color's name to set say, the background color BGCOLOR="red" of a page. Although browsers recognize a few color names, for the most part colors are usually designated using hexadecimal code.

Hexa-what? Hexadecimal is a base-16 numbering scheme in which the numbers run from 0-9 and A-F with 0 representing the least amount of a color and F representing the highest amount. Don't bother asking why and how the letters came into it. Just remember that going from left to right, the values get sequentially higher:

Lowest value 0 1 2 3 4 5 6 7 8 9 A B C D E F Highest value

Each color code in the hexadecimal system contains six digits, broken into three sets, which look like a really wacky locker combination.

Here's how to crack the combination:

- ✔ The first set of two digits in the color code represents the amount of red that's in the color.
- ✔ The second set of two digits represents the amount of green in the color.
- ✔ The third set of two digits represents the amount of blue in the color.

Using *R* for red, *G* for green, and *B* for blue, this is how the color digits are combined:

RRGGBB

If you substitute actual color codes for the representative letters in the previous example, you use the following color code to set the background color of your page to green:

```
<BODY BGCOLOR="#00FF00">
```

Because there's no red, a lot of green, and no blue, the color of #00FF00 must be green.

You won't have to memorize tons of color codes for the exam. You should, however, know how color codes work so you can decipher the most basic colors, such as black, white, red, green, and blue. A code of #FFFFFF is white, while #000000 is black. (That always seems backwards to me, but that's the way colors work.)

Using Web-safe colors

Although you can put most any shade of any color in a Web page, you're safer using Web-safe colors. *Web-safe colors* (also called browser-safe colors) are the colors that look exactly the same regardless of which browser or operating system Web surfers are using. If you choose from the palette of 216 Web-safe colors, you can feel secure that your page colors will render consistently on various viewers' machines.

You could spend a lot of time memorizing all 216 Web-safe colors (that's if you don't have a life), but the easier way to recognize a Web-safe color is to check out the hexadecimal color code. If each two-digit color section (the red section, the green section, or the blue section) is comprised of double digits, it's a Web-safe color. The following color code, for example, is a valid color, but it's not a *Web-safe* color:

```
<BODY BGCOLOR="#09A2F3">
```

In contrast, the following code is a Web-safe color:

```
<BODY BGCOLOR="#AA6633">
```

Don't worry about using Web-safe colors in your graphics. Your browser software doesn't render images; your graphics card does. Your graphics card doesn't care if you choose from the 216 Web-safe color palette.

For the exam, you need to know what a Web-safe color is but you won't be asked to identify whether various colors are Web-safe or not.

You can use the color codes I've been discussing to specify colors for page backgrounds, fonts, and links. Table 11-4 shows how to set colors for each of these page components.

Table 11-4	Adding Colors to Web Pages
What You're Colorizing	*How You Do It*
Page background	In the body tag, add the BGCOLOR (or background color) attribute: <BODY BGCOLOR="#00FF00">
Unfollowed hyperlink	In the body tag, add the LINK attribute: <BODY LINK="#0000FF">
Active hyperlink	In the body tag, add the ALINK attribute: <BODY ALINK="#0000FF">
Followed hyperlink	In the body tag, add the VLINK attribute: <BODY VLINK="#FF00FF">
Text	In the font tag, add the COLOR attribute: <FONT COLOR="#000000">

Dithering

Dithering occurs when your computer is trying to render a color that's outside its regular capabilities or outside a specific color palette you specify for it to use. Say you have an image that contains 5,000 colors and you decide to save it as a GIF file. The image-editing software you're using changes the file to a GIF, knowing that GIF supports only 256 colors, but it needs to try to display 5,000 colors. The image-editing software tries to approximate the colors the GIF palette won't support by combining the 256 colors it does support in different ways. The resulting image won't be as clear and colorful as the original 5,000-color image, but it will approximate the missing colors (sometimes with mixed results, depending on how much dithering the program has to do).

Say you have an image with a large file size that has some purple in it. To minimize your file size, you decide to save it as a GIF, which only supports 256 colors. If that color palette doesn't include the exact same shade of purple as the purple that's in the original image, your computer will attempt to make that shade of purple appear in the image through dithering. The computer takes a pixel, divides it in half, and puts in half a dot of red and half a dot of blue. From a distance, it appears to be purple. Applying dithering can help reduce file sizes because you can apply a high level of compression but eliminate the chunky color changes high compression normally causes (see Figure 11-1). After you apply dithering to a compressed JPEG or GIF image, however, your image's file size may increase slightly — compared to the small file size you can accomplish with high compression levels without dithering. However, if you compress an image a huge amount, the image colors look so bad, you can't use the image anyway, so you might as well add a little file size by applying dithering and end up with an image you can use. Figure 11-1 shows two pictures of me mugging for the camera (that's not dandruff in my hair; it's confetti). The photo on the left was saved with very few colors so the colors look chunky — the color changes aren't nice and or as subtle as they should be. I've applied dithering to the picture on the right, so the color changes are much smoother.

Figure 11-1:
The photo before I dithered it (left) and the photo after I dithered it (right), which looks much nicer.

A noncomputer example of dithering is on stadium or arena color scoreboards. They have only three colors of lights: red, green and blue. When the person in charge of the scoreboard wants it to show the color purple, he turns on the red and blue lights. This makes the glow purple. Your eyes and brain simply take the in-between color as what you see. A computer does the same thing to make colors it normally can't produce or record.

If you get a question about dithering on the exam, it will most likely be just a question asking about the definition of dithering. It's a computer's method of trying to display a color it might not otherwise be able to.

Inserting Image Maps

An image map enables you to make different parts of an image link to different files. Figure 11-2 shows a map of the United States. If you want to create links from each state to a larger image of that state, you use an image map. Image maps can be server-side or client-side. If you create a server-side image map, you utilize a CGI script (I cover CGI scripts in Chapter 17). Most image maps are client-side — all the code for the clickable areas is contained in the HTML code the browser interprets.

Figure 11-2:
Create an
image map
of the
United
States.

In real life, you use a WYSIWYG editor of some type to help you create image maps (sometimes called hotspots). Coding them by hand is a huge pain, so no one (except a few masochists out there) codes them manually. It's extremely unlikely that you'll have to answer specific code questions on image maps for the CIW Foundations test. Just make sure you've got the info in these two paragraphs down, and you should be good to go.

Adding Special Characters

One of the first things you learn about HTML is that most codes are enclosed in less than and greater than symbols <>. But what if you want to put one of these symbols on a page? If you just stick it in your text as you're typing along, the browser's going to assume you're trying to create a tag, and the symbol usually won't display. In this situation, you can use one of the special characters available in HTML.

In addition to less than and greater than symbols, special characters are available to create several non-keyboard characters — the copyright or trademark symbol, for example. One thing that will seem odd — compared to most HTML tags — is that the codes to create these special characters aren't encased in less than and greater than symbols. The tip-off that these are still codes is that they begin with an ampersand (&) and end with a semicolon (;). Table 11-5 shows the most common special characters. These are the ones you need to know for the exam; in real life, your WYSIWYG editor will help you create most of them.

Table 11-5	Special Characters
Character	*Code That Creates It*
< (Less than symbol)	&lt;
> (Greater than symbol)	&gt;
© (Copyright symbol)	&copy;
® (Registered trademark symbol)	&reg;
é (letter e with an acute accent)	&eacute;
Nonbreaking space or hard space	

The Magic Bulleted and Numbered Lists

Just like in a word processing program, HTML allows you to create two types of indented lists: bulleted and numbered. Or, as they're called in HTML-land, unordered (bulleted) and ordered (numbered). To insert an unordered list, you encase the entire list within opening and closing unordered list tags, `<UL>...</UL>`. Each line in the list begins with the line item `<LI>` tag (Although technically the `<LI>` tag is a container tag, closing this particular tag is optional. Prosoft often uses list with no closing `</LI>` tags, so that's what I'm doing in the examples.) Figure 11-3 contains three lines.

```
<UL>
<LI> This is the first item in the list.
<LI> This is the second item in the list.
<LI> This is the third item in the list.
</UL>
```

Figure 11-3:
An
unordered
(bulleted)
list.

By changing just one letter in the preceding code, you can change the list from an unordered list to an ordered list. Figure 11-4 shows what happens when I change the *U* in the opening and closing <UL> tags to an O (make sure you don't use a zero, but the letter O). Now the code creates an ordered list.

```
<OL>
<LI> This is the first item in the list.
<LI> This is the second item in the list.
<LI> This is the third item in the list.
</OL>
```

Figure 11-4:
An ordered
(numbered)
list.

Prep Test

1 One of the primary reasons a Web page has a long download time is

  A ○ Too much bold text
  B ○ Too many graphics
  C ○ Large graphic files
  D ○ Both B and C

2 The correct HTML syntax to insert an image in a page is

  A ○ `<IMAGE SOURCE="myimage.gif">`
  B ○ `<IMG SCR="myimage.gif">`
  C ○ `<IMG NAME="myimage.gif">`
  D ○ `<IMG SRC="myimage.gif">`

3 Which of the following is not true regarding the GIF image compression format?

  A ○ Stands for Graphics Interchange Format
  B ○ Allows 1-color transparency
  C ○ Is the best format for all Web images
  D ○ Supports 256 colors

4 The version of GIF that supports animation is

  A ○ GIF 89A
  B ○ GIF 89B
  C ○ GIF 99A
  D ○ GIF 87A

5 Which image format was created by independent developers?

  A ○ JPEG or JPG
  B ○ GIF 87A
  C ○ GIF 89A
  D ○ PNG

6 What term describes an image that loads gradually on a page?

  A ○ Interlaced
  B ○ Interwoven
  C ○ Progressed
  D ○ Both A and B

7 **The height and width of images can be expressed in**

A ○ Inches

B ○ Pixels

C ○ Percents

D ○ Both B and C

8 **Which is the proper syntax to add alternate text to an image?**

A ○ `<ALT TEXT="Picture of a lion">`

B ○ `<ALT=text, SRC="Picture of a lion">`

C ○ `<TEXTALT="Picture of a lion">`

D ○ `<ALT="Picture of a lion">`

9 **Which of the following descriptions of alignment attributes is not correct?**

A ○ ALIGN="Left" places the image to the left of neighboring text.

B ○ ALIGN="Top" positions the image so its top lines up with the first line of text.

C ○ ALIGN="Middle" aligns the middle of the image with the top of the text.

D ○ <ALIGN="Middle"> aligns the middle of the image with the baseline of the text.

10 **The `<UL>` tag creates which of the following?**

A ○ An ordered or numbered list

B ○ A menu list

C ○ An unordered or bulleted list

D ○ None of the above

Answers

1 **D.** Both B and C. Text, even bold text, takes very little load time and won't be a significant factor in slow load times unless you're including the text from say, a novel in your Web site. *See "Adding Images to Your Page."*

2 **D.** `<IMG SRC="myimage.gif">`. `<IMG SRC>` stands for image source — the file name of your image. *Review "Adding Images to Your Page."*

3 **C.** Is the best format for all Web images. Because GIF supports only 256 colors, it's usually better to save photographic images as JPGs. *Check out "Choosing the Right Image Format."*

4 **A.** GIF 89A. The two valid GIF versions are: 87 and 89A and it's the later version, 89A, that supports the cool stuff like transparency and animation. *Look over "Choosing the Right Image Format."*

5 **D.** PNG. Some independent developers created PNG as a free image format that could take the place of GIF. *Take a look at "Choosing the Right Image Format."*

6 **A.** Interlaced. An image that loads gradually on a page is either interlaced (in the GIF format) or is loading in progressive passes (in the JPG format). Answer C is tricky because it's close to progressive passes, but there's no such thing as a progressed image. *Check out "Understanding the Different Image Format Features."*

7 **D.** Both B and C. Image heights and widths can be specified in either pixels or percents, but usually you use pixels. *Read "Changing height and width."*

8 **D.** `<ALT="Picture of a lion">`. None of the other answers contain valid code. *Review "Including alternate text."*

9 **C.** `<ALIGN="Middle">` aligns the middle of the image with the top of the text. `<ALIGN="Middle" >` aligns the middle of the image with the baseline of the text. *See "Adjusting image alignment."*

10 **C.** An unordered or bulleted list. The `<UL>` tag stands for unordered list and creates what most people would call a bulleted list. *Take a look at "The Magic Bulleted and Numbered Lists."*

Chapter 12

Adding Tables and Forms to Web Pages

Exam Objectives

▶ Creating simple and complex tables

▶ Creating a basic HTML form that accepts user input

*I*f you've been laying out Web pages without *tables,* you're in for a treat. Tables are the key to helping you put images and text exactly where you want them — something that's hard to do otherwise. Tables are also a good way to display grids of information or tabular data.

Just as tables are great for displaying data on pages, *forms* are great for gathering data from visitors. I can think of very few types of Web sites that wouldn't benefit from including a form or two. Whether you use them to enable visitors to order products or you use them to gather demographic and other information, forms are powerful tools.

When you use tables and forms together, you can start playing with the big boys on the Web! You can make a beautiful page all about your company, and when your viewers become hypnotized by your design, you can then gently lead them to your order form page where they'll feel compelled to order millions of dollars of your company's widgets!

For the exam, make sure you know how to code tables backwards and forwards. Pay particular attention to the section on spanning columns and rows. You'll probably get at least a question or two on how to code forms, so know your code.

Quick Assessment

Introduction to tables

1 The _____ tag creates an HTML table.

2 _____ is the tag used to create a row in an HTML table.

3 _____ creates a cell within a row in an HTML table.

4 To make the border surrounding a table invisible, use the code _____.

5 A table header is created with the _____ tag.

6 The _____ attribute specifies how far apart cells will be from each other.

Forms overview

7 The _____ tag creates an HTML form.

8 The type of form field that allows users to select only one of a given set of choices is a _____ button.

9 _____ and _____ are the two values the METHOD attribute can hold in a form.

10 The _____ attribute holds the name and location of a script that will process a form's data.

Answers

1   *Table.* Review "Creating Rows, Columns, and Cells."

2   *<TR>.* Check out "Row, row, row your boat."

3   *<TD>.* Look at "Columns and cells."

4   *BORDER="0".* Review "Columns and cells."

5   *<TH>.* Read "Using other table elements."

6   *CELLSPACING.* Review "Aligning Tables, Cells, and Their Content."

7   *<FORM>.* Look over "Defining the form area."

8   *Radio.* Take a peek at "Radio buttons."

9   *Get and post.* "Finding a method for your madness."

10   *ACTION.* Check out "Here's where the action is."

Creating Rows, Columns, and Cells

I know this is going to come as a surprise, but I gotta tell you anyway. Tables consist of rows and cells. And unless you want a really weird looking table, you have to plan what your table's going to look like — that is, you need to determine how many rows, columns, and cells you want. In this section, I talk about creating rows and columns, and other cool tricks, such as captions and table heads, to make the perfect table. (I can't help you with what to put in your table — you're on your own there.)

The number of rows and columns in a table don't have to match — you can have one row and ten columns if you want — but if you have a ton more columns than you have rows, you might have a hard time fitting such a wide table on-screen.

Tables consist of three important elements, which you code in the following order:

- **Rows:** The horizontal lines in a table
- **Columns:** The vertical lines in a table
- **Cells:** The boxes created by the intersection of horizontal and vertical lines in a table

The main reason you use tables is to help you place graphics and text exactly where you want them in relation to each other. You can also create grids of information — spreadsheet-type data. Say you want to put some text on either side of an image. No problem. Figure 12-1 shows the top half of the Yahoo! home page. Each link and each image at the top of the page is inside its own cell in a table — the borders of the cells are invisible.

Figure 12-1:
The Yahoo!
home page
uses tables.

Cells in tables can contain text, graphics, and even other tables. The tag you use to start and end a table (this will be a shocker) is the <TABLE> tag, which is a standard container tag (one that you have to both open and close). It contains all the information about the rows and columns that make up the table, like this:

```
<TABLE> (Information about rows and columns goes
        here.)</TABLE>
```

Row, row, row your boat

After you've declared, "Hey, I'm gonna make a table now!" by using the <TABLE> tag, you define the rows of the table using the <TR>, table row, tag. For every row you put in a table, you add an opening and closing <TR> tag. To create a table with two empty rows, you'd write this code:

```
<TABLE>
<TR></TR>
<TR></TR>
</TABLE>
```

Columns and cells

After you define the rows in a table, you define cells in each row. You create cells with the <TD> (table data) tag. For each cell, you create an opening and closing <TD> tag. In between the opening and closing <TD> tags, you put the text, links, or images you want to appear in the cell. Here's an example of a table that has two rows and two cells in each row for a phone directory (yes, Tom Cruise is on speed dial on my phone — I wish!).

```
<TABLE>
<TR><TD>Name</TD><TD>Number</TD></TR>
<TR><TD>Tom Cruise</TD><TD>555-6666</TD></TR>
</TABLE>
```

The table displays in a browser, similar to Figure 12-2.

Even though I didn't tell the border to be invisible (using BORDER="0" in the <TABLE> tag), the border is hidden. Don't expect to be tested on this, but be aware that various browser versions interpret a missing border attribute differently. Some browsers display a default, 1-pixel-thick border; others display no border. Make sure you specify a border thickness in your real-life pages, whether you specifically want (or don't want) a border to appear. The following code creates the same table shown in Figure 12-2, except I've added a BORDER="1" attribute to create a 1-pixel-thick border around it, as shown in Figure 12-3.

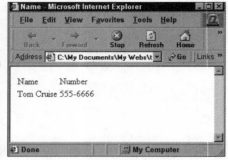

Figure 12-2:
A simple
table as
displayed in
a browser.

```
<TABLE BORDER="1">
<TR><TD>Name</TD><TD>Number</TD></TR>
<TR><TD>Tom Cruise</TD><TD>555-6666</TD></TR>
</TABLE>
```

Figure 12-3:
A phone
directory
table with a
1-pixel-thick
border.

The table in Figure 12-3 has two columns in it, but the code that created the table doesn't mention columns at all. What's up with that? The cells you create in each row create columns. Because each row in that table has two cells, the cells line up under each other and create two columns. Pretty neat, huh? What happens when you don't want all the rows in a table to have the same number of columns? Just hold your horses until the "Spanning Columns and Rows" section, later in this chapter.

Using other table elements

There are two other table elements you need to know for the exam — even though you probably won't use them often in real life. The first is the table caption <CAPTION> tag, which creates a caption above a table like this:

```
<TABLE BORDER="1">
<CAPTION>This is a Caption</CAPTION>
<TR><TD>Name</TD><TD>Number</TD></TR>
<TR><TD>Tom Cruise</TD><TD>555-6666</TD></TR>
</TABLE>
```

When viewed in a browser, the preceding code produces the result shown in Figure 12-4.

Figure 12-4:
A simple table with a caption.

The other table element to memorize for the exam is the table header `<TH>` tag. This tag usually makes the text inside a cell bold and centers it. You can get the same result by using the good old bold `<B>` and center `<CENTER>` tags, but doesn't it make you feel smart to know two ways to do something? To incorporate a table header, you use `<TH>` to define a cell instead of `<TD>` like this:

```
<TABLE>
<TR><TH>Name</TH><TH>Number</TH></TR>
<TR><TD>Tom Cruise</TD><TD>555-6666</TD></TR>
</TABLE>
```

Whatever formatting you apply to text that's not in a table can be used inside a table as well. Surround the text that's inside a cell with one or more of the standard formatting tags: `<TD> Some <B>Bold</B> text </TD>`.

Changing heights and widths

By default, the height and width of a cell will automatically adjust (within reason) to accommodate whatever text or graphics you place inside it. If you want to, though, you can set the height and width to be whatever size you like by using the `HEIGHT` and `WIDTH` attributes. Use these attributes to set the size of a cell, a row, or the entire table. To create a cell that's 100 pixels tall and 120 pixels wide, write the following code:

```
<TD HEIGHT="100" WIDTH="120">Phone</TD>
```

Cell widths and heights can be set in pixels, as in the previous example, or in percents. To create a table that's 50 percent of the width of a page, this is the code:

```
<TABLE WIDTH="50%">Row and cell information</TABLE>
```

Adding colors and images

The background color BGCOLOR attribute can set the background color of a cell, a row, or a whole table. To make a table with a red background, you use the following code:

```
<TABLE BGCOLOR="#FF0000">. . .</TABLE>
```

To place a background image in a cell, row, or table, use the BACKGROUND attribute like this:

```
<TD BACKGROUND="YourImage.gif">Text in cell</TD>
```

Spanning Columns and Rows

Sometimes you want a single cell to span across several rows or several columns. You do this with the ROWSPAN and COLSPAN attributes.

Here's what I mean:

```
<TABLE BORDER="1">
<TR><TH COLSPAN="3">PHONE LIST</TH></TR>
<TR><TD ROWSPAN="5"><IMG SRC="Blily.gif"></TD>
<TD>Name</TD><TD>Number</TD></TR>
<TR><TD>Tom Cruise</TD><TD>555-6666</TD></TR>
<TR><TD>Mel Gibson</TD><TD>555-7777</TD></TR>
<TR><TD>Cindy Crawford</TD><TD>555-8888</TD></TR>
<TR><TD>Reese Witherspoon</TD><TD>555-9999</TD></TR>
</TABLE>
```

In the code, I placed an image in the first cell of a new row — the second cell in this row contains the word *Name,* and the third cell in this row contains the word *Number.* Because the image is going to start on this row and span the other four rows in the table, the total number of rows it's spanning is five. The ROWSPAN attribute is contained within the cell tag <TD> of the cell that you want to span several rows. Lab 12-1 takes you through creating cells that span rows and columns.

Lab 12-1   Creating Tables with Cells That Span

1. Open Notepad and start with standard HTML page code.

For the example, I use this code:

```
<HTML>
<HEAD>
<TITLE>A Table with Row and Column Spanning </TITLE>
</HEAD>
<BODY>
</BODY>
</HTML>
```

2. In between the `<BODY>` tags, create a table with columns and rows.

A table with three columns and four rows looks like this:

```
<TABLE>
<TR>
<TD></TD><TD></TD><TD></TD></TR>
<TR>
<TD></TD><TD></TD><TD></TD></TR>
<TR>
<TD></TD><TD></TD><TD></TD></TR>
</TABLE>
```

3. Add some text in each cell.

I inserted the names of some of my favorite foods. If you want to go ahead and preview this code in the browser, it should produce a table with three rows and three columns with a 1-pixel-thick border.

You should see the full effect when you're finished, similar to the following code:

```
<TABLE BORDER="1">
<TR>
<TD>ice cream</TD><TD>cake</TD><TD>cookies</TD></TR>
<TR>
<TD>steak</TD><TD>lobster</TD><TD>shrimp</TD></TR>
<TR>
<TD>cheese</TD><TD>fruit</TD><TD>bread</TD></TR>
</TABLE>
```

4. Insert a new cell before the first cell in the first row.

I've typed **ice cream** in my example. Inside the `<TD>` tag for the new cell you've just created, add the attribute `ROWSPAN="3"`. Type some text inside the new cell — I typed **Things I love to eat.** The new cell and its content will span all three rows of the table.

```
<TABLE BORDER="1">
<TR>
<TD ROWSPAN="3">Things I love to eat.</TD>
<TD>ice cream</TD><TD>cake</TD><TD>cookies</TD></TR>
```

```
<TR>
<TD>steak</TD><TD>lobster</TD><TD>shrimp</TD></TR>
<TR>
<TD>cheese</TD><TD>fruit</TD><TD>bread</TD></TR>
</TABLE>
```

5. Save the page.

I saved mine as `mytable.htm`.

6. Look at the page in a browser.

Open your browser and then go to the File menu to open and browse for the file. Your page should look something like Figure 12-5.

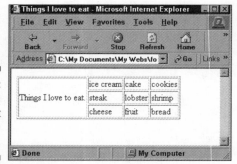

Figure 12-5:
A table with
a cell that
spans three
rows.

Aligning Tables, Cells, and Their Content

After you master basic table structure, you need to know how to place content inside cells the way you want it. The `ALIGN` attribute is just what the doctor ordered! You can use this in `<TABLE>` tags, table row `<TR>` tags, and cell table data `<TD>` tags to control left-to-right alignment. The `VALIGN` attribute controls the vertical alignment and can be used in the same places as the `ALIGN` attribute. The values that `ALIGN` and `VALIGN` can hold are listed in Table 12-1, along with the other table codes you should know for the exam.

Table 12-1		Important Table Codes	
Code	*Values It Can Hold*	*What It Does*	*Example*
`<TABLE>`	N/A	Creates the area for a table in a page.	`<TABLE>`
`<TR>` (table row)	N/A	Creates a table row.	`<TR>`

Code	*Values It Can Hold*	*What It Does*	*Example*
`<TD>` (table data)	N/A	Creates a table cell.	`<TD>`
`BORDER=`	0, 1, 2, 3, 4, 5, and so on	Specifies the width, in pixels, of a border around a table; goes in the `<TABLE>` tag.	`<TABLE BORDER= "1">`
`WIDTH=`	1, 2, 3, 4, 5, and so on or 50%, 100%	Sets the width of a cell, row, or table tag.	`<TABLE WIDTH= "200">` or `<TABLE WIDTH= "50%">`
`HEIGHT=`	1, 2, 3, 4, 5, and so on or 50%, 100%	Sets the height of a cell, row, or table tag.	`<TR HEIGHT= "300">` or `<TR HEIGHT= "60%">`
`CELL PADDING=`	1, 2, 3, 4, 5, and so on	Sets the margin inside a cell.	`<TD CELL PADDING= "2">`
`CELL SPACING=`	1, 2, 3, 4, 5, and so on	Specifies how far apart cells will be.	`<TABLE CELL SPACING= "2">`
`COLSPAN=`	1, 2, 3, 4, 5, and so on	Specifies how many columns a cell will cross or span.	`<TD COLSPAN= "4">`
`ROWSPAN=`	1, 2, 3, 4, 5, and so on	Specifies how many rows a cell will cross or span.	`<TD ROWSPAN= "5">`
`ALIGN=`	Left, Right, Center	Specifies horizontal alignment of a table, row, or cell.	`<TABLE ALIGN= "Left">`
`VALIGN=`	Top, Middle, Bottom of a table, row, or cell	Specifies vertical alignment.	`<TR VALIGN= "Top">`

(continued)

Table 12-1 *(continued)*

Code	Values It Can Hold	What It Does	Example
BGCOLOR=	Some simple color names and any hexadecimal color code	Specifies background colorin a cell.	BGCOLOR= "White" or BG COLOR= "#FFFFFF"
CAPTION	Can contain ALIGN= "Top" or ALIGN= "Bottom" to position caption above or below table	Creates a caption above or below a table. Caption content isn't placed insidea cell, but it is part of the table.	<TABLE> <CAPTION ALIGN= "Top"> Table Caption </CAPTION>

Using the Magic Formula

For the Foundations exam, you need to know what a form is, how it works, and why you include it on a Web page. Unless you live in a vacuum, you're sure to have seen forms on Web pages and have probably filled out at least a few. (Did you win the million-dollar prize? Me neither.) If you use one of the free, Web-based e-mail services such as Yahoo! Mail or Hotmail, you've filled out a small form — one asking for your name and password. If you've ever ordered anything online, you've probably filled out a much longer form with a variety of field types — text boxes, drop-down list boxes, and radio or option buttons. Just as you can lay out a table in any format you can dream of, you can create a form to look and act any way you want. The main reason to include a form on a page is to gather data from visitors — names, e-mail addresses, credit order information, and any other type of data you may be curious about.

There are two main steps involved in working with forms: creating the form fields and then making them work. You can create forms with all kinds of fields all day long, but if you don't specify some way for the data they collect to go somewhere to be stored, you've just wasted your time. The following sections discuss how to create the various form fields you need to know for the exam, as well as the methods you can use to collect the form data.

Putting forms together

There are several standard types of form fields you need to be familiar with for the Foundations exam — text fields, drop-down menus, radio buttons, and textarea fields. All of these fields are inserted in between opening and closing

<FORM> tags, which define the entire form area. Don't expect a ton of questions on how to code each field type, but at least be able to recognize them.

Defining the form area

A Web page form is created with a <FORM> container tag. In between the opening and closing form tag, <FORM>...</FORM>, is where you place the various fields that visitors fill out, which I cover later in this section. Many browsers will not display form elements (fields) that aren't contained within a form tag <FORM>.

Adding text fields

Text fields are the type in which visitors usually type a name or address; they look like standard text boxes and are tall enough to hold one line of text. The box can be as wide as you want — you use the WIDTH attribute to specify how many characters wide you want the text field to be. The following code creates a text field that's 20 characters wide:

```
<FORM>
<INPUT TYPE="text" SIZE="20">
</FORM>
```

The preceding code creates a text field on the screen, but it's missing an important element: a NAME attribute. All fields covered in the following sections have one thing in common — the NAME attribute. You can set the name attribute to equal whatever word you'd like, but you usually use it to describe the type of data a field is collecting. For example, if you create a field to collect visitors' phone numbers, you might type NAME="Phone" so you can tell which data was collected in which field. The following code takes the text field from the preceding example and adds a NAME attribute:

```
<FORM>
<INPUT TYPE="text" NAME="Address" SIZE="20">
</FORM>
```

Just because the SIZE attribute specifies that the field will be 20 characters wide, it doesn't prevent visitors from typing in a much longer address — it just limits how much space the field takes up on the screen. The field allows left-to-right scrolling to accommodate more than 20 characters.

If you previewed the preceding code in a browser, it would display a text field — but that's it. If a rectangular box is the only thing that appears on your page, how will visitors know what kind of information to type in it? You have to add some regular text beside the text box to tell visitors what kind of information you want them to give you, like this:

```
<FORM>
Address <INPUT TYPE="text" NAME="Address" SIZE="20">
</FORM>
```

It's a secret — the password field

A password field is really just a slight variation of a regular text field. It's coded the same way as the text box field, except for the "INPUT" part. The password field also creates a single-line box for someone to type in, but when a person types, say, a password in it, it doesn't display the word; it replaces the letters with stars. The following code alters the text field I created in the previous example: I changed the text beside the field to *Password,* changed the TYPE attribute to equal "Password", and changed the NAME attribute to equal "Password", like this:

```
<FORM>
Password <INPUT TYPE="Password" NAME="Password" SIZE="20">
</FORM>
```

The preceding code creates a password field like the one displayed in Figure 12-6.

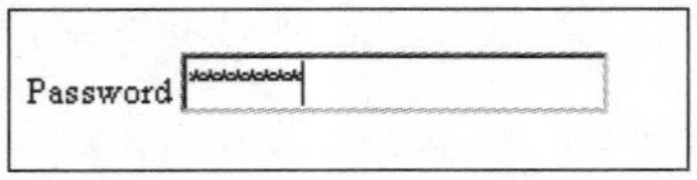

Figure 12-6:
A password
field
containing
a password.

Password [**********]

Using textarea fields

The textarea field creates a standard comment box. By default, it will scroll and scroll, accepting however much text someone types in it. You code this container tag like this:

```
<FORM>
Please tell us what you think:<BR>
<TEXTAREA ROWS="8" NAME="Comments" COLS="51"></TEXTAREA>
</FORM>
```

In the preceding example, ROWS="8" specifies how tall the comment box should be. In this case, it's eight rows, or lines of text, tall. COLS="51" specifies how wide the comment box is. In this case, I decided to make it 51 columns (or characters) wide. The text above the <TEXTAREA> field was inserted to explain to visitors what type of input to add. If you place any text between the starting and ending <TEXTAREA> tags, it will be the default text that initially displays inside the box.

Radio buttons

A radio button (also known as an *option button* in other programming systems) is a little round figure that someone clicks to select one of several options presented in a question. In Figure 12-7, there's a question asking: "What is your favorite part of Web design?" The circles to the left of the answers are radio buttons.

Here's what the code looks like for the radio buttons in Figure 12-7.

```
<FORM>
What is your favorite part of Web design?<BR>
<INPUT TYPE="Radio" NAME="Favorite" VALUE="Design">Design
<INPUT TYPE="Radio" NAME="Favorite" VALUE="Coding">Coding
<INPUT TYPE="Radio" NAME="Favorite" VALUE="Graphics">Graphics
</FORM>
```

Figure 12-7:
Give visitors a choice by having them click a radio button.

Use radio buttons to give the visitor one choice. All the buttons have the same NAME attribute; only one can be chosen at a time. They look similar to the radio buttons in a classic 1975 Buick Century (which is where the name comes from).

Check boxes

Check box fields allow visitors to select several of the options presented in a question. Figure 12-8 displays check boxes under the question, "Why do you want to pass the Foundations exam?"

Figure 12-8:
Visitors can choose more than one option with the check box field.

Here's the code that creates the check boxes from Figure 12-8.

```
<FORM>
Why do you want to pass the Foundations exam?<BR>
<INPUT TYPE="Checkbox" NAME="Job">I want to get a new job<br>
<INPUT TYPE="Checkbox" NAME="Boss">My boss wants me to<br>
<INPUT TYPE="Checkbox" NAME="Love">I just love passing exams
</FORM>
```

Unlike radio buttons, multiple check boxes can be chosen at the same time; you should give them different names as well.

Drop-down list boxes

Drop-down list boxes drop down several choices from which a visitor can choose. The state field in Figure 12-9 is a drop-down list box.

Figure 12-9:
A drop-down list box.

The code that created the fields in Figure 12-9 is

```
<FORM>
Please tell us where you live:<BR>
<SELECT SIZE="1" NAME="State">
<OPTION>. . .</OPTION>
<OPTION>Ohio</OPTION>
<OPTION>Indiana</OPTION>
<OPTION>Virginia</OPTION>
</SELECT>
</FORM>
```

In the preceding code, `size="1"` tells the drop-down list box to be one line high — I clicked the drop-down arrow to display the list of choices in Figure 12-9. The first option: `<OPTION>. . .</OPTION>` tells the box to display three dots (. . .) until someone clicks its arrow.

If the `SIZE` attribute of the drop-down list box is set to be higher than 1, the list becomes a scrollable selection list.

Adding submit and reset buttons

Submit and reset buttons are pretty common features in forms. The submit button sends the form data to wherever you tell it to go. (I cover how to send data where you want it to go in the "Here's where the action is" section, later in this chapter.) The reset button clears all the fields in a form so the visitor can fill them out again. Submit and reset buttons usually go at the end of a form, like this:

```
<FORM >
(Form fields go here)
<INPUT TYPE="Submit" VALUE="Submit">
<INPUT TYPE="Reset" VALUE="Reset">
</FORM>
```

Making forms work

After you've laid out a form containing all the fields you want, you have to tell the form where you want the data to go. It doesn't do you any good to create a form unless you specify how the data will be handled.

Finding a method for your madness

To specify how your data will be sent somewhere, you add the METHOD attribute inside the <FORM> tag. The METHOD attribute can equal either "Get" or "Post" like this:

```
<FORM METHOD="Get">
```

Or:

```
<FORM METHOD="Post">
```

I could probably write a whole chapter about all the details that differentiate the get method from the post method. For the exam, here's what you need know:

- ✔ <METHOD="Get">: Adds the form data to the end of the URL string (the Web page address up in the address bar) and sends the data to the specified location

- ✔ <METHOD="Post">: Creates a separate text file containing the form data that is sent to the specified location

In the examples I create, I use the METHOD="Post".

Here's where the action is

The ACTION attribute tells the form where to send the data when someone clicks the submit button. The ACTION attribute can tell the form to send the data to an e-mail address, or it can tell the form to send it to a database. The ACTION attribute goes in the <FORM> tag, just as the METHOD attribute does. If you want the data to be e-mailed to someone, you use the following code:

```
<FORM METHOD="Post"
        ACTION="mailto:someperson@somecompany.com">
```

Most of the time in HTML, it doesn't matter whether attribute values are in quotes. METHOD=Post works just as well as METHOD="Post". The exception to the rule is when you're referring to file names, URLs, and file paths. In the preceding example, I put quotes around the e-mail address of the recipient because it acts like a file path — telling the data what path to travel. Always put values for the ACTION attribute in quotes.

Attaching scripts to your form

If the data is going to a database, you have to use some method of scripting, which I cover fully in Chapter 17. *Scripts* are little programs that know step-by-step what to do with your form data. A script might be written to do something like this: "First take the data and put it into the database on XYZ server. Then look at the sender's e-mail address and send that person an e-mail saying 'Thanks so much for your order.'" For the exam, you need to be somewhat familiar with CGI scripts, but you won't be expected to recognize any CGI script code.

One of the most important things to know for this section of the exam is what a CGI script is. CGI stands for *common gateway interface*. It's not a scripting language or a programming language, but a method for a computer to deal with a script. CGI scripts can be written in several scripting languages, but they're all handled in roughly the same manner. I compare a computer seeing a CGI script to a human seeing a dog. The main thing is, you know it's a dog. Other than that, you might recognize what breed the dog is or what it happens to be doing, but you're sure it's a dog.

If you're using a CGI script to handle your form data, the name and location of the script goes in the ACTION attribute like this:

```
<FORM ... ACTION="http://www.yourcompany.com/cgi-
        bin/yourscript.cgi">
```

To pass the exam, you definitely want to read Chapter 17. In relation to forms though, you just need to remember that the ACTION attribute holds the location where your data will go when a visitor clicks the submit button.

Prep Test

1 **What two attributes can modify the size of a table?**

A ○ CELLSPACING and CELLPADDING
B ○ HEIGHT and WIDTH
C ○ TALL and WIDE
D ○ ALIGN and VALIGN

2 **What attribute forces a cell to span several rows in a table?**

A ○ ROWSPAN
B ○ COLSPAN
C ○ SPANDOWN
D ○ None of the above

3 **What values can the VALIGN attribute hold?**

A ○ LEFT, CENTER, and RIGHT
B ○ CENTER, MIDDLE, and ABSMIDDLE
C ○ TOP, MIDDLE, and BOTTOM
D ○ Both A and C

4 **Which tag holds the BORDER attribute?**

A ○ <TABLE>
B ○ <TR>
C ○ <TD>
D ○ All of the above

5 **Which tag holds cell contents?**

A ○ <TABLE>
B ○ <CONTENTS>
C ○ <TR>
D ○ <TD>

6 **Choose the statement that best describes the appearance of the following table code:**

```
<TABLE BORDER="1">
<TR><TD ROWSPAN="3"></TD>
TD></TD></TR>
<TR>TD></TD></TR>
<TR>TD></TD></TR>
</TABLE>
```

A ○ A three-row table with a cell on the left that spans all three rows

B ○ A four-row table with a cell on the left that spans all four rows

C ○ A three-row table containing a phone list

D ○ A three-row table with a border that's one-inch thick

7 **Which of the following statements concerning the use of the** SIZE **attribute in a text field is true?**

A ○ It specifies how wide the field will appear on the screen.

B ○ It limits the user to typing in a maximum of 20 characters.

C ○ It creates a text field that's 20 rows tall.

D ○ None of the above

8 **What element calls upon the action specified in the** ACTION **attribute?**

A ○ Reset button

B ○ Action button

C ○ CGI button

D ○ Submit button

9 **To send data gathered in a form to a database, use a(n) _____.**

A ○ E-mail client

B ○ Submit button

C ○ CGI script

D ○ mailto: link

10 **Which** METHOD **attribute sends form data as part of the URL string?**

A ○ GET

B ○ POST

C ○ INPUT

D ○ SELECT

Answers

1 **B.** HEIGHT and WIDTH. *If you're still struggling with this, you may want to review "Changing heights and widths."*

2 **A.** The ROWSPAN attribute spans rows, and the COLSPAN attribute spans columns. *To review this topic, check out "Spanning Columns and Rows."*

3 **C.** Remember, VALIGN stands for vertical alignment, so it specifies top-to-bottom alignment in a cell. *See "Aligning Tables, Cells, and Their Content."*

4 **A.** The border width is set for the whole table at once in the <TABLE> tag. *Take a look at "Creating Rows, Columns, and Cells."*

5 **D.** <TD> stands for table data and defines the cells in a table. All data in a table is displayed in cells. *Review "Columns and cells."*

6 **A.** Remember, when you want a cell to span several rows, add the cell you want to stretch across the other rows to the first row it should span. *Review "Spanning Columns and Rows."*

7 **A.** It specifies how wide the field appears on the screen. The SIZE attribute doesn't limit how many characters the user can type in — by default the field allows left-to-right scrolling. *Look over "Adding text fields."*

8 **D.** Remember, the submit button is always automatically tied to the ACTION attribute. Whatever address or script is listed there will be called upon when someone clicks submit. *Check out "Adding submit and reset buttons."*

9 **C.** CGI, which stands for common gateway interface, is a common type of script used to process form data. It can send data to a database and send an e-mail to customers thanking them for their submission. *Review "Attaching scripts to your form."*

10 **A.** Remember, GET sends the data as part of the URL string or address. POST sends the data as a separate text file. *Take a look at "Finding a method for your madness."*

Chapter 13

You've Been Framed

- -

Exam Objectives

▶ Understanding how frames work

▶ Working with frames and framesets

▶ Linking from one frame to another with target frames

▶ Specifying frame border properties

- -

When frames first came out, they were all the rage — everyone, it seemed, incorporated frames into Web sites. One of the main reasons is that frames allow you to display one area of a screen that remains static and another area of the screen can change. The idea is that you can create an area with hyperlinks or buttons at, say, the top or left side of a page, and no matter what links the user clicks, the area remains on the user's screen while the larger part of the display updates with the new data.

This combination of static and dynamic data enables Web designers to display more than one page at a time. That's right — the static area that contains links is a small, independent page. Hard to imagine? Maybe you've got a channel preview option with your cable provider or a picture-in-a-picture TV. Using one of these features, you can change what's on one screen, but the content of the other screen stays the same. A Web page with frames works much like that. You see two (or more) pages: the area that changes when you follow a hyperlink and another area that doesn't change at all. Both sections of the screen are pages contained in frames.

The material I cover in this chapter shows you how to create, link, and format frames. I also show you what to do if a visitor has a browser that doesn't support frames. Not so coincidentally, that's exactly what you need to know for the Foundations exam.

Because of the nature of this topic, I use a running example. I recommend reading the entire chapter in order, and, if you're unfamiliar with frames, I suggest opening your text editor and following along as you read.

Quick Assessment

<FRAMESET> and <FRAME> tags

1 _____ enable the combination of static and dynamic data by enabling the author to display more than one HTML page at a time.

2 An author can define how many frames he or she wants and where they appear in relation to each other using a _____ document.

3 To specify the layout of horizontal frames, the _____ attribute is used.

4 The _____ attribute specifies the layout of columns (vertical frames).

5 The size of a frame can be specified in percentages or in _____.

6 The _____ tag is used to define which HTML page is to be displayed in a particular frame.

Specifying a base target

7 The _____ attribute of a framed link defines which frame the new page will display in.

8 The _____ tag allows you to specify both the URL and the default TARGET frame for all the links in a file.

9 If the author chooses to provide a message for users with nonframes browsers, the _____ tag must be nested within the frameset.

10 The _____ attribute tells the browser whether to display a border around a frame.

Answers

1   *Frames.* See "Introducing Frames."

2   *Frameset.* Check out "Freeze Frame: Introducing Framesets and Frames Pages."

3   *ROWS.* Take a look at "Getting to know the ⟨FRAMESET⟩ tag."

4   *COLS.* Review "Getting to know the ⟨FRAMESET⟩ tag."

5   *Pixels.* Check out "Getting to know the ⟨FRAMESET⟩ tag."

6   *⟨FRAME⟩.* Read "Getting to know the ⟨FRAME⟩ tag."

7   *TARGET.* See "Playing the Name Game with Target Frames."

8   *⟨BASE TARGET=⟩.* Check out "Defining a base target."

9   *⟨NOFRAMES⟩.* Take a look at "Using the ⟨NOFRAMES⟩ tag."

10   *FRAMEBORDER.* Review "Bordering on the ridiculous."

Introducing Frames

Frame technology allows several Web pages to be displayed together as if they were one page. If you've ever visited a site that had one static area that was visible at all times and another area that you could change by following a link or by scrolling, you've seen frames at work. If you're still not sure what frames are, check out the Wired.com Web site shown in Figure 13-1. See how you can scroll up and down, but you can never scroll past the advertisement? Each screen — the one that scrolls and the one that stays still — is a frame.

Figure 13-1:
You can scroll through the main page on Wired.com but the advertisement at the bottom of the screen won't move.

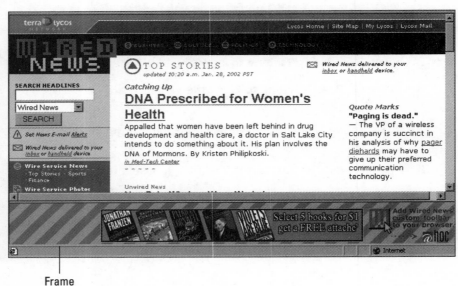

Frame

In Figure 13-1, all frames are separated by obvious borders or scroll bars. In real life, authors often make borders invisible and prevent scroll bars from appearing, so all sections of the page might look like they're part of one static HTML page. The tip off (other than looking at the HTML code) that the site uses frames is scrolling — if you can scroll one section of the page while another section stays still, it's almost a guarantee that the site uses frames.

The discussions in this chapter have nothing to do with Dynamic HTML. When I talk about static pages in this chapter, I mean that a framed page is constantly viewable on-screen. When I talk about dynamic pages or frames that change, I'm referring to the way traditional Web pages can disappear and be replaced on-screen by a new page when a user clicks a link.

The next best thing since betamax?

With every advance on the Web, there are drawbacks, and frames are no exception. Don't expect this information on the exam, but, in real life, frame usage has dwindled a bit because of some of the pitfalls of frames. With frames, users may have difficulty using the bookmark functions to save any page other than a Web site's home page. Also, frames can make it more difficult to get multiple pages of a site listed with search engines.

If you want to find out more about the drawbacks of frames, pick up a copy of *HTML 4 For Dummies*, by Ed Tittel, Natanya Pitts, and Chelsea Valentine (published by Hungry Minds, Inc.).

Freeze Frame: Introducing Framesets and Frames Pages

When you're trying to decide how many frames you want to display on the screen at once, you have a lot of flexibility. The number of frames you can display at one time is, in theory, unlimited. The reality, of course, is if you try to place 50 frames in one screen, the result will be horrible! Keep your frames to a minimum, and use them only when there's a logical design reason to do so.

A *frameset* document is the page you use to define how many frames you want and where they'll be in relation to each other — kind of like a blueprint for a house. I created a simple frames page with two frames shown in Figure 13-2. Both of these frames display a different page — a page you can see in the small frame on the left and a page you can see in the larger frame on the right. What you don't see is a third page at work — the frameset page that contains all the information about how many frames you're creating and where they display on the page. One of the tricky things about creating frames is that you have to create several pages — the frameset and each page that displays in a frame — and make them work together.

Getting to know the <FRAMESET> tag

The tag you use to define the number, height, and width of frames is the <FRAMESET> tag, which creates the <FRAMESET> page. You specify how many horizontal frames you want with the ROWS attribute and the number of vertical frames you want with the COLS attribute. The frameset in Figure 13-2 has two frames; the column (frame) on the left takes up 150 pixels, and the frame on the right takes up the remaining space on the screen. The code for this frameset looks like this:

```
<FRAMESET COLS="150,*">
</FRAMESET>
```

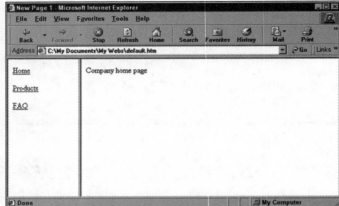

Figure 13-2:
This simple
Web page
has two
frames.

This code defines two vertical frames (columns) — a comma separates the widths of each frame. The first frame is 150 pixels wide and the second frame width is set with the * character, meaning that it takes whatever space remains on the screen.

You can specify column and row attributes in either pixels or as a percentage of the display area. In the following example, I define a frameset with two rows, the top row taking up 25 percent of the height of the page; the second frame fills any remaining space below the first frame. (Check out Lab 13-1.)

```
<FRAMESET ROWS="25%,*">
</FRAMESET>
```

The frameset is the document that should display first if your home page is contained in frames. You name the frameset *default* or *home* as you would any home page, so that it is pulled up first with the pages you specify display-ing in each frame.

The `<FRAMESET>` tag replaces the `<BODY>` tag in the `<FRAMESET>` document. Unless you're using the `<NOFRAMES>` tag (discussed later in this chapter in the "Using the `<NOFRAMES>` tag" section), you won't use the `<BODY>` tag in the `<FRAMESET>` page at all.

Getting to know the <FRAME> tag

You use the `<FRAME>` tag to define which HTML page you want to display or pull into a particular frame. The following code creates the frames shown in

Figure 13-3. The first frame contains an HTML document named top.htm that contains links to a page, and in the lower frame, I added a page named bottom.htm. (The names top.htm and bottom.htm hold no particular significance — they just seemed like good names.)

```
<FRAMESET ROWS="25%,*">
<FRAME SRC="top.htm">
<FRAME SRC="bottom.htm">
</FRAMESET>
```

Lab 13-1 walks you through the process of creating a simple frameset with two frames. (If you're not familiar with basic HTML syntax, review Chapters 9 and 10.)

Lab 13-1 Creating Frames

1. **Open your text editor and type the following code to create a basic frameset page:**

```
<HTML><HEAD>
<TITLE>My Home Page</TITLE>
</HEAD>
<FRAMESET>
</FRAMESET>
</HTML>
```

2. **Create a folder on your desktop named** myweb **and save this document as** default.htm **inside it.**

3. **Leave** default.htm **open and create a standard new HTML document called** top.htm **and save it in the myweb folder.**

4. **In the body section of** top.htm, **type three words with two spaces between them like this:**

```
<BODY>
Home  Products  FAQ
</BODY>
```

5. **Leave the two existing documents open and create another standard new HTML document called** bottom.htm **and save it in the myweb folder.**

6. **In the body section of the** bottom.htm **document, type some filler text like this:**

```
<BODY>
<P>Welcome to my home page.</P>
<P>Page content goes here.</P>
<P>Page content goes here.</P>
<P>Page content goes here.</P>
<P>Page content goes here.</P>
</BODY>
```

7. **In the** `default.htm` **document, in the** `<FRAMESET>` **tag, add the** ROWS **attribute to specify the number of rows in the frameset and the height of each.**

```
<FRAMESET ROWS="25%,*">
```

8. **Specify which pages will display in each frame by adding** `<FRAME>` **tags in between the** `<FRAMESET>` **tags.**

```
<FRAMESET ROWS="25%,*">
<FRAME SRC="top.htm">
<FRAME SRC="bottom.htm">
</FRAMESET>
```

9. **Save the changes to each page and open the** `default.htm` **page in your browser.**

   The end result resembles the page shown in Figure 13-3.

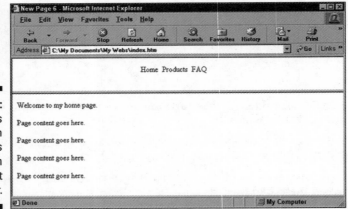

Figure 13-3:
A frames
page with
two rows
displayed in
Internet
Explorer.

Here are two points about frames to remember for the exam:

✔ One `<FRAMESET>` tag can contain either the ROWS attribute or the COLS attribute, but not both within the same `<FRAMESET>` tag.

✔ `<FRAMESET>` code is read from left to right and top to bottom — if you're creating horizontal frames (using the ROWS attribute) the first number represents the size of the top frame and the second number (or sometimes a *) specifies the height of the lower frame. If you're using the COLS attribute to create vertical frames, the first number you list specifies the width of the column on the left, the second number (sometimes a *) specifies the width of the column on the right.

Playing the Name Game with Target Frames

A very common use of frames involves creating a navigation bar on the top or left side of a page that stays visible at all times. Say you have a two-frame page, such as the one I made in Lab 13-1.

You can create a hyperlink from the word *Products* to the products page, but if you do, you will also create a problem. When users click the <u>Products</u> link, the new page will appear inside the small frame on the left, when you wanted the products page to appear in the large frame on the right.

To avoid this problem, you need to create a hyperlink that links one frame to the other. In order for the HTML to distinguish one frame from another, you first name each frame in the frameset page. I've named the frames I use in Figure 13-4; the frame on the left I called *left,* and the frame on the right (you guessed it) *right.* The following code names the frames I use in Figure 13-4.

```
<FRAMESET COLS="150,*">
  <FRAME NAME="left" SRC="left.htm">
  <FRAME NAME="right" SRC="right.htm">
</FRAMESET>
```

To create a link between two frames you must define a *target frame* — the name of the frame you want the new page to display in.

If you have links in a frame on the left and want to link to a new page that pulls up on the right, you target the right frame. Figure 13-4 shows the products page displaying in the right-hand frame. I linked the word *Products* in the left frame to the `products.htm` page and targeted the right frame to specify that the products page should display in the right-hand frame.

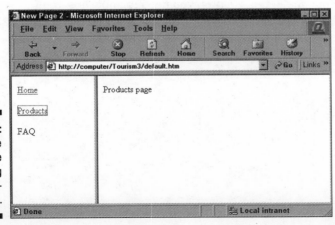

Figure 13-4: A link in the left frame targeting the right-hand frame.

Creating a link to a target frame

After you have named the frames in your page, you can create links between whichever frames you like. In this next example, I create links between the words in the left frame to pages named `default.htm`, `products.htm`, and `FAQ.htm`. I want these pages to come up in the right frame when I click the links.

To make the links work, all you do is add the `TARGET` attribute, like so:

```
<BODY>
<P><A HREF="right.htm" TARGET="right">Home</A></P>
<P><A HREF="products.htm" TARGET="right">Products</A></P>
<P><A HREF="faq.htm" TARGET="right">FAQ</A></P>
</BODY>
```

Defining a base target

In the code in the previous section "Creating a link to a target frame," I linked three words to three different pages. In the code for each link, I had to type `TARGET="right"` to force the page to open the designated frame on the right side of the screen. That wasn't a big deal, considering I only had three links.

But if you have 50 links in a frame on the left side of the screen and you want to create links for every single stinking last one of them — all to pages that should appear in the frame on the right, you'll be coding until the next millennium.

Good thing there's a workaround — using `<BASE TARGET>`. The `<BASE>` tag used with the `TARGET` attribute creates a default target frame for all links created in a particular frame so that you don't have to write target code within each link.

Rather ingenious, don't you think? The CIW people agree. Along with every other line of code in this chapter, you need to know how to use the following code for the exam:

```
<HEAD>
<BASE TARGET="right">
</HEAD>
<BODY>
<P><A HREF="right.htm">Home</A></P>
<P><A HREF="products.htm">Products</A></P>
<P><A HREF="faq.htm">FAQ</A></P>
</BODY>
```

If you use `<BASE TARGET>` to set a default target, you can still create links that target a different frame. Just be sure to include the `TARGET` attribute in the code from the section "Creating a link to a target frame," shown here, to override the default target:

```
<BODY>
<P><A HREF="right.htm" TARGET="right">Home</A></P>
<P><A HREF="products.htm" TARGET="right">Products</A></P>
<P><A HREF="faq.htm" TARGET="right">FAQ</A></P>
</BODY>
```

Add the `TARGET` attribute to the linking code for every link that overrides a default target.

Using the `<NOFRAMES>` tag

Frames have been around for several years, which means that you probably won't encounter a user who uses a browser old enough to not support frames. However, the CIW exam covers the `<NOFRAMES>` tag, so bear with me.

The `<NOFRAMES>` tag enables you to create a message that displays in the window of the antique browser that doesn't support your site's frames. Guess what the message says: It tells visitors that their browser doesn't support frames.

The `<NOFRAMES>` tag is included within the `<FRAMESET>` tag like this:

```
<FRAMESET COLS="150,*">
   <FRAME NAME="left" SRC="left.htm">
   <FRAME NAME="right" SRC="right.htm">
<NOFRAMES>
<BODY>
<P>This page uses frames, but your browser doesn't support
          them.</P>
</BODY>
</NOFRAMES>
</FRAMESET>
```

Formatting Frames

Creating different looks for each frame in a Web page can add an interesting look to your site (refer to Figure 13-1). For example, you can add a colorful stripe along the top of a page by making the background color of a frame different from the main part of the page. You could also place an image in the background. Voila! Instant stripe.

Because each frame in a frameset is actually just a Web page like any other, you don't have to learn many new formatting tricks — just apply the standard formatting, such as background and font specifications, that you would in any other HTML document. (I cover HTML formatting in Chapters 9 and 10.)

The following sections show you the frame-specific formatting tags that you need to know for the exam.

Bordering on the ridiculous

By default, borders appear around every frame as soon as you create them — they act as divider lines between all the frames on the page. You can remove a border from any (or all) frames on a page if you like.

To remove a frame's border, add the FRAMEBORDER attribute to the <FRAME> tag and setting the value to zero, like this:

```
<FRAMESET COLS="150,*">
<FRAME NAME="left" SRC="left.htm" FRAMEBORDER="0">
<FRAME NAME="right" SRC="right.htm">
</FRAMESET>
```

In the preceding example, I specified that the border of each frame is equal to zero, making each border invisible. You can use the same attribute, however, to ensure a border will show. To ensure that a border appears, set the FRAMEBORDER attribute at "1".

Setting frame margins

You can specify the size of a frame's margins with the MARGINWIDTH and MARGINHEIGHT attributes. These attributes set the amount of space between the edge of a frame and the frame's contents like this:

```
<FRAME NAME="left" SRC="left.htm" MARGINWIDTH="5">
<FRAME NAME="right" SRC="right.htm" MARGINHEIGHT="6">
```

The MARGINWIDTH and MARGINHEIGHT attributes set margin widths for the left and right side or the top and bottom, respectively.

Prep Test

1 Which of the following is not true about frames?

  A ○ Frames allow several Web pages to be displayed together as if they are one page.

  B ○ Frames are universally compatible and no longer require the `<NOFRAMES>` tag.

  C ○ Frames allow one area of the user's screen to remain static, while another area can change.

  D ○ Frames allow authors to present documents in multiple views, which may be independent windows or subwindows.

2 Which is not a function of the `<FRAMESET>` tag?

  A ○ Defines the set of links that appear in the frame

  B ○ Defines the number of frames

  C ○ Defines the height and width of frames

  D ○ None of the above

3 Rhonda is designing a Web page with frames and wants two columns to appear. The column on the left must take up one-fourth of the screen and the column on the right must take up the remainder of the screen. Which opening `<FRAMESET>` tag would she use?

  A ○ `<FRAMESET COLS="25,0.75">`

  B ○ `<FRAMESET COLS="75,25">`

  C ○ `<FRAMESET COLS="25%" ROWS="75%">`

  D ○ `<FRAMESET COLS="25%,*">`

4 If an entire Web site is based on frames, what should the author name the frameset document?

  A ○ `default.htm`, `index.htm`, or `home.htm`

  B ○ It depends on what the site is about.

  C ○ `frameset.htm`

  D ○ `top.htm`, `bottom.htm`, or `left.htm`

5 Which of the following statements is accurate regarding the `<FRAME>` tag?

  A ○ The `<FRAME>` tag must come before the `<FRAMESET>` tag.

  B ○ The `<FRAME>` tag defines how many columns and rows appear on the Web page.

  C ○ The `<FRAME>` tag defines which HTML document displays in that frame.

  D ○ `<FRAME>` must always be accompanied by a closing `</FRAME>` tag.

6 When creating a frameset document, the `<FRAMESET>` **tag is positioned**

A ○ Within the `<HEAD>` `</HEAD>`tags.
B ○ Within the `<BODY></BODY>` tags.
C ○ After the `<BODY>` tag.
D ○ After the `</HEAD>` tag.

7 Where should the `<NOFRAMES>` **tag be placed if it is used?**

A ○ Between the `<HEAD>` and `</HEAD>` tags.
B ○ Above the `<BODY>` tag, replacing the `<HEAD>` section.
C ○ Under the `</HEAD>` tag, replacing the `<BODY>` section.
D ○ Between the `<FRAMESET>` and `</BODY>` tags.

8 The `TARGET` **attribute specifies which frame a page loads in and can be contained within which of the following tags:**

A ○ `<FRAMESET>`
B ○ `<NOFRAMES>`
C ○ `<A HREF>`
D ○ `<HEAD>`

9 Which statement describing the use of `<BASE TARGET>` **is not true?**

A ○ It defines the target frame for all links within the document.
B ○ It does not allow any different target frames to be assigned.
C ○ It can be overridden in individual links.
D ○ It's use is optional in a frames page.

10 If an author wants to ensure that a border appears around a specific frame, **which of the following codes should he use?**

A ○ `BORDER="1"`
B ○ `FRAMEBORDER="0"`
C ○ `FRAMEBORDER="1"`
D ○ `BORDER="yes"`

Answers

1 **B.** Frames are universally compatible and no longer require the `<NOFRAMES>` tag. *See "Using the `<NOFRAMES>` tag."*

2 **A.** Defines the set of links that will appear in the frame. *Read "Getting to know the `<FRAMESET>` tag."*

3 **D.** `<FRAMESET COLS="25%,*">`. This code creates two columns (vertical frames); the first one takes up 25 percent of the width of the page and the second column takes up the remaining space. *Check out "Getting to know the `<FRAMESET>` tag."*

4 **A.** `default.htm`, `index.htm`, or `home.htm`. The home page of a Web based entirely on frames must be named with a traditional home page name so it will be pulled up first. *Take a look at "Getting to know the `<FRAMESET>` tag."*

5 **C.** The `<FRAME>` tag defines which HTML document displays in that frame. *Review "Getting to know the `<FRAME>` tag."*

6 **D.** After the `</HEAD>` tag. *See "Getting to know the `<FRAMESET>` tag."*

7 **D.** Between the `<FRAMESET>` and `</BODY>` tags. *Look over "Using the `<NOFRAMES>` tag."*

8 **C.** `<A HREF>`. The `TARGET` attribute is placed inside the tag that creates hyperlinks, which is `<A HREF>`. *Take a look at "Creating a link to a target frame."*

9 **B.** It does not allow any different target frames to be assigned. *Check out "Defining a base target."*

10 **C.** `FRAMEBORDER="1"`. The `FRAMEBORDER` attribute can hold only two values: `"0"`, which removes a border and `"1"` which ensures that a border displays. *See "Bordering on the ridiculous."*

You've Been Framed

Chapter 14

Meet the Rest of the HTML Family

- -

Exam Objectives

▶ Understanding the purpose of Cascading Style Sheets (CSS)

▶ Describing the functions of JavaScript, dynamic HTML (DHTML), and the Document Object Model (DOM)

▶ Explaining the features and use of XML (Extensible Markup Language)

- -

*H*TML revolutionized the Internet by allowing authors to include hyperlinks and images on pages. HTML is still an important part of Web design, but it has limitations.

For the most part, HTML allows only static information to appear on a page. Yes, it allows you to make pages somewhat interactive by creating clickable text and images, but that's about it for user interaction.

Since HTML's creation, technologies that allow Web pages to be more complex and interactive have entered the scene, and I focus on these newer technologies — Cascading Style Sheets (CSS), dynamic HTML (DHTML), JavaScript, and Extensible Markup Language (XML) — in this chapter.

Now, don't freak out about having to know all these new languages and technologies. You only need to be able to recognize a little code for the exam — you don't have to know all the syntax of each language/technology. For the most part, you just need to understand the purpose of each one as well as the benefits and drawbacks. And, as you probably guessed by now, I explain each of these items in this chapter.

If you continue seeking more CIW certifications, you may eventually need to learn how to code some of the languages I discuss here, depending on which certifications you seek. The Site Designer certification, for instance, requires you to have at least a basic knowledge of how to work with the code of these technologies. The Application Developer certification requires you to code several of these in your sleep. For more on these and other CIW certifications, take a look at Chapter 1 or visit the CIW site (www.ciwcertified.com).

Quick Assessment

1 _____ is the ability for changes to *cascade* or flow throughout many pages at once.

2 In CSS, a _____ is the combination of a property and its assigned value.

3 A(n) _____ is the HTML item that formatting is applied to.

4 The _____ is the size, color, or other specific format that is applied to a property.

5 A(n) _____ style is applied within a line of HTML code and applies only to the tag it is used with.

6 _____ or *external* style sheets can apply formatting to many pages at once.

7 Stand-alone, reusable segments of program code that are not part of an object are _____.

8 Dynamic HTML (DHTML) uses _____ to specify how an object will react to user actions.

9 The formatting language that works specifically with XML is _____.

10 JavaScript uses the _____, which contains predefined objects and predefined relationships between those objects.

Answers

1   *Inheritance.* Check out "A large inheritance."

2   *Declaration.* See "Let me count the ways (to apply CSS)."

3   *Selector.* Review "Let me count the ways (to apply CSS)."

4   *Value.* Look over "Let me count the ways (to apply CSS)."

5   *Inline.* See "Keeping you inline."

6   *Linked.* Take a look at "External style sheets."

7   *Functions.* See "JavaScript."

8   *Event handlers.* Check out "Dynamic HTML."

9   *XSL (Extensible Stylesheet Language).* Check out "Extensible Stylesheet Language (XSL)."

10   *DOM (Document Object Model).* Look over "Document Object Model (DOM)."

Beefing Up HTML

Though your knowledge of HTML will be essential for your Web-development career, you may soon find you hit a wall. What I mean is, if you stick to using only HTML content, your pages won't be as dynamic or interactive as the sites the big guys have.

Maybe, when you surf the Web, you don't care for interactive content, so you've decided not to include it in the sites you're building. Many of your site's visitors, however, have come to expect it. You can add features such as a searchable product database with Extensible Markup Language (XML) or customize your page's content based on user preferences with JavaScript. With dynamic HTML (DHTML), you can add fun features, such as rollover buttons. In addition to the end-user benefits, you may also save yourself a lot of development time by using Cascading Style Sheets (CSS).

Throughout this chapter, I reference several standard HTML tags such as the `<HEAD>`, `<BODY>`, `<TITLE>`, and `<H1>` tags. If you need to brush up on these and other basic HTML tags, refer to Chapters 10 and 11.

Understanding Cascading Style Sheets

Cascading Style Sheets (CSS) are comprised of some newer HTML codes that enable authors to create lists of formatting information called *style sheets*. Style sheets can affect as little as a letter or all the content on every page in your site.

One of the key benefits of style sheets is their ability to save you development time because you can make formatting changes in one location that cascade throughout an entire document or an entire Web site. Say you have a 30-page Web site. You want to use a background image on each page, and you've chosen Arial as the font for all your text. If you apply formatting the non-CSS way, you have to apply these settings to each page individually. Later on, if you decide to switch your font to Times New Roman, you have to make that change one page at a time as well. However, you don't have to do it that way with CSS.

Using CSS, you can create a style sheet with all your formatting information and save it as a separate file. You can then link each page to the style sheet, and the pages pull their formatting information from it. If you want to change your font, you have to change it only on the style sheet, and the change then *cascades* to all the pages linked to it. That can save you enough time to catch your favorite TV show!

Although style sheets can add consistent design and cut down on development time, in practice they're far from perfect. The two main browsers sometimes interpret style sheets differently, so make sure you test them in several versions of each browser.

You don't need to know every style sheet code in existence for the exam. The key things for you to know are the differences between inline, embedded, linked, and imported style sheets. You must also be able to glance at a simple style sheet and have an idea of the formatting it will render, which isn't as difficult as it seems. If you see the words *font, red,* and *Arial* placed very near to each other in some code, you can pretty much rest assured that this code is specifying a font of Arial.

There are currently two versions of CSS — CSS1 and CSS2. The first version is concerned primarily with formatting documents — fonts, colors, and so on. CSS2 adds more capabilities to CSS1, such as more precise control over the positions of items on pages and the ability to support media types (such as specific printers). This chapter — and the exam — focus on CSS1. All you need to know about CSS2 for the test is in this paragraph.

A large inheritance

Inheritance is a crucial part of CSS — the ability of changes to flow throughout many pages at the same time is what makes them cascade, hence the name. If you create a style sheet to affect every page in your Web site, it will. Style sheets can override the default formatting information in every Web page and paragraph. For example, using regular HTML, you specify the background color information on each page individually. With a style sheet, you can define the color one time on a separate page — a linked style sheet — and have this background color override any existing background color settings you defined on individual pages. If you want to change the font of the text on one page only, you can create a style that applies only to that page — an embedded style sheet — and overrides any other font settings you may have applied to individual paragraphs.

Style sheets can also override themselves. If you use an embedded style sheet to set a page's font to Arial, for example, you can still set the font of a specific paragraph or sentence on that page to Times New Roman by using an inline style sheet. Or, if you create a linked style sheet in which you set a font to apply to every page, you can override the font settings on only one page using an embedded style sheet, or override the font in just one paragraph using an inline style sheet.

Let me count the ways (to apply CSS)

You can incorporate style sheets into a Web site in several ways. You can create style sheets within your existing HTML pages or as separate documents that link to your HTML pages. The method you choose depends on the results you're seeking.

Style sheet parts and pieces

The syntax of the code you use to write style sheets is different from regular HTML syntax. You don't need to know all the details about style sheet syntax for the exam (the nitty-gritty information on writing style sheet code is covered on the CIW Site Designer exam). However, you will likely be tested on the key parts of a style sheet. Style sheets are made up of several components that combine to create a *rule* — the combination of all the formatting instructions that apply to a specific item. Maybe you want your text to appear blue, 14 points in size, and in the Helvetica font. When you combine all three of these formatting specifics in a style sheet, you've created a rule about how text will display. Before you can really get into working with style sheets, you need to understand five key CSS terms:

- ✔ **Selector:** The HTML item you're applying formatting to.
- ✔ **Property:** The property of an item being changed. If you're changing the size of a font, you're changing the size property.
- ✔ **Value:** The size, color, and so on that you're applying to a property.
- ✔ **Declaration:** The combination of a property and its assigned value.
- ✔ **Rule:** The combination of the selector, property, and its value.

In Figure 14-1, you can see how the first four elements in the preceding list combine to form a rule.

Figure 14-1:
Parts of a
Cascading
Style Sheet
rule.

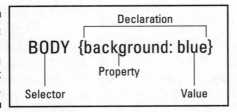

Unlike with regular HTML, you don't usually capitalize most style sheet code. Neither regular HTML nor CSS is case sensitive, though, so you can type it however you like.

Keeping you inline

An inline style is one you apply within a line of HTML code. It applies only within the tag you apply it to. A style applied within one paragraph <P> tag, for example, applies to only that paragraph. Inline styles are used primarily to override embedded and external style sheets. Unless you need to override another style, you may as well use regular HTML to format items — it's just as effective. On the other hand, style sheets are becoming the preferred way to apply formatting (the W3C is encouraging the use of CSS) so the ProsoftTraining folks want you to know about the basics of each type of style sheet for the exam.

You can apply an inline style with either the <STYLE> tag by itself (you use the <STYLE> tag to create all types of styles) or using the <SPAN> and <STYLE> tags together. (The <SPAN> tag creates a section in a document in which you can apply formatting that spans the entire section.) If you want to create an inline style using only the <STYLE> tag, you insert the style sheet code within a standard HTML tag. If you use the <SPAN> and <STYLE> tags together, you don't have to encase the style sheet code within an HTML tag.

In the following example, I'm changing the background color of a section of my document to pink. Because I'm using the <SPAN> tag, I don't include the background color information within the document's <BODY> tag. The <SPAN> tag also allows me to apply a background color to just one part of the background (something you couldn't do with regular HTML).

```
<SPAN STYLE="background: pink">Content goes here</SPAN>
```

If you apply an inline style using the <STYLE> tag without the <SPAN> tag, you have to apply it within a standard HTML tag:

```
<BODY STYLE="background: pink">
Content goes here.
</BODY>
```

The preceding code makes the background of the entire page pink. (With CSS, you can use color names and standard red, green, and blue color values instead of the hexadecimal color codes you have to use with regular HTML.)

For the exam, you need to know that an inline style sheet can override embedded and external style sheets (discussed in the following sections), and embedded style sheets can override external style sheets. Remember that you can apply an inline style by placing the <STYLE> tag inside a regular HTML tag — you insert the <STYLE> tag inside the <BODY> tag, for example, to apply some formatting to the body section of the document — or, alternatively, you can use the <STYLE> tag with the <SPAN> tag, which allows you to apply formatting to a specific section of the document.

Embedded styles

An embedded style sheet is placed in the <HEAD> section of an HTML document and applies formatting to only that document. After you apply an embedded style, it applies to the entire document unless an inline style overrides the embedded style. Embedded styles begin with a <STYLE> tag and are placed between comment tags, like this:

```
<HEAD>
<TITLE>Embedded Styles</TITLE>
<STYLE>
<!--
H1 {color: red; font-family: Arial; font-size: 16pt}
-->
</STYLE>
</HEAD>
```

The preceding code specifies that whenever you insert the <H1> tag in a document, all the text contained within the opening and closing <H1> tags will render on the screen as red text in the Arial font and will be 16 points in size.

External style sheets

External or *linked* style sheets are some of the most commonly used. They make applying formatting to many pages at once a much easier task. They also help you make all the pages in a site look consistent.

External style sheets are also called linked style sheets because you hyperlink external style sheets to the HTML pages in which you want to apply formatting. You create an external style sheet by creating a separate document with your formatting rules. This file can be saved with most any file extension, but normally authors save these files with a .css extension. After you create the style sheet document with all your formatting information, such as the one shown in Figure 14-2, you place code in the <HEAD> section of each Web page you want to apply this formatting to. The code creates a link between the style sheet and the Web page.

Figure 14-2:
Code for an external style sheet.

```
mystyle - Notepad
File  Edit  Search  Help
H1 {color: navy; font-family: Times New Roman; font-size: 18pt}
BODY {background: pink; color: black; font-family: Arial}
```

The code in Figure 14-2 renders the styles shown in Figure 14-3.

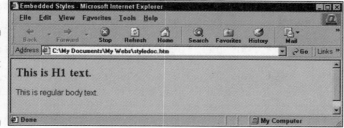

Figure 14-3:
Document
using an
external
style sheet.

Imported style sheets

Imported style sheets are a lot like external style sheets except they don't work as well and people don't use them very often. However, you'll be expected to know what they are for the exam, so here goes.

Imported style sheets, like external style sheets, require you to create a separate file that contains your rules. You import it into your HTML pages using the code `@import url (filename.css);` in the `<HEAD>` section of your HTML document:

```
<HEAD>
<TITLE>Embedded Styles</TITLE>
<STYLE type="text/css">
@import url(mystyle.css);
</STYLE>
</HEAD>
```

The idea behind imported style sheets is that they enable you to link to a style sheet that resides outside your Web site. The reality is, they don't work well in many versions of browsers, particularly Netscape Navigator 4.0, so you probably won't use them in real life. For the exam, just remember that when you see `@import` used with the `<STYLE>` tag in the `<HEAD>` section of a page, it's an imported style sheet.

For more details about Cascading Style Sheets, check out *Cascading Style Sheets For Dummies,* by Damon Dean (published by Hungry Minds, Inc.).

JavaScript

JavaScript is an object-based scripting language created by Netscape that enables you to add dynamic effects and interactivity to Web pages. Scripting languages are like programming languages in that you can use them to make things happen that are beyond the reach of plain HTML. A key difference between them, though, is that a program created in a programming language can run by itself, but a script created in a scripting language must be attached to or embedded in an HTML document to work.

Object-based just means that the JavaScript language contains predefined objects that authors can use when writing JavaScript. This cuts down on development time because you don't have to define every simple object (such as a window or a document) before you can use it in a script.

Compared to a programming language, JavaScript is relatively easy to learn. It also requires no compiling (see Chapter 8 for more on compiling) and doesn't rely on one operating system or another — it's platform independent. Development time is pretty short with JavaScript, too — especially compared to the time you'd have to invest to create similar effects in a programming language.

Some of the effects you can create in JavaScript include

- ✔ (Annoying) pop-up windows and message windows
- ✔ Cookies (see Chapter 7 for more on cookies)
- ✔ Real-time clocks on Web pages
- ✔ Simple Web-based mathematical computations
- ✔ Fun (but primitive) games that play within a browser
- ✔ Image and text rollovers — content that changes when your mouse rolls over certain areas on a page

JavaScript syntax

The first thing you need to know about JavaScript syntax is that JavaScript code is embedded into HTML documents using the <SCRIPT> tag, like this:

```
<SCRIPT>
(JavaScript code goes here)
</SCRIPT>
```

Although the Foundations exam commonly displays JavaScript code embedded into an HTML page using only the <SCRIPT> tag at the beginning, in real life, you normally include the LANGUAGE attribute within the <SCRIPT> tag, like this:

```
<SCRIPT LANGUAGE="JavaScript">
(JavaScript code goes here)
</SCRIPT>
```

Using JavaScript functions

JavaScript, like other scripting languages, uses *functions* to perform its magic. If you were talking to a Prosoft employee, you might hear him define functions as, "stand-alone, reusable segments of program code that are not part of an object." Yikes. In other words, a function is the code that tells objects what to do and how to do it. Much better.

For a good explanation of all the major JavaScript functions, check out _JavaScript For Dummies,_ 3rd Edition, by Emily Vander Veer (Hungry Minds, Inc.). For the exam, there are three functions you need to know about — `alert()`, `document.write()`, and `prompt()`. You don't need to know the specifics of which comma goes where or whether to insert semicolons; if you're presented with some code on the exam that contains one of these functions, you just need to know what the function does.

- `alert()`: Creates an alert box or pop-up message that displays whatever text you want. Figure 14-4 shows an alert box with the message `You will soon pass the Foundations exam!`

- `prompt()`: Displays a dialog box that prompts the visitor to enter some information into a text field. Figure 14-5 shows a `prompt()` box that asks users to type in their names.

- `document.write()`: Displays or _writes_ text on a Web page. Though you can easily place text on a Web page using HTML, the `document.write()` function can work with other functions (such as the `prompt()` function) to dynamically display data on the page.

Figure 14-4:
A
JavaScript
alert dialog
box.

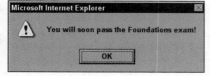

Figure 14-5:
A
JavaScript
prompt box.

Dynamic HTML

Some people think *dynamic HTML* (DHTML) is a language of its own — independent of HTML. It's not. DHTML is just a combination of several technologies — including HTML — that you can use together to make pages more dynamic and interactive. If you look at the definition of JavaScript in the preceding section, you'll notice that DHTML and JavaScript seem similar. That's because you can do many of the same things in each — and JavaScript is part of DHTML.

The technologies that combine to make DHTML are

- ✔ Hypertext Markup Language (HTML)
- ✔ Cascading Style Sheets (CSS)
- ✔ Scripting (as in JavaScript)
- ✔ Document Object Model (DOM), which I cover later in this chapter

Dynamic HTML utilizes *event handlers* to make pages interactive. An event handler specifies how an object or program reacts to user actions or user events.

Using DHTML, you can create rollover effects, move images around the screen, and create text effects, among other things. DHTML, like JavaScript, is *client-based*, meaning that the user's browser reads and runs the code.

Extensible Markup Language (XML)

The main purpose of Extensible Markup Language (XML) is to allow the exchange of data between programs. Exchanging data is key to e-commerce sites, search engines, and other non-Web oriented businesses.

The ability to assemble field-like data (kind of like a database) is what makes XML a great tool for exchanging data between programs. With XML, you can create your own tags. You can also define the meaning of content on your page. If you type your name on an HTML page, for example, you can specify how the name looks, but nothing in the page can let someone know it's a name. With XML, though, you can create a <NAME> tag and place your name inside it. The XML document specifies the meaning of the text — you've essentially created a name *field*.

Because you use XML to create your own language, XML is considered a *meta language* — a language you use to create languages. Like HTML, XML is a derivation of SGML, which I discuss in Chapter 9.

To help you truly understand how to code XML, I'd need to spend a lot more than a few pages on it. For the exam, however, you're not going to need to know how to code XML.

You do need to know two key characteristics of an XML document:

- ✔ **It must be well formed.** A well-formed document contains code that's created using the proper syntax, and it contains a Document Type Declaration (DTD). (DTDs are covered in Chapter 9.) Every comma, bracket, or colon must be in the correct location (just like in every other language you might use).

- ✔ **It must be valid.** For an XML document to be valid, it must contain a DTD. Yes, containing a DTD is part of being a well-formed document, but when an XML document is being judged for *validity,* the information is analyzed more closely. The DTD tag is where you define all your XML tags — what they're called, how they're structured, and how they work together. An XML document is valid only if all tags are completely and correctly defined. You can't use a tag called <NAME> in the body of your XML document, for example, unless you define it first in the DTD.

With HTML, DTDs are optional. With XML, DTDs are required.

Extensible Hypertext Markup Language (XHTML)

You may want to think of Extensible Hypertext Markup Language (XHTML) as a hybrid of two great things: XML and HTML. (It's kind of like the peanut butter and chocolate in a Reese's Peanut Butter Cup — except it doesn't taste as good.) Actually, XHTML is an application of XML that uses HTML abilities — namely the hypertext. In fact, XML 1.0 closely resembles the 4.01 version of HTML. XHTML makes documents adhere to the syntax rules of XML.

Just like with HTML 4.01, there are three flavors of XHTML:

- ✔ **XHTML Transitional:** Allows the use of either older, standard HTML tags or CSS for formatting

- ✔ **XHTML Strict:** Requires the use of CSS only for formatting

- ✔ **XHTML Frameset:** Required for frames pages

Extensible Stylesheet Language (XSL)

Extensible Stylesheet Language (XSL) is a language that allows you to format XML documents. With an XML document, you must use either CSS or XSL — or you can use CSS and XSL together. You don't need to know any XSL code for the exam — just know that XSL is the language used to format XML documents and that it may be combined with CSS.

In real life, XML is not experiencing heavy usage at this time. That's because the predominant browser versions don't fully support all of XML's capabilities. Its usage is expected to increase as more users move up to later generations of the browsers. One reason is that it allows you to integrate data into your documents more efficiently than if you were using a traditional database for data integration. For more information on XML, check out *XML Bible,* 2nd Edition, by Elliotte Rusty Harold (published by Hungry Minds, Inc.).

Document Object Model (DOM)

The Document Object Model (DOM) is a model that includes standard definitions for common objects and the relationships that exist between them. This means objects, such as the document or the window, are already defined, and their relationship — the document is inside the window — is already defined as well. The DOM is used with scripting languages, such as JavaScript or VBScript, in both browsers.

The drawback of using the DOM at this time is that each browser has its own version of it, so it's not completely cross-platform and vendor-neutral — yet. If you're using one browser and try to access a page that was created using another browser's DOM, you may get an Undefined Object Error or the page may render as plain text. However, the big two browsers, Netscape Navigator or Microsoft Internet Explorer, usually do their best to render the page correctly, and if you're using either one, you probably won't know anything is amiss.

Prep Test

1 **Which of the following is not a feature of CSS2?**

A ○ More precise control over positioning of page elements
B ○ The ability to detect the e-mail address of every visitor to a Web page
C ○ The ability to support specific media types, such as printers
D ○ None of the above

2 **What is the CSS term for the combination of a selector, property, and value?**

A ○ Description
B ○ Link
C ○ Declaration
D ○ Rule

3 **Which of the following is not placed in the `<HEAD>` section of an HTML document?**

A ○ Embedded style sheet
B ○ Imported style sheet
C ○ Inline
D ○ Linked

4 **Which of the following is true regarding JavaScript?**

A ○ JavaScript is an object-oriented programming language.
B ○ JavaScript must be attached or embedded within an HTML document.
C ○ JavaScript is a combination of several technologies that make pages more interactive.
D ○ All of the above

5 **Which of the following JavaScript functions can create a dialog box that asks the user to enter data in a field?**

A ○ Alert()
B ○ Prompt()
C ○ Document.write()
D ○ None of the above

6 **Which of the following is not a component of DHTML?**

A ○ Cascading Style Sheets (CSS)
B ○ Document Object Model (DOM)
C ○ Extensible Markup Language (XML)
D ○ Hypertext Markup Language (HTML)

7 **Which of the following statements is true regarding DHTML?**

A ○ DHTML stands for Database Hypertext Markup Language.

B ○ DHTML code is compiled and run on the server.

C ○ DHTML is read and run on the client-side.

D ○ DHTML must always be placed within the `<SCRIPT>` tags.

8 **In order to function, an XML document must be**

A ○ Valid

B ○ Well-formed

C ○ Compiled

D ○ Both A and B

9 **Which of the following best fits the description "a language used to create other languages"?**

A ○ Meta language

B ○ Markup language

C ○ Programming language

D ○ Scripting language

10 **Which of the following is not supported through the DOM:**

A ○ Placing small text files on the end user's computer for reference at a later time

B ○ Opening a new browser instance and controlling its functions

C ○ Creating pop-up windows

D ○ Altering the address bar of the browser

Answers

1 **B.** The ability to detect the e-mail address of every visitor to a Web page. CSS2 allows more precise positioning of items on Web pages and can support specific media types. *See "Understanding Cascading Style Sheets."*

2 **D.** Rule. The combination of a selector, property, and value is a rule. *Review "Let me count the ways (to apply CSS)."*

3 **C.** Inline. Inline style sheets are placed within a line of HTML code. *Take a look at "Keeping you inline".*

4 **B.** JavaScript must be attached or embedded within an HTML document. *Look over "JavaScript."*

5 **B.** Prompt(). The prompt() function creates a dialog box that prompts the user to enter some data. *See "Using JavaScript functions."*

6 **C.** Extensible Markup Language (XML). DHTML is comprised of CSS, HTML, scripting, and the Document Object Model (DOM). *See "Dynamic HTML."*

7 **C.** DHTML is read and run on the client-side. *Check out "Dynamic HTML."*

8 **D.** An XML document must be well formed (contain proper syntax and a DTD) and valid (the DTD must correctly and fully define all XML tags you use). *Review "Extensible Markup Language (XML)."*

9 **A.** Meta language. *Check out "Extensible Markup Language (XML)."*

10 **A.** Placing small text files on the end user's computer for reference at a later time; this is a function of a cookie. *Read "Document Object Model (DOM)."*

Part IV
Networking Fundamentals

The 5th Wave
By Rich Tennant

"It's okay. One of the routers must have gone down and we had a brief broadcast storm."

In this part . . .

The networking fundamentals portion of the exam is by far the hardest part for most test-takers. Because it makes up 40 percent of the exam, you may need to spend most of your study time committing the information in Part IV to memory. But if you're really new to networking, beware. This part of the book covers what I would call an intro to networking. After you know all the information in these chapters, you'll know just enough to be dangerous. In real life, you need to master skills beyond what's covered in this book to administer a network. The point is just to get you familiar enough with how networks and servers work so that you can avoid server-to-Web site communication problems.

To really be ready for the test, you should know the purpose of common network protocols and which software products use which ones. You need to know the connection speeds of various types of Internet connections. You should be able to decide which server products are best in different scenarios and the steps you should take to make a network more secure. Good thing that's what the chapters in Part IV cover! The Open Systems Interconnect Reference Model is another item you need to be very familiar with. The OSI/RM was my least favorite topic to study, so I've tried to make it as simple to understand as possible.

By the way, I've talked to many other test takers, and they, too, have experienced the FOSI/RMP (Foundations OSI/RM Phenomenon). The phenomenon is that you experience one of two extremes — feast or famine — when you take the Foundations exam. I got at least three or four questions on it, but others got none at all. In fact, this phenomenon applies to several topics covered in Part IV. You may leave the testing booth thinking, "Why did I take the time to study XYZ networking topic when I didn't get a single question on it?" But don't think I'm advising you take Part IV seriously just because I have a sadistic interest in watching you squirm. The truth is that the exam pulls questions from a large pool of topics, so as with all mysteries, you just never know. The safest bet is to study it all because you need to know your networking backwards and forwards if you want to continue your career in this field.

Chapter 15

Getting Familiar with Networks

● ●

Exam Objectives

▶ Understanding what a network is and how it works

▶ Explaining the relationship between servers, workstations, and hosts

▶ Describing standard network topologies

▶ Identifying major network operating systems and their clients

● ●

*U*nless you live in a cave (in which case you shouldn't be taking the Foundations exam), you probably already have a working knowledge of what a network is. Basically, a network connects two or more computers so that they can share resources and files. The growth of networks was key to the expansion of the Internet. Prior to the 1980s, most networks were based on the mainframe model — a large, powerful computer connected to a bunch of computers called dummy terminals. Suffice it to say that dummy terminals enabled users to log on to a central computer and use its processing power for various functions, but they didn't have any real juice to work on their own. Back in the '80s, mainframe networks were pretty expensive, so only larger companies could afford to have networks.

When the client/server network model evolved, many more companies could take advantage of networking capabilities. The client/server model was less expensive and allowed more flexibility than the mainframe system because each terminal has its own processing power. With independent processing power, users can customize their terminals to accommodate their needs without having to affect any other terminals. In this chapter, I cover the basics of how networks came to be and how they work.

Although having access to a network might help you understand some of these key concepts, it is by no means necessary for you to understand the concepts covered in this and the other chapters on networking.

Quick Assessment

Networks defined

1   The three main components of a network are _____, _____, and _____.

2   _____ networks use diskless or dummy terminals connected to a powerful, central computer.

3   The _____ network model relies on all the computers within a network to share the work and is often referred to as distributed computing.

4   Network _____ is the ability to easily add network devices.

5   Web-based networking uses both the _____ and _____ server models.

6   In a _____ network, each computer acts as a client and a server.

Networking categories

7   Each point on a network is called a _____.

8   A _____ topology requires that all computers share the same cable.

9   A _____ stops a signal from echoing or endlessly running back and forth on a cable.

10 A _____ topology requires a hub that connects all of the nodes on the network.

Answers

1 *Protocols, transmission media, network services.* See "Knowing Your Networking Architecture."

2 *Mainframe.* Take a look at "Introducing Mainframe Networks."

3 *Client/server.* Read "Introducing client/server networks."

4 *Scalability.* Check out "Introducing client/server networks."

5 *Mainframe, client/server.* Look over "Web-based networking."

6 *Peer-to-peer.* Review "Peeking at peer-to-peer networks."

7 *Node.* Take a look at "Server-based networks."

8 *Bus.* Read "Taking the bus."

9 *Terminator.* Review "Taking the bus."

10 *Star.* Check out "Becoming a star."

Being a Node-It-All: Important Network Terminology

You probably think of a *network* as a group of computers all hooked up so that information can be shared. That's not a bad definition. To get technical, though, you should probably change the word computers to nodes. *Nodes* are what make networks work. Okay, nodes, cables, software, and a bunch of duct tape are what make networks work. Okay, maybe not the duct tape, but whatever. You get my drift — you can't really understand networks without knowing what a node is.

In Geek, a node is any connection point on a network. Translated from Geek to English, a node is a piece of hardware (like a computer or a printer) that's attached to a network and that can process or pass on information and transmissions to other nodes on the network. Nodes include

- **Servers:** Servers, including mail servers, print servers, file servers, database servers, and Web servers, are (really powerful) computers that dedicate their existence to performing certain tasks. A mail server takes care of the entire network's incoming and outgoing e-mail needs. That's all. Nothing else. Not even if you ask real nice. However, a network may have a second (or even third) backup mail server that helps out and takes over if the primary mail server goes down. The backup mail server can't play back up for a Web server, though. (If you're still not sure what I'm talking about here, don't worry; I discuss servers all throughout the rest of the chapter. Check out "Introducing client/server networks.")

- **Workstations:** In the workplace, most people hear the word *workstation* and think of the computer they sit down in front of, log on to a network with, and do work on. That's right — a workstation is a computer that's attached to a network, which is why they're also commonly called terminals, clients, or, more simply, computers. Unlike servers, workstations aren't necessarily dedicated to any specific tasks. You can do a whole bunch of stuff with them.

- **Peripherals:** A peripheral is a piece of hardware that isn't required in order for a computer to function. The most common network peripheral is a printer. Detach the printer from your workstation, and you can still play solitaire until the cows come home. Trying to print something is a different story.

Now here's where things get tricky. A workstation is just a fancy word for computer, right? Well, then a server is a workstation, too, because servers are fancy computers. The difference is that servers are dedicated to specific tasks and individual workstations can do a variety of tasks. To cause even more confusion, servers, workstations, and peripherals are all nodes. To cut through the confusion, I've decided to simplify things for you:

- When you see the word *node*, think workstation, which means computer.

- When you see word *server*, think about how it's dedicated to specific duties.

- When you see the word *peripheral*, think about extra stuff you buy to make your computer cool — a new mouse, a new printer — any hardware that's not required to make your computer run.

In addition to some standard networking terms, you need to know what several common servers do:

- **Mail servers:** Send, receive, and store e-mail.

- **File servers:** Allow users to share files.

- **Print servers:** Allow users to share printers.

- **Web servers:** Host Web sites on intranets, extranets, and the Internet. (For more on intranets and extranets, see Chapter 3.)

The information in this section applies to *client/server* networks. In a mainframe network environment, workstations (usually called *terminals*) don't have the juice to do much of anything. The mainframe computer (which is as close to a server computer as you can get) does all the work. To find out more about mainframe networks, read "Introducing Mainframe Networks."

Knowing Your Networking Architecture

Network architecture is just a fancy term that describes how a network is put together. It's like building architecture — each building will have a unique layout and some unique features, but all buildings will include walls, floors and ceilings — and probably bathrooms. A *network* consists of two or more connected computers that share data (like that file you've been passing from department to department) and/or resources (such as printers and fax capabilities). Networks make it much easier to share data with others. In the early days of computing, you had to save a file on a disk and take it or send it to the recipient (this technology is jokingly referred to as sneakernet).

You need to know about two different network types: mainframes and client/server networks, but remember that mainframe networks and client/server networks come in a variety of flavors. Luckily, I discuss mainframes and client/server networks (and the flavors you need to know) in the following pages. All networks, no matter what their architecture, flavor, or proclivity, are comprised of three main components:

The legacy of CICS

Customer Information Control System (CICS) is a common application that's used on mainframe networks. In fact, CICS, which was written in the COBOL programming language, still lives and breathes in many computer applications on networks because they have been passed down in generation after generation of software upgrades.

In fact, CICS is called a *legacy application* for this very reason. Remember the Y2K computer glitch? CICS programs were at the heart of that whole fiasco because servers using CICS were configured to read only the last two digits of any year, which makes it possible for a computer to interpret the year 2000 as the year 1900 — not a good thing for a computer that holds important records.

You don't need to know much about CICS except that, over the years, it has become the basis for the most common customer transaction applications in use. You also need to know about that little oops-a-daisy that was caused by the CICS programming glitch.

✔ **Protocols:** The rules of communication between two or more computers

✔ **Transmission media:** The hardware (including the cables, routers, and computers themselves) that's necessary for sharing information and resources

✔ **Network services:** The resources (such as files, printers, and Web pages) shared via the network

Introducing Mainframe Networks

For the Foundations exam, you need to have a good idea of the role that mainframe networks played in the history of networking, but you don't need to know the down-and-dirty technical details (say that three times fast) of how mainframes work.

The first networks were called mainframe networks — they used *diskless* or dummy terminals connected to a powerful, central computer. Mainframes are expensive and somewhat inflexible — if the main computer goes down, the whole network collapses like a row of dominoes, and the whole company might as well go home because no one can do any work.

I should probably explain that just because these computers were called dummy terminals doesn't mean that they were dumb, but you know that already. After all, you're a *For Dummies* reader, and you're not dumb.

Mainframe computing is often called centralized computing because of this less-than-healthy (dare I say needy?) relationship between dumb terminals and servers. Most of the work on a mainframe network is done on the back end, the server-side of the network. In other words, the dummy terminals are just windows into the big mainframe computer. Say you're sitting at your computer writing the great American novel (instead of doing your real work). The operating system you're using (probably Windows), application software (probably Word), and hard drive space you use to save your work actually reside on the mainframe — not on your computer. Figure 15-1 illustrates the mainframe model.

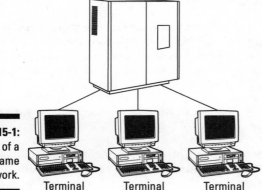
Mainframe

Terminal   Terminal   Terminal

Figure 15-1:
A model of a
mainframe
network.

Mainframes are still in common use, especially at universities and other large institutions because these organizations have invested a lot of time and money into creating and maintaining them. These days, though, when companies decide to invest in networking resources, they're more likely to choose client/server or Web-based networks (which I discuss in the following sections) because mainframes present two key liabilities that can create network congestion:

✔ One part of the network (the back-end or server computer) does most of the work while the other computers sit and stare at users vacantly like extras in *The Stepford Wives*.

✔ Because individual terminal computers don't have hard drives, saving files can be a real chore. The packets of data the server and clients send back and forth are quite large, taking up a great deal of bandwidth.

To retrieve information in a mainframe environment, a terminal makes a request, or *query*. The mainframe processes the query, structures the data, and sends it to the terminal, where you've been waiting patiently for a couple of seconds. This all happens so quickly — when there are no glitches — that you probably don't realize what's taking place in the background.

Introducing client/server networks

By the late 1980s, many offices had started utilizing the *client/server* network model, which consists of computers with their own processing capabilities that don't depend on a central mainframe computer. (For more of an introduction to clients and servers, see Chapter 3.)

The client/server networking model is also called a distributed model because it doesn't rely on one computer to do all the processing as a mainframe network does. Instead, each workstation has its own processing power — the server can focus more on sharing network resources and files. Client/server networks also reduce network congestion by distributing work between the client (the front end) and the server (the back end).

Of course, in any network, the back end still does a little more work than the front end, but the client/server model isn't nearly as lopsided in its workload distribution as the mainframe model. In a client/server environment, the server/back end stores and presents information, and is often a more powerful computer than the front-end workstations.

The client/server model has several advantages when compared with mainframe networks:

- **Reduces network traffic:** The client/server model has the ability to cut down on network traffic by distributing the workload — no one machine has to do all the processing.

- **Increases network flexibility:** Unlike a mainframe environment, a client/server network allows you to use computers with different operating systems — UNIX and Windows 2000, for example — which gives the administrator increased flexibility.

- **Improves scalability:** Scaling a network as needs change over time is much easier with a client/server model than in a mainframe environment. You can add new network devices more easily because each terminal is more independent. And you can remove devices just as easily.

Bottlenecks are specific points in a network where traffic gets jammed up — the file server or the router, for example. This backup slows traffic flow across the network. Distributed networks like the client/server model help clear up bottlenecks.

Web-based networking

Web-based networking is a networking environment that connects users to remote resources via the World Wide Web. In other words, if you get on the Internet using your home computer and access data stored on your company's server, you're taking advantage of Web-based networking. The Web-based networking model is a hybrid of both the mainframe and client/server models:

✔ **Web-based networking is like the mainframe networking model:** Say you're accessing your company e-mail account from your home computer. Your terminal is actually acting much like a dummy terminal. You type in your logon name and password, which are sent to the company's server. The server processes your name and password and, if you enter the correct logon data, formats your e-mail messages and returns the data to your terminal (also called a workstation). This is a good example of how Web-based networking mimics the mainframe model — the server is taking on the bulk of the workload, with your terminal performing only minor formatting.

✔ **Web-based networking is like the client/server networking model:** Say you search the Web to find the user manual for your printer. (You think your dog ate the manual that came with the printer.) You find a PDF version of the manual on the vendor's Web site and download the PDF file. The way your computer and the server are working together more closely mimics the client/server environment model — the server is simply processing a request from your terminal, and the software on your terminal (Acrobat Reader) formats the data to display on your screen.

Knowing Your Network Categories

Network categories are like subcategories of the client/server networking model. Network categories are general descriptions of how clients are connected to the server(s). When I teach a Foundations class, students often confuse network categories with network topologies (which I cover in the "Network Topologies" section, later in this chapter). Topologies are much more specific than categories — specific hardware is connected in specific ways to create a certain type of local area network (LAN), for example. I've found that it helps to think of network categories as network sizes (small, medium, and large). Technically, that's not 100 percent accurate, but it helps get the point across. For example, it's not always the case that a peer-to-peer network is smaller than a server-based network, but usually it is.

Peeking at peer-to-peer networks

In a *peer-to-peer* network, each computer acts as a client *and* as a server. How does that work? Each computer or workstation behaves as a client computer most of the time. You sit at it and type letters and so forth. But each workstation also has some server software installed on it so that any machine can access data from any other machine on the network. Figure 15-2 shows a peer-to-peer network.

Figure 15-2: A model of a peer-to-peer network.

Workstation   Workstation   Workstation   Workstation

Peer-to-peer networks are generally used with a network that contains ten or fewer computers. For a workstation to act as a server, the workstation has to have the right type of software installed.

For the exam, you need to know the names of some common software products used in a peer-to-peer network:

- ✔ Artisoft LANtastic
- ✔ Microsoft Windows 95/98/ME
- ✔ Microsoft Windows for Workgroups
- ✔ Novell NetWare Lite

Server-based networks

Server-based networks are client/server networks that involve one or more machines that act specifically as servers and other machines that act only as clients. Each point on a network (including computers, printers, and other hardware) is called a *node*. A node can be a server, a workstation, or even a printer or scanner (but it doesn't include keyboards, mice, or other peripherals that connect to only one machine).

The server software in a server-based network can keep track of users' activities, like who's playing solitaire and who's accessing which information. A server-based network keeps data more secure than a peer-to-peer network because server-based networks can store all shared data in a central location — on the server — instead of being spread over several computers as in a peer-to-peer network. When data is stored in many places, each of those locations can act as an access point for unauthorized users. Figure 15-3 shows a server-based network. To find out about commonly used server software, check out Chapter 16.

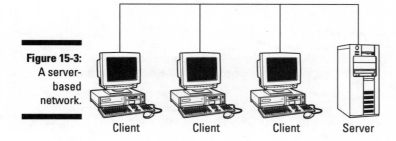

Figure 15-3:
A server-based network.

Client   Client   Client   Server

Enterprise networks

An enterprise network often combines peer-to-peer and server-based network models. According to ProsoftTraining, an enterprise network provides connectivity among all nodes in an organization, regardless of their geographic location, and runs a company's mission-critical applications.

Mission-critical applications are the programs that must run to keep the day-to-day operations of a business going.

In other words, enterprise networks are big, bad networks that can connect different types of networks. Enterprise networks feature two key characteristics:

- ✔ They support multiprotocol systems (you can find out more about network protocols in Chapter 21).
- ✔ They support multiple architectures — topologies. (Topologies are covered in the following sections.)

Network Topologies

Network topologies are ways to configure networks. Network topologies are a lot like house plans — each house (at least all the ones I've ever seen) contains a bathroom, a kitchen, and some bedrooms. How these rooms are laid out in relation to each other, however, is what makes each house unique. Networks almost always use network interface cards, cables, and servers, but the way they're connected varies. Just as there are general categories of house architectures — Cape Cod, Tudor, or ranch — network layouts fall into one of several categories — bus, star, ring, mesh, and enterprise. Just as the house a buyer chooses is based on several factors, the network topology a company chooses is based on several key factors. The three key factors you need to know for the exam are

- **Types of applications used:** The types of programs a company needs to run, such as e-mail programs or Web server programs that might affect the entire network.

- **User requirements:** The needs of the users on a network. Several people within the company, for example, may be responsible for creating and updating a company Web site. Those users would most likely need FTP ability to upload their Web pages from within the company network.

- **Network architecture:** The physical environment the network will be placed in. If an office has 100 rooms spread over 20 floors, for example, this requires a more robust topology than an office with two employees who work in the same room.

Taking the bus

A network laid out in a bus topology has a common cable or backbone that all computers (nodes) are connected to. Bus topologies follow the principle that data can be transferred as if it's riding a bus. Huh? You know how a bus makes all its assigned stops, even if no one is getting on or off? When one node on the network sends out data, the data is broadcast to all nodes on the network, even if the data is really only heading to one of the nodes. This might seem like a real waste of broadcast energy, but only the destination computer actually reads the data. Figure 15-4 illustrates a bus topology.

Each end of the cable in a bus topology is capped off with a terminator. A *terminator* stops a signal from echoing or endlessly running back and forth on the cable. If some data can't find the machine it's headed to (for example, maybe it has the wrong address), the data can't just keep running back and forth along the cable — it would create excess network traffic that could slow down all the other traffic.

The pros of the bus topology include

- It's cheap.
- It's easy to operate.
- It's reliable.
- It uses very little cable.

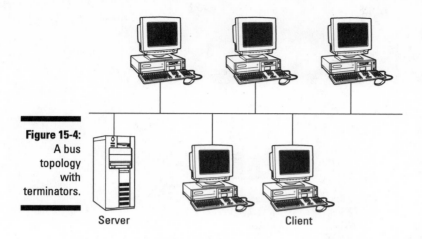

Figure 15-4:
A bus
topology
with
terminators.

Server   Client

The cons include

  ✔ If the cable breaks at some point, the entire network can be affected.

  ✔ It can be difficult to isolate where the problem is.

  ✔ The network slows down during high-traffic time periods.

Becoming a star

The nodes in a star topology are all connected by cables that run through a central device, such as a hub. (A *hub* is a boxlike device that contains several
"holes" for computer cables to plug into. For more on hubs, see Chapter 20.)
The cables running from each node to a central device look kind of like a star,
hence the name. Because each computer has its own cable running into this
central device, the device has to accommodate another cable every time the
need arises to add another computer. Because devices such as hubs can accommodate only a set number of connections, it's more difficult to add nodes to a
star network than a bus network. Often the network has to be completely reor-
ganized to accommodate more nodes. Figure 15-5 illustrates a star topology.

Here are some of the pros of the star topology:

  ✔ One area of the network can go down, and it won't affect the rest of the
    network because each node has its own cable running to the hub.

  ✔ It's easy to expand (within the limits of the central device).

  ✔ It's easy to configure.

  ✔ The network management is centralized around the hub or other device.

The main con is that if the hub goes down, the whole network goes down.

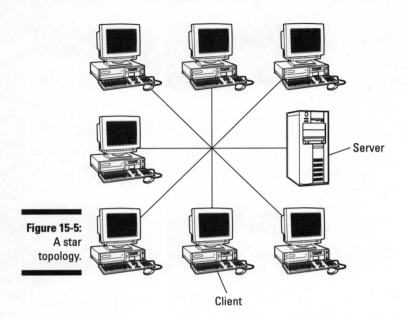

Figure 15-5:
A star
topology.

Server

Client

Giving you a token ring of my affection

A *ring topology* is laid out with a cable running from computer to computer, like a big ring. When a computer sends out a message, it passes a *token* (a specific kind of electronic signal) to the next computer. The token continues to get passed from computer to computer until it finds its destination. (If the token can't find the destination computer to deliver the message to, it loops back around and goes back to the computer that sent it out.) Figure 15-6 illustrates a ring topology.

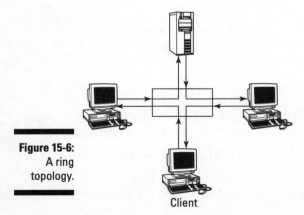

Figure 15-6:
A ring
topology.

Client

The nodes in a ring topology are connected through a multistation access unit, or MAU. A MAU is similar to a hub, but it's made just for ring topology networks. (For more on MAUs, see Chapter 20.)

The pros of the ring topology include

- ✔ All nodes have equal access to data.
- ✔ It can handle heavy traffic well.

The cons include

- ✔ Expansion or reconfiguration can affect the whole network — the ring the token is traveling on has to be broken (at least temporarily) to add or subtract nodes on the network.
- ✔ Isolating problems can be hard because a problem in any section of the ring can affect data transfer over the whole network.
- ✔ If one node fails, the whole network may fail.

Hybrid networks

A hybrid network can combine the bus, star, and ring topologies in any combination or hybridization.

Because each topology has its own unique benefits, two or more topologies are often combined to create a hybrid network. The most common types of hybrids — and, coincidentally, the ones you need to know for the exam — are star bus and star ring:

- ✔ **Star bus:** In this hybrid, two or more star topologies are connected using a bus topology cable commonly called a trunk. The trunk acts as the network's backbone — the main level in a network that all other smaller networks are connected to. Figure 15-7 illustrates a star bus topology.
- ✔ **Star ring:** In a star ring hybrid, two or more star topologies are connected by using a MAU.

The pros of hybrid topologies include

- ✔ They're easy to expand.
- ✔ The whole network usually isn't affected if one node goes down.
- ✔ They can support high-speed media — material that allows data to flow through or be stored on it.

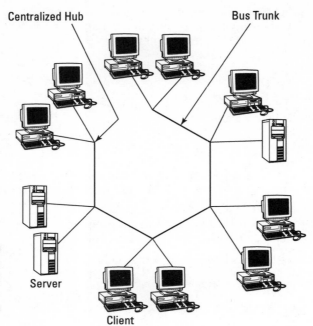

Centralized Hub   Bus Trunk

Figure 15-7:
A star bus
topology.

Server

Client

The main con: If a hub or a MAU is used (and it almost always is), either can malfunction — preventing all the computers connected to that hub or MAU from communicating.

Making everything mesh

A *mesh topology* connects nodes on a network to provide multiple paths for data to travel. The idea is to create redundancy. Yes, I mean that in a good way. In networking terms, *redundancy* is a back-up method for data transmission. The idea is that if there's a traffic jam or a bridge out, data can choose an alternate route to reach its destination.

Here's how it works. Say you have your average, everyday star topology. You can add extra cabling that links every node to every other node (instead of just linking every node to the hub, as is usually the case in a star). In a mesh topology, every node is always connected to every other node on the network, so data always has a good chance of reaching its destination even if one part of the network is down. Figure 15-8 illustrates a mesh topology used with a star bus hybrid.

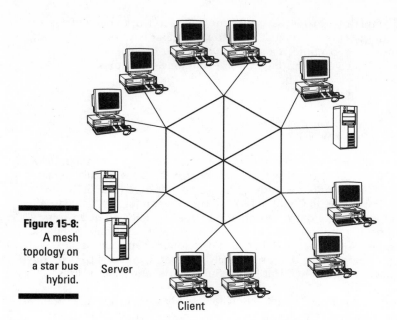

Figure 15-8:
A mesh
topology on
a star bus
hybrid.

Server

Client

One of the pros of a mesh topology is that if one part of message path is down, another may be available to transmit the message. The main con is that the extra hardware that's required to maintain a mesh topology can be expensive.

Network Operating Systems (NOS)

A Network Operating System (NOS) is just that — an operating system. But a NOS runs on every machine in a network, not just on an individual PC. To turn a computer into a server, you must first install a network operating system. After it's running a NOS, a computer can accommodate the server software that performs specific server duties, such as a sharing files, printers, e-mail, and so on.

The full NOS runs on a server, and a NOS-compatible client program (often a slightly different version of the NOS) runs on all clients in the network. Popular network operating systems include UNIX, Microsoft Windows NT and 2000, and Novell NetWare. Many network operating systems can work together — this is called interoperability.

For the exam, you don't have to actually know how to work in any of the network operating systems — you just have to be familiar with their names and any key features. For example, if a question asks you "Which of the following is not a Microsoft server operating system?" and one of the choices is *Red Hat,* you need to know that's the answer.

Using a UNIX NOS

UNIX is a very popular multiuser operating system developed in 1969. UNIX is the most popular NOS used on servers that host Web pages, mostly because UNIX uses the TCP/IP protocol suite for data transmission. (TCP/IP is discussed more thoroughly in Chapter 18.) Another reason for UNIX's general popularity is that the standard version of it is free. Also, it's an open source program — meaning the code that creates the operating system is available to anyone who wants to access it. Because developers can easily access and alter the programming code that created UNIX, several versions of UNIX have been developed, including Red Hat Linux, Sun Solaris, and Digital UNIX.

For the exam, you don't need to know how to actually work in a UNIX system — which screen takes you to which area, for example — but you do need to know three key UNIX terms:

- ✔ **Kernel:** The most basic, essential part of an operating system, the kernel always resides in memory.
- ✔ **Shell:** The shell is a text or command-based interface.
- ✔ **X Windows:** A graphical user interface (GUI), X Windows was developed to simplify working in UNIX.

Using a Microsoft Windows NOS

Many computer users are familiar with the Microsoft Windows operating system. Well, not surprisingly, Microsoft also provides a plethora of NOS options. Although you don't need to know much about Microsoft NOSs for the exam (the Foundations exam, after all, is supposed to be platform-independent), you should know that Microsoft NOSs support both the TCP/IP protocol suite and a proprietary protocol called NetBEUI. (For more on TCP/IP, NetBEUI, and other networking protocols, see Chapter 18). The Microsoft NOSs you need to be able to recognize for the exam are included in the following list:

- ✔ Windows NT is the basis for all the other Microsoft server operating systems in this list. NT isn't based on DOS (Disk Operating System), whereas the client operating systems Windows 3.1 and 95/98 are.
- ✔ Windows 2000 Server replaced Windows NT 4.0.

  ✔ Windows 2000 Professional replaced Windows NT Workstation.

  ✔ Windows 2000 Advanced Server replaced Windows NT Server Enterprise Edition.

The Microsoft network operating systems use the TCP/IP protocol suite to communicate.

Using a Novell NetWare NOS

Novell created one of the earliest, popular network operating systems with NetWare. NetWare is the most widely installed family of network operating systems on local area networks (LAN). (For more on LANs, see Chapter 20.) The current version of the Novell software is NetWare 5. NetWare 5 offers more flexibility than earlier versions, including its use of TCP/IP as its networking protocol. Prior to NetWare 5, the software used a proprietary protocol suite — IPX/SPX — that made it less compatible with other network operating systems. I cover network protocols in detail in Chapter 19.

Prep Test

1 The rules of communication for networks are known as

A ○ Web pages.

B ○ Resources.

C ○ Protocols.

D ○ Drivers.

2 Which network model has a dumb terminal at the client side?

A ○ Mainframe

B ○ Mesh

C ○ Client/server

D ○ Peer-to-peer

3 Identify which network model reduces network congestion by distributing the work between the front end and the back end.

A ○ Mainframe

B ○ Centralized

C ○ Proxy

D ○ Client/server

4 Which of the following is not considered a node?

A ○ Keyboard

B ○ Scanner

C ○ Printer

D ○ Server

5 What kind of network provides connectivity among all nodes in an organization, regardless of their geographic location, and runs a company's mission-critical applications?

A ○ Digital network

B ○ Enterprise network

C ○ Business network

D ○ None of the above

6 **Annie is installing a simple star topology network for a small business. NetBEUI will be the protocol implemented. Annie has purchased category 5 cable and network cards. What else does Annie need?**

A ○ Router

B ○ Node

C ○ Module

D ○ Hub

7 **Which network topology utilizes a Multistation Access Unit (MAU)?**

A ○ Bus

B ○ Centralized

C ○ Ring

D ○ Terminator

8 **Which of the following is a valid type of hybrid topology?**

A ○ Star bus

B ○ Star ring

C ○ Flower ring

D ○ Both A and B

9 **Which network topology connects nodes on a network in a way that provides multiple paths for data to travel on to provide redundancy?**

A ○ Bus

B ○ Star

C ○ Hybrid

D ○ Mesh

10 **Red Hat Linux is a version of which network operating system?**

A ○ Windows NT

B ○ UNIX

C ○ Novell

D ○ Windows 2000

Answers

1 **C.** Protocols. *Check out "Knowing Your Networking Architecture."*

2 **A.** Mainframe. The mainframe model includes one big, powerful computer (the mainframe) and one or more dumb terminals that provide access to the mainframe's processing capabilities. *Review "Introducing Mainframe Networks."*

3 **D.** Client/server. Take a look at *"Introducing client/server networks."*

4 **A.** Keyboard. Peripheral devices such as keyboards aren't network nodes. *Review "Server-based networks."*

5 **B.** Enterprise network. The key phrases in this question that tell you it's an enterprise network are "connects all nodes on a network," "regardless of geographic location," and, the biggest tip-off, "mission-critical applications." *See "Enterprise networks."*

6 **D.** Hub. The type of cable, network cards, and protocols (NetBEUI) are irrelevant. Because Annie wants to create a star network, she has to have a hub. Read *"Becoming a star."*

7 **C.** Ring. A ring topology is the only one that uses a MAU. Look over *"Giving you a token ring of my affection."*

8 **D.** Both A and B. You could combine any of the standard topologies to create a hybrid network. *Check out "Hybrid networks."*

9 **D.** Mesh. A mesh topology reinforces network paths and connects every node to every other node. *Take a look at "Making everything mesh."*

10 **B.** UNIX. *See "Using a UNIX NOS."*

Chapter 16

How May We Serve You?

Exam Objectives

▶ Describing the function and components of a Web server

▶ Describing the functions of various types of servers: file, print, mail, media, and others

▶ Understanding how servers use TCP/IP

▶ Describing how to transmit text and binary files using popular Internet services, including the Web and e-mail

▶ Defining the pros and cons of common server products

Servers can serve up anything that can be accessed from a computer: files, printers, graphics, e-mail, videos, and sound files. Several server products can be, and often are, installed on one computer. The types of servers installed on a network may depend on the needs of the people using the network and the types of data that need to be shared across it. Many software manufacturers offer all-in-one application packages that install several server services at once.

The goal of this chapter (and this portion of the exam) is not to make you an expert server administrator. My goal is to make sure you familiarize yourself enough with server functions so you can integrate many of them into Web sites. If you're creating a Web site that has any type of back-end data integration, you need to understand how to work with various servers to make this integration seamless.

Even if you're only incorporating back-end functions to your site that are as basic as enabling visitors to fill out a form and e-mail it to someone, you may encounter server issues. In real life, almost every time I put up a site that has back-end data involved, I almost always need to make at least a minor adjustment or two to get things going.

Quick Assessment

The role of servers

1 A(n) _____ is a computer with software installed on it that enables specific services on that machine.

2 A(n) _____ allows many users on a network to share a printer.

3 _____ extensions identify the file types of e-mail attachments.

4 The settings configured on servers and operating systems that restrict or allow access to system resources are known as _____.

5 A(n) _____ server can help cut down network traffic and enhance security.

6 A(n) _____ server automatically forwards messages to everyone on a given distribution list, and is sometimes called a reflector.

7 A(n) _____ server allows users to search for information distributed across a network from one central access point.

8 A(n) _____ server resolves domain names to IP addresses.

Popular server products

9 The most widely implemented Web server on the Internet is the open source software called _____.

10 _____ is the Microsoft Web server package that usually runs on Windows NT/2000 machines.

Answers

1 *Server.* Review "What Do Servers Do?"

2 *Print server.* See "Sharing Files and Printers."

3 *MIME.* Check out "Finding out how to MIME."

4 *Permissions.* Look over "Setting permissions on Web servers."

5 *Proxy.* Read "Discovering the proxy server."

6 *Mailing list.* Check out "Getting to know mail servers."

7 *Catalog.* See "Using catalog servers."

8 *DNS.* Review "Understanding DNS servers."

9 *Apache.* Look over "All about Apache."

10 *Internet Information Server (IIS).* Check out "Internet Information Server (IIS)."

What Do Servers Do?

Some people think of servers as powerful computers — the kind that networks use to store and share data. But that's only partially correct. Servers are just computers unless they have the server software installed on them.

Server software enables servers to provide server services. That's why you might hear a network geek (and I use that term with the utmost respect) talk about "Web server service" or "mail server service" being down. When a server's down, it doesn't necessarily mean that an actual machine is down (although it can), but rather there's a hiccup in the server software.

The first servers did little more than store and share files in central sites and databases. Though these services are very important, servers these days are much more powerful. They allow users to access many more types of files than in the past and allow users to access much larger files than before.

Sharing Files and Printers

File and print servers provide access to — you guessed it — files and printers. File and print servers are probably the most common types of servers out there and are often combined as one service. Here are a couple of things you might want to know about these servers:

- **File servers serve up files only.** If you try to access a file created in a program your computer doesn't have installed, you won't be able to open it. The file server only serves up files — it doesn't give workstations access to applications.

- **Print servers manage something called the *print queue*.** A print queue is the area where printing requests are stored until the printer processes them.

Most network operating systems — including Windows NT/2000 and UNIX — use the LPR/LPD protocol combination to send print requests to network printers. The LPR issues the requests, and the LPD executes them.

Introducing Web Servers

Web servers are also known as HTTP servers because Web servers use Hypertext Transfer Protocol (HTTP) to deliver Web pages. (That's why you see http:// preceding Web addresses.)

You may have read in other parts of this book that the Web uses the TCP/IP suite to deliver Web pages. It does — HTTP works within TCP/IP. If TCP/IP confuses you, Web and network protocols are covered in detail in Chapter 18.

Finding out how to MIME

Web servers, of course, can return HTML documents. They can also work with many other types of files including image files, PDF files, and multimedia files like video and sound files. Web servers can actually download any type of file — but a browser won't necessarily know how to render every type of file. A browser can only display a document correctly if it can tell what kind of file it's trying to display. The labeling system most programs on the Internet use to identify file types is the MIME system.

MIME (short for Multipurpose Internet Mail Extensions) is the system that Web servers and clients use to communicate about the types of files they're transferring (kind of like a method of shorthand that everyone agrees to use). Based on the name, you might think MIME works with e-mail, which it does. But MIME is also used to identify nearly all types of files — HTML, plain text, images, and multimedia.

When a Web server uses MIME types to label a document's file type, client browsers can determine how to display the document correctly. If a Web page needs a plug-in, the client browser can tell what kind of plug-in it needs based on the page's MIME type.

The MIME classification system labels files with general headings and then gets more specific. For example, if a Web server sends out an HTML document, the server uses the MIME system to classify the document as a text file in the HTML format or text/html. If it were a PDF file, it would require the Adobe Acrobat Reader application to open; it would be labeled application/x-pdf.

Even though browsers also use MIME, you're most likely going to get exam questions about MIME's use with e-mail. MIME identifies the file type of an e-mail attachment. If you can't open an attachment and you know your computer has software installed that should understand how to open that type of file, the most likely problem is a missing or incorrectly configured MIME type.

Are you using an alias?

An *alias* is a nickname or alternate name. Using an alias allows flexible URL mapping, which means a server administrator can get creative with the locations of Web folders and their names so that they are easier to find.

Say you want to store some HTML documents on the company server for employees to access with their browsers. The server administrator sets up a folder (directory) called *documents* on the server for you to save your documents in, but this folder is a subfolder of the *data* folder, which is a subfolder of the *company* folder. If users tried to access this folder via their browser software, they'd have to type in `www.yourcompany.com/company/data/documents.htm`, which is waaay too long for people to remember. Instead, the administrator sets up a virtual directory with an alias name of *docs* — a pretend folder with a shorter file path that's mapped to the real folder your documents are in. The address of the virtual directory is much easier for users to remember — they can just type `www.yourcompany.com/docs` to access your documents.

Setting permissions on Web servers

An important feature of most Web servers is the ability to restrict user access to files, folders, and directories through the use of permissions.

Permissions are the settings you configure on servers and server operating systems (or both) to restrict or allow a user access to system resources. Permission settings usually include the ability to restrict these three areas:

- **Read:** Gives users permission to see a file's content. Most Web pages are saved in folders with *read* access so everyone can read the files stored in them.

- **Write:** Gives users permission to save to a file on the server. If you want to save your Web site on a Web server, for example, you have to save it in a folder that gives you *write* access.

- **Execute:** Gives users permission to run programs on the server. If you utilize CGI scripts (which I cover in Chapter 17), the scripts must be saved in a folder that has execute permission, because CGI scripts are like small programs.

Web servers can also be configured to deny access to whichever resources you'd like, depending on a network's needs, as well as the needs of the people who use it.

Network operating systems often offer the ability to set permissions such as read, write, and execute as well. When a Web server is installed on a server operating system, either or both of them may contain permission settings, and it's a good idea for those settings to match. If the settings conflict, the network operating system settings usually override the Web server settings. For example, the network administrator creates a folder on the server in which you're supposed to save your Web site. She sets up a server account for you on the FTP server so you can type in your logon information and transfer files to the server. (For more on FTP, see "Using FTP servers," later in this chapter.) She forgot, however, to go into the network operating system and assign write access to that folder, so you won't be able to save any files there after all.

Adding password protection

Most Web documents are available to everyone — users just need to know the correct Web address to access a page. Open access to a document is called *anonymous* access. Sometimes, Web authors place data on a page that they only want certain people to see. Changing the read, write, or execute settings on the network operating system won't help; in order for the Web pages to be seen at all, the files have to be saved in a folder with read access. Because you only want certain people to see the pages, you can password-protect your Web pages using one of two main methods:

- ✔ **User accounts:** The server administrator creates accounts on the server that require the user to know the correct name and password to access private pages. For example, maybe your company has several employees who work from home. The company has set up some Web pages that contain customer account information so home-based employees can access this data. Because only employees should see the data, the server administrator sets up accounts with specific names and passwords that a user must know before accessing these Web pages. The administrator can also allow home-based employees access to other system resources — such as printers — using this protection method.

- ✔ **Database:** A database containing valid user names and passwords is connected to the private pages. Using a database to limit Web-page access is often a better choice because it is easier to restrict access to just given pages and visitors can't access any other system resources. For example, your company allows customers to access their account information such as which product they last ordered and the date of their last order. Because customers won't have any foreseeable need to access other resources on your company's network, using a database to protect the private information would be a better choice than creating user accounts.

Regardless of the method you use to password-protect private data, data on a network is always vulnerable to *password sniffing* — hackers using programs to figure out your passwords. To help prevent this nefarious activity, make sure you encrypt passwords as they're being transferred between the client and the server. (For more on network security, see Chapter 21.)

Logging: The record-keeping kind, not the lumberjack kind

Most servers can keep records of all the requests they receive in a server log. A server log is a record of which users access or try to access which resources and helps administrators determine which users are using which resources and which resources are most popular. Server logs store three main types of data:

- ✔ **Access data:** Keeps track of clients that are making requests. Logs can make a note, for example, of the 50 times you sent the same document to the printer and jammed it up.

- ✔ **Referrer data:** Tracks the Web pages visitors are viewing when making a request to access Web pages. You can determine where people came from — such as a Web page that might have an ad for your company.

- ✔ **Error data:** Logs errors that occur during user requests. For example, the reason you kept sending the same document to the printer is because you kept getting an error message. A log can keep track of all error messages (and help you defend yourself when the administrator barks at you for jamming up the printer — "It wasn't my fault, I kept getting goofy error messages, so I kept resending the document.")

Getting to Know the Plethora of Other Server Types

Servers are abundant — you'll use many different types of servers in a work environment or while setting up a Web site. This section introduces several types of servers you may encounter and the key information you need to know about each one to pass the Foundations exam. You'll get test questions, for example, that outline a specific network problem, and you'll need to choose which type of server would solve the problem. In real life, most Web designers don't have complete authority over which servers a company network will use. If you know the key features of each server, though, you can take advantage of some of them on your Web site — or at least you won't be confused when someone mentions one of these server types.

Discovering the proxy server

A *proxy server* acts as a middleman between an organization's network and the Internet. When part of a network, all transmissions between user machines and the Internet (in either direction) go through the proxy server.

Proxy servers help cut down on network traffic because they can cache (pre-store) Web pages. Proxy servers also increase security because they can mask IP addresses and act as firewalls. The following list explains these and other key features of proxy servers:

- **Caching:** Proxy servers can *cache* (make a copy and store it on the server) commonly used Web pages so the server doesn't have to access the Internet and download the page every time someone on the network wants it. For example, if many people on a network frequently visit a certain Web page (such as www.jokes.com), the proxy server can be configured to download and cache (copy) the www.jokes.com home page every morning (or whenever you want). When employees open their browsers and type in www.jokes.com, the proxy server doesn't have to download the page — it just sends the copy that's already stored. Sometimes a server is setup for this purpose only — called a caching server.

- **IP masking:** Proxy servers hide, or mask, the IP addresses of computers on a network. (For more on IP addressing, see Chapters 3 and 19.) The proxy server essentially replaces a computer's IP address with the address of the proxy server, making it appear as if an Internet request originated from the proxy server even though it didn't. Masking an IP address helps keep all nodes within the network protected from unauthorized outside access.

- **Logging:** Proxy servers can log user requests, as discussed in the "Logging: The record-keeping kind, not the lumberjack kind" section, earlier in this chapter. Proxy server logging primarily tracks user access to the Internet — which users are visiting which Web sites, how much time they spend visiting each Web site, and so on. Logging can also help evaluate network performance.

- **Firewall protection:** Firewalls are software and/or hardware additions to a network that help prevent unauthorized users from entering a network. (For more on firewalls, see Chapter 21.)

- **Filtering:** Filtering is a process that allows network administrators to deny access to certain URLs and IP addresses to any or all clients in the network. Filtering can be based on users' logon names or the IP address of the machines they're using or their computer's name. If a user named Jack Black, for example, spends half the day visiting the www.jokes.com Web site, the proxy server administrator can configure the proxy server to deny the Jack Black user account access to the www.jokes.com Web page.

- **Enhanced administration:** Enhanced administration allows network administrators more control of company servers through logging, monitoring, reporting, and configuring tools. The enhanced administration features provided by proxy server software can also enable administrators to administer company servers from a remote location (from home, for example).

When a network is utilizing a proxy server for Internet access, every client program (every unique program installed on every workstation) that needs to access the Internet must be configured to connect through the proxy server — which means every e-mail program and browser program on every machine.

Using FTP servers

FTP servers allow users to transfer files between computers (even if they're on separate networks) using FTP — file transfer protocol. Authors usually use FTP to publish Web sites because it's easy to use and very efficient at transferring large files.

Users sometimes use FTP to transfer files they might otherwise attach to an e-mail. For example, files that are over 2MB in size may transfer from point A to point B much more quickly using FTP than if they were attached to an e-mail. (That's because FTP is more efficient at transferring large files than e-mail programs are.)

Most Internet server packages include an FTP server. When most administrators configure an FTP server, they usually set up the FTP server with user names and passwords to restrict FTP access to qualified users.

Getting to know mail servers

This may come as a shock, but mail servers allow the transfer of — you guessed it — e-mail. Mail servers use at least two protocols to transfer e-mail — one to send it and one to receive and store it. E-mail is sent out via Simple Mail Transfer Protocol (SMTP). (UNIX uses a sendmail program, which utilizes SMTP.) Mail servers also use either Post Office Protocol (POP) or Internet Messaging Access Protocol (IMAP) to receive and store. For more information on e-mail protocols, see Chapter 5. Mail servers are also in charge of sending, receiving, and storing e-mail attachments. Mail servers use the MIME system (covered earlier in this chapter) to determine file types of many things, including the file type of an e-mail attachment. Two other methods for identifying file types you need to know for the exam are

- **Uucoding:** (Pronounced "you-you-coding.") Developed and run originally only on UNIX, Uucode is the precursor to MIME and was one of the first methods that allowed the transmission of non-text files with e-mail. Like MIME, it identifies and labels file types, but MIME is more efficient, so it has largely replaced Uucode.

- **BinHex:** BinHex originally was used on Macintosh machines to attach non-text files to e-mail. Unlike MIME and Uucode, BinHex applies its own formatting to the attached file and adds its own extension (.hqx).

ProsoftTraining likes to ask a question about the format or method you should use to send an executable file (executable files have an .exe extension and are small applications or executable program) with an e-mail. In real life, I wouldn't normally send one attached to an e-mail; I'd probably send it with FTP, but the Prosoft folks are looking for *Binhex* as the answer. I don't know why they think that's important for you to know (you probably won't use it in real life), but make a mental note of it.

Getting friendly with mailing list servers

Mailing list servers (also called reflectors) automatically forward messages to everyone in a given distribution list. Mailing list servers are SMTP mail servers (like the ones I describe in the previous section) that are configured specifically for mailing list functionality. L Soft LISTSERV is an example of a site that offers access to a public mailing list server. Private companies may add a mailing list server to their network if they want to automatically forward messages to everyone in a given group — all managers, for example, might automatically receive all memos concerning employee productivity. The person who sends out the productivity memos would send them to a specific mailing server address instead of sending the memo to each individual manager.

Mailing lists are a great way for people with e-mail addresses scattered all over the Internet to keep up-to-date on a certain topic. Every message sent to the mailing list's e-mail address is processed by the mailing list server and sent to everyone on the list.

Don't confuse an autoresponder with a mailing list server. Although both automatically send out messages, an autoresponder is a feature that enables users to automatically respond to all messages sent to a specific address. People often use the autoresponder feature to send a reply to everyone who e-mails them while they're on vacation or out of the office. A mailing list server is a specific type of server software that an administrator configures on a network.

Knowing your news servers

News servers are similar to mailing list servers in that they both allow people located in various places to read all messages regarding a certain topic. They use different technologies and slightly different methods to achieve the same goal. A news server uses Network News Transfer Protocol (NNTP) to transfer newsgroup messages. A news server isn't a standard part of most company networks — only companies that are in the Internet news delivery business are likely to have newsgroup servers running on their networks.

Usenet, which is now part of the Internet, was originally an independent network of newsgroups on various topics. These newsgroups can be accessed like messages on a public bulletin board — users look around until they find a topic that interests them.

People can usually subscribe — automatically receive new messages as other members post to the newsgroup — if they want. Newsgroup messages are sent to subscriber e-mail accounts — as long as their Internet service provider (ISP) supports newsgroups.

A newsgroup's name is its network address. Newsgroups use a hierarchal system like this: `biz.ecommerce` is a business newsgroup about e-commerce; `rec.sport.basketball` is a recreational newsgroup about the sport of basketball. To see a list of a wide variety of newsgroup topics, check out Google Groups at `groups.google.com`.

There are three main types of newsgroups you need to know about for the exam:

✔ **Public:** Public newsgroups are open to everyone with no restrictions on content. Google's newsgroups at `groups.google.com`, for example, are public, unrestricted newsgroups.

✔ **Moderated:** All messages are reviewed before they're posted in moderated newsgroups to ensure they're relevant and inoffensive. For example, a company that creates a newsgroup for customers to share information might want to review each message to make sure someone doesn't unfairly criticize the company or its products. (Of course they might remove messages with legitimate criticism, too, but that's their prerogative.)

✔ **Private intranet/extranet:** Some newsgroups are accessible only to users on an intranet/extranet. Private newsgroups can help organize input from various people working together on a specific project. They're often password-protected. As with any password-protection, it's more secure if passwords are encrypted.

Introducing certificate servers

Certificate servers help keep information on a network secure using encryption technology. Encryption is a method of scrambling information so it's unreadable to anyone without the correct descrambling code. Say a user wants to send a file securely over the Internet (or over any network). With a certificate server, the user can use a program that will generate and attach a digital key — an encrypted string of text — to the file. Only a user with a key that knows the encryption algorithm can open the file. Certificate servers create and validate these keys.

Digital certificates not only help prevent unauthorized users from accessing a file, but also help prove a party's identity. I cover digital certificates and encryption more completely in Chapter 21.

Directory servers

Directory servers create directories of all resources on a network so authenticated users can easily access them. Companies commonly use directory servers to create and store lists of employee e-mail addresses and other pertinent information — often called an address book.

Directory servers enable users in many locations — maybe multiple company offices spanning a large geographical area — to access data from a central location. Using a directory server is a very efficient way to share data because each employee doesn't have to keep a running list of employee data.

For the exam, you need to know two protocols that directory servers can use:

- ✔ **X.500:** X.500 was an early protocol used by directory servers to manage user and resource directories. It has had limited success on the Internet because although it has many capabilities, X.500 is difficult to use.

- ✔ **Lightweight Directory Access Protocol (LDAP):** LDAP is based on X.500, is easier to use, and is compatible with TCP/IP, so it's more efficient at allowing access within networks and over the Internet.

Using catalog servers

A catalog server allows users to access resources such as databases and other files. A catalog server is similar to a directory server with one key difference: A catalog server allows users to use one central access point to search for data distributed across a network.

Both directory and catalog servers allow users to search through stored data, but while a directory server stores data in one central location (on one server), a catalog server allows data to be stored in many locations. Maybe a company has a large wide area network (WAN), with offices located in every state. Instead of having employee phone numbers and addresses stored on one server at a company's headquarters, for example, each branch office of a company could store employee data on its local servers; a catalog server would still allow employees all over the country to search through the employee data — even though it's not all stored in one location, as is the case with a directory server.

Using media servers

Media servers allow the transmission of streaming media. Streaming audio and video files can start playing before the whole file loads — only the first part of a song or video clip has to load before it can start playing. The rest of the file continues to load in the background. Streaming media is sometimes said to travel in real time — a media server uses a buffer to cache part of the media file as it downloads.

The protocol often used on media servers is UDP (User Datagram Protocol). Companies can use media servers to enable video conference calls, distribute video and audio files, and broadcast live video feeds such as newscasts. RealNetworks RealSystem, Netscape Media Server, and Microsoft NetShow are common media server products.

Introducing transaction servers

Transaction servers enable transactions such as credit card processing to take place. E-commerce sites often use transaction servers to update all the databases associated with a transaction at the same time.

The following example is included just to give you an idea of how a transaction server can update information in several databases (don't worry about knowing the actual steps of a transaction or how to install a transaction server for the exam):

1. You're having such a great experience with this book, you go online to www.dummies.com to purchase another *For Dummies* book.

2. Not only does your credit card information need to be processed and stored (possibly in one database), but the online store's inventory also needs to be updated (subtract one book), and the company needs to add you to its preferred customer database.

3. If one part of the transaction can't be completed (maybe the book's out of stock), then the transaction server has been configured to cancel the whole transaction so it doesn't charge your credit card.

   Whew! That's a lot going on — and a transaction server takes care of it all.

Understanding DNS servers

Domain names and IP addresses are matched up or resolved using DNS. *DNS* (Domain Name System) is a giant collection of databases called domain name servers that match up the domain name you type with its numeric IP equivalent. (Because both the domain name system and domain name servers use the initials DNS, I spell out which one I'm referring to throughout this section.)

Large networking organizations like ISPs usually have their own domain name servers. Individual companies may also have their own domain name servers, especially if they utilize intranet Web sites — Web sites accessible only to users within an organization's network. (I discuss intranets in Chapter 3.)

DNS is comprised of two main components:

✔ **Name server:** The name server resolves Web addresses to IP addresses. A company with a domain of `www.myabcdcompany.com`, for example, might have an IP address of `64.122.97.001`. (For an explanation of how domain name servers resolve IP addresses to domain names, see Chapter 3.)

✔ **Name resolver:** If the domain name server can't find the Web address requested, the name resolver kicks in and searches other domain name servers on the same hierarchal level. Say you type in `www.hungryminds.com` and the default domain name server your ISP used doesn't recognize the name. The name resolver kicks in and starts searching other domain name servers that contain `.com` addresses until it finds the correct one.

You may get test questions on the three categories of domain name servers:

✔ **Root:** Root-level domain name servers contain databases with the locations of all top-level (primary) servers. There are only about a dozen root-level domain servers out there, and they're updated daily to keep track of any new top-level domain name servers.

✔ **Primary:** Primary or top-level domain name servers keep track of Web sites with top-level domains — for example `.com`, `.edu`, and `.gov`. (See Chapter 3 for more on top-level domains.)

✔ **Secondary:** The secondary level acts as a backup for the primary server. It receives a copy of the information on the primary server and helps provide fault tolerance and helps carry the load.

Implementing DNS on Windows and UNIX

Windows NT/2000 server comes with a DNS component so that network administrators can easily set up DNS within a company intranet. You can also register a company's domain name server with a top-level domain registrar and have the domain name server act as a primary DNS on the Internet.

A feature called the *name daemon* allows a UNIX computer to act as a domain name server. Most of the DNS servers on the Internet are on UNIX systems.

This will go on your permanent record

The information saved on DNS servers is stored in DNS records. DNS records contain routing and resolution data — information on how to get to the Web sites and servers that are listed in their DNS records. (For more on routing and resolution, see Chapter 19.)

Although many types of information (records) about a domain can be saved, only a few are needed for a DNS server to find a site. Table 16-1 lists the DNS records you need to know for the exam.

Table 16-1	Common DNS Record Types
DNS Record Type	*Its Function*
Address (A)	The most commonly used record, the address (A) lists the IP address of a specific machine.
Canonical Name (CNAME)	An alias or nickname for a host. The first section of a URL specifies the server name. Most URLs begin with www, but obviously not every server can have that same name. The CNAME is the server nickname the www is standing in for. (For more information on domain name structure, see Chapter 3.)
Name Server (NS)	Identifies which DNS servers may be used for a given domain name.
State of Authority (SOA)	Specifies which DNS server is the primary server (best one) for a given domain.
Mail Exchanger (MX)	Indicates the mail server the domain uses.

Getting to Know Common Server Products

Many companies make server software, but there are a few that are the most popular. For the Foundations exam, you need to know the pros and cons of several server products; you get scenario questions asking you to choose which server product you would choose in a given situation.

All about Apache

The Apache Web server, originally created for UNIX systems, is the most popular Web server on the Internet. And to even increase the Apache popularity, now there are versions that run on Windows NT/2000. Apache is an open source program. *Open source programs* are free, the code is open and accessible to anyone, and they are usually the result of several developers collaborating. Though no one vendor is responsible for creating the Apache Web server, you can find out more about it at www.apache.org. Here are some of the pros of Apache:

- Apache is well tested, has been around a long time, is used by a lot of people, and has had plenty of time to get any bugs out.

- Apache is free because it's an open source program.

- Apache is easily accessible and will work on virtually any operating system — Windows, UNIX, OS2. If you get questions on the exam concerning which operating systems you can run Apache on, assume you can run it on all operating systems — you won't be presented with some bizarre, off-market operating system.

- Apache has a huge informal support network. With so many people using Apache, there are many Web sites that offer informal product support.

The following are some cons:

- Apache is a Web or HTTP server only. For other server services you have to install other server products such as an FTP server or a mail server.

- Apache doesn't have any formal support. Because no organization sells and profits from Apache, no organization offers a formal help desk or customer support service.

Internet Information Server (IIS)

Internet Information Server (IIS) is a popular server package from Microsoft (www.microsoft.com) that provides server services for Windows NOSs. This free server product supports HTTP, FTP, SMTP, and NNTP protocols; certificate, transaction, and catalog servers; and Active Server Pages (ASP). IIS is now in its fifth generation (IIS5) and is integrated into Windows NT/2000/XP servers. The following lists IIS's pros:

- It's free. You can download it at no charge.

- It has many integrated servers. It can combine many types of servers in one package.

- It has formal support. Microsoft offers fee-based product support.

- It has easy administration. You can administer IIS remotely and with a GUI interface.

Here are some cons:

- It has been only moderately tested. Though it's been around for a while, IIS is still not considered to be as reliable and bug free as Apache.

- It is OS dependent. IIS works best only on Windows NT/2000 servers. (Although in real life it can sometimes work on other operating systems, for the exam, assume it only works on Microsoft systems.)

Personal Web Server

Personal Web Server is a miniature version of IIS, more or less, though it only performs Web server functions. It runs on Windows 95/98/Me, and its main function is to allow administrators to test Web pages and server-side scripts on a development machine, though it can host Web sites in a network environment.

Lotus Domino Series

The Lotus Domino Series is a server package from IBM (www.ibm.com) that includes the most common server services: HTTP, FTP, and SMTP. Lotus Domino servers run on nearly any operating system, including mainframe systems, and offer solid database support using Java servlets. The following lists the pros of the Lotus Domino series:

- Lotus Domino integrates many servers and combines many types of servers in one package.

- Lotus servers can serve applications over intranets and the Internet.

- Lotus servers are flexible to use. They can work on nearly any operating system, including mainframes.

- You get formal support — Lotus is owned by IBM, which offers standard product support.

Here are some cons:

- Lotus Domino servers have only been moderately tested. Though the Lotus Domino series is a solid product, it hasn't been around and tested as long as Apache.

- Lotus servers are not as commonly used as some of the other servers; consequently fewer employee candidates will be familiar with it.

Lotus Go Web server

Lotus Go is a quick startup Web server with a lot of the same functionality as Domino servers. Lotus Go can act as a caching server and is easy to upgrade to one of the Domino servers at a later time.

iPlanet servers

The iPlanet alliance (www.iplanet.com) came about when Netscape and Sun Microsystems joined forces with their server products. (Netscape has since been purchased by AOL.) Servers in the iPlanet family perform standard server services like those performed by IIS or Lotus Domino, but their products are often some of the most tested and dependable. Database connectivity with server-side JavaScript is supported on some iPlanet servers. Although in real life there are always drawbacks to any product, Prosoft lists only a few pros of this product line that you need to know for the exam; those items are included in the following list:

✔ iPlanet servers are well tested. Though Apache still reigns as the most tested Web server, iPlanet server products come close.

✔ iPlanet servers are flexible to use. iPlanet products run on most operating systems, including mainframes.

✔ iPlanet has formal product support. Fee-based product support is available at the iPlanet Web site: www.iplanet.com.

Obviously, in real life, there are more pros and cons to each server product than I've listed. For the exam, though, you just need to focus on the key differences between them — for example, which run on which operating systems, which are easily expandable, and what type of support is offered.

Prep Test

1 Norman is a network administrator for a large company. He must make all the company's documents and spreadsheets available to all employees, both within the intranet and remotely via a browser. Which of the following would not be a server option for Norman?

A ○ Web server

B ○ Print server

C ○ FTP server

D ○ File server

2 Which of the following statements is not true regarding MIME?

A ○ MIME is used only by e-mail clients and is not used by browser applications.

B ○ MIME is an acronym for Multipurpose Internet Mail Extensions.

C ○ MIME identifies the file type of an e-mail attachment.

D ○ If a MIME type is incorrectly configured, the file may not open.

3 Lucy is administering a Web site that allows every user complete access to all the site's pages. What kind of access is she allowing?

A ○ Write

B ○ Anonymous

C ○ Open source

D ○ Alias

4 Which of the following types of data are not typically stored in server logs?

A ○ Error data

B ○ Access data

C ○ Referrer data

D ○ User password data

5 Which of the following statements best describes a proxy server?

A ○ Increases network security and decreases network performance

B ○ Decreases network security and increases network performance

C ○ Increases network performance and increases network security

D ○ Increases network performance and does not affect network security

6 Which of the following protocols is used by mail servers to send mail?

A ○ LDAP

B ○ SMTP

C ○ IMAP

D ○ POP

7 Ralph is the Web developer for his organization. He wants to create an address book that can be accessed by all the employees in the enterprise network. What server would he most likely choose to accomplish this task successfully?

A ○ Directory server

B ○ Transaction server

C ○ Certificate server

D ○ Address server

8 Sarah is a network analyst at her company. The organization plans to host an intranet site, which involves a lot of dynamic functions. Sarah is experienced in Visual Basic and VBScript. What server solution would optimize her skill set?

A ○ Lotus Domino server

B ○ Apache

C ○ Microsoft Internet Information Server

D ○ iPlanet server

9 Which of the following statements is not true regarding Apache server?

A ○ No formal product support

B ○ Well tested, widely used

C ○ Open source software available for free download

D ○ Can serve applications over intranets and the Internet

10 Which of the following DNS server records specifies the primary DNS server for a given domain name?

A ○ Canonical name (CNAME)

B ○ Name Server (NS)

C ○ Mail Exchanger (MX)

D ○ State of Authority (SOA)

Answers

1 **B.** Print server. A print server would only allow employees access to a printer, not to documents. *Review the "Sharing Files and Printers" section.*

2 **A.** MIME is used only by e-mail clients and is not used by browser applications. MIME is used by both browsers and e-mail clients. *Check out "Finding out how to MIME."*

3 **B.** Anonymous. Anonymous access doesn't require a user name or password to access files. *Look over "Adding password protection."*

4 **D.** User password data. *Review "Logging: The record-keeping kind, not the lumberjack kind."*

5 **C.** Increases network performance and increases network security. The caching feature of a proxy server can increase network performance, and the firewall and IP masking features can increase network security. *Check out "Discovering the proxy server."*

6 **B.** SMTP (Simple Mail Transfer Protocol). *Review "Getting to know mail servers."*

7 **A.** Directory server. If the data that employees need to access is stored in one central point, companies can use a directory server to allow employees in various locations access to the data. *Look over the "Directory servers" section.*

8 **C.** Microsoft Internet Information Server. Because VBScript is a proprietary, Microsoft technology, it should be run on a Microsoft server such as IIS. *Check out the "Internet Information Server (IIS)" section.*

9 **D.** Can serve applications over intranets and the Internet. Apache is only a Web server. *Look over the section, "All about Apache."*

10 **D.** State of Authority (SOA). The SOA specifies which DNS server has the most authority or is the one to look to first when searching for a domain name. *Review the "This will go on your permanent record" section.*

Chapter 17

Now Serving Scripts and Database Connectivity

Exam Objectives

▶ Understanding the purpose of server-side scripting

▶ Explaining the difference between server-side and client-side scripting

▶ Describing Common Gateway Interface (CGI)

▶ Identifying common scripting languages and scripting alternatives

● ●

*W*hen you first start creating Web pages, you usually work with only static content — you type some text that appears on the page and update it from time to time. As you become more involved in Web development, however, you may start wishing there were a way to make content more dynamic so that it could pull updated information onto the page for you. That's where server-side scripting comes in.

When you want to connect data stored in a database with a Web page, you need to use something far more capable than HTML. Server-side scripting is the most common method authors use to dynamically pull data to a page or populate it. Nearly all e-commerce sites use databases to store product and order information; that information is then pulled to the page by using server-side scripting.

This chapter focuses on how server-side scripting works and the most common scripting languages used for this purpose. I also discuss alternatives to scripting — other programming techniques that can pull or push data onto a Web page.

For the Foundations exam, you don't need to know how to write scripts by hand. You do need to know the pros and cons of different data-integration techniques and the types of databases that are most efficient for this purpose.

Quick Assessment

Client-side and server-side scripting

1 The most common method of dynamically pulling data to Web pages is _____-side scripting.

2 _____ scripting involves code that is embedded into Web pages and run on the user's machine.

3 Distributing the computing workload between the client and server is called _____.

4 When you use the _____ scripting method to access a database on the server, ActiveX Data Objects (ADO) are used.

5 _____ are usually developed using VBScript and run best on Microsoft Internet Information Server.

Databases and database connectivity

6 _____ allow for complex scripting by using small Java programs that can be chained (linked together) and run on the server.

7 A _____ is a file or series of files that stores data in fields.

8 To pull specific data from a database, a script must _____ the database.

9 The Microsoft method of connecting programming or scripting to a database is _____.

10 When data storage and user interface are on separate computers and the process logic is spread over several computers, you are using the _____ computing model.

Answers

1   *Server-side.* See "Sticking to the Script."

2   *Client-side.* Review "Sticking to the Script."

3   *Load distribution.* Read "Sticking to the Script."

4   *ASP.* Check out "Active Server Pages (ASP)."

5   *ASP (Active Server Pages).* Look over "Active Server Pages (ASP)."

6   *JSP (JavaServer Pages) or Java servlets.* Read "JavaServer Pages (JSP)."

7   *Database.* See "Working with Databases."

8   *Query.* "Querying a database."

9   *ODBC (Open Database Connectivity).* Review "Open Database Connectivity (ODBC)."

10 *N-tier.* Check out "Sharing the workload."

Sticking to the Script

Server-side scripting is the most common technique developers use to pull data from the back end (server) into their Web pages. Many kinds of Web sites benefit from back end data integration — both Internet and intranet sites. E-commerce sites need current product and ordering data, and sports sites need current game scores. Companies often use server-side database integration on their intranet sites, which can, for example, enable employees in various departments to enter data by using a simple HTML form.

Here's an example to help you get a handle on how dynamic data differs from static data. Say you have a page with a table that lists the products and services your company offers along with their prices. If you create this table with HTML, every time you want to raise prices (which, if you're my local cable company is about every week, it seems), you have to open that Web page and add the data, and you may have to change the table dimensions each time if you add or remove items. If you create the same table using server-side scripting, you only need to update the information in your database — it magically updates your Web page with the new information (and can update the table dimensions if necessary).

There are two categories of scripting:

- ✔ **Client-side:** Client-side involves code that's embedded into Web pages. The client browser software interprets and runs the script on the user's machine. Some dynamic data effects can be created client-side — a good example is a message that says "Good Morning" or "Good Evening" based on the time on the visitor's machine.

- ✔ **Server-side:** Scripts are stored, interpreted, and run on the server. After the server processes the script, the resulting data is pulled onto the Web page.

As a general rule, if the data you're accessing is stored on the server, you should use a server-side technique. If the data you need is stored on the user's machine you should use a client-side technique. Say you have a welcome message on your home page that says "Good Morning," "Good Afternoon," or "Good Evening" based on the time of day. You want the message to reflect the current time where the user is, so the script you're using to add the message should be a client-side script because it's accessing data stored on the user's machine.

Some effects can be created either client-side or server-side. Usually, if you can achieve the results you want with a client-side technique, you should choose that rather than placing more demand on the server. Distributing the workload between client and server is called *load distribution*.

Adding Server-Side Scripts

You can choose several technologies to pull back end data onto your Web pages. Some involve scripting languages; others involve programming languages, such as Java or Visual Basic. (For a comparison of scripting languages to programming languages, see Chapter 8.)

Using Common Gateway Interface (CGI)

Common Gateway Interface (CGI) is the standard many Web servers utilize to connect to external programs or scripts. CGI is not a scripting or programming language — it's just the common point or gateway where Web servers and scripts can meet up and communicate.

CGI scripts are usually stored in a folder called the cgi-bin. There's nothing special about the folder name, but the folder must have execute permission. (For more on permissions, see Chapter 16.) Keep in mind that even if you configure your Web server to give the folder execute permission, the operating system can still prevent scripts from running unless you configure it to allow execute permission on that folder too.

CGI, like every technology, has benefits and drawbacks. The following lists the pros and cons of CGI you need to know for the exam.

- ✔ **Pro:** CGI is well tested. CGI has been used almost as long as the Web has existed, so it works well and lots of people know how to use it.

- ✔ **Con:** CGI has a higher risk of malfunction than some other methods. If a user makes an unanticipated entry or choice, the script may not function properly. Only the most well-written scripts perform correctly at nearly all times.

- ✔ **Pro:** CGI can be run on almost any operating system.

- ✔ **Con:** Each script runs as a separate process on the server. With fairly heavy traffic, the server can easily become overloaded because the server has to run a separate instance of the script for every user.

- ✔ **Pro:** CGI uses interpreted languages — often scripting languages — that don't have to be compiled like programming languages. Scripting languages are also easier to learn.

- ✔ **Con:** CGI scripts reside in folders with execute permission. If a malicious user can get access to the folder, he can run destructive programs on the server.

✔ **Pro:** Tons of scripts already exist. Because CGI scripts have been used for years (longer than several other popular scripting methods), you can usually find a script on the Web that does what you want to do. Many Web sites feature hundreds of CGI scripts (most are written in Perl) that handle data in most every way imaginable.

✔ **Con:** CGI scripts are stateless. Scripts can't tell the difference between one session and another. If a user clicks the submit button on a form once, gets impatient, and clicks it again, the script can't tell that it's already processing that user's information so it starts all over again.

CGI scripts are often written in the Perl programming language, but they can be written in any scripting language. Many scripting languages can be used to write CGI and non-CGI server-side scripts. If you write a CGI script in VBScript, for example, you'd probably save the script with a `.cgi` extension. You can also use VBScript to write an Active Server Page (ASP) — a non-CGI, server-side scripting technology.

CGI is a common gateway, as the name implies. Even if you aren't using CGI, however, any server-side script or program you attach to a Web page passes through some gateway, often called a Web or HTTP gateway. You don't need to know specifics about other gateways. You only need to know that for a Web server to pass data back and forth to a Web page, some HTTP gateway is used and it's the common point where the server and the script or program communicate.

Active Server Pages (ASP)

Developers usually create Active Server Pages (ASP) with VBScript, the Microsoft scripting language based on its Visual Basic programming language. Being a proprietary solution (it's from a specific vendor), ASP pages are almost always run on IIS (Internet Information Server) on a Microsoft server. ASP can run on other servers with the help of plug-in programs. (For more information on popular server products, see Chapter 16.)

Active Server Page files end with an `.asp` extension, even though they often contain some regular (static) HTML content in addition to the ASP content. If a Web page has an `.asp` extension but contains no ASP commands, it behaves just like it normally would — the browser reads and displays the HTML content.

When you use ASP to access a database on the server, ASP uses ActiveX Data Objects (ADO). (I discuss how ActiveX can be used client-side in Chapter 8.) Like ASP, ADOs are proprietary bits of code, but as long as they're incorporated on a server running IIS, it doesn't matter which browser the visitor is using.

You can use ASP to create pretty reliable server-side scripts to connect to databases; you can also create server-side includes (covered later in this chapter). Compared to CGI, ASP pages are often easier to create because several Microsoft programs you may already own write ASP for you, which means you don't necessarily need to know how to write any code.

Developers don't use VBScript — ASP's primary scripting language — for client-side scripting often because it's not cross-browser compatible. As long as you use VBScript server-side (and the server is configured to run it), this isn't a problem — only the server needs to understand the script.

Server-side JavaScript (SSJS)

Server-side JavaScript (SSJS) is the Netscape equivalent of ASP. The two methods are similar in that they both rely on object-based scripting languages. The languages they rely on, however, are different. SSJS relies on JavaScript, and ASP relies on VBScript. Where ASP is designed to run on a Microsoft server, SSJS is cross-platform — it can run on Windows, UNIX, Novell, or OS/2 operating systems. Even though SSJS is cross-platform, if you want to run SSJS, you have to install Netscape software, such as Netscape SuiteSpot or Enterprise Server.

The original Netscape server-side scripting language was called LiveWire. Later this evolved into SSJS, but both SSJS and LiveWire were used interchangeably to describe the Netscape server-side scripting technology. Now, however, LiveWire just refers to the database-connection part of SSJS — whenever you use SSJS to connect to a database, you're using SSJS and LiveWire.

Unlike with some other server-side scripting technologies, SSJS allows you to embed server-side JavaScript into HTML pages. Special HTML tags command the server to process the script server-side. You can also utilize this feature to create stand-alone files with a .js extension that are linked to Web pages on the client side.

Personal Home Page (PHP)

Personal Home Page (PHP) is an open source scripting language that's been growing in popularity over the last couple of years. It performs the same types of functions as ASP and SSJS and, just like with ASP and SSJS, you must have the correct software on the server — a PHP interpreter or parser. Free PHP parsers are available for Apache, Internet Information Server (IIS), and several other major Web servers.

ColdFusion

ColdFusion is another server-side scripting language originally created by Allaire. Macromedia later purchased it, and it's now part of Macromedia's Dreamweaver UltraDev program. ColdFusion has its own scripting/markup language called ColdFusion Markup Language (CFML), and ColdFusion pages end with the `.cfm` extension. The ColdFusion GUI was developed for nonprogrammers, so it's easy to use. For ColdFusion to run, you must be hosting on a server that has ColdFusion Server installed.

Connecting a form to a script

If you create an HTML form but don't have any system in place to collect and store the data, you're not accomplishing much (other than maybe aggravating visitors by having them fill out yet another form). If you want the data to be sent to and stored in a database on your company's server (which is pretty common), you most likely need to connect your HTML form to a server-side script. (For more on creating HTML forms, see Chapter 12.) To attach the script to the form, you use the `ACTION` attribute in the `<FORM>` tag. The `ACTION` attribute equals the filepath of your script like this:

```
<FORM METHOD=Post ACTION="http://www.company.com/
          cgi-bin/yourscript.cgi">
```

In the previous example, I use the script called `yourscript.cgi` to send the data to the database I have set up on my company's server. If you're using another type of script — an ASP script for example — the script location (filepath) still goes in the same location like this:

```
<FORM METHOD="Post" ACTION=
          "http://www.company.com/folder/yourscript.asp">
```

In the previous example, the text appears on two lines only because of the space limitations of this book. In real life, you normally type the whole statement on one line.

The `METHOD` attribute can equal either `Get` or `Post` (the Get and Post attribute values are discussed in depth in Chapter 12):

- ✔ `METHOD="Get"`: Adds the form data to the end of the URL string (the Web page address up in the address bar).

- ✔ `METHOD="Post"`: Sends the form data as a separate text file. As a separate file, it can be encrypted to keep the data secure.

Scripting Alternatives

Server-side scripting is the most popular method of connecting back end data with client-side HTML — partially because it tends to be the easiest way to do it. There are, however, several other techniques you can use that may be a little easier on the server and might be more efficient.

Server Application Programming Interface (SAPI)

Server Application Programming Interfaces (SAPIs) are Web server extensions (preprogrammed bits of code) that server administrators can download. SAPIs use *dynamically loaded object libraries* — predefined objects and bits of programming. Because objects and some programming codes are already created, servers have to do less work. Though less work for the server, SAPIs can be more difficult for the developer to implement. SAPIs are proprietary, which means that each Web server has its own version. So if you change the type of server you're hosting on, you have to re-create the effect.

One big benefit of SAPI over CGI is that SAPI applications are *threaded*. This means that each part of the process runs as a subprocess, or a miniprogram, on its own. If the process is interrupted, it can just start over where it stopped — each part of the process can work independently. A CGI script, on the other hand, always has to run as a complete process; if it is interrupted, it has to start all over again. (It's kind of like this story my dad tells about how when he was a kid on a farm. His mule stopped plowing in the middle of a field, so his dad poured dirt in the mule's ear to get it to go and so on. If you interrupt the story, you're going to hear the entire story over from the beginning. By the way, the mule was okay, in case you were worried.)

Internet Server Application Programming Interface (ISAPI)

Internet Server Application Programming Interface (ISAPI) is the type of SAPI that Microsoft servers use. ISAPI applications use shared library files known as dynamic link library (DLL) files. DLL files can be shared and run by several programs at once.

Netscape Server Application Programming Interface (NSAPI)

Netscape Server Application Programming Interface (NSAPI) is the Netscape version of SAPI. Like ISAPI, NSAPI uses DLL files and runs threaded processes.

NSAPI applications generally must run on Netscape servers. The scripting language NSAPI prefers is JavaScript, whereas ISAPI prefers VBScript and JScript (the Microsoft version of JavaScript).

JavaServer Pages (JSP)

A lot of people get JavaServer Pages (JSP) confused with server-side JavaScript (SSJS). SSJS uses JavaScript code; JSPs use *Java servlets* — small, dedicated Java programs that run on the server. Java servlets are capable of performing the same functions that CGI scripts can perform, but JSP has a slight advantage over CGI because it is more *extensible*, or more capable of being customized and expanded.

Java servlets are roughly the server-side equivalent of Java applets (covered in Chapter 8). Whether you're running Java programs client-side or server-side, the machine running the program must have the Java Virtual Machine (JVM) installed. *JVM* is a small operating system that runs on top of a computer's regular operating system. Because Java programs always run on their own operating system (the JVM), they are cross-platform, which is one of the biggest benefits of using Java technology.

Another benefit Java servlets offer over CGI is that you can join several servlets together with a method called *servlet chaining*. When servlets are chained together, one servlet processes its request and then calls upon the next servlet in the chain to do its job. Because each servlet is a separate program, servlets can be saved on different machines within a network to ease the workload on the server.

Java can take advantage of the *Common Object Request Broker Architecture (CORBA)*, a system that allows programs written in different languages to work together.

Working with Databases

A database is essential to data-driven Web sites. Developers can choose from several popular database programs — Access, Filemaker Pro, and Oracle, to name a few. Databases are files or a series of files that store data in fields that users can manipulate — sort, filter, and so forth. All databases fit in one of three categories:

> ✔ **Nonrelational:** A database that contains a table or series of tables that isn't connected or related in any way is nonrelational. If you create several tables in Microsoft Excel, for example, none of the tables are connected or share data. A nonrelational database is the simplest type of Database Management System (DBMS). An example of a nonrelational database is Microsoft Excel — you can store, sort, and filter data, but tables don't share or relate data.

✔ **Relational:** A relational database is also called a Relational Database Management System (RDBMS). In a RDBMS, tables can share data or be related. Relational databases index their data so each record is unique — no duplicates. An example of an RDBMS is Microsoft Access.

✔ **Object-oriented:** A newer type of database is object-oriented, which can be created with object-oriented programming languages, such as Java or C++. An object-oriented database is also called an Object Database Management System (ODBMS).

The goal of all types of database management systems is to allow easy, organized access to the data. All but the most basic databases usually prevent duplicate entries and many allow password protection of files.

Older databases used on mainframes were usually hierarchical — a record can be linked to another record, but only one user at a time can access the record. Newer databases are usually network databases — a record can be linked to another record, but several users can access the record at once.

Querying a database

When you ask a question of a database — show all customers who live in Kentucky, for example — you're performing a *query.* Say you have a customer database filled with customer names and addresses. If you want to find out which customers live in the United States, you perform a query with the criteria of "country = United States".

Queries are written in query languages — languages created specifically to query databases. Queries are kind of like scripts that run within your database program — just as a script written in JavaScript, for example, might run in your browser program. In a Relational Database Management System (RDBMS), the standard language used to write queries is Structured Query Language (SQL). The standard language used to write queries in an Object Database Management System (ODBMS) is Object Query Language (OQL).

Open Database Connectivity (ODBC)

Open Database Connectivity (ODBC) is the Microsoft method of connecting programming or scripting to a database. If you want to connect to a database using ODBC, your database program must be ODBC-compliant, and most commercial database programs are.

After you've created your ODBC-compliant database, you must then register it with the ODBC driver manager. The ODBC driver manager keeps track of where a database resides so that any programs or scripts can be connected to the database.

Currently, there are 16-bit and 32-bit versions of ODBC drivers. Make sure you and your server people are using the same version — otherwise your database won't work with their system.

Java Database Connectivity (JDBC)

Java Database Connectivity (JDBC) is a database connection system developed by Sun Microsystems. JDBC can work with any SQL-compliant database, and it's platform independent, unlike ODBC.

For the exam, you don't need to know the actual steps involved in setting up a database and registering it with the ODBC driver manager. You just need to remember that Microsoft uses ODBC and Sun Microsystems uses JDBC.

Several databases offer to save your data for the Web as HTML. These programs usually have limited scripting/programming capabilities, but they can help in a pinch.

Sharing the workload

Just as you can distribute server duties over a network (covered in Chapter 15), you can also distribute the database workload. Even if all database processes are performed one machine, there are always three parts to a database:

- ✔ **User interface:** The interface the user works with; it formats data on the screen. When you open up a database program, the window or windows you work with are parts of the user interface.

- ✔ **Process logic:** The part of the database program that processes and queries information; SQL and OQL are part of the process logic step.

- ✔ **Data storage:** The tables and/or fields where the data is stored.

If the user interface, process logic, and data storage are all contained on one machine, this is referred to as one-tier computing. To cut down on a computer's workload, you can take advantage of two-tier, three-tier, or N-tier computing:

- ✔ **Two-tier:** Database processes are spread over two computers; one takes care of the process logic and data storage, and the other just formats the data on the screen (user interface).

- ✔ **Three-tier:** Three separate computers each handle one aspect of the database: one contains the user interface, another the process logic, and a third handles the data storage.

✔ **N-tier:** The user interface and data storage are on two separate computers while the process logic — the most demanding step — is spread over several computers.

When you use a Web page to access a database, the browser is often called a *thin client* — a program or interface used to access a database. When the term *thin client* is used, it implies the database functions are spread over at least three computers (a three-tier process).

Prep Test

1 Which of the following statements about client-side scripting is false?

A ○ Client-side scripting is often embedded in HTML code.

B ○ Client-side scripting requires no special software on the server.

C ○ Client-side scripting reduces server overhead.

D ○ Client-side scripting is executed on the server end.

2 Why are CGI scripts stored in a folder separate from images and HTML files for use on the Web?

A ○ CGI scripts are always read in binary mode and must be in a directory with the suffix -bin.

B ○ CGI scripts must be placed in a folder that has execute permission enabled.

C ○ CGI scripts must be in their own folder so that all users can print them.

D ○ All of the above

3 What scripting language is most often used in CGI?

A ○ CORBA

B ○ JavaScript

C ○ DHTML

D ○ Perl

4 Which of the following scripting methods was not created as a cross-platform solution?

A ○ ASP (Active Server Pages)

B ○ PHP (Personal Home Page)

C ○ SSJS (Server-side JavaScript)

D ○ All of the above

5 Which of the following is not true regarding SAPI?

A ○ SAPI applications are threaded.

B ○ NSAPI is the Netscape version of SAPI.

C ○ ISAPI code is generally written in VBScript and JScript for use on Microsoft servers.

D ○ SAPI is the acronym for Software Application Programming Intelligence.

6 Which of the following is not a database category?

A ○ Object-oriented

B ○ Nonrelational

C ○ Object-based

D ○ Relational

7 **How are database queries written in a Relational Database Management System (RDBMS)?**

A ○ OQL (Object Query Language)

B ○ RQL (Relational Query Language)

C ○ XQL (Extensible Query Language)

D ○ SQL (Structured Query Language)

8 **In which type of database structure can linked records be accessed by several users at once?**

A ○ Network

B ○ Dynamic

C ○ Hierarchical

D ○ All of the above

9 **Which of the following is not a component of every database?**

A ○ Process logic

B ○ Data storage

C ○ Syntax query routine

D ○ User Interface

10 **Which of the following could be described as a platform independent database connection system that is able to run easily on any operating system?**

A ○ JDBC

B ○ SQL

C ○ ODBC

D ○ DBMS

Answers

1 **D.** Executed at server end. Remember, a *client*-side script executes or runs on the client side (the browser). *See "Sticking to the Script."*

2 **B.** CGI scripts must be placed in a folder that has execute permission. *Look over "Sticking to the Script."*

3 **D.** Perl. Although you can use any scripting or programming language in CGI, Perl is the most commonly used language. *Review "Adding Server-Side Scripts."*

4 **A.** ASP (Active Server Pages). Although ASP can run on several Web servers with the help of plug-in programs, it was created to work on Microsoft servers. *Check out "Active Server Pages (ASP)."*

5 **D.** SAPI is the acronym for Software Application Programming Intelligence. *Take a look at "Server Application Programming Interface (SAPI)."*

6 **C.** Object-based. Object-based refers to how certain scripting/programming languages handle objects. *Review "Working with Databases."*

7 **D.** SQL (Structured Query Language). SQL is the standard language used by RDBMs. *Check out the section, "Working with Databases."*

8 **A.** Network. The network database structure is much more common than the hierarchal structure because it allows multiple users to access linked records at once. *Look over "Sharing the workload."*

9 **C.** Syntax query routine. *See "Querying a database."*

10 **A.** ODBC is tied to Microsoft operating systems, and JDBC is platform-independent. *Review "Java Database Connectivity (JDBC)."*

Chapter 18

Networking Protocols and Architecture

Exam Objectives

▶ Understanding packets and their makeup

▶ Understanding the Open Systems Interconnection Reference Model (OSI/RM)

▶ Describing common networking protocols and their purposes

▶ Explaining how TCP/IP works

*S*tudying protocols is a lot like studying foreign languages. Protocols, in fact, are kind of like languages — they're the chosen communication method that various parts of networks use to talk with each other. Various network components use different methods to communicate because each method has specific capabilities. Think of the variety of protocols like this: Do you know how you *just know* that you should pick up the phone instead of sending an e-mail when you have something sensitive to say? Well the same principle applies to protocols — different situations call for different protocols.

Chapter 3 is a primer in network protocols — it lists some of the key protocols and their uses. This chapter contains more information about protocols you may have already read about and lists some protocols that haven't been mentioned elsewhere in this book.

Now I have to warn you upfront about something: If you don't have a networking background, it will seem like I'm throwing a lot of new info at you. That's because I am — this chapter is chock full of definitions. Take my advice and know them backwards and forwards. But don't think that this is an everything-you-need-to-know-about-protocols crash course — especially if you plan on becoming a network administrator. This isn't a book on networking protocols, and I couldn't possibly do them justice in just one chapter. If you need more help, check out the CD, where I list Web sites that have more detailed explanations for some of this chapter's content. And check out *Networking For Dummies,* 5th Edition, by Doug Lowe (Hungry Minds, Inc.).

Quick Assessment

Packets

1 When a file is sent across a network, it is generally broken down into small, manageable units of data called _____.

2 _____ is a method — possibly involving the use of several protocols at once — that a destination computer uses to process incoming packets.

3 The standard network architecture model on which most network operating systems are based is the _____.

Choosing and combining protocols

4 The HTTP protocol resides at the _____ layer of the OSI Reference Model.

5 The TCP protocol resides at the _____ layer of the OSI Reference Model.

6 _____ protocols rely on constant connections to communicate and are sometimes referred to as connection-oriented protocols.

7 The suite of protocols adopted as the Internet standard is _____.

8 _____ is a non-routable network protocol used primarily on Microsoft networks that cannot communicate with outside networks.

9 A protocol that is retired because it has outlived its usefulness is in the _____ stage of protocol development.

10 _____ are documents regarding Internet protocols, which are formally published on the Web.

Answers

1 *Packets.* See "Peter Piper Picked a Data Packet."

2 *Demultiplexing.* Review "Peter Piper Picked a Data Packet."

3 *Open Systems Interconnection (OSI) Reference Model.* Read "Introducing the Open Systems Interconnection Reference Model."

4 *Application.* Check out "Knowing Which Protocols Go with Which Layers."

5 *Transport.* Look over "Knowing Which Protocols Go with Which Layers."

6 *Stateful.* See "Connection-Oriented (And Dis-Oriented) Protocols."

7 *TCP/IP.* Look at "Common Networking Protocols."

8 *NetBEUI.* Look over "Combining protocols."

9 *Historic.* Read "Stages of protocol development."

10 *Requests for Comments (RFCs).* Review "Stages of protocol development."

Peter Piper Picked a Data Packet

When you send an e-mail to a friend, the whole message isn't sent over in one big chunk. The message data is broken down into *packets* — the small units that all data is broken down into for transmission.

Every packet has three parts:

- ✔ **Header:** The header contains addressing information, information that transmission protocols need to process the packet, and a signal to alert the destination computer that the packet is on its way. When the packet reaches the destination machine, the corresponding protocols remove the packet's header information and read it.

- ✔ **Data:** A piece of data you're sending.

- ✔ **Trailer:** The trailer contains error-checking data such as the Cyclical Redundancy Check (CRC). The *CRC* is a math calculation that helps validate that a packet is put together right. The sending computer calculates a CRC figure when it sends a packet, and this figure is added to the trailer. The receiving computer calculates a CRC for the packet upon receipt. If the two CRCs match, the packet's valid; if they don't match, it's not valid.

Demultiplexing is the procedure that the destination computer uses to process an incoming packet. Demultiplexing involves all the necessary protocols doing their jobs to process the packet — which may mean several protocols working with the packet at once.

Introducing the Open Systems Interconnection Reference Model

The Open Systems Interconnection (OSI) Reference Model was created by the Organization for Standardization (ISO). It's a standard network architecture model that most popular network operating systems are based on — for example, Microsoft Windows NT/2000, UNIX, and Novell.

Think of the OSI/RM as the different steps in a network connection. The layers of the model are tied to certain protocols, and certain activities happen at each layer.

You may not feel that you completely understand each part of the OSI/RM. In real life, most network administrators are in the same boat. I don't know many who can sit down and explain the OSI/RM in detail. Don't worry about mindlessly memorizing some of this information; you may never need to use it in real life.

The OSI/RM consists of seven layers. The process of packet creation occurs to some degree at each layer. Data starts out in the format that network users create (maybe by typing an e-mail message) and is broken down into smaller and smaller bits throughout the layers. For the exam, you need to know the names and the order of the layers. I use acronyms to help me remember the order of the layers:

> ✔ *All People Should Try New Data Processing.*

> ✔ In reverse order, *Please Do Not Throw Sausage Pizza Away*

I know it's confusing to list the order of the OSI/RM both forwards and in reverse order — but that's how data is sent. The first order (APSTNDP) describes how the sending computer breaks down and sends the data. The reverse order (PDNTSPA) describes how the receiving computer receives and reassembles the data.

Table 18-1 lists the seven OSI/RM layers in order.

Table 18-1		OSI/RM Layers
Layer #	*Layer Title*	*Description*
7	Application	Holds the applications that network users interact with.
6	Presentation	Prepares data for presentation to the user: Text is converted from ASCII to binary, and images are broken down into their pixel counts.
5	Session	Establishes, manages, and ends connections (sessions) between network programs; also provides traffic control.
4	Transport	Provides transport between networked computers; also provides error recovery and flow control.
3	Network	Organizes data packets into frames; adds addresses to packets; begins the routing of packets to their destination.

(continued)

Table 18-1 *(continued)*

Layer #	Layer Title	Description
2	Data link	Completes final preparation of data before it's sent; synchronizes frames. This layer consists of two sublayers — the Logical Link Control layer (LLC) and the Media Access Control layer (MAC). LLC provides error and flow control; MAC places data on the transmission media (physical layer). MAC layer also reads MAC addresses.
1	Physical	Comprises the computers and networking cables and machines that actually send the data as electronic signals.

A precursor to the OSI/RM was the SNA (Systems Network Architecture). Like the OSI/RM, SNA includes a series of protocols; IBM used this architecture with mainframe networks.

To make this OSI/RM stuff a little easier to understand, I offer Table 18-2, which compares the network connection steps to the steps of creating and sending a letter or package. (This may vary a little from the real-life steps you take, but cut me some slack.)

Table 18-2   OSI/RM Is Just Like Sending a Letter — Sort Of

OSI/RM Layer	What It Does	How It's Kind of Like Sending a Letter
Application	User opens e-mail program, types a message, and clicks Send.	You gather paper, pens, and boxes — all the stuff you use to create the letter or package.
Presentation	E-mail message is converted from ASCII text to binary (0s and 1s).	You translate your thoughts to words to put in the letter.
Session	Sending computer makes initial contact with receiving computer to see whether they can communicate.	You call FedEx to make sure that a driver is on the way for scheduled pickup and call the recipient to see whether she's home waiting for your letter.

OSI/RM Layer	What It Does	How It's Kind of Like Sending a Letter
Transport	Sending computer starts organizing packets for flow control and checks for errors.	FedEx driver picks up the letter or package, checks to make sure the address has no errors, and puts your parcel in a box with other packages going to the same state.
Network	Packets of the message are addressed.	FedEx labels each stack of letters with state and zip code information.
Data link	Packets' organization and synchronization are completed; packets are placed on the physical layer.	FedEx office tells delivery drivers which stacks to pick up. FedEx checks road conditions to make sure that the trucks can travel a smooth delivery path; they coordinate departure schedules to make sure that 50 trucks aren't trying to fit through the gate at once. Packages are loaded onto trucks.
Physical	Message moves across the networking equipment and arrives at the receiving computer.	FedEx driver drives your package to its destination and puts it on the recipient's porch. This utilizes all the physical equipment — trucks, roads, and porches.

It's difficult to relate the letter-sending analogy to how data goes through the OSI/RM layers in reverse to get the data to the recipient. When the data hits the destination computer on the physical layer, packets are organized, interpreted, and translated so that they can be viewed in the recipient's program (application).

Knowing Which Protocols Go with Which Layers

Each OSI/RM layer has specific protocols associated with it. Make sure that you know these for the exam. Some protocols work in a couple of layers. If you look at different networking books, you find that, very often, one contradicts another in at least one protocol placement. I've listed the protocol placements as ProsoftTraining defines them. And I define the protocols themselves later in this chapter (see the section "Common Networking Protocols"). Table 18-3 illustrates the protocols that reside at each layer.

Table 18-3	Layers and Protocols
Layer	*Protocols That Reside on That Layer*
Application	SMTP, HTTP, FTP, NFS, SMB, NCP
Presentation	None that you need to know for the exam
Session	NetBIOS
Transport	TCP, SPX, NetBEUI, UDP, NWLink
Network	IP, IPX, NetBEUI, NWLink
Data link	Ethernet
Physical	None

Understanding Internet Architecture

As if all the information about the OSI/RM weren't enough, there's another model you need to concern yourself with for the exam — the Internet Architecture model.

Sometimes called the TCP/IP model, the Internet Architecture model consists of four layers that correspond with layers of the OSI/RM. The protocols of the layers also correspond except for proprietary (vendor-specific) protocols like IPX/SPX and NetBEUI. Table 18-4 illustrates the correspondence between OSI/RM and Internet Architecture layers and lists the protocols that reside at those layers.

Table 18-4	OSI/RM and Internet Architecture Layers	
OSI/RM Layer	*Internet Architecture Layer*	*Protocols at That Layer*
Application; Presentation	Application	HTTP, FTP, TFTP
Session; Transport	Transport (also called the host-to-host, end-to-end, or source-to-destination layer)	TCP, UDP

OSI/RM Layer	Internet Architecture Layer	Protocols at That Layer
Network	Internet	IP
Data link; Physical	Network Access	Ethernet

Connection-Oriented (And Dis-Oriented) Protocols

In order to understand networking protocols, you need to know that some protocols are *stateful*, or connection-oriented, and some are *stateless*, or connectionless.

Here's what these terms mean:

- ✔ **Stateful (connection-oriented):** A *stateful* protocol is one that relies on a constant connection to communicate. Think of stateful protocols as working like telephone calls — you have to remain on the line at the other end while your sister in Cleveland blabs on and on about something or other because you have some bad karma to pay off. If you hang up, your session is broken.

- ✔ **Stateless:** *Stateless* protocols don't rely on a constant connection to work. E-mail works like a stateless protocol. When you send the e-mail message, you don't know whether the recipient is online (and it doesn't matter because his activities are not a factor in whether the communication is successful). The recipient picks up the message whenever it's convenient and replies without having to worry about whether you're online at the moment.

Stateful and stateless protocols work together on the Internet. You don't need to know whether every protocol in the world is stateful or stateless, so I point out just the protocols you need to be concerned with (jump ahead to Table 18-5).

Common Networking Protocols

Several protocols are commonly used in networking environments. Many network operating systems are starting to use TCP/IP — the protocol the Internet is based on — if they don't already. In fact, one key reason that some network systems are more popular than others is this: They've used TCP/IP for years and, as a result, are more compatible with the Internet. Table 18-5 lists the networking protocols you need to know for the exam.

Table 18-5	Network Protocol Definitions
Protocol	*What It Does*
TCP/IP	Suite of protocols that was adopted as the Internet standard in the early 1980s. The Internet currently uses TCP/IP version 4, although TCP/IP version 6 (IPv6) is being tested. (For more on IPv6, see Chapter 3.)
TCP (Transmission Control Protocol)	Manages sessions between computers; helps break down and reassemble packets; ensures packets are reassembled in correct order; makes sure no data is duplicated. Stateful.
IP (Internet Protocol)	Provides Internet addressing for each computer involved in transmission. (For more on IP addressing, see Chapter 3.) Stateless.
UDP (User Datagram Protocol)	Provides datagram form of communication (see note on datagrams following this table); it does a lot of the same things TCP does, but it's stateless and uses the best-effort method of data transfer. That is, UDP gives it a shot, but if the data transfer doesn't work, UDP doesn't retransmit or guarantee reliability.
ICMP (Internet Control Message Protocol)	Troubleshoots within TCP/IP. If there's a problem with a TCP/IP connection, an ICMP message will likely be generated.
NFS (Network File System)	Used on UNIX to share files and printers.
SMB (Simple Message Block)	Used on Microsoft to share files.
NCP (NetWare Core Protocol)	Used on Novell NetWare to share files and printers.
ARP (Address Resolution Protocol)	Matches IP addresses to physical addresses, or determines which computer goes with which IP address. The physical address of a computer is its MAC (Media Access Control) address. A MAC address is the serial number the vendor engraves on a network card — each one is unique.

Protocol	What It Does
RARP (Reverse Address Resolution Protocol)	Does the reverse of ARP. Uses the computer's MAC address to determine its IP address.
IPX/SPX (Internetwork Packet Exchange/ Sequenced Packet Exchange)	Novell's version of the TCP/IP suite. Early versions of Novell Netware supported IPX/SPX instead of TCP/IP; Netware 5 uses TCP/IP as its default protocol although it still supports IPX/SPX. *Note:* The protocol order in IPX/SPX is backwards when compared to the order in TCP/IP: IPX=IP and SPX=TCP. Although TCP/IP is the Internet standard, IPX/SPX is actually more efficient.
NetBEUI (NetBIOS Extended User Interface)	Enables different computers using different programs to communicate using NetBIOS (Network Basic Input/Output System). Used primarily on small Microsoft networks such as a peer-to-peer. Limited use because it's non-routable (see the discussion on routable protocols in Chapter 19.)
AppleTalk	Used only in Apple networks, AppleTalk communicates by dividing groups of computers into zones.
Hypertext Transfer Protocol (HTTP)	Used to transfer Web pages from servers to Web browsers. Supports hyperlinked text and images.
File Transfer Protocol (FTP)	Commonly used to publish Web pages. Publishing transfers pages, images, and folders to a server machine very efficiently. Also used to provide access to larger files on the Internet or within a company.
TFTP (Trivial File Transfer Protocol)	Less-capable relative of FTP. TFTP uses UDP where FTP uses TCP. Often used for initializing diskless systems, it works with BOOTstrap (BOOTP) Protocol.
BOOTP (BOOTstrap Protocol)	An alternative to RARP. Often used by diskless systems to enable workstations to boot from the server.
Simple Mail Transfer Protocol (SMTP)	Used by mail servers to send e-mail. Used with either POP or IMAP, which receive and store e-mail.
Post Office Protocol (POP)	Used by mail servers to receive and store e-mail.
Internet Messaging Access Protocol (IMAP)	Used by mail servers to receive and store e-mail. Not as common as POP, but more powerful. Allows sharing of mailboxes and access to multiple mail servers.

(continued)

Table 18-5 *(continued)*

Protocol	What It Does
Network News Transfer Protocol (NNTP)	Used by news servers to provide access to newsgroups. (For more on newsgroups, see Chapters 3 and 4.)
Serial Line Internet Protocol (SLIP)	Older protocol used with dial-up connections. Widely replaced by PPP.
Point-to-Point Protocol (PPP)	Commonly used with dial-up connections. Often used instead of SLIP because of its flexibility and security.
Telnet	Used with text-only or shell accounts. A terminal emulation program, which enables users to log on to a remote network and access data as if they were actually part of that remote network. Used widely on the early Internet and part of ARPANET, Telnet is still used to administer large networks.
Gopher	Older protocol that has been widely replaced by HTTP. Gopher was the first menu-based program that enabled users to browse for resources and is considered the precursor to the protocols used on the modern Internet.
SNMP (Simple Network Management Protocol)	Used to manage TCP/IP networks; can collect data from any smart network device.
DHCP (Dynamic Host Configuration Protocol)	Assigns IP addresses and other network setup information on a TCP/IP network. Relieves network administrator of having to manually assign IP addresses to nodes within a network.
DLC (Data Link Control)	Originally used by IBM to connect clients to mainframes; currently used by Hewlett-Packard to connect laser printers to LANs. Nonroutable.

People often use the terms *packet* and *datagram* interchangeably — but that usage is not exactly correct. *Packet* is a generic term; *datagram* refers to the kind of packet used in the OSI/RM. Using these terms interchangeably is like using the brand name *Q-tip* to refer to all cotton swabs (which is what most people do).

For more information on the SMTP, POP, and IMAP e-mail protocols, see Chapter 5.

Combining protocols

Why do so many network protocols exist? That's a good question. To make your life miserable when you study? No. Because they proliferate like bunnies?

No, of course not. One main reason for the abundance of protocols is that several software vendors were each pushing for their own method to become the protocol that everyone would use on the Internet. Luckily for us, a vendor-neutral platform, TCP/IP, became the standard.

All of this variety is a good thing, even though TCP/IP is great. For the exam, you should know which other protocols are also great to use.

IPX/SPX, a key protocol in Novell NetWare, is actually more efficient than TCP/IP. On a Novell network, both IPX/SPX and TCP/IP are useful. To communicate outside the Novell network, TCP/IP is the best choice because it's supported by all systems that connect to the Internet. Within the network, however, IPX/SPX can provide communication between network nodes.

NetBEUI is another protocol that, although not as popular as TCP/IP, does have its uses. NetBEUI is a nonroutable protocol, which means that it can communicate only within a single network — it can't communicate with other networks. (I cover routable protocols in Chapter 19.) NetBEUI is still commonly used on Microsoft networks, however, because it is one of the fastest protocols out there. If you need to transmit a message within your network, you might use NetBEUI. If you need to send a message to someone outside of your network, you use TCP/IP.

It's not uncommon for networks to use two or more protocols at once. Keep in mind, though, that whenever you use two different protocols, you also add a lot of network administration work. That is, you have to follow two sets of rules and possibly have two different configurations.

Binding protocols

After you decide what protocol(s) to use on your network, you have to bind the protocol(s) to your network interface card (NIC) so that the NIC knows which protocols it can use to communicate. A *NIC* is the network card that a computer uses to connect to a network. (Network cards and other network hardware are covered in Chapter 20.)

On a UNIX system, binding a protocol involves reconfiguring the kernel. (And I don't mean the guy with the beard that serves fried chicken.) The *kernel* on a UNIX machine contains records of all drivers and protocols on that machine, and you have to update these records to add a protocol.

Stages of protocol development

When someone wants a protocol to become a standard, it doesn't just happen. Protocols go through a formal process on their way to being recognized and used. The IETF (Internet Engineering Task Force at www.ietf.org) is an organization that helps steer the development of Internet architectures and protocols. The IETF has a subcommittee called the Internet Engineering Steering Group (IESG at www.ietf.org/iesg.html) that's in charge of recommending protocols to become standards. The stages that a proposed protocol must go through are

- ✔ **Experimental:** The protocol is being tested in a lab environment only.

- ✔ **Proposed:** The protocol has passed initial lab tests, and several groups begin testing to see what improvements need to be made.

- ✔ **Draft:** IESG begins to consider making the protocol a standard. Test results and feedback are sent to IESG. If additional changes are needed, they're made in the Draft stage, and the protocol returns to the Proposed stage.

- ✔ **Standard:** IESG declares a protocol one of two types of standards: one that applies to the entire Internet or one that applies to only certain networks.

A protocol might also be in one of these two stages:

- ✔ **Historic:** After a protocol has outlived its usefulness, it's retired.

- ✔ **Informational:** A protocol that a vendor or other organization develops for its own use. Documentation about this type of protocol is posted on the Internet for informational purposes.

Requests for Comments (RFCs) are documents about Internet protocols that are formally published on the Internet. Each standard Internet protocol has an RFC paper containing all the details about how that protocol works. RFCs are identified by number — the higher the number, the more recent the protocol development; RFC 1001, for example, was written before RFC 2223. You don't need to know the numbers of specific RFC documents for the exam — just know the information in this paragraph. If you have some spare time on your hands and want to read the laborious details about every Internet protocol in existence, visit www.rfc-editor.org.

Prep Test

1 Which part of a packet contains the CRC error-checking data?

  A ○ Data
  B ○ Trailer
  C ○ Parcel
  D ○ Header

2 At which layer in the OSI Reference Model does the user interact with the network?

  A ○ Physical
  B ○ Transport
  C ○ Presentation
  D ○ Application

3 Which one of the following layers in the OSI Reference Model consists of the LLC and MAC sublayers?

  A ○ Data link
  B ○ Session
  C ○ Presentation
  D ○ Network

4 At what OSI Reference Model layers do the TCP and IP protocols reside?

  A ○ Session and Application
  B ○ Data link and Physical
  C ○ Transport and Network
  D ○ Presentation and Access

5 Which common networking protocol troubleshoots within TCP/IP?

  A ○ ARP
  B ○ TFTP
  C ○ SMTP
  D ○ ICMP

6 Which of the following is a stateless protocol?

  A ○ UDP
  B ○ IP
  C ○ Neither UDP or IP
  D ○ Both UDP and IP

7 **Which of the following best describes DHCP?**

A ○ Used only in Apple networks

B ○ Used with text-only or shell accounts

C ○ Matches IP addresses to physical addresses

D ○ Assigns IP addresses on TCP/IP networks

8 **Joel is a systems administrator at a company that uses Novell NetWare. Joel is developing an extranet component of the company that will allow employees and customers to communicate over the Internet. Which of the following protocols would not be found on Joel's network?**

A ○ IPX/SPX

B ○ AppleTalk

C ○ TCP/IP

D ○ HTTP

9 **Which stage of protocol development directly precedes the Standard stage?**

A ○ Experimental

B ○ Informational

C ○ Proposed

D ○ Draft

10 **Which of the following is true regarding RFCs?**

A ○ RFC stands for Ready For Certification.

B ○ RFCs contain all the details about how protocols work.

C ○ RFCs ask users to submit their opinions about experimental protocols.

D ○ RFCs are published twice a year in paperback format only.

Answers

1 **B.** Trailer. The trailer section of a packet contains the CRC error-checking data. *Check out "Peter Piper Picked a Data Packet."*

2 **D.** Application. Applications the user interacts with are on the Application layer. *See "Introducing the Open Systems Interconnection Reference Model."*

3 **A.** Data link. The Data link layer of the OSI/RM is the only one that contains any sublayers. *Read "Introducing the Open Systems Interconnection Reference Model."*

4 **C.** Transport and Network. Remember that *trans*mission control protocol operates at the *Trans*port layer and IP operates at the Network layer. It might help to remember that because TCP and IP work together, they more than likely operate on layers that are next to each other. *See "Knowing Which Protocols Go with Which Layers."*

5 **D.** ICMP (Internet Control Message Protocol). *Review "Common Networking Protocols."*

6 **D.** Both UDP and IP. *Take a look at "Common Networking Protocols."*

7 **D.** Assigns IP addresses on TCP/IP networks. *Check out "Common Networking Protocols."*

8 **B.** AppleTalk. AppleTalk is used only on Apple networks. *Look over "Common Networking Protocols."*

9 **D.** Draft. The protocol stages, in order, are: Experimental, Proposed, Draft, and Standard. *Review "Stages of protocol development."*

10 **B.** RFCs contain all the details about how protocols work. *Review "Stages of protocol development."*

Chapter 19

Addressing and Routing on the Internet

. . . .

Exam Objectives

▶ Understanding the relationship between IP addresses and domain names

▶ Understanding the assignment of IP addresses within a subnet

▶ Identifying ports and well-known port numbers

▶ Explaining how the routing process works and the equipment used

▶ Describing ports and well-known port numbers

. . . .

*B*efore you tackle this chapter, you should be familiar with the concept of IP addressing. If you need a refresher, check out Chapter 3. This chapter takes the concept of IP addressing further — I show you the rules that IP addresses must adhere to in order to be valid, and I tell you how you can tell the size of a network based on an IP address.

Whenever information is sent from point A to point B on any network, routing is involved. Routing is kind of like driving in a new city. You probably know your local neighborhood so well that you hardly think about the addresses of the buildings. But when you drive around in a new city, you have to consult a map and pay close attention to street addresses (unless you're a man, but that's another topic). Routing takes care of the directions and finding the addresses of data sent to networks outside your local network. In this chapter, I explain how routing works.

One of the first things to do after you enter the testing booth is to *braindump*. Bathroom humor aside, braindumping involves jotting down as much information as you can as fast as you can so that you don't forget it later. One of the most important areas to dump information about is a list of the parameters of network classes. As I explain in this chapter, the numbers in an IP address let you know the classification (or class) of a network. Write down the ranges of numbers that denote each class so that you don't have to think too hard when the test asks which class an IP address belongs to.

Quick Assessment

IP
addressing

1 _____ is the organization that oversees the assignment of IP addresses.

2 IP addresses are comprised of two portions, the network portion and the _____ portion.

3 Class D IP addresses are reserved for _____.

4 IP addresses with 127 appearing in the first quad (127.xxx.xxx.xxx) are reserved as _____ addresses.

5 _____ addresses allow the same message to be sent to all computers on a network.

6 A _____ hides the network portion of an IP address so that only the host portion of the address is visible.

Routing
protocols

7 A router determines where to send packets of data by consulting its _____.

8 The _____ routing protocol selects routing paths based on the fewest number of hops, without regard to network traffic or possible congestion.

9 _____ ports are sometimes called virtual ports and are the dedicated channels over which certain computers and protocols can talk.

10 The _____ command is a diagnostic tool for troubleshooting TCP/IP networks by testing the connection between two computers or nodes.

Answers

1   *ICANN (Internet Corporation of Assigned Names and Numbers).* See "Understanding Internet Addressing."

2   *Host.* Check out "Internet address classes."

3   *Multicasting.* Review "Internet address classes."

4   *Loopback.* Look over "IP addressing rules."

5   *Broadcast.* See "IP addressing rules."

6   *Subnet mask.* Take a look at "Scratching Beneath the Surface with Subnet Masks."

7   *Routing information table.* Check out "Understanding routing information tables."

8   *RIP (Routing Information Protocol).* Review "Knowing your routing protocols."

9   *Logical.* See "Getting to a logical port of call."

10 *PING (Packet Internet Groper).* Read "Keeping your filthy paws off my Packet Internet Groper (PING)."

Understanding Internet Addressing

Just as houses on your street have addresses like 8585 Jaybird Lane or 4 Paradise Drive, every computer connected to the Internet has a numeric address called an IP (Internet Protocol) address. IP addresses are comprised of four numbers separated by periods or dots like this:

```
200.11.71.115
```

IP addresses are not the same as URLs and domain addresses. A URL identifies the type of Internet resource (for example, http:// represents a Web site) and a domain address identifies a particular computer (such as www.thisismycomputerontheinternet.com). IP addresses also identify individual computers on the Internet, but URLs and domain names are much more useful for Web browsers because these names are easier to remember than a string of numbers. IP addresses are important, however, because every URL and domain address is *translated* into an IP address by domain name servers (DNS servers) around the world so that computers will know where to direct data. Computers cannot understand www.hungryminds.com, but they *can* understand 168.215.86.100.

The format for an IP address is called a *dotted quad* because it always contains four numbers separated by dots. The numbers in the dotted quads can range from 0 to 255.

The four numeric sections in an IP address are comprised of the *network* portion — how many networks can have this class of address — and the *host* portion — how many computers can be hooked up on each network. Each network class supports a different maximum number of networks and hosts.

The numbers that make up IP addresses aren't just randomly assigned. A central organization called ICANN (Internet Corporation of Assigned Names and Numbers) oversees the assignment of IP addresses to ensure none are duplicated. ICANN's Web address is www.icann.org.

Internet address classes

You can tell by the number in the first section of an IP address which class a network belongs in. Table 19-1 illustrates the number ranges that indicate various network classes and gives you an idea of how the classes are divided. I get into details about individual classes in the following sections.

Table 19-1	IP Address Classes	
Address Class	**IP Address Range**	**What This Indicates**
Class A	0.0.0.0 to 127.255.255.255	Reserved for really big networks with lots of devices on them.
Class B	128.0.0.0 to 191.255.255.255	Reserved for pretty good-sized networks with some devices.
Class C	192.0.0.0 to 233.255.255.255	Reserved for small networks.
Class D	224.0.0.0 to 239.255.255.255	Reserved for networks of any size which have multicast addresses (computers that send data to many receivers, such as servers that send mailing lists).
Class E	240.0.0.0 to 247.255.255.255	Reserved for an experimental, super-secret network of the future. (Actually, that's no secret.)

Using Table 19-1, you can determine that the IP address 129.19.59.111 is a medium-sized network because it has a class B address: The first number, 129, fits in the number range for a class B address. The IP address 52.109.22.204 is a class A address because it begins with the number 52. Get it?

The separation in starting points of each class range goes down by half each time, like this: 128, 64, 32, 16, 8. To get the next starting point, you add half the previous range's size, like this:

```
  0 + 128 = 128
128 +  64 = 192
192 +  32 = 224
224 +  16 = 240
240 +   8 = 248
```

Moving to the head of the class: Class A

In a class A network, the first quad holds the network portion of the address and the last three quads hold the host portion, which you can see in Figure 19-1.

Each class A network is big enough that it must have a unique network address. In theory, you could have up to 127 uniquely numbered class A networks because the class A number range is 0 to 127.255.255.255. But in the real world, a few IP addresses are reserved for special use. Read "IP addressing rules for determining invalid addresses" and "Addresses reserved for private use," later in this chapter, to find out what those special uses are.

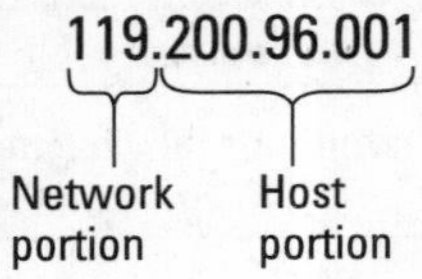

Figure 19-1:
The network
and host
portions of
a class A
address.

119.200.96.001

Network   Host
portion   portion

Because IP addresses beginning with 127 are reserved for special use, the network portion of a class A address can only range from 0 to 126, making 126 the maximum number of class A networks available.

Each computer in a network must have a unique host address as well. There are 16,777,214 ways to combine the digits 0 to 255 in last three quads of a class A address. That means all 126 class A networks can support 16,777,214 hosts (computers).

Being better than average: Class B

In a class B network, the first two quads of the IP address hold the network information while the last two quads hold the host information as shown in Figure 19-2.

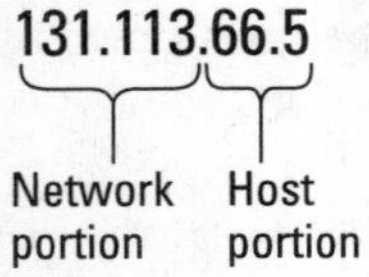

Figure 19-2:
The network
and host
portions of
a class B
address.

131.113.66.5

Network   Host
portion   portion

When you add up all the combinations you can create with the numbers 128 to 191 in the first quad and 0 to 255 in the second quad, you get a total of 16,384 — the maximum number of class B networks. Each class B network supports a maximum of 65,534 hosts.

Getting C-niority: Class C

In a class C network, the first three quads hold the network portion of the address while the last quad holds the host portion of the address, as shown in Figure 19-3.

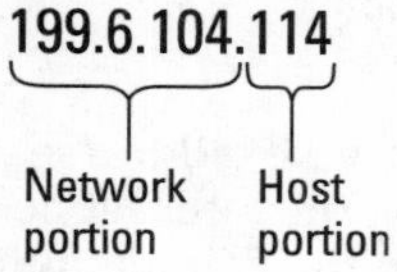

Figure 19-3:
The network
and host
portions of
a class C
address.

199.6.104.114

Network   Host
portion   portion

Add up all the combinations you can get with the first quad ranging from 192 to 223 and the second and third quads ranging from 0 to 255 and you get a total of 2,097,152 class C networks.

The last quad holds the host portion of a class C address. Because IP addresses generally range from 0 to 255, you might be led to believe that there could be 256 host computers on each class C network (including 0); but of course, there are exceptions that prevent you from using the numbers 0 and 255 as the host number in a class C address. The actual number of hosts is 254 on each network.

Whenever you want to refer to an entire network with an IP address, the host section is set to 0. For example, 200.215.86.0 refers to an entire class C network. When the host section is set to 255, it specifies a broadcast that is sent to all hosts on a network. Therefore, any IP address that contains 255 across the entire host portion can be considered a broadcast address. I cover broadcast addressing in more detail later in this chapter.

Digging class D

There is no host portion of a class D address. Class D addresses, therefore, are only good for multicasting. In a *multicast,* all computers in a specific group are sent the same data packet. Class D addresses begin with numbers ranging from 224 to 239.

Note that *multicasting* refers to sending a message to a select group whereas *broadcasting* refers to sending a message to everyone connected to a network.

Class E

Class E addresses aren't in current use — they're reserved for experimental and future use. They begin with numbers ranging from 240 to 247.

IP addressing rules

The Internet Corporation for Assigned Names and Numbers, also known ICANN (www.icann.org), is the organization responsible for assigning names and numbers to all kinds of Internet addresses, including domains (which I discuss in Chapter 3) and IP addresses. Refer to Table 19-1 for a list of IP addresses and a breakdown of IP address classes.

Even though the table seems to account for all of the IP addresses, there are several addresses that are not available for use on the Internet because they are reserved for special use. You may be asked on the Foundations exam to determine whether an IP address is valid for use on the Internet:

✔ **Addresses that begin with** 127.xxx.xxx.xxx **are loopback addresses:** A *loopback address* is an address that enables network administrators to troubleshoot an individual computer's network connection. Loopback addresses are always invalid for use on the Internet. Usually, networks use the loopback function for internal diagnostics and not for anything else.

✔ **Addresses in which all the quads in the network portion or all the quads in the host portion of the address are comprised of** 255 **are broadcast addresses:** A *broadcast address* allows you to send the same message to all computers on the network (a broadcast). Because there are no valid IP addresses that begin with 255, any address with nothing but 255s in the network portion would be nixed from the start. Here's how broadcast addresses look:

    • A class A network broadcast address looks like this:

```
xxx.255.255.255
```

    • A class B broadcast address looks like this:

```
xxx.xxx.255.255
```

    • A class C broadcast address looks like this:

```
xxx.xxx.xxx.255
```

✔ **Addresses in which the entire network or host portion of the address is comprised of zeros are invalid Internet addresses:** Zeros can be part of a valid IP address (120.0.53.0, for example, is a valid IP address), but the entire network or host portion of the address can't be comprised of all zeros (0.xxx.xxx.xxx, for example is not valid). If the entire host portion of an address is comprised of zeros, the IP address refers to an entire network and is therefore not valid for use on the Internet.

For example, the following class C address refers to an entire network, and could not be used as a valid Internet address:

```
xxx.xxx.xxx.0
```

IP addresses that are reserved for private use

Three IP address ranges have been reserved for private networks. A network administrator can assign any of these IP addresses to a machine within a network if the machine's IP address can't be viewed outside that network.

The three IP address blocks reserved for private network use are:

- ✔ `10.0.0.0` through `10.255.255.255`
- ✔ `172.16.0.0` through `172.31.255.255`
- ✔ `192.168.0.0` through `192.168.255.255`

Here are the benefits of using these address ranges:

- ✔ **There are more valid addresses to go around:** Using reserved address blocks for private networks cuts down on the demand for IP addresses that are already in short supply. They allow many network administrators to assign the same IP addresses to computers within their networks because only other computers within that network will see them.

- ✔ **Private addresses create universality:** Using private addresses reminds me of using nicknames within your family. If just you and your spouse are home, it's not hard to figure out whom your spouse is talking to when he/she calls you "Honey." But if you get all the people within a mile radius of your home together, how many people would turn around if someone called out "Honey, over here." Isn't that sweet?

- ✔ **You have more freedom as to how you use workstations:** With private IP addresses, network administrators have the freedom to *not* assign Internet access to individual computers, saving resources for the workstations that do need access. Network administrators also use private network addresses if they're using a proxy server to access the Internet. For more information on proxy servers, see Chapters 16 and 21.

Scratching Beneath the Surface with Subnet Masks

IP addresses are used between computers when transmitting data packets. A subnet mask, on the other hand, has a 32-bit address that looks a lot like an

IP address but has a completely different purpose. *Subnet masks* hide or mask the network portion of an IP address, making only the host portion of the address visible.

Subnet masks serve two purposes:

- ✔ Subnet masks differentiate the network portion from the host portion of an IP address.
- ✔ Subnet masks determine if an IP address is part of the same network or an outside (remote) network.

A subnet mask works somewhat like a phone number. Say your phone number is (555) 111-2222. Unless you live in a very large city, you usually don't have to mention the area code when you share your phone number with someone who lives in your town, because everyone in your neighborhood probably has the same area code.

At many college campuses (and in many companies), you can make a call from one campus phone to another campus number without even having to dial the entire prefix — something like 1-2222. The phone system is, in effect, masking the area code and/or part of the prefix because it only needs to concentrate on the last digits — those are the only digits that differ within the campus calling area. That's why you inevitably hear the question, "Do I have to dial 9 to get an outside line?"

When a network administrator applies a subnet mask, he or she finds the appropriate interface in the computer's operating system and types in the subnet mask number.

The easiest way to apply a subnet mask is to use the default subnet mask for the class of network you're working with. The subnet mask value is generally entered in the Properties interface for the network adapter that's configured to use the TCP/IP protocol suite. Table 19-2 lists the default subnet masks for class A, B, and C networks. You need to know these default values for the CIW Foundations exam.

Table 19-2	Default Subnet Masks
Network Class	*Default Subnet Mask*
Class A	255.0.0.0
Class B	255.255.0.0
Class C	255.255.255.0

Because class D and E networks have no host portion of their addresses, you don't apply subnet masks to those network classes.

Taking the Route Less Traveled

One of the most important IP functions is routing — choosing the path over which to send packets. After all, people wouldn't need networks if they didn't need to transfer data in the first place. Packets may pass through many network devices, or *hops,* to get to their final destination. Packets are routed transparently, which means the process requires no action from users — in fact the routing process happens without users even knowing it.

There are two categories of routing — direct and indirect:

✔ **Direct routing:** Direct routing involves sending packets from one location to another within the same network — no router involved. Direct routing uses ARP (Address Resolution Protocol) to determine where to go.

✔ **Indirect routing:** Indirect routing involves sending packets from a location in one network to a location inside another network. To transfer data between two different networks, you must use a router. When a protocol is described as nonroutable, it can't transfer data outside a network — the protocol is not capable of indirect routing.

Understanding routing information tables

If two or more networks are using the same router, the router can just pass packets from network to network — no big whoop. But if a packet needs to go to a network that's not attached to the same router, things get more complicated: The router has to send the packet to a different router — one that's attached to that other network. This extra step is crucial. A *routing information table* comes in handy because it keeps track of the locations of different networks in relation to the router, allowing for the most effective path to be utilized based on the routing protocol being used.

The information in a routing table can be either static or dynamic:

✔ **Static routing:** In static routing, the network administrator must manually configure and update the routing information. If a router doesn't know how to reach some new point on a network, it just can't send data there.

✔ **Dynamic routing:** A dynamic router dynamically updates routing information. A dynamic router is like the town gossip — the router hangs around and chats with other routers making note of who's new in the neighborhood and who's moving out, and then updates the information as changes occur.

Knowing your routing protocols

Several different protocols may be used in the process of transferring packets from network to network or from one workstation to another within the same network.

In fact, interior routing protocols are only used when packets are transmitted within a network. Accordingly, exterior routing protocols are used to send information to a location outside the current network. The Foundations exam focuses on interior routing protocols, of which there are two:

- **RIP (Routing Information Protocol):** You may rest in peace knowing that RIP is commonly used in small-to-medium sized local area networks (LANs). RIP selects routing paths based on the fewest hops. A disadvantage of RIP is that it doesn't consider that common routes might be clogged with heavy traffic. For example, yes, the freeway may *theoretically* be the fastest way to get from here to there, but not at 8:00 a.m. on a Monday. RIP isn't capable of changing the routing path — its job is done when it's finished counting hops. Also, RIP doesn't do anything to determine whether routes are secure from external threats because routing exchanges are not authenticated. Routing table updates are also restricted to regularly scheduled updates in RIP.

- **OSPF (Open Shortest Path First):** OSPF is superior to RIP in many ways. It takes into account traffic patterns and security issues when choosing routing paths, it updates routing tables as necessary instead of on a regular schedule, and it authenticates routing exchanges. OSPF is most commonly used on large networks, including the Internet.

Getting to a logical port of call

A port is, in essence, a doorway of communication. Ports can be physical or logical. You're probably familiar with physical ports. Those are the adapters on the backside of your computer that you plug your printer into. Don't get confused — I'm not talking about the plugs themselves, but the place where you plug them in.

Logical ports are a little different. Unlike the ones you can see and touch, logical ports, which are the focus of this exam, are called logical (or virtual) because you can't really touch them — they're the dedicated channels over which computers and protocols talk.

Say you multitask like crazy, sending a document to the printer, opening a saved document, browsing the Web, and so on. How does your computer avoid getting confused with all this information going here and there? It uses logical ports to prioritize the activities. The ports, in turn, use protocols to help accomplish their tasks (sending files to the printer, finding documents, and transmitting information to and from the Web). Each protocol uses a specific port.

Information about which port (or ports) are being used is embedded in the headers of packets when they are transmitted. As I discuss in Chapter 18, every packet that is transmitted over a network has a header embedded in it. The header contains a lot of important information, not the least of which is the port information. Logical ports are numbered, and although over 65,000 ports could be utilized, you don't have to memorize all of them. Just know the most commonly used ports. Surprise! The most commonly used protocols have assigned port numbers:

- ✔ **HTTP:** Port 80
- ✔ **FTP:** Port 21
- ✔ **Telnet:** Port 23
- ✔ **SMTP:** Port 25
- ✔ **DNS:** Port 53
- ✔ **Gopher:** Port 70
- ✔ **POP3:** Port 110
- ✔ **NNTP:** Port 119

If you want a round number of logical ports that have been assigned, I can do you one better. I can tell you that the number is 1023:

- ✔ **1 to 1023:** Well-known or reserved port numbers.
- ✔ **1024 to 65,535:** Remaining registered port numbers.

The most commonly utilized ports are also often called well known, reserved, or default ports.

Troubleshooting Commands

What do you do if you send someone several e-mail messages, but the messages aren't getting to the recipient? Or you send jobs to the network printer down the hall, but the document you want to print doesn't come spewing out? Network administrators use several diagnostic tools to troubleshoot a network that's utilizing the TCP/IP protocol suite.

Keeping your filthy paws off my Packet Internet Groper (PING)

People frequently use Packet Internet Groper (less lasciviously called PING) to test the connection between two computers or nodes. PING is executed from the command line of the network operating system, such as the MS-DOS prompt or the Command prompt. PING sends out a packet to the designated IP address, and if the IP address is valid, the destination computer sends back an echo response that looks something like this:

```
Reply from 192.168.5.5: bytes-32 time<10ms TTL=64
Reply from 192.168.5.5: bytes-32 time<10ms TTL=64
Reply from 192.168.5.5: bytes-32 time<10ms TTL=64
Reply from 192.168.5.5: bytes-32 time<10ms TTL=64.
```

Using a trace route command

The trace route command lets you check the path two computers are using to transmit data back and forth. Say your company Web site's home page is taking too long for users' browsers to load, and you know the file sizes aren't the problem. You may want to run a trace route to see how many hops it took for the page to get to your computer, and to see what the address of each device was along the way. (Any computer with an Internet connection will do for this kind of test.) The Web server could be many hops away from the Internet backbone, increasing the page's download time. The Internet backbone is simply the high-speed infrastructure that connects and interconnects all the resources on the Internet.

To perform a trace route on a UNIX machine, you must type **traceroute** at the command line, followed by the destination IP address. On a Windows machine, you type **tracert** at the command line, followed by the IP address of the destination machine.

Working with ipconfig command

If you need to find all the IP-related information about a particular Windows NT/2000 machine, you can use the ipconfig command. The ipconfig command displays a list of the computer's IP address, subnet mask, default gateway, and physical (MAC) address, among other things.

To use ipconfig to list all the Windows NT/2000 computer's IP-related information, you type **ipconfig** at the command line.

On UNIX machines, you type **IFCONFIG** at the command line to yield the IP-related information.

Aside from providing network administrators with IP-related information for troubleshooting purposes, the ipconfig command also releases and renews an IP address from a DHCP server. If your computer's IP address is dynamically assigned, (using DHCP) ipconfig releases your current IP address and prompts the DHCP server to reassign an IP address to it. DHCP (Dynamic Host Control Protocol) allows a network administrator to define the IP configuration scope for all the hosts on the network and dynamically assign IP addresses to the machines within the network, instead of having to manually type in IP addresses on each machine.

Using the winipcfg command

The winipcfg command is similar to ipconfig, except you use it on a Windows 95/98/Me machine. Winipcfg determines the machine's IP configuration and Ethernet address so that the user or an administrator can troubleshoot the TCP/IP connection and/or network. To use winipcfg, you type **winipcfg** at the command line or through the Run interface above the Start button.

Utilizing the netstat utility

The netstat utility displays protocol statistics and current active TCP/IP connections. You can specify one (or several) options to have netstat display configuration information about a network, workstation, or server. This utility is available on both Windows and UNIX operating systems, and allows administrators to isolate network problems in real time.

The netstat utility also displays information about the state of sockets. A *socket* is the combination of a computer's IP address and the port that's in use.

A socket, defined by ProsoftTraining, is the end point of a connection (either side), which usually includes the TCP or UDP port used and the IP address. A socket is used for communication between a client and a server.

Working with the arp command

The arp command uses address resolution protocol (discussed in Chapter 18) to match software addresses (IP) with hardware addresses (MAC). This allows an administrator to figure out what pieces of hardware (network interface cards) belong to what IP addresses. To use the arp command, you type **Arp** at the command line. It then yields a list of IP addresses matched up with MAC addresses, like this:

```
Interface: 192.168.5.5
   Internet Address      Physical Address      Type
   192.168.5.1           00-60-83-7b-24-a1     Dynamic
   192.168.5.10          00-aa-96-8a-11-3c     Dynamic
   192.168.5.11          00-aa-a7-72-22-a2     Dynamic
```

Prep Test

1 **What is the valid IP range for class C IP addresses?**

A ○ 224.0.0.0 to 239.255.255.255
B ○ 128.0.0.0 to 191.255.255.255
C ○ 192.0.0.0 to 233.255.255.255
D ○ None of the above

2 **Which class of IP addresses offers the most possible networks?**

A ○ Class C
B ○ Class A
C ○ Class F
D ○ Class B

3 **Which of the following is not a valid class A address?**

A ○ 19.188.192.0
B ○ 122.255.1.1
C ○ 52.100.22.202
D ○ 128.38.190.1

4 **Evelyn manages her company's network. Twenty users are on her network, and all users access the Internet through a proxy server. Evelyn needs to assign IP addresses for private network use. What IP range would be appropriate for Evelyn to use?**

A ○ 127.0.0.0 through 127.255.255.255
B ○ 192.168.0.0 through 192.168.255.255
C ○ 240.0.0.0 through 247.255.255.255
D ○ 255.255.255.0 through 255.255.255.255

5 **Which of the following statements is not true regarding subnet masks?**

A ○ Subnet masks must always be applied to class D addresses.
B ○ Subnet masks differentiate the network portion from the host portion of an IP address.
C ○ Subnet masks cannot be applied to class E networks.
D ○ Subnet masks hide the network portion of IP addresses.

6 **What is the default subnet mask for class B networks?**

A ○ 255.255.255.255
B ○ 255.255.255.0
C ○ 255.0.0.0
D ○ 255.255.0.0

7 **What routing category uses ARP (Address Resolution Protocol) to determine where to send packets within the same network?**

  A ○ Indirect routing

  B ○ Trace routing

  C ○ Direct routing

  D ○ Node hopping

8 **What port number is commonly dedicated for use by the HTTP protocol?**

  A ○ Port 21

  B ○ Port 80

  C ○ Port 53

  D ○ Port 25

9 **What TCP/IP troubleshooting method checks the path two computers are using to transmit data, recording the number of hops and device addresses between the two points?**

  A ○ PING

  B ○ IPconfig

  C ○ Arp

  D ○ Trace route

10 **Which of the following is not true regarding the netstat utility?**

  A ○ Netstat yields a list of IP addresses matched up with physical (MAC) addresses.

  B ○ Netstat displays protocol statistics.

  C ○ Netstat can show information about the state of sockets.

  D ○ Netstat displays current active TCP/IP connections.

Answers

1 **C.** 192.0.0.0 to 233.255.255.255. *See "Internet address classes."*

2 **A.** Class C. *Read "Internet address classes."*

3 **D.** 128.38.190.1. *Check out "Internet address classes."*

4 **B.** 192.168.0.0 through 192.168.255.255. *See "IP addressing rules."*

5 **A.** Subnet masks must always be applied to class D addresses. *Read "Scratching Beneath the Surface with Subnet Masks."*

6 **D.** 255.255.0.0. *Look over "Scratching Beneath the Surface with Subnet Masks."*

7 **C.** Direct routing. *Review "Taking the Route Less Traveled."*

8 **B.** Port 80. *Take a look at "Getting to a logical port of call."*

9 **D.** Trace route. *Check out "Using a trace route command."*

10 **A.** Netstat yields a list of IP addresses matched up with physical (MAC) addresses. *See "Utilizing the netstat utility."*

Chapter 20

This LAN Is Your LAN, This WAN Is My WAN

Exam Objectives

▶ Understanding the components and standards connected to local area networks (LANs), wide area network (WANs), and wireless networks

▶ Explaining the role of networking hardware and configuring common PC hardware for operation

▶ Identifying the features of various transmission media such as coaxial, twisted pair, and fiber optic

▶ Contrasting various transmission types such as synchronous and asynchronous

*I*n this chapter, I discuss what makes a LAN a LAN and what makes a WAN a WAN. There are several components that determine what type of network you're setting up: the type of network interface card (NIC) you're using, the type of transmission media (a fancy phrase that means the cables or wireless transmission systems you're using) you choose to connect your computers, and the software you install on your machines.

LANs and WANs are the basic types of networks. A local area network (LAN) is ideal for networks within a small geographical region — within an office building, for example. Businesses with several branch offices around the country, however, may connect individual LANs to a wide area network (WAN). A WAN enables users to share files and data over a large geographical area. There's no specific geographical distance that necessitates the use of a WAN as opposed to a LAN, but keep in mind that in a LAN, you most likely are running cables between all computers in the network, whereas in a WAN, your data can be transmitted over phone lines, which can span most any geographical region.

In this chapter, I discuss the hardware specifications for various types of LANs and WANs. I show you how to figure out the type of cabling to use based upon network type and the distance between the machines being connected. I also review the purpose and limitations of standard network hardware — routers, bridges, hubs, and so forth. All of these areas are covered on the exam.

Quick Assessment

Common
network
components

1 Sometimes called a network adapter card, the device that allows a computer to connect to a network is the _____.

2 Any entry or exit point of a network is referred to as a _____.

3 A(n) _____ is the device that usually connects coaxial cable to network devices.

4 In _____ transmission, the access device calibrates precisely to the network by sharing a common clock.

5 With _____ data transmission flow, data travels only one way.

Basics of
LANs and
WANs

6 A _____ is the type of network used to transmit data over a relatively small geographical area.

7 The _____ LAN standard divides the data link layer of the OSI/RM into the logical link control (LLC) layer and the media control layer (MMC).

8 A _____ is the type of network used to transmit data over a large geographical area.

9 _____ is the data transmission method used by the frame relay and ATM WAN technologies.

10 A T1 carrier line has 24 channels that transmit at 64 Kbps (kilobytes per second) each, with a maximum undivided speed of _____.

Answers

1 *NIC (network interface card).* See "Putting Together the Pieces of a Network."

2 *Gateway.* Check out "Putting Together the Pieces of a Network."

3 *BNC connector.* Review "Cozying up to coaxial cable."

4 *Synchronous.* Take a look at "Synchronous transmission."

5 *Simplex.* See "Doing the data transmission flow dance."

6 *LAN (local area network).* Look over "Local Area Networks (LANS)."

7 *802.2.* Look over "802.2 standard."

8 *WAN (wide area network).* Read "Wide Area Networks (WANS)."

9 *Fast packet switching.* Check out "Fast packet switching."

10 *1.544 Mbps (megabits per second).* Read "Give me a T-carrier system."

Introducing LANS and WANS

Depending on the networking situation, you may choose to set up a local area network (LAN) or a wide area network (WAN) or, possibly, both, linking two or more LANs together to create a WAN.

Each type of LAN or WAN is based on a specific standard, which is a specification establishing which types of hardware (and to some degree, software) you use to create a specific type of LAN or WAN. It's kind of like the difference between vehicle classes — a sports car, for example, can be made by lots of companies, but sports cars generally have two doors, high-speed capabilities, and often come with a stick-shift transmission. A luxury vehicle, on the other hand, typically has four doors, a smoother ride, and usually an automatic transmission. The standards that separate car classes are sometimes a little vague (I've heard cars described as "luxury sports cars," for example), but the standards that separate LAN and WAN types are more concrete — specific types of network interface cards (NICs) and cabling are called for with each LAN/WAN type, and I cover those specifications in this chapter.

Don't confuse LAN and WAN standards with topologies. Topologies are the physical configurations used to connect nodes in a network. Using the automobile analogy, topologies are like physical categories such as two-door, four-door, or truck. Standards are guidelines that specify hardware and types of transmissions. A Jeep Grand Cherokee, for example, uses a specific model of steering wheel — there may be a few other vehicles that can use that same steering wheel, but it's the only kind a Grand Cherokee can use. It's the same way with LAN and WAN standards. A specific type of LAN, for example, uses only coaxial cable to connect computers. Other LAN standards may also use coaxial cable, but this specific type of LAN can only use coaxial cable.

Putting Together the Pieces of a Network

Before you can understand the different LAN and WAN standards, you need to know about the different types of hardware they use. Table 20-1 lists the key network hardware components you need to know for the Foundations exam.

Table 20-1	Key Network Hardware Components	
Hardware	**What It Does**	**OSI/RM Layer**
Network interface card (NIC)	Device that allows computers to connect to a network; also called a network adapter card; usually contains a *transceiver,* a device that sends and receives transmission signals.	Works at the data link layer of the OSI/RM
Hub	Device that connects computers in a star topology configuration; several can be hooked together or *daisy-chained;* often acts as a repeater.	Works at the physical layer of the OSI/RM
Repeater	Device that amplifies a signal traveling along a network; prevents signal from degrading so computers can be placed further apart.	Works at the physical layer of the OSI/RM
Bridge	Device that connects two LANs with the same protocol; can divide one network into two segments to reduce traffic; can connect different network segments, such as a token ring to an Ethernet network. Bridges use MAC addresses to determine where to send packets.	Works at the data link layer of the OSI/RM
Router	Device that connects two or more networks; uses IP and other network addresses to determine where to send packets. Various protocol structures need different types of routers; for example one router reads IP addresses, and a different type reads SPX addresses.	Works at the network layer of the OSI/RM
Brouter	Device that combines the functionality of a bridge and a router; can connect two different types of networks (like a WAN to a LAN); protocol-independent.	Works at the network and data link layers of the OSI/RM
Switch	Device that can do most everything a hub, bridge, or router can do, but faster; utilizes entire bandwidth between sending and receiving machines, eliminating bottlenecks.	Can work at any one of the first four OSI/RM layers: Application, Presentation, Session, or Transport
Modem	Device that converts digital signals from a computer into analog signals that can travel over a phone line, and then converts analog signals from the phone line into digital signals so your computer can understand them.	Works at the physical layer of the OSI/RM

(continued)

Table 20-1 *(continued)*

Hardware	What It Does	OSI/RM Layer
Channel Service Unit/Data Service Unit (CSU/DSU)	Device that converts the type of digital signal a digital carrier line (such as a T1) sends into the type of digital signal a computer or network can understand, and then converts the signal the other way. All dedicated circuits, such as a T1 or T3 must use this device. Terminates one type of signal and coverts it to another. Also called a digital modem.	Works at the physical layer of the OSI/RM
Gateway	Device that provides entry and exit points of a network. Many devices can act as gateways — proxy servers, routers — any device that joins two or more networks. Can convert protocols; also called a protocol converter.	Can operate at any layer of the OSI/RM
Patch panel	A device, usually mounted on a rack, that can bring together cables from several rooms or locations within a small geographical area. An office, for example, may have each computer within each room connected to a hub, and that hub may be connected to a wall jack. The cable from each wall jack can run to a patch panel to provide a central location to access all wall-jack cables.	Works at the physical layer of the OSI/RM
RJ-45 (Registered Jack 45)	Device commonly used in Ethernet and token ring networks to connect computers to the network. Larger version of a standard phone jack (RJ-11).	Works at the physical layer of the OSI/RM
Internet-in-a-box	Product many vendors sell that contains all the software and hardware you need to create a network. Easy to install and use.	N/A
BNC connector	Used to connect coaxial cable to NICs, hubs, and other network devices.	Works at the physical layer of the OSI/RM

There are a few more network hardware devices you may encounter on the exam, which you can find throughout this chapter.

Daisy-chaining

Daisy-chaining is a way of connecting several devices, one after the other — like tying sheets together end to end. By daisy-chaining repeaters (or other items, for that matter), you can extend the geographical range that a network with a specific type of cabling can cover. If you encounter a question on the exam asking about the maximum distance that can exist between network computers using a specific type of cabling (each cable type has a specific maximum run length), make sure you note if repeaters are mentioned. If the type of cable you're using can run a maximum of 200 yards, and you use a repeater, you can place computers up to 400 yards apart.

Determining Cable Readiness

You can get a good idea of whether a network is a LAN or a WAN and which type of LAN or WAN it is just by looking at the cable it uses to connect computers to each other. There are a variety of cable types (also called *transmission media*) to choose from, including no cable at all — a cable- free or wireless network. The following sections go into details.

Most types of cable have alternative names that denote the type of transmission they're capable of. For example, a certain type of twisted-pair cable may be referred to as 10baseT. 10baseT cable transmits data at 10 Mbps; the word *base* means it's using baseband transmission, and the *T* at the end stands for twisted pair. As I describe each type of cable, I include any other names the cable may be called.

Becoming a twisted sister (Or brother)

Twisted-pair cable is the Honda Civic of cable types — more Ethernet networks use it than any other type of cable. (Ethernet is a specific type of LAN that I discuss in "Ethernet/802.3," later in this chapter.) Twisted-pair cable consists of pairs of copper wires twisted around each other. You may have seen twisted-pair cable because it's the type used in phone cables.

Two types of wire may be used in twisted-pair cable:

▸ **Stranded:** Stranded wire is the more common type of wire used in twisted-pair cable. Because of its flexibility, it goes around corners easily. If you've ever run cable around corners, you know why this is a good thing.

✔ **Solid:** Less flexible than stranded wire, solid wire breaks if bent too many times. However, it can run over longer distances without *attenuation* — the degrading of a signal as it travels farther from its source. This is a major asset if you're running cable from the 21st floor to the basement. (See "Understanding categories and run length.")

In addition to knowing the two types of wire used in twisted-pair cable, you need to know the two basic types of twisted-pair cabling:

✔ **STP (Shielded Twisted Pair):** The pairs of twisted copper wiring are encased in an additional metal shield — kind of like leftovers wrapped in tinfoil — that prevents signal interference. STP is harder to work with and maintain than UTP.

✔ **UTP (Unshielded Twisted Pair):** UTP cable is less expensive and more common that STP. Because it's unshielded, it's more vulnerable to electromagnetic interference.

There are seven types (categories) of twisted-pair cabling. The first five are accepted as standard cable types used in networks; the last two are expected to be accepted as standards soon.

Understanding categories and run length

Each type of cable has a maximum *run length,* the maximum length that one segment of cable can run between two network devices. If you run a cable over a longer distance than its recommended run length, the signal will degrade, and data transmission may break down. Table 20-2 lists the types (categories) of twisted-pair cables, their descriptions, and their maximum run lengths.

Table 20-2	Twisted Pair Categories and Run Lengths		
Category	**Description**	**UTP/STP**	**Maximum Run Length**
1	Used for voice (phone) only.	UTP	100 meters
2	Comprised of four sets of twisted pairs; sometimes used in token ring networks; transmits at maximum speed of 4 Mbps.	UTP	100 meters
3	Comprised of four twisted pairs; commonly used for Ethernet networks; transmits at maximum speed of 10 Mbps.	Both	100 meters
4	Comprised of four twisted pairs; used in some token ring networks; transmits at maximum speed of 16 Mbps.	Both	100 meters

Category	Description	UTP/STP	Maximum Run Length
5	Comprised of four twisted pairs; used in Ethernet and fast Ethernet networks; transmits at maximum speed of 100 Mbps on Ethernet and fast Ethernet networks, although a newer version called cat5 E can support transmission of up to 1,000 Mbps on a gigabit Ethernet network. Commonly used in Ethernet networks to allow an upgrade to Fast Ethernet.	Both	100 meters
6	Comprised of four twisted pairs; used for Fast Ethernet networks; transmits at a maximum speed of 155 Mbps.	Both	100 meters
7	Comprised of four twisted pairs; used for gigabit Ethernet networks; transmits at maximum speed of 1,000 Mbps.	Both	100 meters

Each type of cable (whether twisted pair or other types such as coaxial, which I discuss later in this section) is used with specific types of LANs and WANs. As I describe specific LAN and WAN standards throughout this chapter, I also mention which type of cabling each LAN/WAN type uses. You may want to refer back to Table 20-2 periodically when I mention that category 3 twisted-pair cabling is used with certain types of LANs, for example.

Note: When referring to twisted-pair cable categories, people often say "cat3" to refer to category 3 or "cat5" to refer to category 5. (I don't want you to sound like a networking newbie.)

Determining TP cable transmission speeds

The maximum speed that data can be transmitted over twisted-pair cable depends on the category of cable and network interface card you're using. For example, if you have a network interface card that only supports 10 Mbps transmission, that's the fastest speed the data can travel at on that network, whether you're using category-6 cable or not.

On the other hand, if you have a network interface card that supports 100 Mbps, but you're using category-3 cable, 10 Mbps is still the fastest the data can travel.

Many network interface cards are 10/100 (pronounced "ten-one-hundred"), meaning they support either transmission speed. For example, if you use category-5 twisted-pair cable (which supports 100 Mbps transmission speed) with a 10/100 card, data can travel at 100 Mbps. In this case, your cable would be referred to as 100baseT because it's transmitting at 100 Mbps over a baseband connection with twisted-pair cabling. If you use category-3 cable, data transfers at the slower rate of 10 Mbps.

Cozying up to coaxial cable

If you've never seen coaxial cable, go take a look at your cable TV connection — it uses coaxial (or coax, pronounced "co-axe") cable. But before you go wild and start plugging the cable cord from your TV into your computer, you should know that there are different standards of coax for different purposes. So unfortunately, you can't use your TV cable to create a home network with all your computers. Big bummer.

Here are some things to know about coax cable:

✔ All coaxial cable is considered *high capacity* because it provides higher bandwidth — it can transmit more data more quickly than twisted-pair cable.

✔ All coaxial cable contains a signal wire in its center that is surrounded by a metallic shield.

✔ All coaxial cable supports either baseband or broadband transmission. Baseband transmission uses all the available wires within a cable to transmit data. Broadband transmission allows the wires within a cable to be sectioned off — certain wires can be used for one transmission, and other wires in the same cable can be used to send other data at the same time. (You can find more on transmission types later in this chapter.)

Coaxial cable comes in two flavors:

✔ **Thinnet,** also called 10base2, transmits at 10 Mbps, supports a baseband transmission, and is about .25 inches in diameter — which is where the *2* at the end comes from.

✔ **Thicknet,** also called 10base5, transmits at 10 Mbps, supports a baseband transmission, and is about .5 inches in diameter — which is where the *5* at the end comes from.

Table 20-3 lists the types of coaxial cable used to network computers, their descriptions, and their maximum run lengths.

Table 20-3	Coaxial Cable Descriptions	
Type of Coaxial Cable	*Description*	*Maximum Run Length*
Thinnet (10base2)	The standard for smaller Ethernet networks; very flexible for corners	185 meters
Thicknet (10base5)	Considered the Ethernet standard; used with 10base5 Ethernet networks	500 meters

The device usually used to connect coax cable to NICs, hubs, and other network devices is called a BNC connector. The BNC (British Naval Connector or Bayonet Neil-Concelman) looks a lot like the cable connector used with cable TV, as shown in Figure 20-1.

Figure 20-1:
A BNC
connector.

Getting your daily dose of fiber-optic cable

Fiber-optic cable is the Speedy Gonzalez of network cabling — it transmits at several gigabits-per-second. Fiber-optic cable sends data as beams of light over threads of glass.

Electromagnetic interference

Electromagnetic interference occurs when a signal emitted from one device interferes with another device's signal transmission. This is similar to how the signal emitted by a powerful radio can "bleed over" into the signal from another radio station. Electromagnetic interference isn't necessarily caused by radio waves, however; electrical appliances or devices (such as hospital radiology equipment or even fluorescent light bulbs) can interfere with signal transmission. If a network's cabling must run close to devices that might interfere (through a room with radiology equipment, for example), it's best to choose a cable that's well-protected from interference such as shielded twisted-pair, Thicknet, or fiber-optic cable, at least for that portion of the network.

Due to its unique transmission method, signals can travel miles without any signal degradation. Because the signals are composed of beams of light, not electrical currents, there's no electromagnetic interference. Two drawbacks to fiber-optic cable: It's expensive, and not as many people know how to work with it compared to twisted-pair or coaxial cable.

Fiber-optic cables are comprised of small glass strands that send data back and forth — simultaneously. The core strands are enclosed in a glass encasement (called glass cladding) and wrapped in plastic reinforced with Kevlar — the stuff bulletproof vests are made of. Fiber-optic cables are somewhat delicate and break easier than twisted-pair or coax cables. Although fiber-optic cable is great for transmitting over long distances, it doesn't go around corners well because the glass strands will break.

Here are the two main types of fiber-optic cable:

- ✔ **Single-mode:** Often used for metropolitan telephone trunks, single-mode fiber-optic cable transmits at only one wavelength or frequency (kind of like a radio station usually broadcasts signals at only one frequency — 590 on the AM dial, for example).

- ✔ **Multimode:** Usually used in LANs and WANs, multimode fiber-optic cable uses several frequencies or modes during transmission (kind of like a radio station that transmits the same program over several frequencies — both 590 AM and 94.5 FM, for example).

Look, Ma, no wires

Wireless transmission media is just starting to become popular with business travelers and others who need to log on to a company network (or the Internet) without the burden of cabling. Wireless transmission media are usually used in conjunction with wired networks — a person uses a laptop with a wireless network interface card to connect to a regular LAN or WAN, for example. When you combine two types of networks — wireless and networks with cables, for example — this is called a *hybrid* network.

Wireless networks aren't covered in detail on this exam. Technology is advancing so quickly in the wireless arena that it almost wouldn't be fair to test you on wireless transmission standards. Two key facts you do need to know about wireless networks are

- ✔ They don't use wires — they send electronic signals kind of like satellites.

- ✔ Each computer connected to a wireless network must have a network access card that includes a *transceiver* — a device that allows the NIC to send and receive wireless signals.

Turning On the Transmission

The cable you choose to configure a network affects transmission rates and the type of transmission. There are several subtle differences in the ways that various cables can transmit data. The next few sections explain the key differences you need to know for the exam.

Asynchronous transmission

Asynchronous transmission is the type of transmission that dial-up modems use to access the Internet. In this type of transmission, the access device (modem) isn't synchronized with the network (your ISP). Because your modem is configured to transmit data at a certain speed, and this speed may not be the same as the speed the network is currently using, the modem sends out data one character at a time so the network can move it along at whatever speed it wants to — regardless of whether that's the same speed your modem is transmitting at.

Synchronous transmission

Synchronous transmission is often used to transmit data within a LAN or WAN. In synchronous transmission, the access device (a modem or NIC) synchronizes with the network by sharing a common clock. (Think of the spies in *Mission Impossible* synchronizing their watches before they begin their mission, only in this case, they're synchronizing to transfer data at the same rate — the fastest rate each device can agree on.) Synchronous data transmission is more efficient than asynchronous transmission because synchronous transmission can send larger packets of data than asynchronous can (although you don't need to know the exact sizes of the packets for the exam). The packets of data that the two exchange are called *message-framed data*. T1 lines use synchronous transmission.

Boogying along with baseband and broadband capacities

A transmission medium's capacity to transfer data is called its bandwidth. The bandwidth of cable and wireless transmission media is often divided into channels — individual sections of the cable. The way these channels are allocated and used fit in one of two categories: baseband or broadband.

✔ **Baseband:** Baseband uses the entire bandwidth for transmission — kind of like having several drinking straws taped together in a bundle, but all the straws have to be used by one person at a time. Baseband transmission is used in most LANs, such as Ethernet and token rings.

✔ **Broadband:** Broadband allows multiple channels with each one carrying its own signal — kind of like having several drinking straws taped together in a bundle, but several users at a time can slurp liquid through one or two straws. High-speed Internet connections such as T1, DSL, and cable Internet connections usually use broadband transmission.

Doing the data transmission flow dance

You know how some roads are two way and some are only one way? Cables have those types of variances, too. Cables support three types of data (traffic) flow or traffic patterns. For the exam, know the definition of each type of data flow and that Ethernet uses half duplex, whereas *full-duplex Ethernet,* a special type of Ethernet, uses — you guessed it — full duplex.

✔ **Simplex:** Data travels only one way — like a one-way street. Simplex transmission is rarely ever used. (Can you think of a network device that only sends data and can't also receive data? I can't.)

✔ **Half duplex:** Data can travel both ways but only one way at a time. This is like a two-lane road that's under construction. Construction workers let traffic use the one good lane to go one way for a few minutes, and then they block that traffic and let cars going the other way travel across the good lane. Ethernet uses half-duplex transmission.

✔ **Full duplex:** Data can go both ways at once, like a typical two-lane road. A type of Ethernet called full-duplex Ethernet can use full duplex transmission, as long as there are switches on the network.

Local Area Networks (LANS)

A local area network (LAN) is the type of network you use to transmit data over a relatively small geographical area — from several inches to approximately two or three miles. Most office environments use LANs.

Within the LAN standard, there are several LAN types you can choose from — each LAN standard you need to know for the exam is discussed in the next few sections. The network cards and types of cable you use determines which type of LAN or WAN you have. The different categories of LANs are called standards. The Institute of Electronics Engineers (IEEE, www.ieee.org) creates the standards LANs and WANs adhere to.

802.2 standard

The 802.2 LAN standard is the one all the others in the 802 series are based on. The one key thing the 802.2 standard does is divide the data link layer of the OSI/RM into two sublayers — the logical link control (LLC) layer and the media access control (MAC) layer. (For more information on the OSI/RM and all of its layers, refer to Chapter 18.) All the LAN standards in the 802 series include this division of the data link layer.

Ethernet/802.3

Ethernet is based on the 802.3 standard. The specifications of an Ethernet LAN include

- ✓ **Data access method:** An Ethernet LAN uses the Carrier Sense Multiple Access/Collision Detected (CSMA/CD) method to place data on the network. When a node on a network communicates using the CSMA/CD method, the sending node transmits a signal to see if the coast is clear before it sends out data. While CSMA/CD does help prevent data collision, if two nodes start transmitting at the exact same time, they still can collide.

- ✓ **Cabling:** Ethernet LANs can use 10base2, 10base5, 10baseT, or even fiber-optic cabling.

- ✓ **Transmission speed:** Ethernet LANs transmit at 10 Mbps.

- ✓ **Transmission method:** Transmissions are broadcast to all network nodes. Only the node intended to receive the message picks it up.

- ✓ **Topology(ies):** Unlike some other LAN standards, there is no set topology an Ethernet network must use, although Ethernet networks are commonly configured in a star, bus, or hybrid star/bus topology. (To review network topologies, see Chapter 15.)

Fast Ethernet/802.3u

As the name implies, Fast Ethernet is a lot like regular Ethernet, but much faster. Fast Ethernet transmits at a minimum speed of 100 Mbps and even faster if you use fiber-optic cable. As network administrators begin replacing worn-out NICs on standard Ethernet networks, they often replace them with Fast Ethernet cards that support both 10 Mbps and 100 Mbps transmissions. After cable is in place that supports 100 Mbps transmission, the network is considered a Fast Ethernet network.

Features of Fast Ethernet include

- ✓ **Data access method:** Fast Ethernet uses CSMA/CD for network access.

- ✓ **Cabling:** Fast Ethernet uses twisted-pair (especially cat5) and fiber-optic cabling.

- ✓ **Transmission speed:** Fast Ethernet supports a data transmission speed of 100 Mbps.

- ✓ **Transmission method:** Fast Ethernet transmissions are broadcast to all network nodes. Only the node intended to receive the message picks it up.

- ✓ **Topology:** Fast Ethernet uses the star topology.

Gigabit Ethernet/802.3z and 802.3ab

Gigabit Ethernet is currently the fastest LAN technology available. A gigabit Ethernet transfers data at 1,000 Mbps or 1 Gbps (gigabit per second). Gigabit Ethernet has two sub-classifications — 802.3z and 802.3ab. The only difference between these two sub-classifications you need to know for the exam is that the two can use different types of cable. The specifics are listed in the following list.

Features of gigabit Ethernet include

- ✓ **Data access method:** Gigabit Ethernet LANs use CSMA/CD for network access.

- ✓ **Cabling:** Gigabit Ethernet 802.3z LANs use specialty copper cable and fiber-optic cabling. Gigabit Ethernet 802.3ab LANs use category 5 UTP cabling.

- ✓ **Transmission speed:** Gigabit Ethernet LANs typically support data transmission speeds of 100 Mbps. If, however, a network is configured using the newest category 5 cabling (cat5e), transmission speeds of 1,000 Mbps (1 Gbps) can be achieved. (ProsoftTraining wants you to know that as a rule, cat5 cable transmits at 100 Mbps, but if you use the highest-grade cat5 (not commonly in use), that gigabit Ethernet can transmit at up to 1 Gbps. If you get an exam question asking which speed cat5 cabling supports, 100 Mbps is the answer unless the question specifically asks if you're using cat5 cabling in a gigabit Ethernet network.)

- ✓ **Transmission method:** Gigabit Ethernet LANs broadcast data to all network nodes. Only the node intended to receive the message picks it up.

- ✓ **Topology:** Gigabit Ethernet LANs are used primarily for network backbones. No specific topology applies.

Token ring/802.5

IBM originally developed the token ring standard for use with its mainframes. The big difference between 802.5 and the other LAN standards in the 802 series is that it uses token passing for data access. A *token* is a specific type of electronic signal that's transmitted a little differently from the electronic signals used in other types of Ethernet networks. In a token ring network, data isn't broadcast to every node in the network at the same time the way it is in an Ethernet or Fast Ethernet network.

Instead, a token is placed on a ring that supports traffic only one way (like a one-way street that goes in a circle). Each node examines the token. If a node isn't the destination computer, the token keeps doing the rounds until it finds the destination computer. Several tokens can be on the ring at once, but they can only travel around the network in one direction (always the same direction).

Features of a token ring network include

- **Data access method:** Token ring LANs use token passing.
- **Cabling:** Token ring LANs use twisted-pair cabling.
- **Transmission speed:** Token ring LANs support transmission rates of either 4 Mbps or 16 Mbps.
- **Transmission method:** Token ring LANs use tokens, which are sent around the one-way ring. Each node examines the token; if the node isn't the destination computer, it allows the token to keep going around the ring until it finds the destination computer.
- **Topology:** Token ring LANs use the ring topology. A ring topology may look like a star topology because all the cables from the computers are usually joined in the center in a hub-like box. Instead of being a hub, though, it's actually a MAU — a multistation access unit. The MAU creates the ring that passes the tokens and helps bypass faulty nodes to keep the network going.

100VG-AnyLAN/802.12

AT&T and Hewlett-Packard originally developed the 100VG-AnyLAN standard. A key difference between 100VG-AnyLAN and the other LAN standards in the 802 series is that it uses *demand priority* for data access. Demand priority uses a hub that decides which message gets through first when more than one is traveling at once.

Here's what I mean. The hub assigns a priority based on the type of data being transmitted. Video files that need to play frames quickly, for example, are assigned a higher priority than, say, an e-mail message, which can wait a few seconds without causing problems. The demand priority access method offers a higher level of security than other Ethernet standards that broadcast to all nodes. Because traffic isn't broadcast to every node, but instead goes through a hub and then on to only the destination computer, data isn't as vulnerable to interception at as many points on the network. Features of 100VG-AnyLAN include

- ✔ **Data access method:** 100VG-AnyLAN uses demand priority for data access.
- ✔ **Cabling:** 100VG-AnyLAN can use most any type of cable including categories 3, 4, or 5 UTP, STP, and fiber optic.
- ✔ **Transmission speed:** 100VG-AnyLAN supports various transmission speeds — the cable choice determines how fast data can travel.
- ✔ **Transmission method:** 100VG-AnyLAN transmissions are sent through a hub, which plays traffic cop — the hub determines which transmission requests are processed first. Data is then sent directly to the destination computer.
- ✔ **Topology:** 100VG-AnyLAN networks aren't tied to any specific topology.

Non-802 LAN standards

At least a couple of LAN standards are not part of the 802 series. Standards outside the 802 series are either proprietary or standardized by an organization other than the IEEE.

Fiber Distributed Data Interface (FDDI)

The Fiber Distributed Data Interface (FDDI) architecture is basically an offshoot of the token ring architecture and uses token passing for data access. But instead of passing data only one way, it uses two rings — one going one way and the other going the opposite direction. This dual-ring architecture speeds data transmission and decreases transmission errors. If one ring goes down, there's another ring that can take over.

A key feature of FDDI is that it supports data transfer over a relatively large geographical area, especially when compared to other LAN standards. Because of this ability, FDDI is often used to cover an entire city or geographical area; it can be used to create a municipal area network (MAN).

Another key feature of FDDI is that it supports both synchronous and asynchronous transmissions. This allows various network devices that may support only one method or the other to transmit data.

Features of FDDI include

- ✔ **Data access method:** FDDI uses token passing on dual rings for data access.

- ✔ **Cabling:** FDDI uses fiber-optic cable. It can function at distances up to 200 kilometers for any one ring; up to 1,000 rings can be connected to cover large geographical areas.

- ✔ **Transmission speed:** FDDI supports data transmission rates of up to 100 Mbps.

- ✔ **Transmission method:** In an FDDI LAN, tokens are placed on one of two rings for transmission. Each node connected to that ring examines a token and, if it's not the destination computer, allows it to keep going around the ring until the token finds the destination computer.

- ✔ **Topology:** FDDI uses an offshoot of the standard ring topology.

Apple LocalTalk

Apple LocalTalk was developed by — drum roll please — Apple. The only thing you need to remember about LocalTalk for the exam is that it uses CSMA/CA (Carrier Sense Multiple Access/Collision Avoided) for data access. CSMA/CA differs from CSMA/CD in that it notifies the other nodes in the network *before* it transmits. CSMA/CD only waits to see if another transmission is in progress before it begins sending. The possibility exists with CSMA/CD that two nodes begin transmitting at the same time and cause a collision. CSMA/CA avoids this by communicating its intent to transmit first.

Wide Area Networks (WANS)

A wide area network (WAN) is used for transmitting data over a large geographical area. Although there's no reason you couldn't use a WAN for a small office, setting up a WAN is more expensive than a LAN, so people usually choose a WAN only if a LAN won't cover the geographical region a network needs to cover. Maybe your company has branch offices in every state in America, and you want to keep a central database of employee e-mail addresses that everyone can use. WAN to the rescue!

Just as there are several types of LAN networks, there are several types of WAN networks. Several protocols that are often used in WANs are covered elsewhere in this book. (See Chapter 18 for information on PPP and SLIP. See Chapter 3 for more information on ISDN.) The following sections focus on the key differences between each WAN standard that you need to know for the exam.

X.25

X.25 is the technology that most automatic teller machines and credit card verification machines use. X.25 is based on the ARPANET 1822 protocol — the original WAN scheme.

X.25 transmits at a maximum of 56 Kbps, so it's not going to win any awards for speed any time soon. But, it is a dependable means of sending error-free data because it checks for errors at several points along the transmission path.

Fast packet switching

Fast packet switching is a method used by two types of WAN technology — frame relay and ATM (not the ATM your bank uses, but a method of transmission I cover in the "Asynchronous Transfer Mode (ATM)" section, later in this chapter). The interesting thing about fast packet switching technology is that the network doesn't perform much error-correction. Because fast packet switching takes hardly any time to correct errors, it can move data along much more quickly than X.25.

Frame relay

The fast packet switching method uses packets called *frames* and allows several companies to share the same high-speed phone line (such as a T1); each message takes up space as needed and then another message takes its turn. Frame relay networks accomplish this by using permanent virtual circuits (PVCs), which are logical dedicated circuits.

Here are some key points to remember about frame relay:

- ✓ Frame relay uses variable length packets.
- ✓ It uses either fiber-optic or digital cabling.
- ✓ Frame relay supports transmission speeds ranging from 64 Kbps to 1.544 Mbps.

Asynchronous Transfer Mode (ATM)

Unlike frame relay, ATM uses fixed-size packets — all packets are a uniform size. Like frame relay, it uses PVCs and works well transferring real-time audio and video.

Remember these important points about ATM:

- It's what Internet backbones usually use.
- ATM supports transmission speeds ranging from 155 Mbps to 1.2 gigabits per second.

Give me a T-carrier system

The T-carrier system is a digital transmission format used in North America, Japan, and Korea. T-carrier systems can carry digital voice and data signals at a maximum transmission rate of 45 Mbps. When you need to connect a LAN to a WAN or to a frame relay network, you'll probably use T-carrier service. Phone companies set up T-carrier lines; customers are allowed to lease all or part of a digital phone line from them. Table 20-4 describes the three categories of T-carrier services — you're most likely to get exam questions about T1 or T3, because T2 and T4 aren't actually used by regular people.

Table 20-4	T-Carrier Services	
Name	**Description**	**Maximum Speed**
T1	Popular leased digital line system; has 24 channels that transmit at 64 Kbps each; can be divided up into a fractional T1 to allow customers to lease just one channel	1.544 Mbps (if not divided)
T2	Equivalent of four T1 lines; not available for public use	6.3 Mbps
T3	Equivalent of 28 T1 lines; can be divided to allow customers to lease just one or two channels; this is called a fractional T3	44.736 Mbps (if not divided)
T4	Not for public use	274.176 Mbps

Give me an E-carrier system

The E-carrier system is the European equivalent of the T-carrier system. The transfer rates of E-carrier services are slightly different than those of T-carrier, but they're considered fairly equal: E1 roughly equals T1; E3 roughly equals T3. Table 20-5 lists the transfer rates of E-carrier systems.

Table 20-5	E-Carrier Systems
Name	*Transfer Rate*
E1	2.048 Mbps
E2	8.448 Mbps
E3	34.368 Mbps
E4	139.264 Mbps
E5	565.148 Mbps

The point at which any two high-speed WANs meet is called a network access point (NAP). For the exam, you don't need to know how many major NAPs exist (at this writing, there are about a dozen along the backbone of the Internet), but you do need to know the definition of a NAP.

Prep Test

1 Which of the following network devices does not operate at the physical layer of the OSI Reference Model?

A ○ Hub

B ○ CSU/DSU

C ○ Repeater

D ○ Brouter

2 Which of the following statements is true regarding a router?

A ○ Works at the network layer of the OSI/RM

B ○ Works at the data link layer of the OSI/RM

C ○ Works at the physical layer of the OSI/RM

D ○ Works at any layer of the OSI/RM

3 What is the point called where any two high-speed networks meet?

A ○ Hub

B ○ NAP

C ○ Backbone

D ○ Patch panel

4 Cyndi is a network engineer who has been contracted to build a LAN for a large company. Approximately 100 users will be on the network, with a maximum of 80 meters between any given nodes. She has been asked to construct the network for the Fast Ethernet standard, with future plans of upgrading to a gigabit Ethernet. What type of transmission media should Cyndi use?

A ○ Category 3 twisted-pair cable

B ○ Thicknet coaxial cable

C ○ Category 5 twisted-pair cable

D ○ Thinnet coaxial cable

5 Which of the following statements is not true regarding fiber-optic cable?

A ○ Multimode fiber-optic cable uses several frequencies to transmit data.

B ○ The core strands of glass are wrapped with Teflon.

C ○ Data is sent as beams of light.

D ○ Signals don't degrade due to electromagnetic interference.

6 Which of the following statements best describes the half-duplex type of data transmission flow?

A ○ Data can travel two ways, but only one way at a time.
B ○ Data can travel only one way.
C ○ Data can travel two ways at once.
D ○ None of the above.

7 Which type of data transmission uses the entire bandwidth of the network cable?

A ○ Baseband
B ○ Broadband
C ○ Wireless
D ○ Packet

8 Which of the following LAN standards is not based on the 802.2 LAN standard?

A ○ Token ring
B ○ Fast Ethernet
C ○ 100VG-AnyLAN
D ○ FDDI

9 What WAN standard do most automated teller machines use?

A ○ Frame relay
B ○ ATM
C ○ X.25
D ○ Gigabit Ethernet

10 A T3 carrier line is equal to how many T1 lines?

A ○ 14
B ○ 28
C ○ 3
D ○ 4

Answers

1 **D.** Brouter. There are a lot of hardware devices to know about, but if you remember that of all the intermittent devices (routers, bridges, repeaters, hubs, and brouters), brouters and routers are the only ones that don't work on the physical layer. (A brouter operates at the network and data link layers of the OSI/RM.) *Look at "Putting Together the Pieces of a Network."*

2 **A.** Works at the network layer of the OSI/RM. See "Putting Together the Pieces of a Network."

3 **B.** NAP. *Check out "Putting Together the Pieces of a Network."*

4 **C.** Category-5 twisted-pair cable. *Review "Gigabit Ethernet/802.3z and 802.3ab."*

5 **B.** The core strands of glass are wrapped with Teflon. *Read "Getting your daily dose of fiber-optic cable."*

6 **A.** Data can travel two ways, but only one way at a time. *See "Doing the data transmission flow dance."*

7 **A.** Baseband. Remember, baseband is like a bundle of straws that only one user can slurp out of at a time. *Look over "Boogying along with baseband and broadband capacities."*

8 **D.** FDDI. FDDI and Apple LocalTalk are the only LANs mentioned on the exam that aren't based on the 802.2 standard. *Check out "Non-802 LAN standards."*

9 **C.** X.25. I always think about withdrawing $25 from the ATM. (Even though it really has to be an increment of 20, it makes it easier for me to remember.) *Take a look at "X.25."*

10 **B.** 28. *Review "Give me a T-carrier system."*

Chapter 21

Keeping Networks Secure

• •

Exam Objectives

▶ Identifying network security threats

▶ Describing common types of security threats

▶ Understanding encryption and SSL

▶ Discussing common Internet security issues, including user-level and enterprise-level concerns

▶ Working with firewalls and other protective measures

• •

*E*ven if you've got the best Web site possible on the fastest network in the world, you still need a good security system to protect it. All Web sites (and, therefore, the networks they're on) are vulnerable to security breaches. For some reason that escapes me, certain types of people (those notorious hackers) can't stand for you to have an attractive, functional Web site or an efficient network. They feel compelled to ruin your week by bringing down either or both.

In this chapter, I describe steps that server administrators can take to secure data that's transferred to and from your Web site. I also discuss the most common ways that hackers get into networks and explain the steps that can be taken to prevent people from breaching a network.

Although you will likely get questions concerning almost every topic in this chapter, pay particular attention to the section on firewalls. Knowing about firewalls helps you not only in real life, but also on the Foundations exam. Nearly everyone gets questions about firewalls.

Quick Assessment

Defining
security
and assets

1 When defining network assets, desktop computers on the network are considered _____.

2 In regard to network assets, all the data stored on a network is defined as _____.

3 The most common type of network security attack is the _____ attack, in which the network resources are overloaded by the hacker.

4 During the _____ stage of hacking, information needed to infiltrate the network is gathered.

Defeating
attacks

5 Thorough _____ of a network should be the first step in securing network resources.

6 _____ is software that monitors system traffic and detects unusual patterns.

7 _____ is the method of scrambling data by using math algorithms.

8 A _____ encapsulates every data packet inside an encrypted packet for private transmission over long distances.

Under-
standing
firewalls

9 A _____ is a hardware and/or software solution that protects trusted network resources from outside networks.

10 A _____ virus contains programming code that changes every time it runs.

Answers

1 *Local resources.* Look over "Defining a Network's Assets."

2 *Information resources.* Check out "Defining a Network's Assets."

3 *Denial of Service (DOS).* See "Having a Hack Attack."

4 *Discovery.* Read "Defining the stages of the hacking process."

5 *Auditing.* Take a look at "Auditing a network's security measures."

6 *IDS (Intrusion Detection Systems).* See "Using detection software."

7 *Encryption.* Review "Using encryption."

8 *VPN (Virtual Private Network).* Check out "Virtual private networks (VPNs)."

9 *Firewall.* Look over "Putting Out the Firewall."

10 *Polymorphic.* Review "Achoo! Catching a Nasty Virus."

Network Security: Knowing Thy Enemy

Simply explained, network security is the protection of a network's assets. But (as with most things) network security usually involves much, much more. Because protecting all network assets requires time and effort, it needs to be done right the first time. To set up good security, a network administrator first needs to determine which aspects of the network are most at risk.

There are methods of determining if and when network security has been compromised; a network monitoring system is essential to help network administrators determine which specific areas of a network may have been compromised, and which areas are receiving extra (possibly unwanted) attention. This chapter covers all the key methods of securing a network that you need to know for the exam. No one method or technology constitutes a complete security solution; several are usually combined to cover all the bases. (The techniques I discuss in this chapter are often combined with permissions and network access rights, which I cover in Chapter 16.)

Although numerous types of viruses and hackers may threaten your network assets, security threats fall into two main categories:

- ✔ **Accidental threats:** Accidental threats occur when, for example a user accidentally stumbles upon something that threatens the network. A user may unknowingly bring in a virus-infected disk from home, for example, and infect the network.

- ✔ **Intentional threats:** Intentional threats are threats that occur when a hacker purposely tries to invade and/or control your network.

Defining a Network's Assets

The first step to implementing excellent network security is to figure out what the network's existing assets are. Call it accentuating the positive to eliminate the negative — but only if you're into musicals.

Network assets can be divided into the following groups:

- ✔ **Local resources:** Local resources consist of desktop computers (workstations) on the network.

- ✔ **Network resources:** The network connections that join your company resources are network resources. NICs and routers, for example, are network resources.

- ✔ **Server resources:** All the types of servers that a company utilizes, such as e-mail, Web, and FTP servers.

✔ **Information resources:** Information resources are the data (including databases and other company documents) that are stored on a network.

Having a Hack Attack

Hackers have all kinds of programs available to them that help them invade systems. The most dangerous hackers aren't necessarily the ones who put the most effort into their chosen profession, but the ones who have the largest collection of hacking programs. The reasons hackers try to gain unauthorized entry into a network are as varied as the hackers themselves — to prove they can, to gain valuable data, or maybe someone dared them to do it. Whatever a hacker's motivation, a big part of a network administrator's job is to prevent hackers from getting what they want.

Defining the stages of the hacking process

Although there are many types of hack attacks, the hacking process has three distinct stages. The stages are

✔ **Discovery:** In this stage, the hacker gathers the information needed to infiltrate the network. Some information can be gathered by legitimate means, such as a Whois search; other information can be gathered by using a technique like pinging. (The PING utility is discussed in Chapter 19.)

✔ **Penetration:** The hacker infiltrates the network system in this stage.

✔ **Control:** After the system has been infiltrated, the hacker tries to control the target of the hack: data, servers, and so on. The control stage is also the stage in which a hacker usually tries to cover his tracks by destroying any evidence of his activity.

Whois searches

A Whois search helps you find out information about a company and/or its Web site. You can go to almost any certified domain name registrar (such as www.register.com) to perform a Whois search. Find the location on the Web site that allows you to perform a Whois search, and type in a domain name. If it's a registered domain name, the site will return information about the owners of that domain name, such as where the company is located, what type of company it is, who registered the domain name, and the e-mail address you can use to contact the person who registered the domain name.

Hacking strategies 101

Hacking attempts fall into several standard categories. The ones you need to know for the exam are

- ✔ **Denial-of-Service (DOS):** The most common type of attack occurs when a hacker overloads network resources to the point the network can't function properly. Overloading can be accomplished by many methods, including mail bombing — a technique where the hacker floods one or more e-mail addresses on a network with mail, overloading the network. Hackers sometimes combine this with spoofing.

- ✔ **Spoofing:** Spoofing occurs when a hacker invades a system and makes one network device (or program) pretend to be another. For example, a hacker may situate on a network a program that can pretend to be a printer, and then this program can read every document users send to the printer.

  Hackers can also infiltrate a system through *IP spoofing* — a hacker sends a packet to the network with an altered header, making it appear as if the packet came from a trusted network. Once inside, the hacker can snoop around the system and map its contents.

- ✔ **Hijacking:** Also called a *man-in-the-middle* attack, hijacking occurs when a hacker intercepts a packet while it's traveling around a network. The key item to remember is that the hacker grabs the packet while it's between network hosts. Hijacking is often used with spoofing.

- ✔ **Brute-force:** A common type of brute-force attack occurs when a hacker tries to access a password-protected area by just trying every password he (or she) can think of. Often, hackers use password-sniffing programs that randomly generate passwords until they find one that works.

- ✔ **Trapdoor:** A hacker looks for a trapdoor to get into the system. System administrators usually password protect top-secret company data, but may forget to password protect some system defaults. For example, when someone installs Internet Information Server, IIS creates a folder called WWWROOT in a certain location. If an administrator fails to change that default, the hacker knows exactly where to look for it.

- ✔ **Trojan horse:** A variation of the trapdoor attack, the Trojan horse attack involves embedding a malicious program into a legitimate-looking program to cause a system breach. A fake logon screen is a common type of Trojan horse attack. When you see a logon screen on your office computer, you probably type in your name and password without even thinking about it. What if that logon screen were actually created by a hacker? You probably wouldn't notice and you'd type in your name and password just the same. If you then got an identical-looking logon screen that's actually from your network, you'd probably just fill out the information again, never realizing the data from the first screen provided a hacker with access to your network.

✔ **Replay:** A replay attack occurs when a hacker gets a hold of a message or part of a message (a packet) and replays it. While replaying the packet, the hacker gains valuable information about the network.

✔ **Insider:** Insider attacks occur when an insider (often a company employee) uses inside information to access network resources. An insider, especially one with high-level access to server resources, can often easily gain access to other information they're not supposed to have.

✔ **Social-engineering:** Social-engineering attacks occur when a hacker uses tricky methods (often acting) to gain access to network resources. Attacks could involve finding out when the system administrator is out of the office and pretending to be a contract worker whom the administrator hired to help with a project. The hacker then convinces people he needs to start on this project right away. Bam! He's got network access. I think of social-engineering attacks as the kind a classic movie con man would try to carry off. *Very* film noir.

Preventing Hack Attacks

No prevention method is 100-percent effective against hackers. If it were, very secure sites, such as the White House Web site, wouldn't have been hacked.

You can, however, take several steps to make your network much less likely to get hit. This section covers key security concepts you need to know for the Foundations exam.

Auditing a network's security measures

A network administrator should do a good thorough audit of a network before setting up network security.

The three key steps in the auditing process are

✔ **Status quo analysis:** Analyze the current security of your network. What measures are already in place? What security breaches have already occurred?

✔ **Risk analysis:** Figure out the weakest points in the network. For example, if only two people in the office are supposed to know the password to access certain data, but one of the users often writes the password on a sticky-note pasted to his monitor, an unauthorized user can easily gain access.

✔ **Threat analysis:** Inventory what a hacker would most likely try to come after. Whether you're worried about a particular database or a proprietary program, knowing what attackers are most likely to come after lets you focus your attentions there first.

After completing an audit of your network, you're ready to take steps to keep your network resources secure.

Using detection software

Intrusion Detection Systems (IDS) have recently become popular in response to the growing threat of hacker attacks. IDS software monitors system traffic and detects traffic patterns that are unusual. It contains a database of rules. If a rule is broken, the program is prompted to take specific actions. For example, whenever someone unsuccessfully tries to access a private database, the IDS application may sever all communication between that user and the network.

Another benefit of IDS software is that it usually contains a database of *attack signatures* — a series of activities that have, in the past, indicated the onset of an attack. The only drawback with this feature is that innocent users may take similar steps as part of their routine, so IDS systems often detect false alarms.

Authenticating

To authenticate a user is to determine a user's true identity. Only if users have been authenticated can they gain access to protected data.

You need to know three main types of authentication, which are described in the following list:

✔ **Authenticating what you know:** This type of authentication won't give users access to a network (or part of a network) unless they know the correct information, such as a user name and password. This is the most common method of maintaining security. The problem with it is that people are fallible. They forget passwords, share them with others, and so on.

✔ **Authenticating what you have:** This type of authentication requires users to have the necessary equipment before they can access information. For example, requiring users to have a swipe card or a key to access the server room falls into this category.

> ✔ **Authenticating who you are:** Physical features are scanned to ensure that users are who they say they are. This kind of security can include retinal scans, fingerprint scans, or voice recognition software. (Move over, James Bond — it's not just in the movies anymore.)

If someone says they're applying *strong encryption,* they're usually using some combination of the three authentication methods with added encryption. I discuss encryption in the following section.

Using encryption

Encryption involves scrambling data so that anyone who doesn't have the proper decryption program can't read the data. Encryption is one of the most important methods you can use to protect network resources.

Encryption protects data by using math algorithms. Yuck. These algorithms keep out hackers by depressing them with memories of high school algebra. No, that's just me. The algorithms may scramble an entire file or just a password attached to the file so that a hacker can't easily figure it out.

To open a file that's encrypted, the user must have the correct key — some data stored on the user's computer that's created by the same program that encrypted the data in the first place. In most cases, if the recipient's machine has the correct decryption data on it, the user can open the protected file as usual. Only the correct key — the one that understands the algorithm used on the protected file — can enable the encrypted file to be opened. The following sections cover the specific types of encryption you need to know for the Foundations exam.

Symmetric-key (single key) encryption

In symmetric-key encryption, one key both encrypts and decrypts the data, much like a house key can both lock and unlock your door.

Also like a house key, everyone that needs to access the data is sent a copy of the key — the algorithm that scrambles and unscrambles the data.

The key to successfully using this encryption method (no pun intended) is to make sure no one intercepts the keys as they're being sent. The methods used to actually create and send the keys vary from program to program — you don't need to know how to use any specific encryption program for the exam.

The pros and cons of symmetric-key encryption include the following:

✔ **Pro:** It's fast and strong. Common single key algorithms contain any-where from 40 to 128 bits. Bits are the smallest unit of data storage on a computer. The more bits an algorithm can contain, the longer it is; the longer it is, the harder it is to break. (Just like a longer network password is more secure than a short one; that's why network administrators are notorious for harassing users to use long passwords. It's for your own good, as Mom might say.)

✔ **Con:** Users must be provided with keys. If they're sent over a network, keys can be intercepted. It's often too difficult for users to meet in person to exchange keys saved on disks — otherwise, they'd just exchange the private data that way to begin with.

Asymmetric (dual key) encryption

Dual key encryption uses one key to encrypt and another key to decrypt. When you use dual key encryption, you keep one key (the private key) and make the other one (the public key) available to others you want to send secret messages to. Only the combination of the private and public key can encode and decode messages; others who have only the public key can't share secret messages because they don't have the private key. Pros and cons of asymmetric encryption include:

✔ **Pro:** Dual key encryption is more secure than single key encryption because you distribute only one key. You can distribute the public key to anyone who needs it, but the system works only if the private key stays private.

✔ **Con:** Because two separate keys must work together, dual key encryption is slower than single key encryption — possibly many minutes slower.

Hash (one way) encryption

Hash encryption is more of a method to alert you if a message has been altered than a method of keeping the message out of unauthorized users hands.

Hash encryption uses a *hash table* — a table of complex math functions to scramble information. Data that's encrypted using the hash method is never decrypted. That doesn't seem to make sense at first — why would you take the time to encrypt something if you couldn't decrypt it?

You don't actually encrypt the valuable message — just the password attached to it. A password's hash sequence, when calculated, returns a certain value. When the message is received, the value of the hash sequence is recalculated. If the resulting value is the same as the value that was calculated in the first place, the message is considered unaltered and, therefore, safe.

Secure Sockets Layer (SSL)

Secure Sockets Layer (SSL) is a protocol that uses dual key encryption and a special type of single key encryption called a *digital certificate* to protect data during transfer. If you've ever used a Web browser, you've used SSL.

SSL uses *digital certificates,* digital IDs that are issued by a certificate authority and that prove the identity of an individual or company on the Web, kind of like how a drivers license proves your identity.

A certificate is digitally signed by the certificate's creator to authenticate a user's identity. A third party, such as VeriSign (www.verisign.com), can issue certificates, or a company may have its own certificate server that creates certificates for users within the company's network.

During an SSL session, public and private keys are exchanged between the Web server and a user's computer. The user probably doesn't even realize his computer is receiving a public key because the transfer is usually seamless. As long as the certificate attached to the Web site is valid, the user most likely won't be asked whether they want to accept the public key.

Pretty Good Privacy (PGP)

The Pretty Good Privacy (PGP) program is a good example of how several methods of encryption can be combined for enhanced security.

Here's the technology PGP uses and how it works:

- ✔ Single key encryption to scramble the message being sent.
- ✔ Dual key encryption to scramble the single key encryption that was just added by single key encryption.
- ✔ Hash encryption signs the message so the recipient can detect if anyone has tampered with the message between Point A and Point B.

Country-specific standards

A security company called RSA, Inc. (www.rsasecurity.com) creates the most common public encryption algorithms in the United States. RSA public encryption is usually 40-bit or 128-bit. Different countries, however, have different encryption standards.

Until 1999, the United States outlawed the export of 128-bit encryption for fear that malicious users would start using it against the U.S. As of this writing, governments of countries around the world haven't agreed upon a common standard, though they're talking about it.

Many governments are discussing a controversial idea at this time. All users of 128-bit encryption would be required to give the government a copy of that encryption standard. In theory, the government could use that information only to open a document under court authority.

Virtual private networks (VPNs)

If people on a network routinely need to transmit private information over long distances, a virtual private network (VPN) may be the best security solution.

A VPN uses the Internet as its backbone and can connect networks located far away from each other — much like a standard WAN, only VPNs have a little more Vroom. Before transmission, a VPN encapsulates each data packet inside a separate encrypted packet that's kind of like a strong envelope — super strong.

VPNs, unlike WANs, allow users to transfer data that wouldn't normally work on the Internet. The VPN embeds each data packet — no matter what kind of packet it is — into its own encrypted TCP/IP packet. This enables people to send all types of files over the Internet — something that might not be possible in certain other network environments. A VPN usually uses a VPN server to communicate with VPN clients.

The protocols VPN uses to communicate are called *tunneling protocols*. The three VPN tunneling protocols you need to know for the exam are

- **Point-to-Point Tunneling Protocol (PPTP):** PPTP is the most common tunneling protocol used in VPNs. It creates a private channel between two computers for private data transfer.

- **Layer 2 Tunneling Protocol (L2TP):** L2TP takes PPTP one step further — it combines PPTP with Cisco's Layer 2 Forwarding Protocol (L2F), which enables you to create a VPN over WANs such as X.25 or frame relay.

- **Internet Security Association Key Management Protocol (ISAKMP) or (IPSec):** IPSec has all the abilities PPTP does, but it's expected to eventually become the VPN standard because it's designed for use with IPv6.

Putting Out the Firewall

A firewall acts as a barrier between your trusted network and unknown networks, including the Internet. Firewalls filter what goes in or what goes out of your network — kind of like a guard at a pay parking lot.

Whether a firewall consists of hardware, software, or a combination of the two, all firewalls can perform many functions, including the following functions that you need to know for the exam:

✔ **Filtering packets:** Packet filters examine source and destination IP addresses and source and destination TCP/UDP port information to determine if the packet has authorization to be forwarded. Other devices, such as routers, can also act as packet filters. One weakness of packet filters is they don't examine packet data. They're usually used with other security because they don't sufficiently guarantee safe data transfer on their own.

✔ **Circuit level gateway:** Acting much like a proxy server (see the section on proxy servers later in this chapter), circuit level gateways mask the source address of packets so that the packets appear to have come from the firewall.

✔ **Application level gateway:** Application level gateways are similar to circuit level gateways, but they act at the application level. Application level gateways can act as an SMTP firewall; they examine outgoing e-mail, verify the source, and scan any attachments for viruses. This distinction is important because SMTP, by itself, doesn't do this.

✔ **Detecting unauthorized access:** Firewalls can prevent access from several types of addresses that a server administrator denotes — certain IP addresses, Web addresses, or a range of IP addresses.

✔ **Added password authentication:** Firewalls can add an extra layer of password authentication when users attempt to access the protected network.

✔ **Logging and reporting:** Firewalls log network traffic and create summary reports. Monitoring a network for increased or peculiar traffic patterns is an important part of keeping a network safe.

✔ **Permitting encrypted access:** Firewalls allow the type of encrypted access VPNs use, so a network can have a firewall and still communicate through a VPN without interference from the firewall.

Firewall topologies

You can find as many firewall programs out there as you can count. With every firewall program comes a different *topology* (system architecture).

In the following sections, I discuss the four main categories that firewall topologies fall into: simple packet filter, single-homed bastion, double-homed bastion, and screened subnet.

Simple packet filter

A simple packet filter, often called a *packet-filtering router,* is the simplest of firewalls. It inspects network header fields and then analyzes only IP addresses and port numbers, but it still filters out most unwanted traffic.

Here are the drawbacks of using a simple packet filtering firewall topology:

✔ The effectiveness of the simple packet filter depends entirely on the skill of the people who configure it. Network administrators frequently configure existing routers to act as packet filters as well. If this isn't done correctly, traffic within the network can be unnecessarily inhibited.

✔ If the only device protecting a network from the outside is a simple packet filter, it's the only barrier a hacker has to overcome before infiltrating the network. Not a huge challenge for pros.

Figure 21-1 shows the layout of a typical packet-filtering router.

Figure 21-1:
A packet-filtering router topology filters out most unwanted traffic.

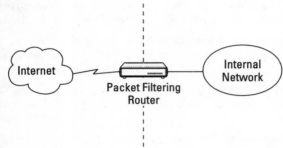

Single-homed bastion

Another popular firewall topology is the single-homed bastion, also called a screened-host firewall. (A *bastion* is just another word for firewall.) This layout first filters incoming packets with a packet-filtering router, which determines if packets need to be sent to the bastion or whether they can go directly to the Web or FTP server.

When packets reach either the Web-server or FTP-server node, the data is made available to the entire internal network. Outgoing packets go through the reverse process.

Benefits and drawbacks to a single-homed bastion:

✔ **Pro:** Compared to a simple packet filter, a single-homed bastion offers much more protection.

✔ **Con:** Single-homed bastion software costs more than a simple packet filtering router and can decrease network performance because it spends more time examining incoming and outgoing data.

✔ **Con:** If a hacker can alter a packet so that it doesn't seem to need the firewall's analysis, the hacker gets access to the company's Web or FTP server. From there, it's hog heaven — the hacker can get to the whole network.

Figure 21-2 illustrates the layout of the single-homed bastion. Notice that after data passes through the packet-filtering router, it moves to either the bastion host (firewall device) or to the Web server. From there, the packet is available to the internal network.

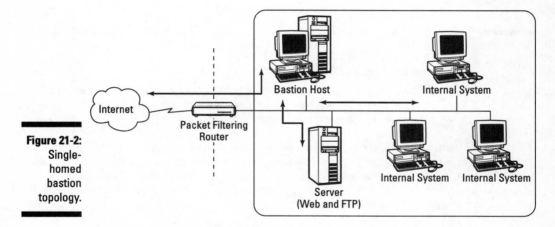

Figure 21-2:
Single-homed bastion topology.

Dual-homed bastion

A dual-homed bastion is also called a *screened-host firewall.* (Yes, I know that's the same alias a single-homed bastion uses. I don't make up the names, I just tell you what they are.)

The dual-homed bastion topology offers much more security than the two other methods listed previously. With all three topologies, data first passes through a packet-filtering router. A key difference between the single-homed bastion and the dual-homed bastion, however, is with a dual-homed bastion, *all* incoming and outgoing traffic must pass through the firewall device before moving on. Neither incoming nor outgoing traffic can reach the network's Web or FTP server without first passing through the firewall.

A hacker has to overcome at least two devices before infiltrating the network. Figure 21-3 illustrates a dual-homed bastion topology.

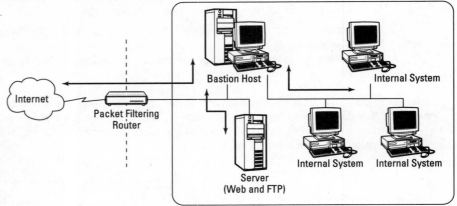

Figure 21-3:
Dual-homed
bastion
topology.

Demilitarized zone (DMZ)

A demilitarized zone, also called a *demarcation zone* or a *screened-subnet firewall,* offers yet another step of protection against network intruders — the most secure of the firewall topologies.

Demilitarized-zone topologies are kind of like quarantines. The technology creates a protected area or *demilitarized zone* where all incoming and outgoing traffic is placed under several stages of scrutiny before it can pass through. The data packet must survive every test to make it into or out of the internal network.

A screened-subnet firewall topology ensures that incoming traffic passes through a packet-filtering router and then on to either the firewall or to the network's servers. Data must then pass through another packet-filtering router before the data is available on the internal network.

Although incoming data can go from the first packet-filtering router to a server, the data can't continue on to the internal network unless the bastion analyzes it. The secondary packet-filtering router rejects any data that doesn't first pass through the router *and* the bastion. In effect, the process used by screened-subnet firewalls creates a subnetwork that sits between the trusted network and the Internet. Hence the name.

On the way out of the network, data first passes through a packet-filtering router, and then onto the firewall or Web or FTP server; finally the data passes through another packet-filtering router. If any data reaches the outer packet-filtering router without passing through the firewall first, that's the end of that — the data is rejected. Figure 21-4 illustrates the demilitarized zone.

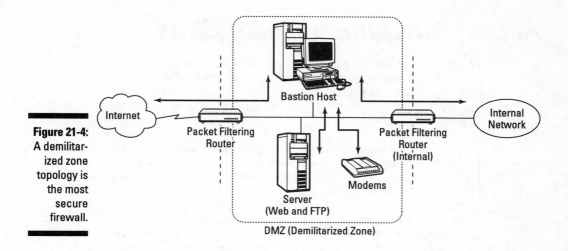

Figure 21-4:
A demilitar-
ized zone
topology is
the most
secure
firewall.

Proxy servers

A proxy server acts as a middleman between an organization's network and the Internet. When part of a network, all user machines go through the proxy server to access the Internet. Proxy servers can perform some of the same types of duties as firewalls — certain types of filtering, for example. But proxy servers also perform several other functions, such as helping to reduce network traffic through caching and further increasing security through added logging. The following list explains the security components of proxy servers. (For more on other duties of proxy servers, see Chapters 7 and 16.)

- ✔ **IP masking:** Proxy servers hide, or mask, the IP addresses of computers on a network. The proxy server essentially replaces a computer's IP address with that of the proxy server, making it appear as if an Internet request originated from the proxy server. By masking addresses, the proxy server helps keep all nodes within the network protected from unauthorized outside access.

- ✔ **Logging:** Proxy servers log user requests. Logging allows administrators keep track of which users on a network are accessing which features and when, as well as which Web pages network users are accessing. Logging can also help evaluate network performance.

- ✔ **Filtering:** Filtering allows network administrators to deny access to certain URLs and certain IP addresses to any or all clients in the network. Filtering can be based on users' logon names, the IP address of the machines they're using, or their computer's name.

Achoo! Catching a Nasty Virus

A virus is a malicious program specifically designed to damage computers and other network resources. Viruses sometimes get past standard network security measures such as firewalls. Viruses are most often distributed by legitimate network users who accidentally open infected files and let them loose on the network.

Viruses are the reason system administrators often discourage company employees from bringing disks with data from home systems. Most users don't have the same level of security on home systems as companies do on network Internet access points.

I don't want to mention specific virus names because that's one of the main reasons people create viruses — to achieve some level of fame. But I'm sure you've heard of many of them. During the past couple of years, viruses that send infected e-mails to everyone in your Outlook address book have become common.

People use several standard methods to transmit viruses (and for you to catch them):

- ✔ **Executables:** Executable files are miniprograms. Because they're full-fledged programs, there are many ways these files can damage information on your computer.

- ✔ **Macros:** Macros are miniprograms that can damage a system's files. Macros are written in code specific to a program like Microsoft Word or Excel. As long as the recipient has the program that the macro was created to run in, the macro can do whatever dirty work it's programmed to do.

- ✔ **Boot sector:** This type of virus loads into the boot sector of a hard drive so that it can be loaded into memory every time the system reboots. Boot sector viruses can infect the media in other drives, such as disks in a disk drive, CDs in a CD drive, or other connected hard drive.

- ✔ **Polymorphic:** A polymorphic virus contains programming code that morphs or changes every time it runs. This type of virus is one of the most difficult to detect because the virus runs as a different process each time it attempts to infect an application.

- ✔ **Stealth:** A stealth virus protects itself from detection by redirecting any requests by antivirus programs to read the hard drive. It can also change a system's directory structure to further complicate the detection process.

Antivirus Software

The best way to keep a network virus-free is to install good antivirus software and keep it updated. Just as new strains of human viruses can be immune to existing drugs, new strains of computer viruses need to be attacked with the newest antivirus detection available. After you purchase an antivirus package, return to the vendor's Web site periodically to download any updates. Symantec (www.symantec.com) and McAfee (www.mcafee.com) sell two popular antivirus programs.

Users can take steps to help the network's antivirus software be more effective. ProsoftTraining likes to reinforce the point that one of the most important things that server administrators can do to keep a network safe is to educate network users. Users can do the following to keep the security on a network top-notch:

✔ If you receive an executable file from someone you don't know, don't open it. It's as simple as that. If more people had followed this advice in the last couple of years, some of the most common viruses wouldn't have infected nearly as many systems.

✔ If you receive an executable file that appears to be from someone you know, but you weren't expecting, scan it before you open it.

✔ Always scan incoming and outgoing e-mails.

Prep Test

1 Which of the following is considered a network asset?

A ○ Human resources

B ○ Global resources

C ○ Multimedia resources

D ○ Server resources

2 When John opened an Excel file that was attached to an e-mail, a series of events occurred within the Excel program on his computer that damaged the data on John's hard drive. What type of virus has John encountered?

A ○ Boot sector

B ○ Stealth

C ○ Macro

D ○ Polygraphic

3 Slacker is a hacker who gains access to a network's resources by telephoning the network's support department and posing as a trusted third-party contractor who needs vital information about the network. What method of attack is Slacker using?

A ○ Spoofing

B ○ Trojan horse

C ○ Social-engineering

D ○ Hijacking

4 What stage of the hacking process occurs when the hacker actually infiltrates the target network?

A ○ Penetration

B ○ Discovery

C ○ Control

D ○ Trap door

5 Which of the following statements describes hash encryption?

A ○ It uses one key to encrypt the data and another to decrypt the data.

B ○ It uses a table of math functions to encrypt data that is not intended to be decrypted.

C ○ It authenticates data based on an attached digital certificate.

6 **Which of the following is not one of the main types of authentication?**

   A ○ What you know

   B ○ Who you are

   C ○ What you have

   D ○ Where you are going

7 **Xavier is setting up a new component of his company's network that must send all types of the company's data over long distances and do it with minimal security risk. What method of transmission should Xavier choose?**

   A ○ Fast Ethernet

   B ○ VPN

   C ○ IDS

   D ○ Symmetric-key encryption

8 **Which of the following is not a function of a firewall?**

   A ○ Encrypting and decrypting data using single and double key encryption

   B ○ Packet filtering

   C ○ Detecting unauthorized access

   D ○ Logging and reporting

9 **Which of the following firewall topologies decreases network performance and is also called a screened-host firewall?**

   A ○ Dual-homed bastion

   B ○ Single-homed bastion

   C ○ Both A and B

   D ○ Neither A nor B

10 **What is the name of a screened-subnet firewall that creates a subnetwork between a trusted network and the Internet and offers the highest security of all the firewall topologies?**

   A ○ Simple packet filter

   B ○ Extranet

   C ○ Proxy server

   D ○ DMZ

Answers

1 **D.** Server resources. Network assets include local, network, server, and information resources. *See "Defining a Network's Assets."*

2 **C.** Macro. Because it's an Excel file that works in John's Excel program, that is a tip-off that it's likely a macro virus. *Check out "Achoo! Catching a Nasty Virus."*

3 **C.** Social-engineering. When a hacking method involves acting or "faking out" people, it involves social-engineering. *Review "Having a Hack Attack."*

4 **A.** Penetration. *Read "Defining the stages of the hacking process."*

5 **B.** Hash encryption uses a table of math functions to encrypt data that is not intended to be decrypted. *Look over "Hash (one way) encryption."*

6 **D.** Where you are going. *See "Authenticating."*

7 **B.** VPN (Virtual private network). Virtual private networks are one of the most secure ways to send any type of data over short or long distances. *Take a look at "Virtual private networks (VPNs)."*

8 **A.** Encrypting and decrypting data using single and double key encryption. *See "Putting Out the Firewall."*

9 **C.** Both A and B. Single-homed bastions and dual-homed bastions can slow down network performance because data must go through several extra steps. *Review "Firewall topologies."*

10 **D.** DMZ (Demilitarized Zone). Remember that demilitarized zone equals screened subnet; if a test question asks about a firewall that creates its own *subnetwork,* think subnet and you'll remember the right answer. *Check out "Demilitarized zone (DMZ)."*

Part V
The Part of Tens

The 5th Wave   By Rich Tennant

"What I'm looking for are dynamic Web applications and content, not Web innuendoes and intent."

In this part . . .

In Part V, I do what all books in the *For Dummies* series do — I give you ten (count them, ten) of everything. No extra charge to you! I'm just doing my part to participate in a long-standing tradition. Look for ten Web sites that have sample exams, discussion areas for test-takers, or other helpful information. Before you head to the testing booth, look at The Part of Tens for ten great test-taking tips, like what to do an hour before the exam, what to do right before you start taking the exam, and more.

No certification exam is perfect, but I feel this exam is a fair one; you are not going to be purposely misled by tricky questions. If you know the core information about each topic, take the practice exam, and follow the advice in this part, then you should be able to recognize the correct answers right off the bat — at least most of the time.

Chapter 22

More Than Ten Really Great Web Sites to Help You Study

In This Chapter
▶ Finding study materials on the Web
▶ Locating additional resources

*T*here's a saying about different strokes for different folks (I think that was a TV show, too, wasn't it?), and when it comes to taking an exam, that's certainly true. Although the Hungry Minds people and I have worked diligently to make this the best test-preparation product on the market, I'm going to mention several other useful tools. If you utilize all the resources you can get your hands on, you'll have the best chance of passing the Foundations exam with flying colors.

You can find a bunch of good sites on the Web to help you prepare to take the exam. (Consider yourself lucky because when I took my exam in the early days of the program, Web resources like the ones I list in this chapter weren't available.) Many of the sites offer free information, but some of them charge anywhere from $26 to nearly $500 for materials.

Think carefully about the amount of money you're willing to throw at this exam. I truly believe that most people can get away with studying this book and the free sites and be very well prepared.

I list the Web sites in this chapter in order of my personal preference, and I list the pay sites last because I'm too cheap to spend any more money than I have to and I'm sure some of you feel the same way.

Like every other Web site, certification prep sites come and go. Please keep in mind that each of these sites existed at the time I wrote this chapter. Use search words like *CIW Foundations brain dump* or *CIW Foundations exam cram* to get the best results searching for resources on your own.

When you look over the study notes and sample tests on these sites, pay close attention to the way the questions are worded. I've tried to be faithful to the CIW syntax when writing this book and asking questions. However, questions can be asked a lot of different ways. If a sample question on a site uses wording that's different from what you've seen/heard before, pay attention to the wording and the answer the question is trying to elicit. Make sure you understand why the answer presented is the correct one, and make a note of the phrasing the question uses so you won't be surprised if the same wording appears on the exam.

CIW Resources

The first ten Web sites I list are targeted specifically towards the CIW exam and its contents. Some offer great study notes, some offer sample exams, and others contain glossaries of common CIW terms.

CIWCertified.com

www.ciwcertified.com

CIWCertified.com is probably a good place to start your Web quest on CIW materials because this is ProsoftTraining's Web site. If there are any major changes in the CIW program, you'll find that information here. Prosoft also offers self-study kits online, but, in my humble opinion, they're a bit pricey (several hundred dollars).

CIW Cram

www.ciwcram.com

CIW Cram is one of my favorite test-preparation sites. It has an overview of the CIW program, discussion areas on several CIW exams, study guides, and sample tests. Best of all, it's free. You do have to give your e-mail address and log on to access some features, but that's a minor inconvenience compared to how much great information is on this site.

TestFree

www.testfree.com

TestFree offers lots of free tests on many CIW exam topics. One of the best things about its exams is that TestFree usually has a bank of several hundred questions, so you can work your brain for hours. You'll need to give your name and e-mail address, but, once again, that's not much for access to a lot of good practice questions.

CertifyExpress

www.certifyexpress.com/prosoft/foundation

CertifyExpress is another great free site that offers study notes and sample exams. You can read the study notes online or download PDF versions for printing.

MC MCSE

www.mcmcse.com/ciw/index.shtml

The MC MCSE site has a great synopsis of terms and topics covered on the Foundations exam and a very good practice exam. It offers excellent study information for several CIW exams and several other exams such as MCSE certification.

CIW Study

www.ciwstudy.com

CIW Study is a great site put up by a friend of mine who also teaches CIW classes. The site includes a great forum with postings from several of my friend's students and lots of other test-takers who are willing to share helpful information. In addition to the forum, study guides, and sample exams, there are tons of helpful links to more information about various topics like HTML. It also has a nice glossary of terms if you need a quick review of some geek-speak. Some of the basic information is free; otherwise, you can pay about $25 to get full access to extra sample exams.

IntelInfo

www.intelinfo.com

At IntelInfo, you'll find study guides for most every CIW exam. It's not free but very inexpensive, only ten bucks for six months of access to its information. It also offers cheap access to study guides for Microsoft, Cisco, Novell, and Oracle exams.

MCSEguide

www.mcseguide.com/ciw.htm

MCSEguide offers good free study guides for the CIW Foundations, Site Designer, and E-Commerce Designer exams. The focus of the site, as you might guess from the name, is the Microsoft MCSE exams, but it does a good job with the few CIW exams it offers.

Transcender LLC

www.transcender.com

Transcender LLC has been offering practice certification exams for years. The service is very good, but not cheap. The practice Foundations exam, as of this writing, costs $129. You can get a whole lot of information and help for free elsewhere, so think carefully before pouring too much money into even the best resources.

ExamsOnline

www.examsonline.com

ExamsOnline offers practice exams for the CIW Foundations exam. You can find a few free exams, but most of them are available for a fee.

ExamsOnline also offers a salary survey so you can compare what you earn with your current skills to what you might earn as you acquire new skills.

Non-CIW Resources

If you need more information on some Web design basics like HTML or server-side scripting, you may want to check out some other great Web sites. I've included a few of my favorite sites that offer tutorials and/or online instruction.

Webmonkey

www.webmonkey.com

Part of the Terra Lycos network and a spinoff of Wired.com, Webmonkey was one of the first sites written by Web developers for Web developers. Webmonkey has great free tutorials on HTML, JavaScript, and several other scripting languages. It also includes how-to articles on several Web-creation programs. Webmonkey starts all of its articles and tutorials with the bare-bones basics so you won't feel overwhelmed from the start.

Webopedia

www.webopedia.com

Webopedia is a wonderful site to look up just about any Web or computer-oriented term you can think of. You just type in the term you're curious about in the Search box and hit Enter. It's free and very easy to use.

WhatIs.com

www.whatis.com

Another great site along the lines of Webopedia, WhatIs offers clear, easy-to-understand definitions of just about every computer-related term you can think of. WhatIs also offers links to sites related to the term you're searching for.

E-online Training

www.eonlinetraining.com

E-online Training offers online classes on the CIW Foundations, Site Designer, and E-commerce exams. It costs about $50, but you get an instructor to answer any questions you have within 24 hours.

New Horizons

www.newhorizons.com

If you really feel the need to attend a hands-on class, New Horizons has training centers all over the country. It was one of the first companies to teach instructor-led CIW classes. (As a matter of fact, that's where I taught my first CIW classes.) Certification classes aren't cheap, but you'll be performing hands-on exercises on most topics on the exam.

Chapter 23

Ten Test-Day Tips

*I*f you're reading this chapter, you've probably decided to schedule and take your exam. In this chapter, I give you tips to help keep you calm and make sure you do your very best on the exam.

The test costs $125. I don't know about you, but I don't relish the thought of having to pay another $125 to retake a test just because I ran into a minor snafu on test day.

Now that I've warned you about not blowing your money, I want to emphasize that you can take the test again, if necessary, as many times as you need. Whenever I get a little overwhelmed by the idea that I might, in fact, fail an exam, I just remind myself that the worse thing that could happen is I'd have to take the test again. After you've taken an exam, you have a much better idea of what areas you need to review. Now, honestly, I've never failed a certification exam (as of this writing), but telling myself that it won't be the end of my career if I happen to fail one seems to calm me down so that I can focus on the exam.

Knowing Where to Go

When you schedule your exam, you get to choose the most convenient testing center because there are tons of testing centers throughout the United States (and quite a few overseas). You can schedule your exam close to your home or near a resort area and make a vacation of the whole grueling process!

The two most popular testing centers are Thomson Prometric (www.prometric.com) and VUE (www.vue.com). See Chapter 2 for information on Web sites and phone numbers for test scheduling.

Whichever option you choose, take the time to drive to the testing center a day or two before the exam. Think of how disappointed you'd be if you mapped out a route to the testing center and found out on the day of the test that the road's closed and you don't know another way to get there.

Before You Leave Home

Before you head out the door, make sure you take these two items with you:

- ✔ **Two pieces of identification.** One must have your photo and name; the other must have your name. A driver's license and a credit card will do.

- ✔ **Your study materials.** Be sure to bring all your notes, the Cheat Sheet from the front of the book, and this entire book, if you'd like. You can do some last-minute cramming (see "Scan Your Notes One Last Time") and if you have a momentary anxiety issue because you've forgotten some term or concept, you have the book with you to look it up before you sit down at the testing computer.

The Early Bird Gets the Cert

Plan on getting to the testing center at least a half an hour early. You'll have time to do some of that last-minute cramming that many are so fond of or have a cup of coffee, tea, or my favorite, chamomile tea, which helps keep me calm. (Can you tell I get pretty worked up before an exam?)

By being early, you can avoid being rushed and adding to your test-day anxiety. Also, if the tester ahead of you finishes early or cancels, you may be able to start your test a little early. If you're one of those people who'd rather get things over with than sit around worrying (like me), you might like this opportunity.

Scan Your Notes One Last Time

Right before you take the test, review any items that still concern you. Even if there's some term you're a little confused about, just remembering a key descriptive phrase may be enough to help you choose the right answer. You don't have time to learn new concepts at this stage, but I've found that a quick scan of my notes before I enter the testing room implants a snapshot of some of that information into my brain — almost like a mental table I can refer to.

Check In with the Test Administrator

After you arrive, don't just wander aimlessly around the testing center. Check in with the test administrator or the person at the front desk. You can find out if the tests are running on time or if the test room is flooded or if the heater's broken and set at 95 degrees.

After you check in, right before you head into the testing room, you have to hand over all your valuables. No, you're not being burgled; it's just the testing center's way of ensuring that no one cheats. You'll have to hand over your notes, books, and your purse or backpack (if you brought it with you).

Don't give the testing administrator a hard time because you have to surrender your belongings. For one thing, this isn't a conspiracy against you. Test administrators do this all the time and are most likely going to protect your stuff with, well, if not with their lives at least with their best intentions. If you run into the rare testing center that won't keep an eye on your belongings while you're testing, just bring in your IDs and any notes you could live without getting back after the exam.

Spill Your Guts

At most testing centers, you can get a blank plastic test tablet (or as many as you want) and a grease pencil to take into the testing room. As soon as you sit down, write down everything you can remember about some of the tough topics. I suggest including these stimulating topics:

- ✔ The layers, in order, of the OSI/RM
- ✔ Maximum run lengths of cables and their transmission speeds
- ✔ Transmission speeds of T1-T5 and E1-E5 connections
- ✔ The ranges of various IP address classes

Any topic that requires a lot of rote memorization is a good candidate for your own private brain dump. The process of dumping all these lists onto a tablet frees your mind to focus on the question at hand (instead of trying to remember which layers the session layer comes between). You've got access to this great information without having to actively concentrate on it.

Do the Tutorial!

Before the test actually begins, you are given the opportunity to go through a tutorial. The tutorial shows you how different types of questions look, shows you various screens you may see, and explains how the testing process works.

Take the tutorial.

Even if you've taken several other exams, take the tutorial. Each exam has a few of its own unique features. Also, the testing center may have changed its procedures since the last time you took a test. The only way to find out is to take the tutorial.

You lose nothing by taking the tutorial — literally. The time you take to go through the tutorial doesn't take up any of your allotted 90-minute test time.

I find that going through the tutorial is another step that helps me calm down and focus. Must be the idea of interacting with the computer — it's such a common activity for me that I find it calming. (I'm a lot of fun on a Saturday night, aren't I?)

By the way, did I mention that I think you should take the tutorial?

Go for the Gold

When you're ready to get serious and really take the test, take a deep breath, clear your head, and get to it. Read every answer before you choose one. Your first instinct is often right, but if you don't read carefully, you may miss the fact that two answers are correct and that the question was written so that you may choose both.

Don't worry too much about the 90-minute time restriction. Most people find they have plenty of time. Some of the questions are very easy and take about three seconds for you to answer. That gives you all kinds of time to focus on the hard questions.

Is That Your Final Answer?

If you're presented with a completely confounding question that blows your mind, don't be thrown. You don't want to get so anxious about one question that you can't easily focus on all the other questions you know the answers to.

You can get up to 15 questions wrong (actually 25, if you include the beta questions) and still achieve a passing score of 75 percent, so don't get too worked up about not knowing a few.

You can always mark the question to return to later. (***Hint:*** The tutorial shows you how.) I've found that if I skip a question early in the exam, another question later in the exam gives me a clue to the right answer.

Say you can't remember the correct syntax to insert an image in an HTML document. You skip that question and later, you get a question on the correct syntax of the ALT="attribute". The answers are

A. `<IMG SRC="myimage.jpg" ALT="My text">`

B. `<IMG SRC="myimage.jpg" TEXTALT="My text">`

C. `<IMG SRC="myimage.jpg" ALTERNATE="My text">`

D. `<IMG SRC="myimage.jpg" TEXT="My text">`

You can tell from the answers to this question that the correct syntax to insert an image must be: `<IMG SRC="myimage.jpg">`.

So now you can go back and mark the correct answer to the first skipped question. (In case you're wondering, the correct answer to the question above is A.)

Just make sure to return to all questions you've marked for review — always give yourself at least a chance of getting the question correct by giving some answer to every question.

And the Certification Goes To. . . .

After you finish the exam, there's an area you can click to indicate you're done. One of the best (or worst, depending on your perspective) features of taking a test at a Prometric or VUE testing center is that you find out how you did immediately after the exam ends. You even get a handy printout that shows how many questions you missed in each section. If you don't pass, you may not like these gut-wrenching details, but hang onto this document. You can use this information when you review for the test the next time around.

If you pass the exam (which I'm betting on), you receive your official certificate in the mail within a few weeks.

After you pass your exam, Emily Post suggests that you not do a victory dance in the middle of the testing center. After all, people may be trying to concentrate. Congratulations!

Appendix
About the CD

• •

On the CD-ROM

▶ Practice tests, to make sure you are ready for the real thing

▶ Trial versions of several Web creation programs

▶ Trial and full versions of Web promotion software and FTP utilities

• •

The CD-ROM that accompanies this book is filled with all sorts of goodies and tools, and this Appendix is your starting place for information on navigating and using the CD. From system requirements to installation instructions — and everything in between — if you are curious about the CD, look no further — you've come to the right place.

System Requirements

Make sure that your computer meets the minimum system requirements in the following list. If your computer doesn't match up to most of these requirements, you may have problems using the contents of the CD.

✔ A PC with a 486 or faster processor.

✔ Microsoft Windows 95 or later.

✔ At least 32MB of total RAM installed on your computer.

✔ A CD-ROM drive — double-speed (2x) or faster.

✔ A sound card for PCs.

✔ A monitor capable of displaying at least 256 colors or grayscale.

✔ A modem with a speed of at least 14,400 bps.

Using the CD with Microsoft Windows

To install the items from the CD to your hard drive, follow these steps:

1. **Insert the CD into your computer's CD-ROM drive.**

2. **Choose Start➪Run.**

3. **In the dialog box that appears, type** D:\SETUP.EXE.

   Replace *D* with the proper drive letter if your CD-ROM drive uses a different letter. (If you don't know the letter, see how your CD-ROM drive is listed under My Computer.)

4. **Click OK.**

   A License Agreement window appears.

5. **Read through the license agreement, nod your head, and then click the Accept button if you want to use the CD — after you click Accept, you'll never be bothered by the License Agreement window again.**

   The CD interface Welcome screen appears. The interface is a little program that shows you what's on the CD and coordinates installing the programs and running the demos. The interface basically enables you to click a button or two to make things happen.

6. **Click anywhere on the Welcome screen to enter the interface.**

   Now you are getting to the action. This next screen lists categories for the software on the CD.

7. **To view the items within a category, just click the category's name.**

   A list of programs in the category appears.

8. **For more information about a program, click the program's name.**

   Be sure to read the information that appears. Sometimes a program has its own system requirements or requires you to do a few tricks on your computer before you can install or run the program, and this screen tells you what you might need to do, if necessary.

9. **If you don't want to install the program, click the Back button to return to the previous screen.**

   You can always return to the previous screen by clicking the Go Back button. This feature allows you to browse the different categories and products and decide what you want to install.

10. **To install a program, click the appropriate Install button.**

    The CD interface drops to the background while the CD installs the program you chose.

11. **To install other items, repeat Steps 7 through 10.**

12. **When you've finished installing programs, click the Quit button to close the interface.**

    You can eject the CD now. Carefully place it back in the plastic jacket of the book for safekeeping.

In order to run some of the programs on the *CIW Foundations For Dummies* CD-ROM, you may need to keep the CD inside your CD-ROM drive. This is a Good Thing. Otherwise, the installed program would have required you to install a very large chunk of the program to your hard drive, which may have kept you from installing other software.

What You'll Find

In addition to the terrific test engine to help you study for the exam, I wanted to include other products you may find helpful in your Web development career. Several of these are trial versions that you could have downloaded yourself from the Internet, but I put them on the CD so you wouldn't have to. Aren't I nice? Here's a summary of the software on this CD.

Macromedia products

You'll find 30-day trial versions of the most popular Macromedia Web development products:

- ✔ Dreamweaver is an extremely popular GUI editor that enables you to easily add sophisticated effects with JavaScript and DHTML. It's a very clean-coding program that allows you to edit as much or as little of your HTML as you like.

- ✔ Fireworks is an easy-to-use image editor that does a great job of compressing image file sizes that you can use to easily create rollover effects with images.

- ✔ Flash is the industry standard in vector-based image animation. Flash enables you not only to animate and morph images, but also to attach programming to image files.

- ✔ ColdFusion Server Enterprise Edition is the server you'll use if you include ColdFusion server-side scripting in your Web site.

HotDog Professional

HotDog, by Sausage Software, is a well-known text and HTML editor for those of you who prefer to do most of your page coding yourself. HotDog helps type code by having a library of HTML codes in its memory and can fill some codes in for you if you'd like. The version on the CD is a trial version.

BBEdit

BBEdit, by Bare Bones Software, Inc., is an HTML and text editor for Macintosh users. In my opinion, it's not quite as easy to use as a standard GUI editor, but for Mac users who like exact control of their HTML, it can't be beat. The version on the CD is a 30-day trial.

J-Bots

J-Bots, by Webs Unlimited, is a great plug-in for FrontPage 2000 users. This 14-day trial plugs into your FrontPage interface and adds lots of JavaScript capabilities — pop-up windows, scrolling text, and form field validation, just to name a few. If you decide you like it, the full version is only $99. A new version for FrontPage 2002 should be out by the time this book prints.

Web Position Gold

Web Position Gold is used by nearly every Web marketing person I know. It helps to analyze your Web pages to see how various search engines will rank them and can submit your site to search engines. The version on the CD is the 30-day trial by FirstPlace Software, Inc.

WinZip and Stuffit Expander

WinZip, by Nico Mak Computing, Inc., and Stuffit Expander, by Aladdin Systems, help you zip and unzip files so you can store large files in less space.

FTP Utilities

I've included two of the most common FTP utilities on the CD: CuteFTP by GlobalSCAPE and WS-FTP Pro from IpSwitch. Both do a great job of helping you FTP your files from one location to another.

Adobe Acrobat Reader

Adobe Acrobat Reader allows you to read files that are in PDF format. PDF is a great format for distributing many types of files over the Internet. Everyone can access files if they have Adobe Acrobat Reader installed on their machine, which everyone can download for free from its Web site: `www.adobe.com/products/acrobat/main.html`.

Shopfitter

Shopfitter, a nifty program by Cedalion Ltd, is a freeware program that helps you create e-commerce sites. It's fully functional and contains wizards to help you make catalogs and other e-commerce related stuff. After your site is up, you pay 50 cents a transaction no matter how much the transaction is. I think it's a pretty good deal.

Dummies Test Engine

This CD contains questions related to the CIW Foundations exam. The questions focus on fundamental Internet, Web, and networking topics that you can expect to be on the test.

The Dummies Test Engine is designed to help you get comfortable with the certification-testing situation and pinpoint your strengths and weaknesses on the topic. You can test your knowledge by accepting the default setting of all questions, or you can choose a specific number of questions by selecting a category (Web Page Authoring Fundamentals, Networking Fundamentals, or Internet Fundamentals).

The Dummies Test Engine lets you mark questions that you're not sure about. Just choose an answer and then click Mark Question. When you've had enough of the exam experience, click Review Test; you can see which questions you've marked so that you can go back to them. (Click any question number to see the question again and make last-minute changes.)

When you click Grade Test, you see your percentage score. You can also see which questions you got right and which you got wrong. (If you got a question right, it appears in green; wrong answers are represented by the color red — we're really into Christmas colors.) Click a question number at this point to review the correct answer and see an explanation.

If You've Got Problems (Of the CD Kind)

I tried my best to compile programs that work on most computers with the minimum system requirements. Alas, your computer may differ, and some programs may not work properly for some reason.

The two likeliest problems are that you don't have enough memory (RAM) for the programs you want to use, or you have other programs running that are affecting the installation or running of a program. If you get error messages like Not enough memory or Setup cannot continue, try one or more of these methods and then try using the software again:

✓ **Turn off any antivirus software that you have on your computer.** Installation sometimes mimics virus activity and may make your computer incorrectly believe that it is being infected by a virus.

✓ **Close all running programs.** The more programs you're running, the less memory that's available to other programs. Installers also typically update files and programs; if you keep other programs running, installation may not work properly.

✓ **In Windows, close the CD interface and run demos or installations directly from Windows Explorer.** The interface itself can tie up system memory, or even conflict with certain kinds of interactive demos. Use Windows Explorer to browse the files on the CD and launch installers or demos.

✓ **Have your local computer store add more RAM to your computer.** This is, admittedly, a drastic and somewhat expensive step. However, adding more memory can really increase the speed of your computer and enable more programs to run at the same time.

If you still have trouble with the CD, please call the Hungry Minds Customer Care phone number: 800-762-2974. (Outside the U. S.: 317-572-3993.) You can also contact Hungry Minds Customer Service by e-mail at techsupdum@wiley. com. Hungry Minds will provide technical support only for installation and other general quality control items; for technical support on the applications themselves, consult the program's vendor or author.

Index

Hungry Minds, Inc. End-User License Agreement

READ THIS. You should carefully read these terms and conditions before opening the software packet(s) included with this book ("Book"). This is a license agreement ("Agreement") between you and Hungry Minds, Inc. ("HMI"). By opening the accompanying software packet(s), you acknowledge that you have read and accept the following terms and conditions. If you do not agree and do not want to be bound by such terms and conditions, promptly return the Book and the unopened software packet(s) to the place you obtained them for a full refund.

1. **License Grant.** HMI grants to you (either an individual or entity) a nonexclusive license to use one copy of the enclosed software program(s) (collectively, the "Software") solely for your own personal or business purposes on a single computer (whether a standard computer or a workstation component of a multi-user network). The Software is in use on a computer when it is loaded into temporary memory (RAM) or installed into permanent memory (hard disk, CD-ROM, or other storage device). HMI reserves all rights not expressly granted herein.

2. **Ownership.** HMI is the owner of all right, title, and interest, including copyright, in and to the compilation of the Software recorded on the disk(s) or CD-ROM ("Software Media"). Copyright to the individual programs recorded on the Software Media is owned by the author or other authorized copyright owner of each program. Ownership of the Software and all proprietary rights relating thereto remain with HMI and its licensers.

3. **Restrictions On Use and Transfer.**

   (a) You may only (i) make one copy of the Software for backup or archival purposes, or (ii) transfer the Software to a single hard disk, provided that you keep the original for backup or archival purposes. You may not (i) rent or lease the Software, (ii) copy or reproduce the Software through a LAN or other network system or through any computer subscriber system or bulletin-board system, or (iii) modify, adapt, or create derivative works based on the Software.

   (b) You may not reverse engineer, decompile, or disassemble the Software. You may transfer the Software and user documentation on a permanent basis, provided that the transferee agrees to accept the terms and conditions of this Agreement and you retain no copies. If the Software is an update or has been updated, any transfer must include the most recent update and all prior versions.

4. **Restrictions on Use of Individual Programs.** You must follow the individual requirements and restrictions detailed for each individual program in the About the CD appendix of this Book. These limitations are also contained in the individual license agreements recorded on the Software Media. These limitations may include a requirement that after using the program for a specified period of time, the user must pay a registration fee or discontinue use. By opening the Software packet(s), you will be agreeing to abide by the licenses and restrictions for these individual programs that are detailed in the About the CD appendix and on the Software Media. None of the material on this Software Media or listed in this Book may ever be redistributed, in original or modified form, for commercial purposes.

5. **Limited Warranty.**

   (a) HMI warrants that the Software and Software Media are free from defects in materials and workmanship under normal use for a period of sixty (60) days from the date of purchase of this Book. If HMI receives notification within the warranty period of defects in materials or workmanship, HMI will replace the defective Software Media.

   (b) **HMI AND THE AUTHOR OF THE BOOK DISCLAIM ALL OTHER WARRANTIES, EXPRESS OR IMPLIED, INCLUDING WITHOUT LIMITATION IMPLIED WARRANTIES OF MERCHANTABILITY AND FITNESS FOR A PARTICULAR PURPOSE, WITH RESPECT TO THE SOFTWARE, THE PROGRAMS, THE SOURCE CODE CONTAINED THEREIN, AND/OR THE TECHNIQUES DESCRIBED IN THIS BOOK. HMI DOES NOT WARRANT THAT THE FUNCTIONS CONTAINED IN THE SOFTWARE WILL MEET YOUR REQUIRE-MENTS OR THAT THE OPERATION OF THE SOFTWARE WILL BE ERROR FREE.**

   (c) This limited warranty gives you specific legal rights, and you may have other rights that vary from jurisdiction to jurisdiction.

6. **Remedies.**

   (a) HMI's entire liability and your exclusive remedy for defects in materials and workmanship shall be limited to replacement of the Software Media, which may be returned to HMI with a copy of your receipt at the following address: Software Media Fulfillment Department, Attn.: *CIW Foundations For Dummies*, Hungry Minds, Inc., 10475 Crosspoint Blvd., Indianapolis, IN 46256, or call 1-800-762-2974. Please allow four to six weeks for delivery. This Limited Warranty is void if failure of the Software Media has resulted from accident, abuse, or misapplication. Any replacement Software Media will be warranted for the remainder of the original warranty period or thirty (30) days, whichever is longer.

   (b) In no event shall HMI or the author be liable for any damages whatsoever (including without limitation damages for loss of business profits, business interruption, loss of business information, or any other pecuniary loss) arising from the use of or inability to use the Book or the Software, even if HMI has been advised of the possibility of such damages.

   (c) Because some jurisdictions do not allow the exclusion or limitation of liability for conse-quential or incidental damages, the above limitation or exclusion may not apply to you.

7. **U.S. Government Restricted Rights.** Use, duplication, or disclosure of the Software for or on behalf of the United States of America, its agencies and/or instrumentalities (the "U.S. Government") is subject to restrictions as stated in paragraph (c)(1)(ii) of the Rights in Technical Data and Computer Software clause of DFARS 252.227-7013, or subparagraphs (c) (1) and (2) of the Commercial Computer Software - Restricted Rights clause at FAR 52.227-19, and in similar clauses in the NASA FAR supplement, as applicable.

8. **General.** This Agreement constitutes the entire understanding of the parties and revokes and supersedes all prior agreements, oral or written, between them and may not be modified or amended except in a writing signed by both parties hereto that specifically refers to this Agreement. This Agreement shall take precedence over any other documents that may be in conflict herewith. If any one or more provisions contained in this Agreement are held by any court or tribunal to be invalid, illegal, or otherwise unenforceable, each and every other pro-vision shall remain in full force and effect.